INSIGHT GUI

ARIZONA
& THE GRAND CANYON

APA PUBLICATIONS L

Part of the Langenscheidt Publishing Group

INSIGHT GUIDE
ARIZONA

Editorial

Project Editor
Astrid deRidder
Series Manager
Rachel Lawrence
Publishing Manager
Rachel Fox
Art Director
Steven Lawrence

Distribution

UK
Dorling Kindersley Ltd
A Penguin Group company
80 Strand, London, WC2R 0RL
customerservice@dk.com

United States
Ingram Publisher Services
1 Ingram Boulevard, PO Box 3006,
La Vergne, TN 37086-1986
customer.service@ingrampublisher
services.com

Australia
Universal Publishers
PO Box 307
St Leonards NSW 1590
sales@universalpublishers.com.au

Worldwide
**Apa Publications GmbH & Co.
Verlag KG (Singapore branch)**
7030 Ang Mo Kio Avenue 5
08-65 Northstar @ AMK
Singapore 569880
apasin@signet.com.sg

Printing

CTPS-China

© 2012 Apa Publications (UK) Ltd
All Rights Reserved

First Edition 2002
Third Edition 2012

CONTACTING THE EDITORS
We would appreciate it if readers
would alert us to errors or out-
dated information by writing to:
**Insight Guides, PO Box 7910,
London SE1 1WE, England.**
insight@apaguide.co.uk

www.insightguides.com

ABOUT THIS BOOK

The first Insight Guide pioneered the use of creative full-color photography in travel guides in 1970.
Since then, we have expanded our
range to cater to our readers' need
not only for reliwable information
about their chosen destination but
also for a real understanding of the
culture and workings of that destination. Now, when the internet can
supply inexhaustible (but not always
reliable) facts, our books marry text
and pictures to provide those much
more elusive qualities: knowledge
and discernment.

How to use this book

*Insight Guide: Arizona and the Grand
Canyon* is structured to convey an
understanding of the state and its
people as well as to guide readers
through its attractions:

◆ The **Features** section, indicated
by a pink bar at the top of each
page, covers the natural and cultural history of the region, together
with illuminating essays on outdoor
adventure, cowboy lore, and exploring ghost towns and Indian ruins.

◆ The main **Places** section, indicated by a blue bar, is a complete
guide to all the sights and areas
worth visiting. Places of special
interest are coordinated by number
with the maps.

◆ The **Travel Tips** listings section,
with a yellow bar, provides full information on transportation, hotels,
activities from culture and shopping
to sports, and an A–Z section of
essential practical information. An
easy-to-find contents list for Travel
Tips is printed on the back flap,
which also serves as a bookmark.

The contributors

This new and updated edition was
managed by **Astrid deRidder,**

Left: Monument Valley.

restaurants of New York City, while exploring the Western states by backpack and river raft. He has written and contributed to numerous guidebooks and is the author of two novels for young people, *DWEEB* and *The Only Ones*.

Arizona writer **Rose Houk** covers familiar territory – the Grand Canyon, where she worked as a park ranger before embarking on a writing career, and Flagstaff, her home for more than 15 years.

Nora Burba Trulsson has lived in Arizona long enough to see golf courses outnumber dude ranches. She writes about both in "The Arizona Cowboy" and "Golfer's Paradise."

Santa Fe writer **Richard Mahler** guides readers to "Arizona's West Coast," a stretch of the Colorado River on the state's western border. Mahler is a columnist for *Desert Exposure* and the author of 11 books.

With more than 30 years' experience as an editor and writer, **Edward A. Jardim** knows how to transform a complex story into a concise narrative. Here he condenses four centuries of history into an engaging chronicle of Arizona's past.

The photography in this book is the work of some of the most distinguished photographers in the Southwest. The two principal photographers are **Richard Nowitz**, a frequent Insight Guide contributor whose recent assignments include guides to China, Peru, and Florida, and **Kerrick James**, a Phoenix-based photographer whose work has appeared in *National Geographic Adventure*, *Arizona Highways*, *Sunset*, and others.

This book was proofread by **Catherine Jackson** and indexed by **Helen Peters**.

whose earlier books include guides to Colorado, Florida, and New England. Copy-editing this text was a joint venture between Insight Guide editors **Rebecca Lovell** and **Rachel Lawrence**.

Updating her work from the original edition of this book was **Nicky Leach**, an award-winning travel writer and long-time Insight Guide contributor whose work appears in guides to Colorado, Florida, US National Parks West, USA on the Road, and numerous other destinations. Leach covers a host of Arizona topics, from geology and archaeology to ghost towns and cultural history.

Aaron Starmer updated the Travel Tips for this book, combing the canyons and rivers of Arizona for the best accommodations and activities. He has spent the last twelve years haunting the streets, parks, and

Map Legend

‒ ‒ ‒ ‒	State Boundary
‒ ‒ ‒ ‒	County Boundary
⊖	Border Crossing
‒•‒	National Park/Reserve
✈ ✈	Airport: International/Regional
🚌	Bus Station
ℹ	Tourist Information
🕆 † ⳨	Church/Ruins
†	Monastery
☾	Mosque
✡	Synagogue
🏰	Castle/Ruins
∴	Archeological Site
∩	Cave
🗿	Statue/Monument
★	Place of Interest
🏠	Mansion

The main places of interest in the Places section are coordinated by number with a full-colour map (eg ❶), and a symbol at the top of every right-hand page tells you where to find the map.

Contents

LEFT: Mather Point,
Grand Canyon National Park.

Maps

Inside front cover: Arizona
Inside back cover:
Arizona's National Parks and
Monuments.

Travel Tips

THE BEST OF ARIZONA: TOP ATTRACTIONS

Spectacular scenery, thrilling adventures, a mix of Native American, Hispanic, and Anglo cultures, plus more than 300 days of sunshine a year, make Arizona a classic Southwestern destination

△ Check into one of **Arizona's famous resorts** and pamper yourself with spa treatments, fine cuisine, and lounging by the pool. For the adventurous, dude ranches are a uniquely western experience. *Pages 112 and 222*

▽ The backdrop of countless western movies, **Monument Valley** is one of the iconic landscapes of the American West and an epicenter of traditional Navajo culture. *Page 185*

△ Words can't easily express the scale and grandeur of the **Grand Canyon**, one of the world's natural wonders, millions of years in the making. *Page 127*

△ Set within stunning red-rock formations, **Sedona** has a lively arts scene, lots of shopping and dining, and a reputation for New Age vibrations. *Page 235*

◁ Strangely carved rhyolite rocks and rare Mexican flora and fauna mingle in the spectacular "sky island" mountains of **Chiricahua National Monument** near the US–Mexico border. *Page 293*

△ Boaters can explore more than a million acres of sandstone wilderness on **Lake Powell**, created by the flooding of Glen Canyon. *Page 169*

△ In the heart of the Navajo Nation is **Canyon de Chelly**, a spectacular gorge where Navajo shepherds tend flocks and fields and ancient pueblos are perched on cliffs. *Page 189*

△ The most thrilling way to experience the Grand Canyon is whitewater rafting on the **Colorado River**, a multiday journey on one of the mightiest waterways in the western US. *Page 143*

◁ Sun-baked Arizonans escape to the **White Mountains**, where cool forests, leaping streams, and an abundance of outdoor recreation offer a welcome break from the desert heat. *Page 257*

▷ Native American art and culture are interpreted with intelligence and sensitivity at the **Heard Museum,** site of the annual Indian Fair and Market. *Page 232*

THE BEST OF ARIZONA: EDITOR'S CHOICE

Awe-inspiring landscapes including the Grand Canyon, Sedona's red rocks, and the Sonoran Desert ... here, at a glance, are our top recommendations for a visit

BEST SCENERY

Grand Canyon National Park. One of the must-see wonders of the world, the "Big Ditch" delivers sublime scenery and glimpses of 2 billion years of earth history. *See page 189.*

Kartchner Caverns State Park. A wet, living cave system in the Whetstone Mountains, the beautiful caverns below this former ranch make it Arizona's top state park. *See page 298.*

Monument Valley Navajo Tribal Park. The wind-sculpted buttes and mesas in this park on the Arizona-Utah border have sheltered Ancestral Pueblo and Navajo people for millennia and inspired movie Westerns since the 1930s. *See page 185.*

Petrified Forest National Park. Moody badlands of the Painted Desert and petrified tree trunks with mysterious gem-laden centers created during the Age of the Dinosaurs are spread below the Hopi Mesas of northern Arizona. *See page 258.*

Saguaro National Park. Like Jolly Green Giants, these one-ton cacti march across southern Arizona's Sonoran Desert hills in likeable profusion and provide photo opportunities in two different park units. *See page 282.*

Sedona. These eroded red sandstone mesas are a magnet for outdoor-lovers, artists, and New Age spirits drawn by the rocks' famous healing energies. *See page 234.*

Antelope Canyon. Hike northern Arizona's most alluring slot canyon with Navajo guides, then enjoy a meal at the Antelope Marina on Lake Powell, whose architecture and waterfront dining facilities showcase Navajo culture. *See page 170.*

BEST FOR FAMILIES

Arizona Science Center. With an IMAX theater, planetarium, and over 300 hands-on exhibitions, this vibrant science center in an Antoine Predock-designed building next to Heritage Square is a must for hyperactive kids. *See page 220.*

Challenger Learning Center. Fly simulated space flight missions as a flight crew, mission controller, or scientist at this educational space center in Peoria, near Phoenix, affiliated with the Smithsonian Institution. *See page 285.*

Grand Canyon Railway. Ride a steam train and experience a staged ambush and shootout on the way home on the historic railroad between the town of Williams and the Grand Canyon. *See page 140.*

Lowell Observatory. Walk through a re-creation of the solar system, look at the stars through a telescope, play with interactive exhibits, and take part in special presentations at this nationally known planetarium in Flagstaff. *See page 153.*

Phoenix Zoo. The annual ZooLights holiday display and the chance to view 1,200 animals, from white rhinos to desert tortoises, make this private zoo the top-rated kid's destination in Arizona. *See page 224.*

Tombstone. "The Town Too Tough to Die" now offers staged gunfights, stage coach and wagon rides, live music in some of the saloons, Boot Hill Cemetery, and a museum with exhibits on the Shootout at the OK Corral. *See page 296.*

ABOVE: the glory of the Grand Canyon.

BEST WILDLIFE VIEWING

Arizona-Sonora Desert Museum. Not really a museum but a huge zoo in Tucson celebrating animals of the Sonoran Desert, which are housed in naturalistic enclosures and star in well-conceived presentations.
See page 283.

Grand Canyon condors. Restored populations of endangered California condors regularly visit the South Rim to pose for pictures on the guard rail.
See page 84.

Kofa National Wildlife Refuge. Relict California palm trees, stranded during the Ice Age, and even rarer desert bighorn sheep inhabit this nature refuge at a former mine near Phoenix.
See page 211.

Chiricahua Mountains. Apache fox squirrels, Chihuahua and Apache pines, and neon-hued neotropical migratory birds like the rare elegant trogon live cross-cultural lives amid southern Arizona's "sky islands."
See page 293.

San Pedro Riparian National Conservation Area. This river corridor on the US–Mexico border is a layover for an astonishing 4–10 million migratory birds each year. *See page 299.*

Willcox Playa. Birders flock to flooded Willcox Playa each winter to view the spectacular landings and takeoffs of over 10,000 migrating sandhill cranes, Canada, and snow geese.
See page 297.

ABOVE: Navajo textiles on display.

ART AND CULTURE

Grand Canyon Music Festival. The South Rim is a musical mecca for a month every September with world-class chamber music and the occasional jazz and blues concert by professional musicians.
See page 328.

Tubac Festival of the Arts. Arizona's oldest festival of the arts takes place over four days every February and in the old Spanish presidio town of Tubac, near the border with Mexico, and showcases artists from across the US and Canada. *See page 326.*

ASU Gammage Auditorium, Tempe. Designed by Frank Lloyd Wright, Gammage offers a full roster of performing arts events.
See page 223.

Tempe Center for the Arts. This beautifully designed community center houses two theaters, an art gallery, a restaurant, and a pleasant riverwalk with a sculpture garden. *See page 223.*

MUST-SEE MUSEUMS

Heard Museum. The perfect introduction to Arizona's Indian cultures through an award-winning multimedia presentation, special collections, contemporary exhibits, and Indian arts and crafts festivals, all in historic setting Phoenix. *See pages 221 and 232.*

Museum of Northern Arizona. Founded in Flagstaff by archaeologist Harold Colton, MNA is the major repository for artifacts unearthed at nearby Wupatki Pueblo and other archaeological digs and has exhibits on northern Arizona's geology, history, and cultures, as well as juried Indian art shows. *See page 154.*

Phoenix Art Museum. PAM has become a major venue for international traveling art exhibits. *See page 221.*

Titan Missile Museum. This missile silo is the only site in the US with a (disarmed) nuclear missile still on its underground launch pad. *See page 286.*

Best Historic Sites

Bisbee. Visit historic underground and open-pit mines, take a historic walking tour of Bisbee's steep streets, and visit museums, art galleries, retro restaurants, and quaint hotels in old (and sometimes haunted) buildings. *See page 295.*

Hubbell Trading Post National Historic Site. This restored working trading post in Ganado, is run by the National Park Service and has a store, bullpen, rug room, and craft demonstrations, revealing trading life on the Navajo reservation over the last century. *See page 189.*

Pipe Spring National Monument. A preserved 1870s Mormon fort, cattle ranch, Ancestral Pueblo settlement, and cultural remains from the adjoining Kaibab Paiute Reservation all tell a fascinating history on the lonely Arizona Strip situated north of the Grand Canyon. *See page 173.*

Presidio Historic District, Tucson. Visit a series of restored buildings housing museums, restaurants, B&Bs, and businesses in Tucson's downtown to experience its

lively Mexican and Territorial American past. *See page 276.*

Taliesin West. A visit to Frank Lloyd Wright's Scottsdale home and school is *de rigueur* for fans of the master's organic architecture. *See page 225.*

Tumacacori National Historical Park and San Xavier Del Bac Mission. One of several missions founded by Father Kino, the ruined Tumacacori mission was built near the Spanish presidio of Tubac, an early American boomtown and now an arts center. San Xavier Del Bac church, near Tucson, still serves the San Xavier Reservation and has a beautiful white-carved facade. *See pages 301 and 302.*

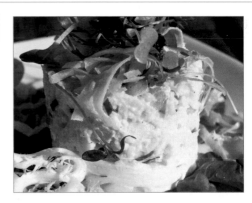

ABOVE: Arizona resorts promote fine cuisine.

Best Wining and Dining

Brix Wine Bar and Restaurant, Flagstaff. This charming fine-dining restaurant in an old carriage house mesmerizes with its locally sourced Mediterranean cuisine and exceptional wines. *See page 160.*

Café Poca Cosa, Tucson. Susana Davila's vibrant café offers a taste of Mexico City in downtown Tucson, with imaginative tamales, mole sauces, and daily specials. *See page 288.*

Canela Bistro, Sonoita. The location may be rural, but the European-inspired dishes created by the chef-owners of this weekends-only, backcountry, borderlands bistro are world class – a perfect marriage of local foods and wines, sophisticated culinary techniques, hard work, and passion. *See page 306.*

Kai, Sheraton Wild Horse Pass Resort, Chandler. Phoenix's top fine-dining restaurant leads the pack by reimagining traditional Native American cuisine

for the 21st century, sourcing foods locally, executing dishes perfectly, and creating a beautiful setting in which to enjoy them. *See page 229.*

Turquoise Room, La Posada, Winslow. English-born John Sharpe's award-winning cuisine plays on local ingredients and cross-cultural dishes to magnificent effect in his attractive restaurant inside Winslow's historic trackside La Posada hotel. *See page 269.*

Barrio Café, Phoenix. Chef Silvana Salcido Esparza's delicious new takes on traditional southern Mexican dishes led to a James Beard Award nomination in 2010 for this hip eatery in downtown Phoenix. *See page 229.*

Heartline Café, Sedona. Classically trained chef-owner Chuck Cline crafts fresh-sourced dishes with heart and soul in this unpretentious, garden-style restaurant among Sedona's red rocks. *See page 244.*

RIGHT: a gunfighter in authentic clothing.

OFF THE BEATEN TRACK

Biosphere 2. This experiment in futuristic living inside a 3-acre building is now a research center managed by the University of Arizona. *See page 286.*

Grand Canyon Skywalk. A 75ft (23-meter) -long Plexiglass viewing platform, 4,000ft (1,200 meters) above the Colorado River on the Hualapai Indian Reservation, offers vertiginous views of the western Grand Canyon. *See page 208.*

Greer. This remote Mormon village has charming log cabins, historic lodges, hearty ranch food, fishing on the Little Colorado River, cross-country skiing, downhill skiing and one-of-a-kind history museums. *See page 261.*

Hopi Mesas. Hopi farmers and craftspeople live in 12 villages on or below isolated mesas surrounded by the Navajo Nation. Second Mesa has a cultural center, restaurant, and examples of each mesa's pottery, *kachinas*, and jewelry. *See page 190.*

Patagonia. A favorite Tucson getaway, this laid-back former mining community offers backroads for biking, top birdwatching, art galleries, historic B&Bs, great eateries, wine tastings, and healing retreats. *See page 301.*

ABOVE: marina at Lake Mead.

ABOVE: Biosphere 2, center for scientific research.

SPORTS AND OUTDOOR ADVENTURE

Grand Canyon rafting and hiking. Guides offer trips highlighting the quintessential Grand Canyon experience: paddling the Colorado River. Hikes into side canyons, including tropical Havasu Falls, are a bonus; rim-top hikers will enjoy the North Rim's cooler, forested trails. *See pages 143 and 134.*

Lake Powell house-boating. Its waters are gradually evaporating, but Lake Powell is still a mecca for boaters of all stripes, including laid-back houseboaters and more active kayakers. *See page 169.*

MONEY-SAVING TIPS

America the Beautiful Federal Lands Pass: If you plan to visit more than a couple of US national parks, national forests, or Bureau of Land Management sites in the next year, be sure to buy an annual federal lands pass, which offers admission for one vehicle containing four passengers to sites across the country for $80. **National parks on the Navajo reservation:** Entrance to spectacular Canyon de Chelly and Navajo national monuments on tribal lands in northern Arizona is free. **Flagstaff Festival of Science:** Lectures, star-gazing, hands-on archaeological digs, hikes to local pueblos, and other events are free for the whole family at Flagstaff's annual 10-day celebration of science. **Camping in national forests:** Primitive camping is free on national forest lands, if you're willing to bring your own food, water, supplies, and practice "Leave No Trace" camping ethics. **Summer rates at resorts:** Locals flock to southern Arizona's swankiest resorts when summer temperatures hit 100°F (37°C) to enjoy all the amenities for a fraction of the high-season rates.

THE GRAND CANYON STATE

One of the world's great natural treasures, the
Grand Canyon is just the first of Arizona's
many wonders

Visiting the Grand Canyon in 1903, Theodore Roosevelt delivered a speech that would become a classic summation of conservation principles. "Leave it as it is," he declared. "You cannot improve on it. The ages have been at work on it, and man can only mar it. What you can do is keep it for your children, your children's children, and for all who come after you, as the one great sight which every American…should see".

Five years later, President Roosevelt declared the Grand Canyon a national monument to prevent it from being "improved upon" by human hands. And though a clutch of hotels and parking lots now stand on the rims, and the Colorado River has been restrained by dams, this amazing canyon remains an emblem of the grandeur of the American West, its formal protection a watershed in the history of environmental stewardship.

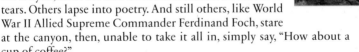

Today, nearly 5 million visitors a year journey to view this natural wonder – "the Big Ditch", as locals call it. Most arrive at the easily accessed South Rim, via the gateway community of Tusayan, where hotels, restaurants, and services are abundant. At Mather Point, the first overlook into the canyon, some fall into awed silence. Some are moved to tears. Others lapse into poetry. And still others, like World War II Allied Supreme Commander Ferdinand Foch, stare at the canyon, then, unable to take it all in, simply say, "How about a cup of coffee?"

Monoliths and malls

Even more wondrous is that the Grand Canyon is just one of Arizona's many natural treasures. From the sandstone monoliths of Monument Valley and the soaring walls of Canyon de Chelly to the trees-turned-to-stone of the Petrified Forest and the giant saguaros of the Sonoran Desert, the state is a catalog of wonder.

The human imprint is just as fascinating and, despite the proliferation of strip malls, tract housing, and other modern developments,

PRECEDING PAGES: Havasu Canyon; the Grand Canyon; aspen leaves in the Autumn.
LEFT: Monument Valley. **ABOVE LEFT:** Arizona Biltmore Resort & Spa.
ABOVE RIGHT: Thomas Moran's *Chasm of the Colorado*, 1873–74.

surprisingly ancient. The mesa-top villages of the Hopi include the oldest continuously inhabited town or village in the United States (since AD 1150), and their culture is filled with echoes of the long-vanished Sinagua and Ancestral Pueblo people, or Anasazi, whose abandoned dwellings are strewn throughout the northern canyons.

The Navajo and Apache, both descendants of Athabascan nomads who migrated into the Southwest perhaps a thousand years ago, integrate traditional values into their modern lives, as do the descendants of the Spanish and Mexican immigrants who settled the missions and ranchos of the south. Cowboys still ride the range in remote corners of the state, and a few lone prospectors scratch a living from played-out mines. Even Phoenix, the country's sixth-largest city and a prime example of the New West, sits atop an ancient Hohokam settlement, whose elaborate irrigation system, once used to water fields of maize and melon, now serves corporate towers and shopping malls.

Iconic landscapes

For many people, a visit to the Navajo and Hopi reservations, east of Flagstaff, is the highlight of their trip to northern Arizona. Time seems to stand still in this epic landscape, whose stone landmarks and secret canyons are sacred to the people who have called this home for centuries. The 29,817-sq-mile (77,226-sq-km) Navajo Nation is the largest Indian reservation in the country. The crown jewel in the Navajo tribal park system is undoubtedly Monument Valley, instantly familiar to everyone who has seen classic John Ford movies such as *Stagecoach*, *She Wore a Yellow Ribbon*, *The Searchers*, *Sergeant Rutledge*, and *Cheyenne Autumn*.

Dwelling in the park

A number of Navajo families live inside the boundaries of the parks, on traditional homesteads usually consisting of a frame house, a *hogan* (log and earth hut), a shade *ramada* (shelter), a nearby sweat lodge, and livestock corrals for sheep, goats, and horses. Many local Navajos are licensed to offer horseback and Jeep tours of their homeland. Almost every family makes turquoise and silver jewelry, rugs, baskets, sand paintings, and folk art, and the seasonal income from tourists is their principal means of support.

The big picture

Travelers with a taste for creature comforts will find no lack of plush resorts and trendy restaurants in Arizona, and enough golf courses to keep them occupied for years. But those who venture beyond the usual tourist trails will discover that the state, like its best-known feature, is a place of uncommon depth. Seeing the big picture can be overwhelming at first. Only by descending beneath the rim, exploring the state layer by layer, is its true nature revealed.

ABOVE LEFT: palm-shaded beach at Lake Havasu City. **ABOVE RIGHT:** underground mine tour, Bisbee. **RIGHT:** a climber clings to a limestone cliff.

THE CULTURAL LANDSCAPE

A colorful combination of Indian, Hispanic, and Anglo cultures is enriched by immigrants from all over the world

Early in 1856, an eastbound stagecoach arrived in a cloud of dust in Tucson, then a Spanish-speaking adobe village. Arizona had passed from Spanish to Mexican rule in 1821, and just two years before, as part of the 1854 Gadsden Purchase ending the Mexican War, become American territory. Papers signed thousands of miles away had little impact on residents of northern Mexico and southern Arizona, then as now united by a shared landscape and ancient cultural ties. Not until the arrival of the railroad in 1880 and the end of the Apache Wars in 1886 would Arizona Territory attract the flood of white settlers that dominate the state ethnically today. Statehood, granted in 1912, was still 56 years away.

Aboard that stagecoach in 1856 was one of Tucson's first Anglo immigrants. Sam Hughes, a 28-year-old Welshman, had been working in a bakery in a California gold-rush town. He was dying of tuberculosis and, in a last-ditch attempt to save his life, started making his way to Texas, hoping the warm, dry air would improve his health. The stage driver didn't share his faith. Expecting the sickly foreigner with the sing-song accent to expire at any moment, he dumped him in Tucson. Of the 500 or so residents, Hughes was assured, five spoke English.

Founding father

Hughes didn't die. Just the opposite. Like the thousands who would later come here for their health, he was cured by the Arizona desert. Grit and determination made up for formal education in frontier Tucson, a town where,

as journalist J. Ross Browne observed in 1864, "Every man went armed to the teeth, and street-fights and bloody affrays were of daily occurrence".

Hughes's weapons were a steel will and a capacity for hard work. He made friends with his Mexican neighbors, learned their language, married a young Sonoran girl, and had successful careers in ranching, real estate, and politics. By the time he died, at the age of 88, he was considered one of Tucson's founding fathers.

At about the same time, in the opposite end of the state, Mormon colonists, recently settled in Utah, were now setting their sights on Arizona. In 1858, Mormon missionary Jacob Hamblin traveled across the Arizona Strip to

LEFT: a young girl dances in celebration of Cinco de Mayo. **RIGHT:** San Xavier del Bac Mission.

the Hopi Mesas in search of Indian converts and new farmland along the Little Colorado River. He was warmly welcomed at Moenkopi by Hopi chief Tuva, who became the first of many Hopis to convert to Christianity. Hamblin's trip laid the groundwork for settlements in the 1870s, when government persecution in Utah led Mormons to establish communities all the way down to St David in the San Pedro River Valley. In one of the odd twists of history that seem to abound in this state, the Mormons were convinced that the Hopi spoke Welsh, and Hamblin brought with him a Welsh-speaking translator. Had they met,

hunter-gatherers in the Sonoran Desert and shared information about farming, pottery, and religion that would be passed along to tribes throughout the state. Without this exchange among cultures, it's unlikely the Mogollon, Hohokam, and Ancestral Pueblo would ever have come to dominate the prehistoric Southwest.

It must have been opportunity, too, that lured nomadic Athabascans – today's Navajo and Apache – from northwest Canada between the 12th and 15th centuries. Around the same time, Shoshoneans and the Utes and Paiutes were also moving in from the Great Basin. In the 1600s

the translator and Hughes would undoubtedly have enjoyed the joke.

Opportunity knocks

For immigrants, Arizona has always been a land where dreams could come true, a "blank slate on which they could etch their visions of the future", according to historian Thomas Sheridan. Nor is this a recent phenomenon. Opportunity undoubtedly spurred the very first paleo-hunters to venture into Arizona's game-rich grasslands after the retreat of the Ice Age glaciers 12,000 years ago. It may have been what motivated people from Mexico to travel north to Arizona and begin trading some 3,000 years ago. They mingled with Archaic

it was the promise of gold and silver, timber and fertile land that lured first Spaniards and Mexicans, then Anglos and other immigrants to the state. Though they didn't always find what they were looking for, pioneers of every race stayed and made a life for themselves.

The trend continues. Arizona is the second-fastest growing state in the country, posting a growth rate of 40 percent between 1990 and 2000. It has an ethnic diversity rare even in the West. Of the state's 6.6 million residents, Hispanics constitute 31 percent, American Indians 5 percent, African Americans 4.5 percent. Most of the others are white people of various nationalities and religions. The result isn't so much a melting pot, in which ethnic groups are boiled down to a bland homogeneity, but a tossed salad in which distinct groups coexist and occasionally come into conflict.

The first Arizonans

Though American Indians are a relatively small minority, no other group is more closely identified with the state or, ironically, more misunderstood. For starters, there is no one over-arching Indian culture. Each of the 21 tribes in Arizona has its own history, traditions, and language, though almost all now speak English and many hold jobs off their reservations. While some tribal members have chosen to maintain

Indian people have traditionally employed to reach consensus. Casinos, resort developments, and other businesses on Indian reservations have let tribes get ahead economically but may also represent a compromise of traditional values.

Ironically, one of the keys to sustaining cultural values has been embracing positive change. Every tribe has borrowed cultural traits from its neighbors, creating dynamic societies that not only survive but, surprisingly, thrive in the face of change. Navajo kids use computers to learn their native tongue. Indian youth go away to law school, then return to the reservation to represent their tribes in centuries-old disputes over land and water rights,

traditional ways of life, the influence of modern culture is unavoidable and often produces unexpected and calamitous results.

Introduced diseases, substance abuse, and domestic violence – while not uniquely Indian problems – have devastated many tribes already struggling to hold onto cultural identities after years of government-sponsored re-education, land reallocation and, during the 19th century, extermination. Tribal councils, introduced in the early 1900s, are frequently at odds with themselves or mired in the long debates that

housing, subsistence hunting and gathering, and access to public lands for traditional religious uses. Reservation doctors and nurses combine modern medicine and traditional healing in the treatment of diabetes and other modern ailments.

The trick for most tribes is to engage the outside world without being overwhelmed by it. As more tribes take over the management of their institutions and natural resources, and encourage the development of tribal businesses, there is a shift in decision-making from federal policy-makers to tribal governments.

The Navajo

The 250,000-strong Navajo Nation, the largest in the country, grapples with this issue daily.

FAR LEFT: a Navajo dancer, 1904. **LEFT:** Apache men, 1909. **ABOVE:** a Navajo silversmith works inside a hogan, 1915.

The Navajo, or *Diné*, as they call themselves, live on a 29,000-sq-mile (47,000-sq-km) reservation that encompasses the mesas, canyons, black lava promontories, and high-desert grasslands of northeastern Arizona, northwestern New Mexico, and a sliver of southern Utah. A matriarchal society, where women own all the property and men move in with the wife's family, Navajo life is governed by complex clan relationships and the pursuit of traditional religious beliefs, often referred to as the Beauty Path. Modern Navajos still strive for *hozho*, a state of harmony with all things, taught by the Holy People who created First

Man and First Woman, and later, Changing Woman, the ideal Navajo woman whose spirit is evoked in the *kinaalda*, a puberty ritual observed by Navajo girls.

The ancestors of the Navajo were Athabascan nomads who migrated into the Southwest from Canada perhaps as early as the 12th century. In addition to hunting and gathering, they raided Pueblo settlements, a practice that intensified after they acquired Spanish horses in the 1600s. But they also saw the merits of Pueblo agriculture and, during times of peace, intermarried, traded, learned weaving, and adapted some aspects of Pueblo religion. They were such proficient corn farmers that the Pueblo called them *Navajú*, a Tewa word meaning "great fields." Corn remains central to Navajo rituals, and corn pollen is used in all blessing ceremonies.

Early colonizing efforts by the Mormons led to permanent Latter Day Saints settlements in Arizona. Mormons and the LDS church remain a strong presence along the Arizona–Utah border.

Culture and conflict

Though relations between Navajo and Pueblo people are cordial in most day-to-day interactions, tensions have simmered over the years – particularly between the Navajo and Hopi. In 1680, the Navajo united with Pueblo people in a revolt against the Spanish and, for a time, lived with them in small defensive *pueblitos* in

NAVAJO CODE TALKERS

Navajos have fought bravely in every major American military engagement in the last century, but their most important contribution came during World War II, when 400 Navajo Code Talkers served with the US Marine Corps throughout the Pacific, sending and receiving messages in a disguised version of their native language. The code, which was never broken by the Japanese, is now recognized as having been one of the keys to victories at Iwo Jima and other major battles.

It was the brainchild of Philip Johnston, a white missionary's son who had grown up on the Navajo reservation and spoke the language fluently. In 1942, Navajo recruits at Camp Pendleton, California, devised their own

code, using three Navajo words for each letter – e.g., ant, ax, and apple for A, or badger, bear, and barrel for B.

So secret was their work, Code Talkers didn't receive national recognition until 1982, when President Ronald Reagan proclaimed August 14 National Navajo Code Talkers Day. In 1999, President Bill Clinton visited the reservation and gave a speech that included a few words in Navajo code. For Navajos, the symbolism of that speech lay not so much in a recognition of their people's patriotism but in the use of a language that, for years, the US government actively worked to stamp out as un-American.

New Mexico. But in 1868, after the Navajo's four-year incarceration at Fort Sumner in New Mexico, following the U.S. Army's operation against them known as the Long Walk, relations between the Navajo and Hopi soured fast (see Cowboys, Indians, and Miners chapter). The reservation created for the Navajo was rapidly expanded to accommodate a rebounding Navajo population and its hungry livestock. Eventually, Navajo grazing lands surrounded the compact cornfields and villages of the much smaller Hopi reservation. A long and complex land dispute over boundaries and the relocation of families in some joint-use areas

This created opportunities for merchants, who opened trading posts on the reservation in the 1870s. Early entrepreneurs like Lorenzo Hubbell in Ganado befriended the Navajo, became intermediaries between the tribe and federal government, and developed a market for Navajo weaving by suggesting improvements and selling finished rugs to eastern buyers. Rugs woven by women (and several men) all over the reservation now command top prices. Not far behind is the beautiful silver jewelry made by Navajo artisans, along with pottery, kachina dolls, and other crafts learned from the Pueblo people.

is still being adjudicated today, and there are ongoing concerns about how overgrazing of fragile desert grasslands by Navajo sheep and goats exacerbates erosion on Navajo land.

What we now regard as traditional Navajo culture was also profoundly influenced by Europeans. The Spanish introduced not only horses but shepherding, rug weaving, and silversmithing. After the Long Walk, the Navajo adopted a version of the tiered Mother Hubbard dress they saw army wives wearing at Fort Sumner and developed a taste for flour, canned goods, and other consumer products.

LEFT: American Indian at UCLA Pow Wow.
ABOVE: horses at Wickenburg.

The Western Apache

The *Indé*, or Western Apache, are descended from the same Athabaskan stock as the Navajo and live in the mountains of Arizona. Historically, there were five groups of Western Apache. The four territorial bands of the San Carlos Apache inhabited the rolling high desert surrounding the Pinal, Apache, Mescal, and Catalina Mountains. The Eastern and Western bands of the White Mountain group occupied the area from the Pinaleno Mountains to the high plateau north and east of the White Mountains. The Cibecue, Southern Tonto, and Northern Tonto groups lived in the high country from the Salt River north to present-day Flagstaff. Though they shared resources and recognized ties to each other, the bands owed no political allegiance to the larger group. Conflicts with white settlers in the 1850s and 1860s led to the establishment of Fort Apache in the White Mountains in 1868. The White Mountain and Cibecue Apache allied with whites and served as scouts in the wars against the Tonto, Chiricahua, and Pai groups. Beginning in 1874, the federal government forced Apaches from four reservations to walk to the San Carlos reservation, where tensions eventually arose between the 20 independent bands. In 1886, Victorio and Geronimo escaped with their bands of Chiricahua Apache and hid

The White Mountain Apache Reservation has over 12,000 members and operates a successful logging and recreation economy. The adjoining San Carlos reservation is slightly larger, at 1.8 million acres (730,000 hectares), and has 9,400 residents. The San Carlos reservation is known for its cattle and cowboys, a tradition that dates to the 1870s, when people accumulated their weekly allotments of beef to obtain a live steer. By the 1880s, the Indian agency was encouraging a cattle industry at San Carlos, which has grown to 20,000 head managed by five cattle associations. The reservation produces more cowboys than any area of comparable size in

out in the Chiricahua Mountains and Mexico's Sierra Madre. They were forced to surrender in 1886 and were shipped to Florida. Most never returned to Arizona. Eventually, the White Mountain, Cibecue, and Tonto groups were allowed to return to their own reservations. The Tonto Apache population was much reduced, however, and merged with the Yavapai in the Verde Valley. Some members of the Eastern White Mountain band stayed on the San Carlos Apache reservation, while others returned to the Fort Apache (now White Mountain) Reservation. The Cibecue group merged with the White Mountain Apache.

Today, Arizona's Apache live on three reservations and maintain strong links with the land.

Texas or Oklahoma. The San Carlos Rodeo is one of the highlights of the year.

The Tonto Apache are now officially known as the Yavapai Apache Tribe and inhabit a small reservation in the Verde Valley. While they were on the San Carlos reservation in the 1870s, the Tonto lost most of their land to white settlers. Today, Cliff Castle Casino is the tribe's main source of income.

Like the Navajo, the Western Apache believe the world was made by the Creator, or Sun, and that it was first inhabited by animals and monsters. Central to Apache belief are the *Gaan*, Mountain Spirit people who live beneath sacred mountains. They serve as protectors, teachers, and role models. At special ceremonies, *Gaan* dancers with elaborate headdresses appear in groups of five – four *Gaan* representing each of the sacred directions and a messenger who communicates with them.

The Hopi

The Navajo and Western Apache are newcomers compared with the Hopi, whose ancestors – the *Hisatsinom* or Ancestral Pueblo people – have lived on the Colorado Plateau for millennia. The Hopi moved to these stone villages atop the Hopi Mesas in the 1100s. Each village was founded separately during a period of contraction that saw many Southwest

Tohono and Akimel O'odham

If the Tohono O'odham (Desert People) and Akimel O'odham (Water People), who live on reservations in southern Arizona, are indeed descended from the ancient canal-building Hohokam, they rival the Hopi for ancient origins. We may never know. The Hohokam disappeared around 1400 and the O'odham encountered by the Spanish were hunter-gatherers who knew nothing of pottery making, city building, and the construction of canals. In historic times, Tohono O'odham, or Papago, farmers relied on irrigation from the Santa Cruz River and dry farming at the base of *bajadas*, or

Pueblo clans seeking refuge in larger, more easily defended sites. Hopis identify primarily with their village rather than with a single tribe. People in different villages speak different languages but have an overarching Pueblo culture centered on agriculture, seasonal ceremonies, and the making of pottery, basketry, jewelry, and *kachinas*. Many Hopi have embraced education and professional jobs but frequently stick to traditional dress, which, like so many aspects of Pueblo culture, has strong symbolic meaning.

Left: San Carlos Apache Gaan dancer. **Above:** a Pima activist protests freeway construction on the edge of the Salt River Indian Reservation.

BUFFALO SOLDIERS

In territorial times, about a quarter of Arizona's cowboys were black. Many black soldiers fought during the Apache Wars and assisted General George Pershing when he rode into Mexico after Pancho Villa. Their physique and character impressed the Apache, who called them "buffalo soldiers." The 24th and 25th Infantry regiments, as well as the 9th and 10th Cavalry regiments, were stationed at Fort Huachuca, including the first black graduate of West Point, Henry O. Flipper. Black soldiers constituted 20 percent of all cavalry forces on the American frontier.

mountain slopes. In the early 1900s, non-Indian settlers dug channels from the Santa Cruz River to intercept the water table, destroying O'odham agriculture in the process. Lawsuits filed by the tribe finally led to settlements in the 1980s that require the City of Tucson to negotiate with the O'odham on returning some of the water.

The Akimel O'odham, or Pima, who live on the Gila Indian reservation with the Maricopa, south of Phoenix, were highly successful irrigation farmers along the Salt and Gila rivers. They became the first agricultural entrepreneurs in Arizona during the US–Mexico War, when

they traded flour and other goods with the US Army, and later supplied gold miners headed for California. They too saw their farms wither as white settlers dug canals and diverted water. By the late 1800s, the people who had once fed a whole state found themselves poverty-stricken and in need of aid.

Coolidge Dam, built in 1924, was designed to return water to the Akimel O'odham but was an expensive failure. Built during a long drought, its reservoir not only never filled but prevented seasonal flooding, one of the last viable means of agriculture on the reservation. Today, the Akimel O'odham are farming again, and in 2003 they opened a multimillion-dollar resort, the Sheraton Wild Horse Pass, on their land.

The Colorado River Yumans

The struggle for access and control of the Colorado River was also at the root of fighting between Quechan Indians and Spanish and later Anglo settlers. The Quechan, who had historically manned the ferry crossing at Yuma, were forced to cede control to Americans in the mid-1800s, after the construction of Fort Yuma. In the late 1800s, irrigation projects brought Anglo farmers to the desert and forced the Yumans to share newly created reservations with refugees from the Navajo, Hopi, and other tribes.

The Yumans' ancestors covered their bodies in elaborate tattoos, wore shells in their ears, and made beautiful painted effigy pottery. They were guided by powerful dreams about every aspect of daily life, including institutionalized warfare. The most important battle waged by the Colorado River Tribes in recent times has been a legal one in the 1980s over zoning of tribal lands – a fight they won handily.

The Pai

The Yavapai, Havasupai, and Hualapai tribes were nomads who once occupied nearly a third of northern and central Arizona. They speak closely related languages. Hualapai means Pine Tree People, Havasupai means People of the Blue Green Water, and Yavapai means People of the Sun. They believe themselves to be "the only true human beings on earth".

The Havasupai live in the western Grand Canyon in one of the most beautiful and remote settings in the Southwest. Access to the village of Supai is by foot or mule from the rim of the canyon, or by boat. The Havasupai receive provisions by mule but also farm in the canyons. Their neighbors, the Hualapai, live atop the rim and have embraced the modern world with a large-scale resort and airport. The Yavapai merged with the Tonto Apache in the Verde Valley. Both groups are known for fine basketry.

The Southern Paiute

The Southern Paiute are also superb basket makers. When encountered by explorer Major John Wesley Powell during his 1869 and 1871 surveys of the area around the Colorado River, they were still hunting and gathering seasonally on the North Rim and using tightly woven burden baskets for collecting seeds and plants, winnowing, and headgear. Only the San Juan Paiute Tribe keeps the tradition alive today. They do a lively trade in Navajo wedding baskets, an essential part of Navajo nuptials. Arizona's Kaibab Paiute tribe lives on a very small reservation, north of the Grand Canyon, and is embracing cultural tourism as its main means of support, next to Pipe Spring National Monument.

Spanish legacy

Unlike New Mexico, which became the headquarters of Spanish government in the north in the 1600s, Arizona was never dominated by New Spain. The earliest explorers were mainly interested in finding the fabled Seven Cities of Gold. There were no such places in arid, over-

The *conquistadores* did not stick around. They hurried northeast to what is now New Mexico, where Spanish culture would change New Mexican pueblos forever, a fate that never befell Arizona's fiercely independent Hopi on their remote mesas in northern Arizona.

The mission era

Spanish missionaries returning to Arizona 150 years after the first Spanish explorers also found their work cut out for them. That Indian missions at Tumacacori and San Xavier del Bac in the Santa Cruz River valley south of Tucson were established in the 1690s was entirely due

heated southern Arizona – only abandoned Hohokam towns melting back into the caliche soil. Poor Pimas and Papagos (today's O'odham people) wandered around the Sonoran Desert, hunting and gathering and sleeping in makeshift shelters. Warlike Yumans repelled the foreigners in the Mojave Desert along the Colorado River, and bands of Apache warriors hid in every corner of the mountains and staged lightning raids on livestock. To the north, there seemed to be nothing but mountains, mesas, and the impenetrable Grand Canyon.

LEFT: an Indian woman weaves a basket. **ABOVE:** Hopi girls gather water in 1906. Their whorled hairstyles indicate that they are unmarried.

to the charisma of Father Eusebio Kino, an Italian-born Jesuit, who was warmly received in Indian communities throughout Sonora and southern Arizona. His respect for the Indians was largely undone by the Franciscan priests who replaced Jesuit missionaries in the 1700s. These priests taught Indians livestock ranching, farming, Old World construction techniques, and the rituals, paraphernalia, and icons of a paternalistic new religion.

But this hardly mattered when the Indians were dying in huge numbers from introduced diseases and driven to exhaustion by the incessant demands of Spanish priests, soldiers, and land grantees who expected the *encomienda*, or tribute, promised them by the Spanish Crown.

Pima rebellions occurred twice, but even worse, Apache raiding constantly posed a serious threat to the missions, even when garrisons were built to protect them.

In the end, Arizona proved too full of recalcitrant Indians and too wild a place for Spanish colonial efforts. When Mexico won its independence from Spain in 1821, the aristocrats who had sought their fortunes there headed home. Three hundred years after Spanish Conquest, Mexico had become a country of Spanish-speaking Catholic Indians. It is this Mexican culture that pervades southern Arizona today.

Mexican influences

Ironically, Mexicans did not begin to filter up into Arizona until the land passed into American hands and US soldiers were dispatched to defend settlers from marauding Apaches. People from Sonora, many of them Yaqui Indians, now felt safe heading north to find new lands to farm, ranch, and mine. The strong Sonoran influences that still pervade Tucson culture began during the early territorial period. Extended families lived in cool, thick-walled adobe compounds with saguaro and ocotillo rib ceilings, dirt floors, courtyards, and shade *ramadas* like those preserved in downtown's colorful historic districts. People of all races socialized with each other, two-stepped to Norteña music played by mariachi bands, and ate *carne asada* (barbecued beef) and other typically Sonoran dishes made with beef raised on the huge Spanish land grants along the border.

At the center of Mexican life was a deep Catholic faith, which, after being introduced by the Spanish, had taken permanent root with the miracle of the Virgin of Guadalupe, the dark-skinned madonna who appeared to an Indian man, Juan Diego, in 1531. The Virgin of Guadalupe is a ubiquitous presence throughout southern Arizona, in colorful murals, shrines, and dedicated churches. The miracle of Guadalupe is celebrated every December 12 with food, music, prayer, and a midnight Mass.

Most families still celebrate a daughter's *quinceañera*, the traditional puberty observance that probably dates back to Indian "coming of age" ceremonies not unlike those of the Navajo and Apache tribes. Another pre-Columbian

A TASTE OF MEXICO

It's a balmy summer night at El Charro, Tucson's oldest Mexican restaurant. Waiters move through the old adobe bearing warm tortilla chips, guacamole, and salsa – a piquant blend of chopped tomatoes, onions, jalapeño peppers, and cilantro. Diners are tucking into platters of meat- and cheese-filled tacos, enchiladas, tamales, flautas, burritos, and chillis rellenos, accompanied by rice, beans, flour tortillas, and sopaipillas, doughy deep-fried puffs doused with honey. The more adventurous are trying the house specialty, carne seca – sun-dried beef simmered with onions and peppers – and flan, a creamy custard.

Ranch-style, Sonoran beef dishes have been a staple since Arizona was part of Mexico. Chili colorado and chili verde (red and green chili beef stew) are longtime favorites. But other Mexican regional dishes are increasingly popular: huachinango à la Veracruzana, fish simmered in a sauce of garlic, tomatoes, capers, and nutmeg from Veracruz; pan de cazon, a kind of shark-and-bean sandwich from the Yucatan; birria, a goat pot roast from Guadalajara.

At the heart of most dishes is the alpha and omega of Mexican spices: the chili pepper, which has been grown by Indians in Central America for thousands of years. Ranging from incendiary orange Habañeros to mild Anaheims, chilis add complexity to dishes that bring the tastebuds alive.

ritual that remains popular is the Day of the Dead, held around November 1, All Souls Day. Celebrants honor the deceased, celebrate life, and acknowledge death by lighting candles, decorating graves, and offering food at altars, along with sugar representations of skulls.

Important festivities in Hispanic culture include Cinco de Mayo (the Fifth of May), which commemorates the Battle of Puebla, and Mexican Independence Day on September 16.

was an opera singer with an international reputation. His great-granddaughter is the pop singer Linda Ronstadt.

Worldwide appeal

Arizona attracted a great variety of other immigrants as well, some seeking refuge, others seeking fortune or adventure in the far West. Even before the Civil War, African-Americans were escaping to Arizona to find a new life. Wiley Box and his wife came to Tucson from Louisiana in the 1850s. A runaway slave named Ben McClendon found gold in the Superstition Mountains in 1862.

Unlike the Mexican peasants and laborers attracted to the agricultural fields of Phoenix, those who came to Tucson were often from ambitious, upper-class Sonoran families. One such immigrant was Federico Ronstadt, the son of a Sonoran mother and German father, who had trained as an engineer in his native land. Ronstadt opened a successful coach works in Tucson and, like Sam Hughes, became one of Tucson's founding fathers. Future generations of Ronstadts went on to fame and fortune, too. Federico's daughter

The promise of overnight riches drew prospectors from all over the world, making mining one of the most multicultural occupations in the West. A gold rush along Arizona's Gila River in the 1850s lured many hopefuls from California, including Chinese cooks, laundry workers, and miners, as well as Jewish traders, who set up shop in the boomtown of Gila City. A 1918 survey in the copper-mining town of Jerome found that foreign-born mine workers outnumbered Americans by more than two to one. The nationalities listed on the report included 401 Mexicans, 393 Americans, 96 Slavs, 98 Spaniards, 60 Austrians, 57 Italians, 53 Irish and 32 Serbs. The ethnic makeup of Bisbee in southeastern Arizona was equally diverse.

LEFT: Mission San Xavier del Bac, Tucson.
ABOVE: a mariachi musician at a Cinco de Mayo celebration.

DECISIVE DATES

c.10000 BC
Paleo-Indians enter the region, hunting big game such as woolly mammoth and giant ground sloth with stone-tipped spears.

AD 1
The earliest evidence of pottery dates to this period. Living in pithouses, people of the Cochise culture sustain themselves by hunting, gathering, and farming.

AD 50
Hohokam begin building irrigation canals near present-day Phoenix.

1064
Sunset Crater Volcano erupts. Sinagua farmers return to the region attracted by increased rainfall and moisture-retaining, ash-covered soil.

1250
Ancestral Pueblo people, or Anasazi, begin construction of Betatakin and Keet Seel in Tsegi Canyon, now part of Navajo National Monument.

1250–1450
Settlements in the Southwest are abandoned due possibly to drought, disease, or overuse of resources.

1250–1450
Athabascans migrate from the north, and later diverge into Navajo and Apache tribes.

1540
Coronado expedition extends Spanish domain to the Southwest in futile search for reputed cities of gold.

1582
Antonio de Espejo finds some of the silver and copper deposits that would yield immense riches three centuries later.

1598
Juan de Oñate crosses Arizona and establishes the first European settlement in the Southwest, near Santa Fe, New Mexico.

1680
A sudden rebellion by Pueblo Indians costs the lives of more than 400 settlers in Arizona and New Mexico.

1687
Father Eusebio Francisco Kino begins the wide-ranging efforts that make this "Padre on Horseback" and founder of Tumacacori and San Xavier del Bac the most celebrated of the Spanish missionaries.

1751
Pima Revolt leads to establishment of a presidio at Tubac – which was moved to Tucson in 1776 – to protect missionaries and settlers from Indian attack.

1805
A Spanish military expedition into Canyon de Chelly results in the massacre of 115 Navajo, virtually all of them women, children, and old men.

1821
Mexico wins independence from Spain, thereby ruling Arizona.

1848
The United States, victorious in war with Mexico, takes over most of Arizona.

1854
The southern strip of Arizona is acquired from Mexico in the Gadsden Purchase.

1858
Discovery of gold nuggets in a prospector's pan on the Gila River gives rise to Gila City, first of many Arizona mining boomtowns.

1859
The first of Arizona's Indian reservations is established at Gila River. The greatest of all will be the Navajo Nation, covering nearly 16 million acres (7 million hectares), the largest reservation in the United States.

1863
President Abraham Lincoln signs a statute recognizing Arizona as a territory separate from New Mexico.

1869
Civil War veteran Major John Wesley Powell leads a path-finding three-boat expedition down the Colorado River through the Grand Canyon.

1877
Arizona enters the era of trans-continental railroading with erection of a bridge over the Colorado River at Yuma for the Southern Pacific. Three years later, the line's arrival in Tucson sets off a grand celebration.

1881
Wyatt Earp, two of his brothers, and Doc Holliday survive shootout at the O.K. Corral in Tombstone that becomes a Western legend.

1884
Two mining companies, Phelps Dodge and Copper Queen, tap into a rich vein in Bisbee, one of many deposits that will produce vast fortunes and make Arizona famous as one of the world's greatest sources of copper.

TOP LEFT: Hopi priest, c.1910.
TOP RIGHT: Sinagua pueblo ruins at Tuzigoot National Monument. **LEFT:** San Xavier del Bac. **ABOVE:** Thomas Moran's *Chasm of the Colorado*. **RIGHT:** Fort Defiance was an Army outpost on the Navajo Reservation.

"CACHESE."

1885
University of Arizona established.

1886
Surrender of Apache warrior Geronimo marks the end of Indian resistance.

1889
Phoenix becomes Arizona's state capital.

1911
Dedication of Roosevelt Dam is first step in a federal irrigation project in the Salt River Valley that spurs development of the region.

1912
Arizona becomes the 48th state in the Union.

1917
About 1,200 striking copper miners and their supporters are removed from Bisbee by

train and deposited in a desert hundreds of miles away as labor-management conflict intensifies.

1919
Grand Canyon National Park established.

1937
Frank Lloyd Wright, consultant on the spectacular Arizona Biltmore Hotel in Phoenix, establishes a home and studio, Taliesin West, where he works until his death in 1959.

1941
The nation's entry into World War II makes Arizona a busy location for defense purposes,

stimulating population growth and transforming the state's socioeconomic character.

1960
Sun City, a new community near Phoenix equipped with golf course and shopping center for "active" senior citizens, puts five model homes on display on January 1 and is besieged by thousands of prospective buyers.

1963
Arizona's claim to a major portion of the water from the Colorado River is upheld by the United States Supreme Court.

1968
Congress approves the Central Arizona Project, a large-scale effort to deliver water to the state's most populous region.

1983
Governor Bruce Babbitt calls out the National Guard after strikers shut down the Phelps Dodge mine in Morenci. The company eventually sells part of the mine and closes operations in Ajo and Douglas.

1990
London Bridge is rebuilt at Lake Havasu in western Arizona. The improbable import, rebuilt stone by stone, makes the reservoir area the

then-governor Janet Nepolitano's appointment as head of Homeland Security in President Obama's cabinet.

2010

Governor Brewer signs into law the nation's toughest immigration law, aimed at identifying, prosecuting, and deporting illegal aliens. Controversy erupts nationwide. A year later the federal court of appeals upholds a ruling against the law, stating that it is a violation of the Constitution.

2011

Following the deadly shooting of six attendees at a meet-and-greet in Tucson by a disturbed young man, which left popular Congresswoman Gabrielle Giffords with serious head injuries, Governor Brewer vetoes a state law allowing concealed hand guns on campus. She also vetoes a law requiring proof of US citizenship for presidential candidates, a "birther law" promoted by the Tea Party, an activist right wing of the Republican party.

most popular tourist attraction after the Grand Canyon.

2000

Arizona's population reaches 5.1 million, an increase of 40 percent in 10 years; it is second only to Nevada as the fastest-growing in the nation.

2005

Grand Canyon's El Tovar hotel observes its centennial on January 14.

2006–08

Forests around Sedona are struck by severe fires that force many residents to evacuate. Volunteer groups known as Minutemen protest illegal immigration and organize

patrols of the US–Mexico border in Arizona and other western states.

2008

Arizona Senator John McCain loses the race for president to Senator Barack Obama.

2009

Jan Brewer is sworn in as Arizona governor following

TOP LEFT: a popular melodrama in 1907 romanticized frontier life. **LEFT MIDDLE:** Geronimo in 1886. **LEFT BOTTOM:** mining town of Bisbee, 1916. **ABOVE:** completed in 1911, the Roosevelt Dam impounds the Salt River. **RIGHT:** a protestor at a Border Patrol Station in Naco.

NATIVE HERITAGE

Archaeologists studying Arizona's prehistoric peoples find evidence of complex societies engaged in an ever-shifting network of cultural exchange and conflict

Hakataya cultures, influenced by the powerful Pueblo and Desert cultures, yet different enough to keep everyone guessing about who they were, where they came from, and where they went. Far from being monocultural, prehistoric Arizona was a melting pot of highly adapted cultures interacting with each other through trade, marriage, warfare, and overlapping territorial boundaries.

> *The Hohokam traded for seashells from the Pacific Coast, which they etched with fermented saguaro juice, strung into bracelets and necklaces, or decorated with a mosaic of semiprecious stones.*

People have lived in Arizona for at least 11,000 years, perhaps longer. In southern Arizona are remnants of hunting camps, cave shelters, bones of extinct megafauna, and stone tools from paleo and archaic times, as well as Hohokam pithouses, great houses atop platform mounds, and 1,000-year-old irrigation systems. To the north, colorful sandstone canyons and high-desert knolls are the settings for pithouses, multistory cliff dwellings, and granaries that blend so seamlessly with their settings that they seem more like natural outcroppings than man-made structures.

In between, atop and below central Arizona's Mogollon Rim and along the Colorado River, are the remnants of the Mogollon, Salado, and

This fact was lost on early 20th century archaeologists. Impressed by the beautifully built pueblos discovered at Mesa Verde in Colorado and Chaco Canyon in New Mexico, they came to believe that a single, evolving culture migrating through different environments and developmental stages was responsible for the ruins of the Southwest. They spent time among the Hopi and other contemporary Pueblo tribes and used them as a basis for understanding prehistoric Pueblo people, forgetting that modern Pueblos have also undergone a great deal of cultural change over the past four centuries.

By the late 1940s, the single-culture model was out of favor, and the prehistoric picture in the Southwest was beginning to look far more complex. It remains so today, as archaeologists continue to identify distinct and shared traits among the Southwest's cultures.

Ancient hunters

The earliest people in Arizona were paleo-hunters at the end of the last Ice Age, when the climate was cooler and big game lumbered across grasslands and forests in what are deserts today. These ancient hunters trapped mammoths and other prey in marshy areas or drove them off cliffs, making their kills using percussion-flaked Clovis arrowheads attached to spears. They butchered their prey on the spot, leaving behind tools and bones that have been uncovered at the Murray Springs Clovis Site in the San Pedro River Valley and in the recesses of Ventana Cave on the Tohono O'odham Indian reservation, both in southern Arizona.

The big-game bonanza didn't last. Eventually, overhunting and a drier climate doomed the woolly mammoth, ground sloth, and other large mammals to extinction.

With the loss of their main prey, paleo-hunters were forced into a different lifestyle. The Southwestern Archaic period (8,500 BC–AD 300) was a widespread hunting-gathering adaptation to the changing climate. The Archaic people were autonomous groups with defined territories. They moved around seasonally, taking advantage of a wide range of wild plants and small game, which they killed using spear-throwers known as atlatls. Artifacts from this period include chipped stone tools and debris, and occasionally sleeping circles and cleared areas.

In southwestern Arizona, the San Dieguito I period of the Archaic is represented in the Barry Goldwater Bombing Range (north of Cabeza Prieta National Wildlife Refuge), which preserves evidence of mortar holes in rocks, where stone and wooden pestles were used to grind seeds and bean pods into flour. In northern Arizona, split-twig willow figurines, thought to be hunting fetishes, were secreted in caves high above the Grand Canyon.

Cochise culture

In southeastern Arizona, University of Arizona archaeologist Emily Haury dubbed people of this Archaic period the Cochise culture and divided them into three phases: Sulphur Springs, Chiricahua, and San Pedro.

Left: O'odham women in the early 20th century harvested cactus fruit. **Right:** a medicine wheel placed at a vortex in Sedona.

As the culture advanced technologically, such artifacts as stemmed points, storage pits, and heavy millstones indicate that farming became an influential factor in the subsistence of the culture. Irrigated and dry farming of squash and teosinte, a Mexican grass that later developed into corn, produced reliable food supplies and resulted in permanent settlements.

About 2,000 years ago, the introduction of pottery from Mexico offered desert dwellers a new technology, allowing for storage of water and dried food. By the final San Pedro phase, Cochise people were living in small pithouses.

It is believed that the San Pedro phase of the Cochise culture evolved into the Mogollon tradition of the central highlands.

The Mogollon

The Mogollon people lived in early pithouse pueblos in the rugged mountains along the Arizona–New Mexico border and south into Mexico from 100 BC to the AD 1400s. Considered the least complex of the three main cultures that came to dominate the prehistoric Southwest, the Mogollon were farming and making pottery earlier than any other group in the region. They are distinguished by their rectangular kivas, or underground ceremonial chambers,

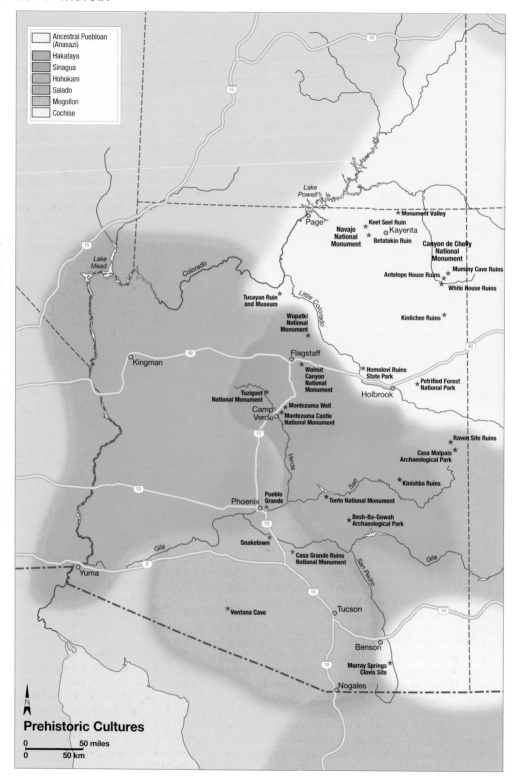

	Ancestral Puebloan (Anasazi)
	Hakataya
	Sinagua
	Hohokam
	Salado
	Mogollon
	Cochise

Prehistoric Cultures

0 ————— 50 miles
0 ————— 50 km

which developed from pithouses. Perhaps it was merely their isolation in remote mountains that prevented the mobility and exchange of ideas that allowed other cultures to advance.

Sometime between AD 900 and 1100, the Mogollon culture merged with that of the Ancestral Pueblo people (formerly known as the Anasazi) to the north and ceased to exist as a separate entity. The Mogollon began constructing multistory pueblos but continued to favor rectangular kivas, such as the great kiva found at Casa Malpais in Springerville, Arizona, built in AD 1277. In New Mexico, around the

The Hohokam

In the Sonoran Desert, around 300 BC, Archaic people were evolving into the Hohokam, a Pima word for "all used up", proposed by archaeologist Jesse Fewkes in 1910, while he was excavating the Hohokam "great house" of Casa Grande, south of Phoenix. Like other archaeologists of his day, Fewkes made no cultural distinction between the Hohokam and the Pueblo people to the north, believing that the same culture had built all the ruins, a theory that has since been discarded.

All that changed in the late 1920s, when Harold Gladwin, a Wall Street financier and

same time, they built the unusual Gila Cliff Dwellings beneath canyon overhangs.

Their basic red pottery also evolved into beautiful black-on-white vessels, perfected by a branch of the culture living on the Mimbres River of New Mexico. It featured human-like figures, lizards, birds, and scenes that depict trade in tropical birds. It is believed that the merged Pueblo and Mogollon culture contributed to the cultural background of the Hopi, Zuni, and Acoma Pueblos and the Tarahumara Indians of Mexico.

Above: petroglyphs adorn the Vermillion Cliffs in northern Arizona. Evidence of human habitation in the region stretches back more than 10,000 years.

archaeology enthusiast, financed the excavation of sites in the Sonoran Desert. The breakthrough for Gladwin and his research organization, the Gila Pueblo Foundation, came in 1935, during the huge Snaketown dig. Project archaeologist Emil Haury and his team used recently developed dating techniques and comparisons of building styles, pottery, and burial practices to establish the Hohokam as a distinct prehistoric culture. In the 1930s, and during a second major excavation of Snaketown in the 1960s, Haury refined the definitions of the Hohokam cultural sequence, consisting of four main phases: Pioneer (300 BC–AD 550), Colonial (550–900), Sedentary (900–1100), and Classic (1100–1450).

Hohokam dwellings were single-story oval or rectangular huts built over shallow pits using a framework of poles, brush, and reeds, covered with caliche mud. They included entryways, living areas with basin-shaped firepits, and storage space for single families. An outdoor shade structure, or *ramada*, protected residents from the sun. More than 60 pithouses were uncovered at Snaketown, a site in use for almost the whole of the Hohokam period. Pithouse dwellings have been found in Organ Pipe Cactus National Monument and as far north as Montezuma Well in the Verde Valley.

The Sinagua were dry-land farmers living near Flagstaff a thousand years ago. They built the lovely but lonely pueblos of Wupatki National Monument and cliff dwellings at Walnut Canyon.

The Hohokam specialized in a distinctive red-on-buff micaceous pottery, coiled on an anvil support and smoothed with a wooden paddle. Large storage jars, flat-bottomed dishes, jars with narrow openings, and legged containers such as incense burners were covered with geometric designs, curved motifs, and animal or human figures.

The Hohokam also invented a process for etching shell imported from the Gulf of California, using fermented cactus juice and wax to create lizard, toad, and other motifs; they traded these prized artworks for red argillite and other resources. Macaw feathers, pyrite mirrors, and copper bells, probably used in rituals, were imported from tribes in Mexico and distributed throughout the Southwest.

More than 200 Mesoamerican-style ball courts have been found at various Hohokam sites. Casa Grande has the earliest known ball court. Introduced in the 700s and aligned to the four points of the compass, ball courts were probably used for games that involved keeping a heavy rubber ball in play without using either the hands or feet. Ball games likely provided an opportunity to poeople interact with neighboring villages, arrange marriages, exchange goods, and mediate disputes, but they probably also had a symbolic aspect: the movements of the ball and players reenacted the annual passage of the sun, moon, and planets around the heavens and ensured cosmological harmony.

The importance of astronomy to desert farmers may also account for the introduction of multistory adobe structures atop platform mounds during the final Classic period. The four-story Casa Grande building, the only great house to survive, is 35ft (11 meters) high and contains 11 rooms. The existence of window alignments suggests that such structures may have been inhabited by ritual specialists who tracked the movements of celestial bodies and predicted rainfall, the desert's most precious commodity, during times of increased drought.

Platform mounds like the one at Casa Grande have been linked to the Hohokam's sophisticated canal irrigation system and may have played a part in regulating water use along the Gila and Salt rivers. More than 85 miles (135km) of irrigation canals have been mapped at Casa Grande, with many more lying beneath the freeways, buildings, and modern canals of Phoenix. These canals were undoubtedly the key to supporting the estimated 24,000 people who eventually concentrated in the Salt-Gila River Basin in the early 1300s – a remarkable population for such an arid region. It may have been the collapse of this irrigation system, perhaps during a major flood, that spelled the end for the Hohokam. When the Spanish arrived in the 1500s, they encountered Akimel O'odham (Pima, or Water People) and Tohono O'odham (Papago, or Desert People), probable descendants of the Hohokam who had reverted to a simpler life of hunting and gathering.

The Puebloans

It's not hard to understand the appeal of the Pueblo people's dramatic stone villages for 19th century archaeologists, who perhaps interpreted the move from simple pithouses to highrise "apartments" as an orderly progression in the rise of civilization. But, like the Hohokam and Mogollon, the Pueblo people started out as hunter-gatherers during the long Archaic period and gradually evolved into farmers.

Around the start of the Christian era, ancestors of the Puebloans were living in scattered pithouse villages and making baskets, which led cowboy-archaeologist Richard Wetherill to name them Basketmakers. By the Pueblo I period, between 700 and 900, people living in small hamlets of multistory dwellings had incorporated earlier pithouses as underground ceremonial chambers, known as kivas. They were now hunting with bows and arrows and farming more extensively.

During the Pueblo II (900–1100) and Pueblo III phases (1100–1300), larger towns appeared and, in the 1200s, the cliff dwellings that spark our fascination today. Pueblo civilization seems to have benefited from coalescence and the exchange of goods and ideas. Each community began to have its specialties and to reach new heights of invention, building more sophisticated structures, creating beautiful baskets, weaving fine cotton cloth, firing distinctive pottery, and refining tools. Centralized towns could stockpile and share food with surrounding villages during times of shortage and demand tribute and manual labor in return. This may have led to the rise of the Chaco Canyon site in New Mexico, which may have functioned as a kind of redistribution center orchestrated by ritual specialists whose understanding of astronomy allowed

them to predict favorable planting and harvesting times.

At the height of Pueblo civilization, the fertile bottomlands of the Colorado, Little Colorado, San Juan, and Virgin Rivers quickly filled up with farmers. The Tsegi Canyon-Marsh Pass area near Monument Valley, on today's Navajo reservation, was occupied for centuries by Kayenta Anasazi people, a western branch of the Pueblo culture. The Kayenta were less celebrated for their architecture than the Chacoans or Mesa Verdeans to the east and north but were distinguished by their resourcefulness, adaptability during hard times, and fine polychrome

Left: Wupatki National Monument encompasses several Sinagua pueblos. **Right:** Pueblo Grande Museum and Archaeological Park.

pottery. In the mid-1200s, increasing drought and shrinking resources forced families to engineer the impressive Betatakin and Keet Seel sites of Navajo National Monument. Nearby Canyon de Chelly and Monument Valley also contain Kayenta Anasazi ruins.

The Sinagua

First investigated by Harold Colton, founder of the Museum of Northern Arizona, the Sinagua ("without water") straddled the frontier between Anasazi, Hohokam, and Mogollon territories, apparently absorbing aspects of each culture. They began as pithouse dwellers near Sunset Crater around AD 500, but were forced to flee south to the Verde Valley following the 1065 eruption of the volcano. While in the Verde Valley, contacts with the Hohokam and other tribes exposed the Sinagua to new ideas and influences. The large Tuzigoot Pueblo, built on a defensible knoll above the Verde River in AD 1000, is Sinaguan, as are nearby Montezuma Castle and the multistory cliff dwellings around Sedona's picturesque red-rock country.

Land rush

When Sunset Crater Volcano stopped erupting, a prehistoric land rush seems to have occurred

THE ABANDONMENT

They built great cities of stone, became successful traders, and reached heights of aesthetic brilliance. Then, between 1300 and 1450, the major cultures of prehistoric Arizona simply disappeared. What happened?

The straw that broke the camel's back seems to have been a severe drought between 1276 and 1299. Crop failures would have been a disaster for civilizations that had risen to power during times of plenty, specialization of labor, and adequate leisure time to create trade goods. Now it was every man for himself. The hilltop pueblo of Tuzigoot shows clear signs of battening down the hatches. The cliff dwellings at Navajo National Monument hide in plain sight in their alcoves. Add to this the environmental havoc caused by overuse of resources, the subsequent social breakdown, and you get the picture. Time to move on.

Where did they go? Clan by clan, the Ancestral Puebloans migrated to the Hopi Mesas and the 19 pueblos strung along the Rio Grande. The Hohokam probably never left. When the Spanish arrived in the mid-1500s, the O'odham claimed to know nothing of their predecessors, yet lived in houses that resembled 1,000-year-old Hohokam dwellings. A coincidence? Archaeologists doubt it. The old way of life was simply, as the O'odham say, hohokam, "all used up."

in northern Arizona, attracting the Sinagua and other tribes eager to take advantage of the fertile volcanic soil and increased rainfall. This combination of cultures may have been responsible for development of Wupatki Pueblo, near Flagstaff, which contains Chaco-style masonry and over-scaled public architecture. The pueblo also has a Hohokam-style ball court, the northernmost ball court in North America and the only one lined with masonry.

Also noticeable is the loosely mortared, blocky style of Kayenta Anasazi construction in the many small outlying pueblos and field houses scattered between the main pueblo and the Little Colorado River. Ceremonial burials of high-status leaders and the presence of Mexican macaws and other imported items suggest that Wupatki may have functioned as an important trade and ritual center following the abandonment of the Chaco Canyon pueblos. By 1250, after just a century of use, the Sinagua had abandoned Wupatki and Walnut Canyon. They probably resettled on the Hopi Mesas to the east and at Zuni and other pueblos along the Rio Grande in New Mexico, where their descendants still live.

The Arizona Strip was the domain of the Virgin River Anasazi. Perhaps related to the Kayenta Anasazi, the Virgin River people built pueblos like the one at Pipe Spring National Monument and grew corn or maize.

Prehistoric puzzles

Similarly enigmatic in their origins and disappearance is the Salado ("salty" in Spanish), a name given to the tribe by Padre Eusebio Kino when he discovered its people living along the Salt River in the late 1600s. Known for their beautiful cotton cloth and polychrome pottery, the Salado originated in Pueblo territory, along the Little Colorado River, and settled in the Salt River Basin, picking up Mogollon traits along the way. Filling a niche between the Mogollon to the east and the Hohokam to the west, the Salado seem to have influenced the Hohokam during the Classic period, from about 1300 to 1450. They built the multistory cliff dwelling of Tonto National

Monument and the large pueblo of Besh-ba-Gowah in the city of Globe, which has yielded large quantities of pottery.

Athabascan immigrants

The cultural picture was complicated further by the arrival of Athabascan hunter-gatherers from western Canada possibly as early as the 12th century. The Athabascans diverged into two groups: the Navajo, who settled in the plateau country of northern Arizona, and the Apache, who roamed southern Arizona and New Mexico.

The Navajo were deeply influenced by their

Pueblo neighbors, taking up corn farming, weaving, and various aspects of Pueblo religion, and later by the Spanish, from whom they adopted shepherding and silversmithing. The Apache, on the other hand, remained hunter-gatherers and broke up into wide-ranging bands. The Apache acquired horses from the Spanish in the 1700s and some bands, like the Jicarilla of northern New Mexico, took on some of the cultural traits of the Plains tribes.

The best-known group, however, was the Chiricahua. Led by warriors such as Cochise and Geronimo, they were the last Indians in the Southwest to be pacified by yet another wave of immigrants – the white, English-speaking invaders from the East.

LEFT: Wupatki Pueblo National Monument sign.
RIGHT: a doorway leads into a Sinagua ruin.

THE SPANISH ERA

Seeking mythical cities of gold and pagan souls,
the Spanish planted the seeds of European
culture throughout the Southwest

Anew chapter in Arizona's history began
to unfold on February 22, 1540. Its main
character was a young and by all reports
dashing Spaniard named Francisco Vásquez
de Coronado. He was leading an expedition
of some 1,300 men and two or three women
– Spaniards, Indians, and Africans – heading
north from Mexico.

Coronado, governor of New Galicia in western
Mexico, hoped to find the "Seven Cities of Gold".
He was one of the *conquistadores* who followed
in the wake of Columbus in that swashbuckling
age sometimes known as the Spanish Century,
their names once familiar to every Iberian
schoolboy: Balboa, discoverer of the Pacific
Ocean; Cortés, who wrested control of the Aztec
empire in Mexico from Montezuma; Pizarro,
the harsh ruler of Peru who exacted an immense
ransom before killing off the Inca emperor; de
Soto, whose own expedition traipsed across the
American Southeast from Florida as far west as
Oklahoma between 1539 and 1542.

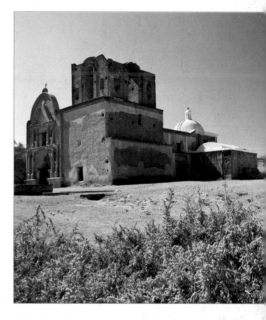

> *Cárdenas, the first European to see the Grand
> Canyon, discovered a basic truth about the
> chasm: it's bigger than it looks. Failing to reach
> the bottom, he reported "what seemed easy from
> above was not so, but instead very … difficult."*

Coronado had been born into a wealthy
family in the old university town of Salamanca
about 1510. He became an assistant to the viceroy of New Spain, António de Mendoza, and

LEFT: St Augustine Cathedral, Tucson. **RIGHT:** Tumacacori
was founded in 1691 by Father Eusebio Francisco Kino.

married into one of Mexico's wealthiest and
most powerful families. It was Mendoza who
picked him to head the expedition to the north.
That region never held much appeal for Spanish
colonials, but their interest could be piqued
by any reports suggesting that the otherwise
unpromising El Norte might turn out to be an
El Dorado brimming with precious metals.

Cities of Gold

The notion of Seven Cities of Gold persisted
in the imagination of those times. There were
variations on the theme, but one basic Iberian
legend involved Seven Bishops who fled the
peninsula to escape persecution by Moorish
infidels, crossed the Sea of Darkness, and wound

up on an island named Antilia that was blessed with gold. One of those who helped keep that legend alive was Alvar Nuñez Cabeza de Vaca.

Sailing from Florida in 1528 after having survived one great shipwreck, Cabeza de Vaca became shipwrecked again in the Gulf of Mexico, off the land that would become Texas. He and three surviving companions were taken in by Indians before embarking on a long trek across Texas into the New Mexico–Arizona region. When, after eight long years, they met up again with Spaniards, Cabeza de Vaca and his companions had become very knowledgeable about Indians and recounted

of Esteban's behavior – including his appetite for their women – objectionable and swiftly cut him to pieces.

Great expectations

Friar Marcos continued on and, according to his much exaggerated account, came upon the Zuñi pueblo of Cíbola. He described it as a dazzling place that was larger than Mexico City, and his glowing report stirred new interest in the legend of the seven great cities. It was his report that prompted Mendoza to mount the ambitious Coronado expedition of 1540, plus two additional ships commanded by Hernando

stories of supposedly great Indian kingdoms to the north.

The stories got back to Mendoza, who, before sending forth Coronado, dispatched two men on a reconnaissance mission. One was a Franciscan friar, Marcos de Niza. The other, as guide, was Esteban, a North African slave who had accompanied Cabeza de Vaca. They set out in March 1539, traveling up the west coast of northern Mexico. Esteban, going ahead of the friar, crossed into southeastern Arizona, probably through the San Rafael Valley, and followed what is now the Arizona–New Mexico border. But his luck soon ran out. The Zuñi Indians he was now encountering were less pacific than those of the south, and they found much

de Alarcón – a venture that resulted in the discovery of the mouth of the Colorado River.

And so Coronado set forth, amid much fanfare, a large financial investment by several parties and great expectations of a rich reward. After a public pledge of allegiance to Coronado, the expedition proceeded from southern Nayarit up the coast of the Gulf of California. It reached the Sonora River and followed it, then crossed the Gila River to Cíbola, in what is now western New Mexico.

Unfortunately, there was nothing imposing about Cíbola, which turned out to be a plain Zuñi pueblo. Coronado determined that Marcos de Niza had lied, and in disgrace the friar was ordered to return to Mexico City. The mission was deemed a fiasco. In actuality, it was the first systematic exploration of the Southwest and extended Spain's empire into North America. The expedition traveled as far into the interior as the land that would become central Kansas.

Coronado sent one of his lieutenants, García López de Cárdenas, and 25 comrades to search for a great river to the west that had been described by the Hopi Indians, and they became the first Europeans to encounter one of the world's great natural wonders – the Grand Canyon. For three days Cárdenas and his men tried to descend into that great abyss to reach the Colorado River, but the effort was futile and they turned back.

They also encountered herds of buffalo for the first time, to which the Spaniards were directed by a Pawnee Indian guide they called El Turco. And there was another, though far more tragic, precedent – the first of many battles that would pit Indians against whites in what is now the United States was fought on July 7, 1540, in New Mexico.

El Turco spun a tale of a great city of gold called Quivira that also turned out to be illusory – it seems that Indians were finding it convenient to tell the Spanish intruders what they wanted to hear – and his mendacity cost him his life. Then, on December 7, 1541, Coronado was thrown from his horse during a race with one of his lieutenants and badly injured. Struck on the head by the horse's hoof, he was never the same again. The expedition returned home in 1542, without precious metals, and Coronado died 12 years later in Mexico City.

It would be 40 years before another exploration was undertaken. In 1582, Antonio de Espejo led a party of nine soldier-prospectors and a hundred or so Zuñi Indians up the Rio Grande to what is now New Mexico in search of three missionary priests – they had been killed, as it turned out – and deposits of precious minerals. His party visited Hopi villages as Coronado's group had done four decades earlier, and the territory was officially claimed for Spain's King Philip II. Silver and copper deposits were discovered in the area that came to be known as Jerome, east of present-day Prescott. Three centuries later Jerome would be the site of a copper bonanza.

Spanish colonization of the Southwest began in earnest in 1598 under Juan de Oñate, a wealthy Mexican-born miner with important connections – his wife was a descendant of both the *conquistador* Hernán Cortés and Montezuma, the Aztec emperor. Oñate, who had received a contract from Philip II, led 130 families, 270 single men, and several thousand head of cattle up the Rio Grande to San Juan Pueblo, just north of present-day Santa Fe, New Mexico. This was probably the first European settlement in the Southwest. The settlers were mostly Mexicans and *mestizos* (of European and Amerindian racial descent) who had come in search of a new life.

Oñate traveled across Arizona and got as far east as Kansas, where he fought an unsuccessful

THE CROSSING OF THE FATHERS

Missionaries did a lot of traveling in the old days. A case in point is the journey made in 1776 by the intrepid Franciscan priests Silvestre Valez de Escalante and Atanasio Dominguez, who hoped to find a good route from Santa Fe to California. The priests journeyed north from New Mexico into Colorado and then over to Utah but failed to find their way to the Pacific.

Disappointed, they headed for home, whereupon they became the first white men to encounter one of the few places along the 1,500-mile (2,400km) Colorado River where it could be crossed on horseback. It is in northern Arizona, at Lake Powell, and known today as the Crossing of the Fathers – El Vado de Los Padres.

LEFT: Indians bring gold to conquistadores in this 17th-century depiction of Spain's New World conquest. **RIGHT:** the Hopi resisted Spanish dominance.

battle against Indians. Meanwhile, a small troop of men under the command of one of his officers, Captain Marcos Farfán de los Godos, found a rich deposit of silver ore near present-day Prescott.

Heavy metal

Farfán and his eight companions, in addition to some Hopi guides, headed into the timberland of the Mogollon Rim. They encountered Jumana Indians who led them to the Verde River valley. Farfán's group came close upon the mineral deposits that had been discovered years earlier by Espejo and that were being

mined by the Indians themselves. It was the Europeans' introduction to Arizona's mineral wealth. Farfán returned in 1604 with another expedition, and over the next two years the locations of much of the area's mineral deposits were found.

Oñate's achievement was to solidify Spanish control over a vast area that encompassed Arizona, New Mexico, Texas, Colorado, Nevada, Oklahoma, and Kansas. He has been called the Last Conquistador. After him, and for much of the 17th century, a missionary fervor took hold in the Americas, which sought to bring the Indians into the Christian fold through spiritual persuasion and peaceable means.

Indian revolt

Three religious orders become dominant in the American southwest – the Franciscan, Dominican, and Jesuit orders. The Franciscans came first, reaching Arizona approximtely 20 years after Oñate's visit. Arriving at the Hopi villages in 1629, they established the first permanent structures erected for use by Europeans in Arizona.

Colonization was enhanced by the Catholic priests, their missions, and their peaceable ways. But among some Indian tribes, such as the Hopi, resentment simmered. A major rebellion erupted in 1680 in the Pueblo Revolt, owing mainly to unhappiness over Spanish inability to protect the tribes against guerrilla attacks by nomadic Apache and Navajo warriors. The leader of the revolt, Popé, was determined to drive the Spaniards entirely out of northern New Spain. In a surprise, well-planned attack, Pueblo Indians in Arizona and New Mexico arose. Some 400 settlers, including 22 priests, were slain, and the remainder were driven all the way back south to El Paso.

There were other major outbreaks of native violence. In 1700, Hopis killed priests and sacked Awatovi, ending Spanish colonization of northern Arizona. The Apache and Pima resisted the gradual entry of miners and farmers in Santa Cruz Valley. In 1751 a revolt by Pima warriors resulted in the death of a hundred or so people and the destruction of missions and farms. Spanish soldiers caught up to, and defeated, the Pima in the Santa Catalina Mountains north of Tucson.

Holy mission

The Jesuit era in Arizona ended in 1767 when the powerful order was expelled by Spain's King Carlos III. Taking their place in the Southwest missions were the Franciscans, and the priest assigned to the Arizona missions was Francisco Tomás Garcés. He proved to be a tireless presence who established a strong rapport with the local tribes. He sought to establish a link with the missions newly founded in California by another Franciscan who would become equally renowned, Father Junípero Serra.

Garcés accompanied Captain Juan Bautista de Anza on two major expeditions to California in the mid-1770s. Garcés explored the westernmost reaches of the Grand Canyon and named the great river that coursed through it Río Colorado ("ruddy-colored"). He then headed east and reached the Hopi villages. His journey lasted 11 months and covered about 2,000 miles (3,200km). Sadly, this popular priest who came to know Indian ways so intimately was martyred in the great Yuma Revolt of 1781 in which Quechan Indians rebelled against their Spanish oppressors. The revolt shut the land route to California via Arizona, at the strategic Yuma Crossing for four decades.

Tucson was chosen as the site for one of 15 *presidios* along a route stretching west from San

to dependency on Spanish largesse. It was an effective, if cynical, strategy.

The Spanish colonial phase was nearing its end. At the peak of its power, as historian David J. Weber observed, Spain claimed an area in North America alone, from ocean to ocean, that was larger than all of Western Europe. Now the tide was receding. And as political problems mounted for the Spanish governors in Mexico City, less attention could be paid to the outermost reaches of the empire. Shifts in power were looming that would reconfigure the political map of the American Southwest.

Antonio, Texas. Construction began in 1775. Seven years later the fort was attacked by a large war party of Apache Indians. Under the leadership of Don Pedro Allande, the *presidio* withstood the attack.

Apache resistance to Europeans was strong, but a Spanish policy initiated in 1784 by Viceroy Bernardo de Galvez took a new tack designed to improve relations with the Indian tribes. Indians were now encouraged to settle near trading posts, amply supplied with alcoholic beverages, and generally reduced

LEFT: Navajo petroglyphs at Canyon de Chelly depict the coming of Spanish soldiers.
RIGHT: the interior of Mission San Xavier del Bac.

THE PADRE ON HORSEBACK

Father Eusebio Francisco Kino, an Italian-born Jesuit, was renowned as the "Padre on Horseback." He arrived in Mexico in 1681, established his first mission six years later in Sonora, and first visited Indian villages in Arizona (Pimería Alta) in 1691. Father Kino rode thousands of miles in the course of introducing European crops and teaching Indians how to farm and raise livestock, exploring and map-making in addition to tending to spiritual needs. By his death in 1711 he had started 25 missions, three of them between Tucson and Nogales in Arizona – including the future sites of the architecturally renowned San Xavier del Bac and San Jose de Tumacácori.

COWBOYS, INDIANS, AND MINERS

Spurred on by nationalism and the promise of mineral wealth, Americans take possession of a harsh and violent land

The 19th century brought a major change of identity for Arizona and the Southwest. What had long been a Spanish colonial outpost would now become an Anglo-American homeland. The old order of Iberian *conquistadores*, missionaries, and remote bureaucrats yielded to an influx of North American gringos – the mountain men at first, then miners and merchants, farmers and ranchers – driven by materialism and Manifest Destiny.

Behind the transformation were such main historic currents as Anglo expansion and Iberian decline, an American self-confidence imbued with revolutionary fervor, even the nationalist sentiment of the tumultuous Napoleonic period. Those same nationalist winds of change that swept over all of Latin America were felt by Mexicans, who rebelled against their Spanish overlords in 1810 and achieved independence by 1821.

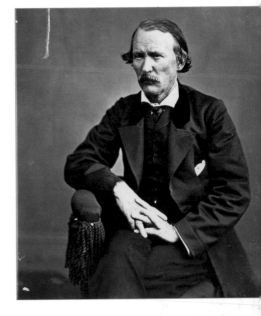

> Territorial governor Anson P. K. Safford returned all but $5,000 of a $25,000 bribe intended to secure a land grant for the Southern Pacific Railroad; the briber apparently over-estimated the legislature's price.

Oddly enough, the last years of Spanish rule in the Southwest had been relatively peaceful and productive. There had been good relations with the Pima. Farming and ranching activities were prospering, especially in the Santa Cruz Valley of southern Arizona. Minerals were

discovered and missions erected – San Xavier del Bac was completed in 1797, San José de Tumacácori dedicated in 1822.

Mexican independence

This era of good feelings lasted about a quarter of a century, starting to dissipate about the time Mexicans began agitating for independence. When it was achieved, Arizona became Mexican territory. Ironically, the break with Spain helped open the Southwest to the gringos, who were at first welcome to enter the region. Mexico's regime, unlike the aloof and suspicious Spaniards, favored not only commercial relations with the Americans but settlement as well.

LEFT: a Hopi man ascends a kiva ladder, 1897.
RIGHT: Christopher "Kit" Carson.

In pre-independence Texas, for example, large tracts of land were made available – as long as prospective settlers swore fealty to Mexican rule and Catholic belief. For their part, what the Mexicans sought were large numbers of home-steaders whose presence would mitigate the threat of depredations by Apache, Comanche, and other hostile Indians.

Anglos, disposed to free trade and com-merce, began trickling into the territory. Many were trappers – beaver fur was profitable at a time when men generally wore that type of hat. The basic trade route, the Santa Fe Trail, became an American landmark. It stretched

from Independence, Missouri, to Santa Fe, New Mexico, where it picked up the Chihuahuan Trail south to Mexico City. Some trappers added California to their itinerary, as did Christopher "Kit" Carson, who became a renowned frontier guide and Indian agent and served as a Union general in the Civil War. Traders came, mated – many with Mexican brides – and settled, laying down a foundation for a different Arizona that emerged after mid-century.

American takeover

The turning point came when war erupted in 1846. Mexicans had become unnerved by all the Americans they had once welcomed, and Texas was already lost. War was declared and the US Government sent troops, including the Army of the West headed by General Stephen Watts Kearny. Kearny seized Las Vegas, a village on the Santa Fe Trail, and announced on September 22, 1846, that henceforth New Mexico and Arizona were US territory.

Kearny was assigned the task of opening up a wagon route across the Arizona wilder-ness to California, and the work was carried out efficiently by a specially formed unit of Mormon volunteers. Traveling more than 1,000 miles (1,600km) in just 102 days, the Mormon Battalion of 340 men and a few women hacked out a road from Santa Fe through Tucson and on to San Diego. Some of the Mormons settled in Arizona, largely as farmers and ranchers.

Mexico lost a lot of ground – nearly half of her land – when the Treaty of Guadalupe Hidalgo ended hostilities on February 2, 1848. The lost acreage included Arizona north of the

ONE HUMP OR TWO?

The US Army's Camel Corps was born in 1855 when Congress agreed that camels would be useful in exploring arid lands. So 33 of the desert animals were shipped to Texas, with another 44 to follow. All were the one-humped dromedary type, as opposed to the 20 bactrians (two humps) later imported by mine owners in Nevada.

The camels could haul heavier loads than mules, could work at a faster pace, and could go for long periods of time without water. They came in handy when the Army opened a road across the Arizona ter-ritory to the Colorado River. But, alas, these large, shaggy creatures also had a way of startling horses

and mules, not to mention people, and the cavalry-men disliked them. Most of the camel drivers imported to handle the animals proved to be inept, although one of them achieved prominence – Hadji Ali, a Syrian known as Hi Jolly who was honored following his death in Arizona in 1902 with a grave monument at Quartzsite.

Unfortunately the camels used to explore the West were generally mistreated and malnourished. The Civil War caused the War Department to lose interest in the experiement and the camels were auctioned off. Not all of them found owners, and a few were relegated to a nomadic existence.

Gila River. Six years later, the Gadsden Purchase brought all of the Arizona territory under US control. James Gadsden, a railroad promoter serving as American minister to Mexico, purchased on behalf of the United States some 29 million acres in southern New Mexico and Arizona south of the Gila River. The cost: $10 million. The land was wanted, mostly, for a southern railroad route to California, but the project was never carried through.

Gold diggers

What really stimulated traffic across the Arizona territory was the gold rush, that frenzy which

Settlement remained sparse in the 1850s. In southern Arizona there were some mining communities but only two military posts (Fort Buchanan and Fort Breckinridge). The beginning of American occupation of the lower Colorado Valley occurred in February 1852, with the establishment of Fort Yuma on the California side of the Colorado River. More military forts would be constructed to protect travelers from attack by hostile Indians.

Most of the Anglos who were settling in Arizona were Southerners. With the outbreak of the Civil War, Confederate leaders noted that the territory was poorly defended by federal

seemed to lure half the world to California after James Marshall found some bright metal in a stream at Sutter's Mill on January 24, 1848. The quest for mineral wealth attracted settlers to Arizona. Transportation was by wagon, stagecoach, and even, on the Colorado River, steamboat. Tracks were laid by the Southern Pacific and the Atlantic and Pacific (later called Santa Fe) Railroads, and direct connection with the California coast was made in 1883, at San Diego. Arizona became inextricably linked to the rest of the United States.

LEFT: Indian scouts pursue Geronimo in a Harper's Weekly illustration by Frederic Remington,1886.
ABOVE: a stylized depiction of an Apache raid.

troops and sought to take advantage of that fact. Citizens of Tucson voted to join the secessionist cause, and Confederate troops occupied the town in February 1862. They withdrew, however, when Union forces from California arrived.

Most of the entire western half of the New Mexico territory was controlled by Indians, and they were not thrilled by the wave of fortune-seekers intruding on their land like a plague of locusts. Before the Forty-niner fever ran its course, the region would be visited by an estimated 50,000 gold diggers and tradespeople.

Indian relations with settlers had waxed and waned ever since the Spanish arrival. The chaotic period that followed Mexican independence in 1821 brought a breakdown in relations, especially with Apaches. They made assaults on farms and ranches in Mexico's Sonora region and in southern Arizona, running off herds of horses and dislocating commerce and agriculture. There would be many notorious incidents. One of them, in 1837, involved a group of Mexicans led by an Anglo settler, John Johnson, who abruptly ended two days of peace talks by suddenly gunning down their Apache counterparts, about 20 in all.

Apaches, who conducted their raids from mountain strongholds, had waged an especially fierce resistance against all invaders. To a Spanish missionary writing in 1630, they were "fiery and bellicose and very crafty in war", and so they appeared to the Anglo-Americans who inherited the territory and with it Indian hostility.

Apaches were greatly skilled in handling the horse – a once-native species, which was reintroduced to the New World by Spaniards – and were accustomed to moving about freely. Now, however, their way of life was threatened – miners were a particular thorn in their side – and they struck back.

Hostilities worsened in the 1860s. Bounties were paid for Indian scalps, and Arizona's territorial legislature called on the federal Department of War to carry out a policy of extermination.

A GRAND RIDE THROUGH THE CANYON

Exactly 100 years before Neil Armstrong became the first earthling to step on the Moon, a one-armed Civil War veteran was making his own fantastic voyage down the Colorado River. Major John Wesley Powell, 35, and his boating expedition traveled 900 miles (1,450km) from Green River, Wyoming, through the Grand Canyon in Arizona in 1869. It was a grueling, dangerous journey that had been considered impossible, even by Native Americans. Indeed, the expedition was given up as lost before Powell and five comrades emerged from the mouth of the Virgin River three months later. The date was August 30, 1869. Four men had dropped out along the way, three of them killed by Indians in apparent retaliation, wrongfully, for the murder of an Indian woman.

Powell's right arm had been amputated after he was wounded at Shiloh, but he remained in active service on the condition that his bride, Emma, accompany him. After the war, she became the first woman to climb Pike's Peak, as part of an expedition headed by her husband. Powell, a geology professor, explored the Green and Colorado rivers again in 1870–71. He took up the frustrating duties of a government official, founding and directing the US Geological Survey and later the Bureau of Ethnology, a post he held until he died in 1902.

The request denied, a citizens' mob took it upon itself to slaughter 75 unarmed Apache women and children near Tucson.

Massacre of innocents

A more notorious incident occurred in the Camp Grant Massacre of April 1871. A posse organized in Tucson to avenge Indian raids rode 60 miles (95km) northeast to the abandoned military camp, where Aravaipa Apaches were confined. The posse attacked at dawn, when most of the Apache men were out hunting, and caused as many as 100 deaths. Virtually all of the victims were women and children. The raiders were tried for murder in Tucson but acquitted. Bent on revenge, Apaches launched their own raids and ambushes against settlers and soldiers, with terrible atrocities committed.

In 1864, Colonel Kit Carson headed an army operation that rounded up some 9,000 Navajo at Canyon de Chelly in Arizona and forced them on an infamous 300-mile (500km) "long walk" to a desolate area in New Mexico known as Bosque Redondo, where they were incarcerated for four years. Seven years later, President Ulysses S. Grant sent General George Crook to Arizona. He proved adept at reining in roving bands of Apache marauders while at the same time winning Indian acceptance of the reservation concept.

The so-called Indian Wars in effect tied down America's military establishment before subjugation of Native Americans was completed by 1890. Three names are particularly prominent in most accounts of Indian leaders at this period in Arizona's history: Mangas Coloradas, Cochise, and Geronimo. All were Chiricahua Apaches who fought fiercely against the takeover of their land and the subjugation of their people, though it was a struggle doomed to failure.

Mangas Coloradas ("Red Sleeves"), a giant of a man at 6.5ft (2 meters) tall, had conducted campaigns against Mexicans and even offered to help General Kearny when they met in 1846. Turning in later years against Anglo-Americans, Mangas Coloradas attacked a 126-man army unit at Apache Pass in the Chiricahua Mountains and was wounded by gunfire. Captured in January 1863, he was imprisoned

at an abandoned fort in New Mexico and gunned down by soldiers when he resisted being taunted with heated bayonets.

Cochise, who married a daughter of Mangas Coloradas, was captured in 1861 at Apache Pass by an army lieutenant named George Bascom who had pretended to be friendly. The notorious Bascom Affair involved the abduction of a 12-year-old boy from a ranch for which Cochise was wrongfully accused. Cochise escaped, but hostages on both sides were killed, including his brother and two nephews. Apaches took 150 lives in two months, and hostilities raged until 1872, exact-

ing 4,000 casualties and causing entire settlements to be abandoned.

Geronimo was the last Indian to surrender to the United States, in 1886. Earlier in his life his mother, wife, and children were killed in an attack by Mexican soldiers on an Apache camp. In 1877 he was arrested and confined to a reservation in Arizona. He broke free with a band of followers and for five years conducted raids that harassed army troops and terrorized southeastern Arizona and neighboring areas in Mexico and New Mexico.

General Crook pursued Geronimo and his Apache force and twice attempted to negotiate the terms of a surrender. A compromise allowing a return to the Arizona reservation

LEFT: Navajo men. **RIGHT:** Geronimo (fourth from left) discusses surrender with Gen. George Crook (second from right), 1886.

was overruled by President Grover Cleveland, who suggested that Geronimo be hanged. The Apache warrior slipped away again. With his fourth and final surrender, this time to a less sympathetic General Nelson Miles, harsh terms were imposed on the Apache warrior and his cohort. They were shipped in chains to a prison camp in Florida, and later to Alabama.

Late in life Geronimo performed in Wild West shows, took part in President Theodore Roosevelt's inaugural parade in 1905, dictated his memoirs for a biography published in 1906, and died three years later of pneumonia, still a prisoner of war, at Fort Sill, Oklahoma.

places in New Spain. In 1736, a rich lode of silver was found about 25 miles (40km) southwest of what is now Nogales, Arizona, by a Spaniard who was guided to the site by a Yaqui Indian.

One of the first of the latter-day Arizona miners to hit pay dirt was Charles D. Poston, a Kentuckian who came to be known as the "father of Arizona". Poston went to California about 1850 and four years later visited southern Arizona, taking ore samples at Tubac and Ajo. With him was Herman Ehrenberg, a German-born mining engineer he had met.

The high quality of the ore led to creation of the Sonora Exploring and Mining Company,

Mining bonanza

If the Anglo-American takeover was Arizona's most important development in the 19th century, not far behind was the fact that the territory turned out to be so rich in precious metals – gold, silver, and copper. Mining activity on a serious scale got under way right after the Gadsden Purchase fixed boundaries in 1854. The gold strike in California a few years earlier had made prospecting a popular activity in the region, and western Arizona was one of the nearby areas being searched.

Spaniards had made discoveries as far back as the 16th century, but the means of taking out the ore were limited. There were silver mines at Alamos, Zacatecas, Guanajuato, and other

excavation near the old Spanish *presidio* at Tubac, and a booming business in silver. About $3,000 worth was extracted daily before the start of the Civil War in 1861 necessitated the removal of federal troops from the Santa Cruz area and, with no protection against hostile Indians, shutdown of the mines. Arizona saw fighting during the Civil War. The Battle of Picacho Pass, the westernmost battle in the Civil War, was fought around Picacho Peak on April 15, 1862, between Unionist cavalry from California and Confederate pickets from Tucson.

Poston pushed for territorial status for Arizona, going to Washington in 1862 to lobby. The territory and the name "Arizona" became official on February 24, 1863, and

Poston was elected its first delegate to Congress. Whatever profit he accrued was dissipated by the time of his death in 1902.

Another silver miner was Sylvester Mowry, an ex-soldier who built a thriving business in the late 1850s. He kept it operating despite the removal of troops at the start of the Civil War and in the face of harassment by Apaches. The Mowry Mine was one of the nation's richest producers early on, but wartime complications deprived its founder of any lasting fortune.

Arizona was found to have ample deposits of both placer gold, the surface kind easy to get at, and lode gold, which requires a large-scale min-

1863 near what is now Congress Junction when in just three months more than a quarter of a million dollars in placer gold was found.

Rich copper deposits

There were many gold and silver strikes worth millions of dollars in the latter years of the 19th century, but the metal that became Arizona's most valuable resource was copper. The first substantial effort at open pit mining was undertaken at Ajo in 1854 by the American Mining and Trading Company – the ore was shipped via Cape Horn all the way to Wales for smelting.

ing enterprise. Placer gold became scarce after a relatively short period, and serious mining was left to the big companies. The territory's first gold rush occurred in 1858 when rich deposits of placer gold were discovered by Jake Snively, a Texan, about 20 miles (32km) beyond the junction of the Gila and Colorado rivers.

A boomtown known as Gila City arose, but by 1864 the site was virtually cleaned out. Another rich strike was made in 1862 at La Paz, some $8 million worth of gold being taken there before it too ran dry. The richest discovery was made in

ABOVE: the town of Clifton (shown here in 1909), together with nearby Morenci, was part of one of the richest copper-mining districts in the country.

Bisbee, in southeastern Arizona, turned out to be one of the richest copper areas in the world. Here the Copper Queen company began mining in 1880. The site had been chanced upon by an army scout from nearby Fort Bowie, and ownership eventually passed to a San Francisco group of financiers. They formed the Copper Queen Mining Company, a huge deposit of rich ore was unearthed, and thus was born the boomtown of Bisbee, which took its name from the company's attorney, who never set foot in the place.

Now entering the picture was Phelps, Dodge & Company, a small metal-importing firm based in New York that had been urged to set up mining operations in southern Arizona.

It bought out Copper Queen and reaped a fortune. By 1908 copper totaling 730 million pounds (330 million kg) and worth millions of dollars was mined. It has been estimated that by 1975 the Bisbee area alone produced gold, silver, copper, lead, and zinc worth over $6 billion.

Fortunes were made. James Douglas, the assayer-consultant who steered Phelps Dodge to Arizona and became president of Copper Queen Consolidated, was worth $20 million at his death in 1918. Douglas and Phelps Dodge did, however, miss out on one opportunity: a mine operation in Jerome that became the prodigious United Verde company.

Its principal figure was New York financier Eugene Jerome, whose offer to sell for $300,000 was met by the Montana mining tycoon and politician William A. Clark after Douglas held off one day too many. Clark eventually took in more than $100 million from United Verde. The company was bought by Phelps Dodge in 1935 for $21 million.

The town too tough to die

Most famous of all the boomtowns that grew out of the mining bonanza was Tombstone. Ed Schieffelin, who arrived in Arizona in 1876 with nothing to show after 20 years of prospecting, hit it rich in 1877. He discovered rich silver deposits in the San Pedro Valley about 70 miles (110km) southeast of Tucson. Joining him in the enterprise was his brother Albert and Dick Gird, an assayer who realized the value of the ore. Schieffelin was warned that the territory was Apache country and "all you'll find will be your tombstone". The name stuck.

With support from Eastern investors, the Tombstone Mining District was established. By 1888, some $30 million worth of silver had been taken out. At least 50 mines were lodged in the hills around Tombstone by 1886, and they employed hundreds of teamsters, millworkers, and miners.

Schieffelin and his brother Albert sold their claims for a half million dollars each in 1880, and Gird, too, cashed in handsomely the next year. Ed Schieffelin kept trying his luck over the years in various places, including Alaska. He died in a shack in Oregon and is buried in Arizona near the site of one of his strikes, a

---

THE ENIGMA OF TOMBSTONE

Hero? Villain? None of the above? Wyatt Earp is a hard man to pin down – buffalo hunter, gambler, gold-digger, sometime lawman who, craving excitement, lit out for Arizona and enduring notoriety. One thing is certain: he had a knack for survival. He alone emerged unscathed in the bloody shootout at the O.K. Corral and then beat the rap, along with brothers Virgil and Morgan and their hot-tempered friend Doc Holliday. Then, when Morgan was mysteriously dispatched by a bullet while shooting pool, a second one went sailing by Wyatt. In another shooting, Virgil's arm was crippled. And in 1900, younger brother Warren was terminated by a bullet in an Arizona bar.

Wyatt outlasted all of his eight siblings. He and Josie Marcus, the showgirl who became his lifetime companion, knocked about mining camps in Colorado. They joined the Idaho gold rush in 1884, and ran a saloon in San Diego. In 1896, Earp took to the boxing ring in San Francisco to officiate at a match between heavyweights Bob Fitzsimmons and Tom Sharkey – in the process exposing the .45 Colt he packed under his frock coat. Then it was off to the Alaska gold rush and a profitable saloon-gambling venture. After further prospecting, Wyatt and Josie settled in Los Angeles, where he died in 1929, an 80-year-old Western legend.

monument 25ft (8 meters) tall towering over his grave. Tombstone's mines started to flood in 1883 and were shut down completely by 1909.

Tombstone attracted a variety of people, many with rough edges. Its population soared to 15,000 in a short time and the town acquired a notorious reputation – President Chester A. Arthur once threatened to impose martial law in the entire territory. This was the heyday of the cowboy, that Anglo version of the *vaquero* character Spaniards introduced to the American West. Pulp fiction and Hollywood fantasy would transform the drab, proletarian cowboy into a mythical hero-gunfighter.

Wyatt Earp is a good example. Born in Illinois in 1848, he worked at various jobs in the West, hunting buffalo, fighting Indians, and occasionally running afoul of the law. In 1876 he was a deputy policeman in Dodge City, the wild and woolly Kansas cattle town. Here he met Doc Holliday, Luke Short, and Bat Masterson. They, Earp, and his four brothers gravitated to Tombstone, became known as the Dodge City Gang, and made political friends and enemies: Virgil Earp was appointed town marshal. Differences with the Clantons, a rowdy family of small ranchers and cattle rustlers, simmered into a poisonous enmity that finally exploded in a deadly shootout.

The shootout happened near the O.K. Corral in Tombstone on the night of October 25, 1881. When it was over, three members of the Clanton faction lay dead, Earp's brothers Virgil and Morgan were wounded, and Holliday was creased by a bullet. Wyatt Earp was unhurt. The gunfight lasted less than 30 seconds but the legend has endured. Virgil Earp was later wounded in an ambush and Morgan Earp shot to death while shooting pool in a saloon.

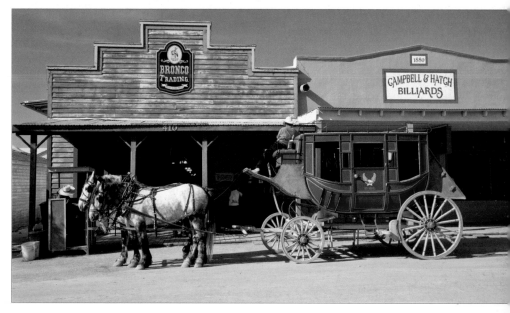

Bloodier yet was the Graham-Tewksbury feud that raged for six years between cattlemen and sheepmen in Pleasant Valley, in the Tonto Basin, starting in 1886. It exploded when sheep by the thousands were allowed to graze in the valley despite a strict prohibition. Ambushes, shootouts, and other violence left dozens of casualties, some of them innocent victims. One woman lost a husband and four sons.

Hollywood burnished the myth on screen in a steady flow of shoot-'em-ups – *Fort Apache*, *Arizona Kid*, *Broken Arrow*, and, of course, *Gunfight at the O.K. Corral*. But the times were a-changin' for Tombstone and Bisbee and all the get-rich-quick boomtowns as another century dawned over Arizona Territory.

LEFT: staged in 1907, the drama *An Arizona Cowboy* romanticized the rigors of frontier life.
ABOVE: Tombstone recreates frontier life.

BIRTH AND REBIRTH

Reclamation projects, wartime industry, and a
cool new invention called air-conditioning
powered Arizona through the 20th century

Gunfire flared in Arizona on St. Valentine's
Day in 1912, but it wasn't triggering any
Chicago-style gangland massacre, nor was
it a resurgence of frontier lawlessness. It was a
celebration of something happening in far-off
Washington, D.C. A proclamation admitting
Arizona to full-fledged membership in the
Union was being signed there by President
William Howard Taft.

After half a century as a territory, it was
becoming the 48th and last of the continental
United States. Taft's ceremonial signing was a
good photo-op, and a motion-picture camera
was on hand to film the historic moment. And
who could blame the armed citizenry back in
Arizona for being fired up? They had waited
a long time. There were too many Democrats
out there to suit the Republican gate-keepers
in Congress, who had voted "Nay" on statehood
in 1906, and who even considered wrapping
Arizona and New Mexico together and labeling
the package "Montezuma".

> *George Warren lost his claim to the Copper
> Queen Mine in a drunken bet that he could
> outrun a man on horseback. It later became
> one of the most productive mines in the his-
> tory of the West.*

Taft had his own reservations about some
progressive features in Arizona's new constitution. But the day finally arrived and the old

---

LEFT: miners at work in a Bisbee tunnel.
RIGHT: workers inspect a diversion tunnel during the
construction of Hoover Dam, 1934.

territory became the so-called "Baby State". It
was a new chapter in the Arizona story, and
there would be more transforming moments
ahead as this hot, dry desert started blossom-
ing into a modern-day El Dorado for sun-seek-
ers and fun-seekers who came and stayed in
increasing numbers.

Bringing up baby

A year before admission to the Union, another
important event occurred. Taft's predeces-
sor as president, Theodore Roosevelt, came to
Arizona to dedicate a great dam named in his
honor. Roosevelt, champion of conservation,
had been a vital force behind the Reclamation
Act of 1902 authorizing the federal government

to build reservoirs and stimulate irrigation projects in the West. The first major effort was the Salt River Project in Arizona. It was the same area in which Hohokam Indians a couple of thousand years earlier had carried out their own irrigation project, building an extensive canal system to bring water to their fields of corn, beans, and squash.

Roosevelt Dam was built on the Salt River about 90 miles (145km) upstream of Phoenix. Work began in 1905, and the dam was dedicated on March 18, 1911. It is the world's tallest masonry dam at 280ft (85 meters), and it cost $10 million to build on rough terrain where it could

Hoover Dam in 1947 (the name changed back and forth for years). Arizona's claim to a major share of Colorado River water was affirmed by the US Supreme Court in 1963.

In 1968 Congress approved the Central Arizona Project, a grand federal undertaking to funnel water from the Colorado River to the state's populous central region, which includes Phoenix and Tucson. Total cost for the canal system? About $4 billion.

Prosperity and conflict

Railroads unified the state and stimulated its development starting in the late 19th century.

Deportation of I.W.W's July 12, 1917.

MARCHING PAST LOWELL.

get extremely hot. It allowed for water to be stored, floodwaters controlled, arid land turned into an agricultural oasis, and Phoenix to bloom into a big city. Three more dams would be built along the Salt River and two on its major tributary, the Verde, storing water to irrigate vast acres of cotton, citrus, vegetables, and other crops. The dams helped to spur farm acreage in the state by almost 400 percent between 1910 and 1920.

Also harnessed was the Southwest's mightiest waterway, the 1,450-mile (2,330km) -long Colorado River, with the construction of Boulder, Glen Canyon, Parker, and Davis dams. Arizona is one of seven states served by Boulder Dam, which was dedicated by President Franklin D. Roosevelt in 1935 and renamed

North-south tracks were put down to connect the transcontinental lines – the Southern Pacific in Arizona's south, the Santa Fe in the northern part, where it was the dominant economic force. The powerful copper interests, faced with the need to transport larger ore extractions, built their own connections when necessary, as Phelps Dodge did when it fought over terms with the transcontinental companies.

The livestock industry prospered as large ranches were established, their chief customer being the army forts. Mining companies thrived but were beset with labor problems – a shortage of manpower early on; ethnic and racial antagonisms involving Anglos,

Mexicans, Chinese, Italians, and others; and union militancy. That militancy usually brought a harsh response from mine owners. When, for example, Mexican and Italian workers went on strike in 1903 at the Clifton-Morenci mines, Arizona's governor was enlisted to call out both the National Guard and the Arizona Rangers.

There were many labor-management conflicts in Arizona's mining areas during the early decades of the 19th century. Patriotic fervor during World War I engendered a fear of industrial sabotage and a hatred for militants like the "Wobblies"– the radical agita-

mines supplying half of the total demand in the nation. The most productive year was 1929, when mine extractions totaled more than $155 million. Only a fraction of that was realized a few years later when the industry and the country was hit hard by the Great Depression. The economic downturn affected Arizona as severely as it hurt other places around the United States. Cotton had been the state's leading crop, but revenues now fell sharply. The cattle industry was hurt as well. Some of the copper mines were shut down, the communities they had spawned turning into ghost towns.

tors, real or alleged, popularly associated with the Industrial Workers of the World.

The most notorious labor-management incident, known as the Bisbee Deportation, occurred in July 1917. As many as 1,200 people were rounded up by 2,000 "sheriff's deputies" and armed citizens, herded like cattle into railroad cars, shipped to Columbus, New Mexico, and unloaded in the dark of night.

More copper was produced in Arizona than in any other state in the Roaring Twenties, its

LEFT: striking miners are forced out of Bisbee during the "deportation" of 1917. **ABOVE:** Arizona, New Mexico, and Oklahoma wait for their stars, signifying statehood, in a 1911 political cartoon.

CARL HAYDEN

No one played a more enduring role in Arizona's development than Carl Hayden. He was present at the state's creation in 1912, when voters chose him to be the new state's first representative in Congress. He went off to Washington at the age of 34, and 56 years later he was still on the job. Hayden served in both the House and Senate, his long career capped by congressional approval of the Central Arizona Project in 1968. His life spanned the Indian Wars to the Vietnam War, and the family's history stretches as far back as 1858, when his father, Charles, settled in Tucson and became a prominent merchant and civic leader.

Wartime stimulus

Despite a reputation for rugged individualism, Arizona traditionally has benefited from a good deal of federal largesse – settlers were protected from Indians by army troops, farmland was irrigated, floodwaters restrained, cotton growers subsidized. And it was the federal government once again that played a prominent role in the state's phenomenal development, which started with the onset of the World War II period.

The war itself was a major stimulant. Defense plants and research laboratories launched operations in Arizona that created jobs and brought

prosperity. Air bases and other military installations were established in the state out of fears for security posed by its location near the West Coast. (The federal government is the largest landowner in the state, possessing a major portion of its 113,642 sq miles (294,331 sq km.)

After the war, veterans returned to settle and start families. Homes went up, and businesses attracted by the labor pool opened plants, among them electronics giants like General Electric and Motorola. Mining production was revitalized in the war years.

Even before the war there were factors in play that opened Arizona to outsiders and made it the "Grand Canyon State". Railroad construction was at its peak from 1880 to 1920 and brought many visitors. The automobile had an even greater impact, stimulating road-building. Great vistas and spectacular scenery, once the preserve of explorers and then the privileged class, began attracting masses of ordinary people.

Theodore Roosevelt had created Grand Canyon National Monument in 1908, seven years after a passenger train first brought tourists there. It became Grand Canyon National Park in 1919, drew 56,000 tourists the following year, and three times that number within a decade (currently the park receives nearly 5 million visitors). Other national parks and monuments established in the 1906–08 period were Petrified Forest, Montezuma Castle, Tonto, and Tumacácori.

Birth of the cool

Arizona was once regarded as so forbidding that General William Tecumseh Sherman recommended starting another war with Mexico to "make her take it back". But during the first two decades of the 20th century, the state began attracting people suffering from tuberculosis and other respiratory ailments. The dry climate had been sought out as early as the mid-1800s by a few health-seekers. But now churches and other groups, especially in Phoenix and Tucson, were starting facilities that cared for the afflicted. The state's climate was giving southern Arizona a national reputation as a health haven.

Great change also came with the advent of air-conditioning. In the 1930s, attempts were made to provide relief from the searing heat by evaporative devices. These so-called "swamp coolers" began appearing in windows and on roofs, and Phoenix billed itself as the "Air Conditioned Capital of the World". The city

MR CONSERVATIVE

He was either a plain-speaking hero or a loose cannon in scary nuclear times. Such were the depictions of Barry Goldwater (1909–98), grandson of a Russian Jewish emigrant, who became the champion of an effort to outduel Soviet communism, revive American conservatism, and save Western Civilization. Goldwater gave up a career managing the family business in favor of public service. Starting out on the Phoenix City Council, he rose to become the Republican standard-bearer for president in 1964. He was defeated handily, returned to the US Senate, and ultimately won the public's admiration for his steadfast conviction as "Mr Conservative."

was a leading center for production of the artificial coolers, which were later replaced by the superior technique of refrigeration cooling. Air-conditioning made work conditions more pleasant and were an inducement for out-of-staters to relocate to southern Arizona.

One man attracted to Phoenix for health reasons played a major role in the Arizona transformation. Del Webb was born in California and moved to Phoenix in 1927. Forming the Del Webb Corporation, he entered the housing field and won fame and fortune by designing Sun City, a vast community of homes for retired people and a model for similar developments throughout the Southwest.

Encompassing 30,000 acres (12,000 hectares), it offered ranch-style houses with carports, golf courses, swimming pools, shopping centers, and other attractions. All were tailored to the needs of active senior citizens eager to enjoy the rewards of their "golden years" (a term popularized by Webb) and possessing the resources to do so. It was a major innovation in the American social landscape.

Arizona was transformed once again, propelled by an explosive growth in population. The population ballooned from 335,000 in 1920 to 3.6 million in 1990, and a decade later it exceeded 5 million. In just seven years (1990–97) it grew by 24.3 percent.

The most exceptional growth has been experienced by Phoenix, which did not exist until 1867 and now has more than 1.5 million inhabitants. Its founding came as part of an effort to clean out the old Hohokam canals, an action seen as breathing new life into an ancient settlement, hence the adaptation of the name of the mythical Egyptian bird that rose from the ashes.

Phoenix, the capital since 1889, surpassed Tucson as Arizona's largest city in 1920. Both are among the fastest-growing in the nation. And both are burdened with helter-skelter urban development and suburban sprawl as well as the traffic congestion and smog that arise from a near-exclusive reliance on the automobile for transportation.

21st century challenges

By 2011, Arizona had become a daily feature in national news – usually for controversial

reasons. In early 2009, the popular former governor Janet Napolitano was tapped as the new head of Homeland Security by President Barack Obama and departed for Washington. Her successor, Republican governor and Tea Party favorite Jan Brewer, was sworn in on January 20, 2009, and lost no time provoking a firestorm among civil rights groups and concerned citizens for supporting an immigration bill designed to identify, detain, and deport undocumented migrants that was later deemed unconstitutional by the federal government. But the governor has also vetoed legislation allowing guns on school campuses (an emotive issue

following the shooting of Congresswoman Giffords in Tucson in January 2011) and a bill attempting to shape the next presidential election by demanding presidential candidates produce US birth certificates. Arizona's partisan politics are set against a backdrop of escalating drug activity spilling across the US–Mexico border, which has triggered a mounting death toll in border towns like Nogales, and the economic crash of 2008, which has led to record unemployment and home foreclosures. Arizona has been forced to sober up, downsize, and reassess its needs – in that respect, at least, it's no different from the rest of the nation, attempting to recover from the longest recession since the Great Depression.

LEFT: suburbs sprawl around downtown Phoenix.
RIGHT: the Phoenix skyline.

THE NAKED EARTH

Arizona bares its geological bones in some of
the West's most spectacular landscapes

For Arizona's Indian tribes, the state's mountains, mesas, and eroded formations aren't just rocks; they are sacred touchstones. The Tohono O'odham believe their creator god lives on Baboquivari Peak near Tucson. Traditional Navajo rarely feel at home beyond the boundaries of the four sacred mountains that encircle their homeland and view rock formations as petrified gods, monsters, or the settings of creation myths and legendary battles. Hopi dances honor to the *kachinas*, spirit helpers whose summer home is the San Francisco Peaks near Flagstaff and whose intercession with the creator spirit ensures good crops and survival. The Paiute learn the song of every rock in the territory they "own" and act as caretakers of the natural world.

You don't have to be an Indian to feel the drama of this desert landscape. Thousands make pilgrimages to Sedona each year seeking to be healed by mud, crystals, and the powerful vortexes said to vibrate out of the red rocks. Geologists make their own pilgrimages to view the world's oldest and best-preserved rock formations in the Grand Canyon. Miners continue to risk their lives to extract precious minerals from within the earth. A caver shines his headlamp through a tiny opening deep beneath the Whetstone Mountains, discovers an elaborate, untouched limestone cave system laid out in front of him, and spends 14 years fighting to protect it, as if it were his firstborn child.

PRECEEDING PAGES: the Grand Canyon. **LEFT:** petrified wood in the Badlands. **RIGHT:** fluted schist and granite patterns can be seen on the wall of the Grand Canyon.

A tale of two regions

Arizona's extraordinary geology can be explained partly by its geographic location between the faults that created the Rocky Mountains and Sierra Nevada, its diverse topography (a 12,000ft/3,700-meter elevation span), and its dry climate, which leads to unvegetated rocks that clearly show what's going on in the ground beneath our feet. The state divides neatly into two broad geological provinces: the basin-and-range country of southern Arizona's deserts and northern Arizona's Colorado Plateau region.

The Colorado Plateau, the dramatically carved sandstone country of the north, covers 130,000 sq miles (340,000 sq km) of Arizona,

Utah, Colorado, and New Mexico. A relatively stable, monolithic landmass a mile high and rising, it began to be pushed up about 75 million years ago, when the collision of the Pacific and North American Plates, on which the continent sits, reverberated east. This caused movement in faults that forced up the modern Rocky Mountains, a process known as the Laramide Orogeny. Localized uplifts split the region into highland areas known as the Coconino, Kaibab, Kanab, Shivwits, Kaibito, Defiance, and Paria plateaus.

The area has been subject to continued volcanism, visible as lava flows in the western

Though restrained by Glen Canyon and Hoover dams, the Colorado River continues to rasp away at the Grand Canyon, transporting an average of half a million tons of sand and silt per day.

Carving the canyon

The Grand Canyon, centerpiece of the Colorado Plateau, is not geologically ancient – it was carved by the Colorado River within the past 6 million years. The ancestral Colorado flowed south into Arizona from Utah, staying

Grand Canyon, along the southern edge of the plateau at the 2,000ft (600-meter) -high Mogollon Rim, and as volcanic necks, dikes, and other magma-intruded rocks and upwarps across the Navajo and Hopi reservations. At Flagstaff, hundreds of cinder cones were thrown up in the large San Francisco Volcanic Field. The state's highest point, 12,633ft (3,850-meter) Humphreys Peak, is part of the San Francisco Peaks, an ancient collapsed stratovolcano. To the east, Sunset Crater Volcano, which erupted between 1064 and 1065, was given its evocative name by geologist John Wesley Powell, the first man to run the Colorado River through the Grand Canyon and explore the region in 1869.

east of the Kaibab Upwarp. Another stream flowed west of the Kaibab Upwarp, cut back through the newer, steeper route.

At this point, sediment-heavy waters began to carve the Grand Canyon in earnest, deepening the chasm to its present mile depth. The Colorado, the "Red River" in Spanish, churned tawny and soupy with sediments that it carried all the way down to the Gulf of California. Downcutting has slowed now that the river has reached resistant schists and its erosive force has been tamed by the construction of Glen Canyon Dam.

Different types of erosion – tributary streams, flashfloods, rockfalls, rain, ice, dust, wind, animal movements – have been responsible for widening the canyon to its 10 mile

(16km) width. Differential erosion of rocks of various composition, thickness and hardness have created ledges, cliffs, dramatic mesas, buttes, totems, spires, and other features.

Little rivers

The Little Colorado River now runs along the ancestral course of the Colorado, which it joins within the canyon. The Little Colorado is today a major river on the Navajo reservation, winding through the Painted Desert and tumbling over Grand Falls during heavy spring snowmelt. It has carved its own beautiful gorge, visible just west of Cameron. The Paria River, on

with lava flows, in a sea that washed onto a shore at the western edge of the continent. These rocks were buried up to 12 miles (19km) deep, then uplifted 725 million years ago and folded into a mountain chain, injected with veins of molten rock, eroded to their roots, redeposited, and then uplifted and folded again. This created strata that are today banded and contorted in some places, and platey and shiny in others.

Resting directly on top of the Vishnu Schist are sandstones that are only 545 million years old. What happened to the intervening 1.2 billion years of rocks? Were none deposited?

ABOVE: Desert View Overlook.

the Utah–Arizona border, has also gouged out a distinctive course for itself through a uniform bed of sandstone, creating a picturesque 2,000ft (600-meter) -deep slot canyon barely 30ft (9 meters) wide, in which sunlight rarely reaches the sandy floor.

Layer upon layer

Almost half of the earth's 4.5-billion-year history is contained within the horizontal layer cake of sedimentary rocks found in the Grand Canyon. The 1.7-billion-year-old Vishnu Schist in the Inner Canyon was laid down as sandstone, shale, and limestone, interleafed

CHIRICAHUA'S RHYOLITE ROCKS

One of southeastern Arizona's most violent volcanic events occurred 27 million years ago, when six ash flows shot out of Turkey Creek Caldera near present-day Chiricahua National Monument, producing a 2,000ft (600-meter) -thick layer of volcanic rock, known as rhyolite. Subsequent erosion sculpted the rhyolite into columns, balanced rocks, and hoodoos. The Heart of Rocks trail in the national monument offers a look at the most unusual named formations; Duck on a Rock, Punch & Judy, Kissing Rocks, and Big Balanced Rock, while over on the east side of the mountains, dramatically carved sheer cliffs mark the entrance to Cave Creek, a prime birding area.

Were they laid down and then eroded away? The Great Unconformity is one of the mysteries of the Grand Canyon. These 500-million-year-old layers of sandstone were deposited at the start of the Paleozoic era, and were located at the edge of a Cambrian sea. The Tapeats Sandstone, Bright Angel Shale, and Muav and Temple Butte Limestones contain fossil sponges, brachiopods, mollusks, corals, crinoids, and trilobites up to 3ins (8cm) in size.

Ancient seas

During the Devonian Period (408–360 million years ago), the North American continent straddled the equator, and a tropical sea covered much of the Southwest. Fish with armored heads began to appear, which has led geologists to call the Devonian the Age of Fishes.

The Redwall Limestone, formed in Mississippian times (365–330 million years ago), contains crinoids, related to sand dollars and sea urchins, that looked like plants, with a base, a stem, and a flowerlike top. It is a gray rock stained red by iron deposits in overlying Supai rocks, a group of siltstones and sandstones produced in a swampy environment, and the Hermit Shale, which was deposited about 280 million years ago.

TRIASSIC PARK

Her name is Gertie, and she is one of the oldest dinosaurs known to science. When her bones were found eroding out of the crumbling hills of Petrified Forest National Park in 1984, she had been resting silently beneath the Painted Desert for 220 million years.

Gertie was a chindosaur – a small, fast-moving dinosaur that ate flesh and walked on two feet – and she represented a world in transition, from gentle herbivores like the heavily armored aetosaur to the giant carnivores whose bones thrill museum-goers to this day. Even the 30ft (9-meter) -long crocodile-like phytosaur, which patiently stalked its prey in the swamps, could not compete. Gertie, and descendants such as the three-toed, 10ft (3-meter) -tall dilophosaurs, whose tracks are preserved in the red sandstone west of Tuba City, ruled the world for another 150 million years.

The park's Rainbow Forest Museum and the Museum of Northern Arizona in Flagstaff have exhibits of dinosaur skeletons and eggs. Arizona's southern deserts have also yielded their share of dinosaur remains. The 97-million-year-old Sonorasaurus thompsoni, a new species of brachiosaur, was recently found in the Sonoran Desert and are displayed at the Arizona-Sonora Desert Museum. Mesa Southwest Museum, near Phoenix, is also worth a visit. It has one of the largest exhibits of dinosaur skeletons in the West.

Near the rim of the canyon is the yellow, crossbedded Coconino Sandstone, which was deposited in a desert filled with large sand dunes. The Toroweap and Kaibab Formations, laid down in Permian times (286–245 million years ago), make up the rim of the canyon. The fossil-rich Kaibab forms terraces that are cloaked with ponderosa pine forests.

Where dinosaurs walked

Younger rocks of the warm, tropical Triassic era (245–208 million years ago) dominate the Navajo reservation. The soft, banded Moenkopi Formation was born in a delta, when stream uranium, but with groundwater that was silica-rich, creating quartz. Fossilized dinosaur skeletons are often found preserved in the Chinle Formation, while dinosaur tracks are nearly always found in the red Kayenta Formation, a rock that was laid down in damp, interdunal areas as the climate dried and desert sand dunes started piling up.

Deserts at the end of the Permian era, 260 million years ago, formed the De Chelly and Wingate Sandstones that make up the buttes, totems, and mesas in Monument Valley. A significant period of desertification also took place during the Jurassic period (208–144 mil-

sediments mixed with marine deposits. It is barely distinguishable from the overlying Chinle Formation, which is well exposed near Canyon de Chelly. A crumbly purple, yellow, and brown formation, the Chinle contains large quantities of uranium, produced from groundwater and likely leached out of volcanic ash. Certain plants, such as milkvetches, are an indication that uranium is present.

The Chinle also preserves a lot of petrified wood, formed in a process similar to that of

LEFT: lava fields and a cinder cone at Sunset Crater Volcano National Monument north of Flagstaff.
ABOVE: spring runoff sends a torrent of muddy water over the Grand Falls of the Little Colorado River.

lion years ago), when a Sahara-like desert of 3,000ft (900-meter) -high sand dunes covered 150,000 sq miles (390,000 sq km) of the West, eventually hardening into the beautiful pink Navajo Sandstone. Dune-formed sandstones have been eroded into distinctive shapes by the "exfoliation" process that occurs in porous sandstone. Groundwater passes easily through the rock and, when it encounters the impervious layers below, exits as dripping springs and seeps that undermine the sandstone, causing it to peel away like an onion.

Water-loving plants are attracted to these seeps, where they form hanging gardens of moss, fern, monkeyflower, and columbines, which contribute to the destabilization of overlying rocks.

Volcanic remnants

Igneous intrusions of hot molten lava (magma) along faults beneath layers of sandstone have pushed up and deformed much of Monument Valley into anticlines (upwarps), monoclines (dropping on one side), and synclines (downwarps). Also clearly visible are laccolithic ranges like Navajo Mountain, where magma has risen along a zone of weakness, spread laterally between sedimentary layers, pushed them up into a dome, and been uncovered by erosion.

A San Juan River trip, from Mexican Hat to Clay Hills Crossing, offers an opportunity to view these rock strata and float through the Goosenecks of the San Juan, technically an entrenched meander, where uplift of the Colorado Plateau has caused an older river to cut down several thousand feet into its Cedar Mesa Sandstone course and form hairpin bends. Rivers won't meander for long without seeking a more direct route past obstacles in their way. In this case, the grinding action of the river currents punches a hole in a meander wall, widens it, and eventually leaves behind a natural bridge like those at nearby Natural Bridges and Rainbow Bridge National Monuments.

Basin and range

Southern Arizona's basin-and-range country is much younger than the Colorado Plateau and largely the result of pulling apart, not pushing up. Starting about 20 million years ago, the Earth's crust beneath these deserts began to extend, stretch thin, overheat, and crack along a roughly north-south trend. The mountains in this region have been described as a swarm of "giant caterpillars marching northwest", so linear are these volcanic ranges.

Some blocks of earth started to break and tilt, forcing huge chunks of land to rise and others to drop. The ones that dropped formed the basins and began to fill with sediments washing down in huge alluvial fans called bajadas from the Huachucas, Chiricahuas, Dragoons, and other sky island ranges. Some basins contain 15,000ft (4,600 meters) of fill and rubble. Movements of the Earth's crust along these faults continue to the present day.

Volcanic action along a northwest-southeast trend within sedimentary rocks, such as limestones, is thought to be the reason Arizona has deposits of porphyry copper. One theory is that the continent drifted northwest over a hot spot in the Earth's mantle. Copper ores may have been the last substances to crystallize out of the magma. The copper-bearing minerals dissolved in the hot water that permeates most magma, making them able to penetrate narrow fissures and fractures in the channels of adjacent rocks. Most copper deposits were injected by a molten granite batholith, or deep igneous intrusion, into nearby limestone rocks, such as the Mule Mountains around Bisbee, where beautiful turquoise malachite deposits have been found.

DESERT VARNISH

Sandstone is frequently stained with desert varnish, a shiny dark brown or black coating made up of manganese oxides (black) and iron oxides (reddish brown). It is unclear how the manganese and iron are bonded to the rock surface. Many geologists believe that the process involves bacteria that oxidize minerals and cement them to the rock; others believe that a purely chemical reaction occurs between the iron, manganese, and water. New evidence points to a combination of both. Prehistoric people found desert varnish a perfect canvas on which to carve petroglyphs, or incised rock art, which are visible throughout Arizona.

LEFT: view over Tsegi Canyon to Anasazi cliff dwellings in Navajo Monument National Park.

Arizona Volcanoes

Spectacular eruptions have occurred at various periods in the geological formation of the Southwest's extraordinary landscapes

When hot, molten rock, or magma, rises along vents and erupts at the Earth's surface, an extrusive mountain, or volcano, is created. Volcanoes that erupt violently and shower ash and lava over a large area are called composite, or strato, volcanoes and have a classic cone shape. Volcanoes that erupt in slow-moving lava flows and build up gradually are known as shield volcanoes.

Cinder cones erupt along side vents, which explains why they seem to cluster in chorus lines around the mother volcano. Magma that never reaches the surface forms an intrusive, domed mountain, or laccolith. Laccoliths are common on the Arizona–Utah border, at places like Navajo Mountain on the Navajo reservation, where sedimentary layers are thick and hard to break through.

Dark, jagged volcanic "necks" or "plugs" provide additional evidence of older volcanism on the Colorado Plateau. Erosion has uncovered the volcanic cores inside the sediments at places like Agathla Peak in Monument Valley, Church Rock in nearby Kayenta, and the Hopi Mesas.

Volcanic activity is greatest at the southern margin of the Colorado Plateau and may indicate that volatile basin and range activity in the southern part of the state is beginning to affect the relatively stable plateau along the Mogollon Rim, the 2,000ft (600-meter) -high dividing line between the low deserts and the high country. Arizona's highest mountains are all found here. The highest, 12,633ft (3,850-meter) Humphreys Peak, one of the San Francisco Peaks outside Flagstaff, is a stratovolcano that was built of lava and ash over a period of 1.5 million years.

The Peaks stopped erupting about 400,000 years ago, but they are skirted by a 2,300-sq-mile (6,000-sq-km) volcanic field – the largest in the US – with more than 400 younger cinder cones. The best known is 1,000ft (305-meter) -high Sunset Crater. It was one of the last volcanoes to erupt, some 900 years ago, leaving behind lava flows that were used by the Sinagua Indians as mulch for their crops.

RIGHT: cinder cones near the San Francisco peaks.

The state's second highest mountain, 11,403ft (3,476-meter) Baldy Peak, is at the center of the White Mountain Volcanic Field, which erupted 8 million years ago. The nearby 1,158-sq-mile (3,000-sq-km) Springerville Volcanic Field is the third largest in the continental United States and contains 405 vents, craters, and shield volcanoes, which began erupting 3 million years ago. The state's third highest mountain, 10,912ft (3,326-meter) Escudilla Mountain, is found here.

Just below the Mogollon Rim, 10,720ft (3,270-meter) -high Mount Graham, the tallest of the Pinaleno Mountains, towers 8,000ft (2,400-meter) above the cottonfields of Safford – the greatest verti-

cal rise in Arizona. The most violent volcanic episode in southern Arizona's geological history, the eruption of Turkey Creek Caldera, occurred nearby about 27 million years ago. Ash covered a large area and settled as rhyolite, which eroded into the strange totems and balanced rocks of the Chiricahua Mountains.

The Earth's crust is undergoing far more heating, extension, and deformation here than anywhere else in the state. The result is younger and craggier mountains, rising as "sky islands" from flat desert basins. The clarity of the desert air has attracted astronomers, perhaps since ancient times. Powerful telescopes are found atop Kitt Peak in the Baboquivari Mountains, Whipple Observatory in the Santa Ritas, and Mount Graham in the Pinalenos.

DESERT LIFE

Though Arizona's deserts may at first seem
stark and lifeless, they sustain a fascinating
array of plants and animals adapted to extreme
heat and aridity

panning 118,000 sq miles (306,000 sq km), and with elevations ranging from 70ft (21 meters) above sea level at Yuma to 12,643ft (3,854 meters) at Humphreys Peak near Flagstaff, Arizona is much more than the searingly hot desert flats, saguaro cacti, and howling coyotes of popular myth. In fact, it is the most biologically diverse state in the American Southwest, with 137 species of mammals, 434 different species of birds, 48 snake species, 41 lizard species, 22 types of amphibians, thousands of arthropods, and a stunning 3,370 species of plants.

Such diversity can be attributed to the state's wide range of habitats, which include four converging deserts – the Sonoran, Chihuahuan, Great Basin, and Mohave – basin-and-range topography, and unusual ecozones, from lava flows to caves, where species have had to make special adaptations. In addition, a large number of plants and animals have migrated permanently north of the US–Mexico border to occupy protected niches in riparian corridors.

Only one of Arizona's 30 scorpion species, the bark scorpion, is considered life-threatening, though no deaths have been attributed to the species in the state for more than 30 years.

This is remarkable because when one thinks about Arizona, one instantly thinks of aridity. The Sonoran Desert of southern Arizona is found at the 30th parallel north of the equator, which creates atmospheric circulation patterns that lead to desertification. Another leading factor is that Arizona is a long way from the coast, too far to benefit from moisture. Moreover, any coastal moisture it might have received is effectively blocked by California's 14,000ft (4,300-meter) Sierra Nevada, placing the Grand Canyon State in a rain shadow. Even high-elevation areas often receive less than 15ins (38cm) of precipitation a year – the high desert range.

Precious water

Finding and holding on to water is what life is all about here, especially for those plants and animals that, unlike people, birds, and larger

LEFT: Joshua tree cactus (*Yucca brevifolia*) growing alongside Desert Marigold (*Baileya multiradiata*).
RIGHT: rattlesnakes are often found under rocks, logs, and other protected places.

predators such as wide-ranging coyotes and mountain lions, cannot leave. Desert plants and animals have developed strategies for survival. The kangaroo rat gets all its water from seeds. Spadefoot toads encase themselves in slime in the bottom of dried-up potholes, or *tinajas*, and wait months for heavy rains. Cacti gave up leaves in favor of protective spines and large water-saving waxy trunks that also help them photosynthesize food.

The lay of the land

The southern part of the state is "basin and range", a land of craggy, young volcanic moun-

to pinyon-juniper dwarf forest between 5,500 and 7,000ft (1,700–2,100 meters) in areas like Sedona on the Mogollon Rim.

> "In the desert ... the very fauna and flora proclaim that one can have a great deal of certain things while having very little of others." – Joseph Wood Krutch, The Desert Year.

Most of southern Arizona is in the Sonoran Desert, at 10,000-years-old a relatively young desert, averaging 3,000ft (900 meters) in elevation,

tains that form verdant "sky islands" above huge desert basins and ephemeral playa wetlands, such as those around Willcox, that attract thousands of migratory waterfowl each winter. By contrast, northern Arizona's Colorado Plateau soars from 5,000 to 12,000ft (1,500–3,600 meters) in a sprawling high country of volcanic peaks and uplifted plateaux, expansive ponderosa pine forest, glittering lakes, alpine meadows, and sandstone canyons carved by the Colorado River and its tributaries. In between, at 3,500 to 5,000ft (1,100–1,500 meters), are sweeping grasslands around the fast-growing communities of central Arizona's Payson and Prescott and the US–Mexico border around Patagonia (Arizona's historic cattle country), transitioning

that slices diagonally from the southwest quarter of Arizona down to the Sea of Cortez in Sonora, Mexico, as far as the Sierra Madre in the east and the lower southeast corner of California in the west. Because of its location, the Sonoran receives moisture twice a year – summer "monsoons", as they are dubbed (incorrectly), from July to September, and winter storms – making it the greenest of the West's deserts.

In the drier western Sonoran Desert, around Organ Pipe Cactus National Monument, dominant plants include foothill paloverde, saguaro, cholla, and ironwood; in areas with more moisture, such as the Arizona Uplands around Tucson, add to the mix blue paloverde, mesquite, catclaw, desert willow, and desert hackberry, and shrubs such as bursage, creosote, jojoba, and brittlebush. When previous summer and early winter rains have been adequate, the Sonoran no longer seems a desert but a flower garden, with poppies, brittlebush, desert marigolds, lupines, fairyduster, fleabane, and other beauties blooming in waves, beginning in February.

A lush desert

More than 100 species of cactus call the Sonoran home, including organ pipe, Mexican senita, cholla, pricklypear, beavertail, pincushion, claret cup, hedgehog, and the symbol of the Sonoran Desert: the many-limbed saguaro.

hours, or visit the sprawling Arizona-Sonora Desert Museum, west of Tucson, where naturally landscaped enclosures house rarely seen mountain lions, bobcats, and jaguarundis, kit foxes, desert bighorn sheep, and black bears, as well as the utterly charming coati, a type of ring-tailed cat from south of the border that likes to curl up in a ball in a tree and snooze during the day. Most visible are squirrels and crepuscular hunters and browsers like large-eared mule deer and bands of javelina, or desert boar, which congregate along sky island back-roads and feed on prickly pear cactus fruit in late summer. Javelina, with their little tusks and

Cacti like these are the most successfully adapted of all desert plants. They take advantage of infrequent but hard rains by employing shallow root networks to suck up water, which is then conserved, accordion-like, in the gelatinous tissues of their waxy trunks. Cacti use their broad trunks to photosynthesize sunlight for food and have modified leaves into spines, which are much more useful as protection.

Three-quarters of desert animals are nocturnal. Your best chance of close-up encounters is to visit a water hole in the cool dusk or dawn

ABOVE: desert plants employ such formidable defences as spines and bitter-tasting or bladelike leaves, but their blossoms are often large and brightly colored.

stout bodies, are delightful to encounter as you drive the desert, but they have poor eyesight and can charge if threatened. Don't approach them.

More than 400 species of birds live in the Sonoran Desert and include the topknotted Gambel's quail, roadrunner (the state bird), mourning dove, phainopepla, and birds that carve out cool nests in saguaro trunks, such as the Gila woodpecker, northern flicker, cactus wren, curved-bill thrasher, and elf owl. Birds of prey and other avian species that can move easily from shade to sun are visible in daytime desert skies soaring on thermals. Often spotted are Harris's and red-tailed hawks, peregrine falcons, and golden eagles on the lookout for darting jackrabbits, cottontails, or ground squirrels.

Be careful where you walk and put your hands during daytime hikes. Mottle-skinned rattlesnakes, brightly hued collared lizards, whiptails, chuckwallas and the impressive-looking Gila monster keep cool under rocks and bushes during the day. Lizards have a variety of strategies to evade capture, including detaching their tails when caught and later growing a new one. Gila monsters can live for several years on fat stored in their tails.

An unforgiving environment

Parts of southeastern Arizona are in the Chihuahuan Desert, two-thirds of which is found in Mexico. At a mean elevation of 3,500 to 5,000ft (1,100–1,500 meters), this desert has relatively long, chilly winters, with occasional snowfalls that melt quickly. As with the Sonoran Desert, summer temperatures in the Chihuahuan exceed 100°F (38°C) but are cooled by violent summer monsoons, which drop 8–12ins (20–31cm) of annual rainfall in places like Bisbee, Tombstone, and the Willcox Playa area. Limestone caverns, such as those at Kartchner Caverns State Park near Benson, are found in this area, which was inundated by a Permian Sea 250 million years ago. Ocotillo, prickly pear, and cholla cactus do well in these

GIANTS OF THE DESERT

The many-armed saguaro cactus seems as timeless as the Sonoran Desert it inhabits. Indeed, saguaros may live for more than 150 years, given warm southern exposures and sufficient rain on mountain slopes, or bajadas. They don't even begin to grow their appendages until they are 75 years old. Their shallow roots suck up moisture into barrel-like torsos that swell like an accordion, storing as much as 200 gallons (750 liters).

Saguaros take summer highs in excess of 100°F (38°C) and freezing winter temperatures in their stride. Spines protect them from intruders, trap cool air, provide shade, and along with the cacti's waxy coating, protect them from dehydration. Unlike leafy plants, saguaros photosynthesize food along their arms and trunks, the latter often reaching 35–40ft (11–12 meters) in height. In spring, saguaros sprout white blossoms that attract visiting Mexican long-nosed bats, which pollinate the cactus with their wings as they sip nectar. In late summer, saguaros sport ruby-red fruit that, for centuries, have been made into syrup and jelly by the Tohono O'odham. Their ancestors made shelters from saguaro ribs, glue from the flowers, and treated arthritis with saguaro poultices. Urban sprawl, pollution, and vandalism threaten saguaros. Millions are protected in the two units of Saguaro National Park, outside Tucson.

calcium-rich soils. The signature vegetation of the desert is the lechuguilla agave, which has thick spikes rising from a rosette of fleshy, swordlike "leaves." After exiting the Mule Mountains tunnel, north of Bisbee, watch as the Chihuahuan Desert starts to blend with the Sonoran, with ocotillo and agave neighboring with saguaro.

Mohave and Great Basin

The Mohave Desert extends into Arizona along the Colorado River on Arizona's western border. The least colorful and most overheated of all the deserts in summer, the Mohave can trans-

form overnight into a wildflower extravaganza with enough rainfall. Ironwood, desert holly, creosote, blackbrush, and bursage are spaced evenly to take advantage of available moisture. The indicator species here is the shaggy Joshua tree, a giant yucca named by Bible-minded Mormons passing through in the 1800s. Relict palm trees have found a niche in a canyon in the Kofa Mountains, along with a thriving population of endangered desert bighorn sheep. A herd of about 500 bighorns lives in Cabeza Prieta National Wildlife Refuge, on the

LEFT: the common raven, the subject of much Native American folklore, is extremely intelligent and displays complex social behavior. **ABOVE:** wildflowers bloom.

US–Mexico border. Every June, as temperatures soar, volunteers count the sheep – the true calling of "desert rats".

The northwestern corner of Arizona is primarily Great Basin desert, which extends all the way to eastern Utah and Oregon. A cool desert, found at elevations of 4,000ft (1,200 meters) or higher, the Great Basin was once dominated by lush, tall native bunchgrasses such as Indian rice grass, sideoats, and blue grama. Today, most of these native grasses have given way to disturbance species such as sagebrush, saltbush, snakeweed, rabbitbrush, and the ubiquitous cheatgrass after more than a century of grazing by cattle and sheep. Grasslands in protected parcels of southern Arizona like Las Cienegas National Conservation Area are beginning to recover.

Animal magnetism

Arizona's southern desert "sky islands", with their higher elevations and thick stands of ever-green-deciduous forest, are a powerful magnet for living things trying to escape the heat of the desert. For every 1,000ft (300 meters) gain in elevation, the temperature drops 4°F (2°C) and precipitation increases about 4ins (10cm). In the sheltered canyons of the Chiricahua and Huachuca Mountains, near the Mexican border, Arizona cypress and alligator juniper mingle with Mexican natives like Chihuahua and Apache pine, while at higher elevations, Douglas fir, aspen, and ponderosa pine provide food for white-tailed deer and cover for sulphur-bellied flycatchers, Mexican chicadees, and long-tailed elegant trogons.

Wildlife (and human residents) in the desert borderlands are particularly drawn to cool riparian areas, where perennial streams offer that most precious of gifts: reliable water. Southeast of Tucson, places like Ramsey Canyon in the Huachucas and Madera Canyon in the Santa Ritas are oases, attracting 14 of 19 hummingbird species that winter in Mexico and nest in the huge sycamores, maples, and oaks that line the creeks.

San Pedro River is one of the country's most important waterways, protecting cottonwood-willow bosques for hundreds of resident birds and literally millions of migratory waterfowl, such as sandhill cranes and snow and Canada geese, which also use flooded desert basins, or playas, in Sulphur Springs Valley, near Willcox in southeastern Arizona. In northern Arizona, bald eagles are often found wintering on alpine lakes and reservoirs near Flagstaff, where cold-water fish are plentiful.

Northern uplands

Glorious though southern Arizona's desert mountains are, the most spectacular area of Arizona is the canyon country of the Colorado Plateau, the uplifted region north of the Mogollon Rim that takes in the White Mountains, the San Francisco Peaks, and the Coconino and Kaibab plateaux of the South and North Rims of the Grand Canyon. The largely sedimentary layers of the monolithic Colorado

The bottom of the Grand Canyon is as torrid as the Lower Sonoran Desert in summer, with temperatures exceeding 100°F (38°C). Life concentrates along the river, where willow and tamarisk form bowers for large numbers of songbirds, including the endangered Southwest willow flycatcher. Small canyon wrens flit around the rocks, their presence announced by their haunting descending songs.

It's a different story on the rims. Huge, airy forests of ponderosa pine and Gambel oak sweep across the Coconino and Kaibab plateaux, forming the largest ponderosa forest

Plateau began to be pushed up by faulting in the mid-Cretaceous period, some 75 million years ago. The area continues to rise and has been further uplifted and sculpted by local faulting into breathtaking high peaks and plateaux.

The Colorado River has carved canyons through the uplifted plateaux creating the Grand Canyon, an abyss that drops from an elevation of 8,200ft (2,500 meters) at the North Rim to 1,300ft (400 meters) at the Colorado River. This kind of sudden elevation change has created a unique situation for wildlife, which has had to adapt to vastly different environments, from desert to montane, and corresponding changes in temperature, moisture, soil type, slope angle, and exposure to sun and wind.

in the continental United States. The forests are home to Steller's jays, mule deer and two species of tassel-eared squirrels, the Aberts of the South Rim and Kaibab of the North Rim, whose destinies diverged millennia ago, when the Grand Canyon separated them. In high country, black bear are common, though grizzlies no longer roam the peaks. The last grizzly, nicknamed Bigfoot, was sighted on Escudilla Mountain near Springerville, in the White Mountains, in the 1930s.

Return from the brink

A number of endangered species are now once again roaming their natural habitats in Arizona. California condors were successfully introduced to the Arizona Strip area, 30 miles (48km) north of the Grand Canyon, in 1996, after a 10-year captive breeding and release program guided by the Arizona Game and Fish Department, federal wildlife and land management agencies, and private conservation groups. California condors are the largest land birds in North America, with a wingspan of more than 9ft (3 meters) and weighing up to 22lbs (10kg). Members of the vulture family, they are opportunistic scavengers, feeding exclusively on carrion, traveling 100 miles (160km) or more per day in search of food. The birds managed to maintain a strong pop-

virtually eliminated from the wild by ranchers concerned about livestock predation. Since March 1998, six packs of radio-collared wolves have been released into Apache-Sitgreaves National Forest in eastern Arizona. Today, there are 50 wolves in the wild. As of 2011, legislation is pending in Arizona that weakens Endangered Species designation for the wolf.

Other reintroduction efforts include a black-footed ferret breed-and-release program in the Aubrey Valley, in northwestern Arizona, and the release of endangered Sonoran pronghorn antelope in the Buenos Aires National Wildlife Refuge, southwest of Tucson.

ulation until the settlement of the West, when shooting, poisoning from lead and DDT, egg collecting, and general habitat degradation began to take a toll. Today, they may often be seen soaring over Marble Canyon and House Rock Valley in northern Arizona.

The reintroduction of the endangered Mexican wolf remains controversial. Mexican wolves once ranged from central Mexico to West Texas, southern New Mexico, and central Arizona, but by the mid-1900s had been

LEFT: endangered California condors have been reintroduced to northern Arizona and are occasionally seen at the Grand Canyon. **ABOVE RIGHT:** coyotes prey mostly on small animals but will eat just about anything.

ARIZONA'S STATE REPTILE

Arizona offers prime habitat for rattlesnakes (which can be found on some menus in the state); 13 of 36 identified species of rattlesnake are found in Arizona, including western diamondback and massasauga rattlesnakes, more than any other state. The state's official reptile since 1986 is the relatively unvenomous Arizona ridge-nosed rattlesnake, a small, primitive, brown rattlesnake only found in the Santa Rita and Huachuca Mountains of southern Arizona. The rattle that serves as a warning of a rattlesnake's presence is a segmented keratinous extension of the tail.

A Mountain in Reverse

The ecology of the Grand Canyon is determined largely by elevation, ranging from sere desert along the Colorado River to forested plateaus at the canyon's rims

Hiking into the Grand Canyon offers intimate views of the plants and animals that live at different elevations. Dwarf piñon-juniper thickets grow below the rim, and airy forests of virgin ponderosa pine and gambel oak dotted with natural clearings called "parks" dominate the 7,000ft (2,000-meter) South Rim, alongside native grasses, cliffrose, sagebrush, prickly pear cactus, scarlet Indian paintbrush, and purple lupine. The higher, moister 8,200ft (2,500-meter) North Rim supports fir and aspen, biological pioneers that grow up in the sunlight at the margins of meadows. Alpine fir-spruce forests are found at the North Rim's highest elevations.

Rim residents include Steller's jays, woodpeckers, great horned owls, huge desert ravens, and restored populations of California condors. Cottontails, gophers, and other rodents form the diet of nocturnal coyotes and bobcats. Long-eared mule deer emerge at dusk to feed. They are the principal prey of cougars, one of the West's most timid creatures. Look for two distinct species of squirrel, which evolved as the canyon widened: the Abert's on the South Rim and the Kaibab on the North Rim.

In the canyon bottom, adjoining desert and riparian habitats create a striking contrast. Shy bighorn sheep are sometimes seen among rocks, picking among cacti and yucca, startling chuckwallas, collared lizards, and the occasional rattlesnake. Mingling with the sound of trickling water is the sweet, descant song of the canyon wren, which hops among rocks, native willows, and exotic tamarisk. Birds rely on the Colorado River for survival and include ducks, sandpipers, endangered Southwest willow flycatchers, great blue herons, and bald eagles attracted by coldwater fish like rainbow trout and carp. Where water seeps through sandstone, look for lovely "hanging gardens" of maidenhair fern, monkeyflower, and columbine.

Above: bighorn sheep thrive in the vertical terrain of the canyon. Sharp, cloven hooves allow them to stand on ledges only inches wide, and powerful legs propel them away from predators at speeds up to 30mph (48kmh).

Below: hikers pass through a ponderosa pine forest on Widforss Trail on the North Rim of the Grand Canyon; ponderosa pines grow at elevations between 6,500ft and 8,200ft (2,000–2,500 meters).

Left: the endangered California condor is the largest flying bird in North America. The Arizona population numbered 74 birds in 2011. A second population has been established on the California coast.

MERRIAM'S LIFE ZONES

In 1889, naturalist Clinton Hart Merriam hiked down the Old Hance Trail to the bottom of the Grand Canyon, climbed the surrounding San Francisco Peaks, and explored the badlands of the Painted Desert. Merriam concluded that plants and animals in the Southwest live in habitats that can broadly be arranged in horizontal bands, or life zones, according to elevation and temperature, that normally would only be found by crossing the United States from northwest Mexico (lowest) to Canada's Arctic Circle (highest).

The 7,000ft (2,000-meter) elevation difference at the Grand Canyon accounts for five of the seven life zones and includes the Lower Sonoran (up to 4,000ft/1,200 meters), Upper Sonoran (4,000–6,800ft/1,200–2,100 meters), Transition (6,800–8,000ft/2,100–2,400 meters), Canadian (8,000–9,500ft/2,400–2,900 meters), and Hudsonian (9,500–11,000ft/2,900–3,350 meters). Typically today, biologists refer to life zones in terms of the specific plant associations within each zone: cacti in the Lower Sonoran, piñon and juniper in the Upper Sonoran, ponderosa pine in the Transition, aspen and fir in the Canadian, and alpine fir-spruce in the Hudsonian.

These broad-brush categories don't account for the numerous ecotones found throughout the park, where a change in soil type, exposure, or moisture allow small islands of wildlife to get a foothold. More than 1,500 plant, 355 bird, 89 mammalian, 47 reptile, 9 amphibian, and 17 fish species are found in the park.

ABOVE: bald eagles returned to the Grand Canyon in the mid-1980s, possibly attracted to the presence of trout in the Colorado River and an increase of migratory waterfowl. The Fish and Wildlife Service removed the bald eagle from Endangered Species in 2010, even though only 50 breeding pairs survive in Arizona.

TOP: snow blankets the South Rim.
RIGHT: rattlesnakes use their fangs for both hunting and defense. Their venom prevents blood from clotting; a bite should be treated immediately.

OUTDOOR ADVENTURE

Arizona offers great opportunities for backpacking, rock climbing, mountain biking, river running, and even skiing – but you need to be prepared

The first thing to remember when contemplating an outdoor adventure is that "adventure" is a relative term. When it comes to exploring the outdoors, are you more inclined to challenge yourself physically, to find out what you're made of, to test your mettle against the elements? Or do you prefer an adventure that emphasizes personal discovery instead of physical challenge, that focuses on getting close to nature, exploring new places, and opening yourself up to novel experiences?

The American West, and Arizona in particular, is known for the dual, seemingly contradictory, nature of its people. On one hand, this is a place of laid-back landscape and nature lovers who are drawn to slow-paced reflective days. On the other, it is a land of camelback-wearing adrenaline hounds, who scurry from their SUVs to the wilderness carrying kayaks and mountain bikes over their shoulders. You will get plenty of advice on how to spend your time outdoors, and almost all of it will be valid. It is simply a matter of finding what best fits your goals and personality.

A good start

The opportunities for adventure travel are more abundant than ever, and it's never been easier to get started. Schools and clubs are available that will teach you the basics of wilderness safety as well as adventure sports such as rock climbing and kayaking. There are also a growing number of tour companies that specialize in "light adventures" for people who want to experience the thrill and beauty of the outdoors without

committing themselves to months of training or the hassles of planning a trip.

If you're a few years (or several pounds) past your prime, don't despair. Though the ads in outdoor magazines may lead you to believe otherwise, you don't need to be an energy drink-swilling 20-something with washboard abs. A minimal level of fitness may be required, but in most pursuits good judgment and a willing spirit count for more than brawn and bravado. Which is not to say you'll be dangling by your fingertips or wheeling down a mountainside on your first day out. Making an honest assessment of your limitations – including your tolerance for danger – is an essential first step in any adventure, as is learning to say no when more

---

LEFT: hot air ballooning over the Sonoran Desert.
RIGHT: a rock climber in the Santa Catalina mountains.

experienced companions try to pressure you into situations that exceed your abilities.

A walk in the park

For some, hiking is adventure enough. They owe no apologies. A walk in the desert is not to be taken lightly, and even a short jaunt can turn ugly if you're not properly prepared.

What gets most people into trouble isn't snakebite, flash floods, or falling off cliffs but the far more mundane risk of dehydration – a critical loss of moisture due to extreme heat and aridity. When the sun is bearing down, sweat evaporates almost as soon as it reaches the sur-

easy to stray from even a well-marked trail. Coupled with the symptoms of mild dehydration – fatigue, light-headedness, disorientation – losing your way can quickly spiral into a life-threatening situation. Carry high-energy food, maps and a compass (and, ideally, a GPS unit) and know how to use them, and leave a travel plan with someone at home, so they know when and where to start looking if you don't turn up at the expected time.

Other basics you'll need are a hat, sunglasses, and sunscreen with a high SPF. The Arizona sun is unrelenting, and shade is scarce. Left unprotected, your skin will be burned in no time.

face of the skin. The condition is particularly insidious because in the desert even mild exertion, like hiking, can cause the body to lose moisture faster than the brain can generate an urge to drink. In other words, you become dehydrated before you feel thirsty.

Prevention is simple enough. Carry plenty of water and drink it at regular intervals, whether or not you feel thirsty. The rule of thumb is one gallon (four liters) per person per day, but it's best to take more than you think you'll need just in case you extend your trip or lose your way. Getting lost is notoriously easy to do in the desert, where the absence of trees and other landmarks leaves you with few reference points and the abundance of bare ground makes it

Seasoned hikers set out early, often before dawn. The desert sunshine of mid-afternoon accelerates dehydration . It is best to complete a hike by 1 or 2pm, or to find a shady spot to rest until early evening before tackling the last few miles.

Getting into gear

As a hiker, you will rely almost entirely on your feet, so keep them in good shape with the best hiking boots you can afford. Modern boots are waterproof and lightweight but sturdy enough to protect your feet from cactus and thorny underbrush and need little or no breaking in, which helps avoid painful blisters. A thin, inner polypropolene sock and a thick, outer sock will help keep your feet dry and comfortable on long hikes. If blisters or sore spots develop, quickly cover them with moleskin or surgical tape, available at most pharmacies or camping supply stores. As for attire, wearing technical wicking fabrics will make you rue the day you ever took to the wilderness draped in absorbent and chafing cotton. Shirts, pants, socks, even undergarments, come in synthetic fabrics that keep you dry and comfortable.

Overnight trips are naturally more complicated to plan and require a rather daunting list of additional equipment, including a backpack, sleeping bag and mat, head-lamp, tent, water-purifying and first aid kits, and camping stove. The design and quality of gear has never been better, though choices (and prices) can quickly become overwhelming. Unless you have an experienced friend to show you the ropes, the best advice is to start by doing a little research, then go to a reputable camping-supply retailer and work with a salesperson who's willing to take the time you need to make the right decisions.

Remember: comfort is key. A backpack with 40 pounds of supplies feels a lot different than an empty one, just pulled off the store wall. Test multiple models, weighed down and adjusted to fit your frame. Roughing it in the outdoors shouldn't be rough at all. The idea is to simplify your life, unload stress, and enjoy the place, people, and moment, not aggravate yourself with ill-fitting or poor-quality equipment that leaves you cold, hungry, achy, and generally miserable.

Now that you're properly equipped, you can begin making the tough decisions about where to go. Trail conditions, topography, and weather vary widely in Arizona, so gathering accurate information about a destination – the length and difficulty of your route, the availability of water, the location of facilities – is essential for planning a successful trip. Many parks have websites with trail descriptions and weather reports, and often visitor centers with knowledgeable rangers and local volunteers. Heed their warnings and advice, and never attempt something foolhardy like hiking to the very bottom of the Grand Canyon and back in a single day. It may seem like a good idea when

you're enjoying a cool breeze on the South Rim, but it's another story when, a few hours later, your strength is sapped by the searing heat of the inner canyon and you're facing a long steep slog back to the top.

The best approach is to let your interests be your guide. Do you enjoy hiking in forests? Consider a trip through the aspen groves of the San Francisco Peaks or among stands of juniper and ponderosa pine on the Mogollon Rim. Have an interest in birding? More than 350 avian species, including a dazzling variety of hummingbirds, have been recorded at Madera and Ramsey canyons in Coronado National

Forest south of Tucson. Red-rock country? Explore the swirling sandstone formations of Paria Canyon-Vermilion Cliffs Wilderness. Fly-fishing? Pull on your waders and cast a line into Oak Creek just north of Sedona.

Pedal power

The possibilities become even more enticing when you consider alternate modes of transportation such as mountain biking or boating, which usually free you from the burden of lugging a backpack and open up territory that may have been unreachable on foot. Improvements in the design of mountain bikes have made them lighter and more mobile than ever. The advantages are obvious in a place like

LEFT: exploring a lost canyon outside Page.
RIGHT: winter camping is a cold but rewarding experience.

Golfer's Paradise

Arizona is an above-par place for the sport, which has been a growth industry since the first official course opened over 100 years ago

olf isn't usually considered an adventure sport, but in Arizona there's a rich tradition of rugged play. Up until recent years, an annual Cowboy Golf tournament in Springerville, a rural community in the White Mountains, featured

nine holes on a working cattle ranch. Players would ride horseback between holes and use cowpies as tees. There was the risk of having their "cart" gallop off mid-swing or twisting an ankle in a tumbleweed-filled arroyo. In fact, the first Arizona courses were "true desert courses" with "greens" composed of sand (doused with recycled french-fry oil to keep the dust down). Golfers made their way between creosote bushes and cacti, and when they were done playing a hole, they would have to drag a piece of carpet across the sand to erase their footprints.

These days, the adventure has more to do with withstanding the unrelenting heat. Book a tee time in Phoenix or Tucson at midday in July, and you may face temperatures of 110°F (43°C) or higher.

Arizona's longest-operating course, Turquoise Valley in Naco, opened in 1908, and since then the state has slowly transformed into a golf mecca. There are now more than 400 courses statewide, and most are public. Couple that with more than 300 days of sunshine a year and mild weather between October and May, and you have plenty of opportunities to hit the links.

Golf courses are as varied as the terrain. Phoenix and Tucson feature dramatic courses set at the base of desert mountains, with greens surrounded by boulders and saguaro cacti. In the mountainous communities of northern Arizona, such as Flagstaff, Payson, Prescott, and Pinetop, courses are surrounded by pine and juniper trees and cooled by mountain breezes. One of the state's most challenging public courses is said to be Las Sendas in Mesa, which has a rating of 73.1 and a 144 slope.

For some people, golf is also a spectator sport, and in Arizona, there are plenty of tournaments to watch. The two biggest tournaments are played in metro Phoenix during peak golf season. The PGA's Waste Management Phoenix Open, held in late January and early February, draws the nation's top golfers as well as hundreds of thousands of enthusiastic spectators. In March, it's the women's turn with the LPGA's RR Donnelly Founders Cup tournament.

There are still a few more ways to turn golfing into an adventure. Heli-golfing involves a chopper picking up a foursome in one town, dropping them off in an exotic locale, and returning in time for cocktails at the clubhouse. Then there's night golfing, which includes fluorescent golf balls and lighted fairways. But perhaps the most adventurous of all is encountering one of the state's wild residents on a green – a javelina, a coyote … maybe even a rattlesnake.

For more information about golf in Arizona, contact the nonprofit Arizona Golf Association at 602-944-3035 or www.azgolf.org

LEFT AND ABOVE: lush golf courses in the desert.

Arizona, where much of the backcountry is crosshatched with logging and mining roads. You'll cover more ground on wheels than on foot, and, unlike motorized travel, biking is easy on the environment (so long as you stay on prescribed trails), and lets the landscape unfold at a speed that's more akin to hiking than driving.

While it can take years to master, the basics aren't all that different from riding a standard road bike. As long as you steer clear of extremely steep, tortuous or rocky routes and technically demanding single tracks, beginners shouldn't encounter too many difficulties.

Many of the same safety issues pertain to biking as to other wilderness travel. Bring plenty of water and nutritious food, keep abreast of weather conditions, and don't overtax your skills or endurance. Carry a pump, as well as repair and first-aid kits, and be courteous to jeeps, horseback riders, and hikers who may be sharing the trail. Be wary of logging trucks, which often barrel down backroads at breakneck speeds.

Wet behind the ears

If, as naturalist Loren Eiseley wrote, there's magic in water, then the rivers of Arizona are truly a miracle. They bring life to sun-blasted deserts,

ABOVE: a helicopter tour is a great way to get a bird's-eye view of the landscape.

Best of all, opportunities for mountain biking in Arizona are virtually endless. Even business travelers confined to offices in Phoenix or Tucson will find good biking in classic Sonoran landscapes only a short drive from downtown. Farther afield, bikers can explore the alpine meadows of the White Mountains, the stark desert ranges of Organ Pipe Cactus National Monument, the slickrock trails of Sedona, the volcanic highlands of Coconino National Forest, and the "high, wide and lonesome" backroads of the Kaibab Plateau to little-visited overlooks of the Grand Canyon and Colorado River.

sculpt rock into breathtaking canyons, and serve as natural corridors for travelers and wildlife.

The premier river trip in Arizona – and arguably in all of North America – is a whitewater rafting trip through the Grand Canyon on the Colorado River. The full 225-mile (362km) journey from Lees Ferry to Diamond Creek takes about two weeks (although motorized rafts take about half as long) and is filled with wild rides through heart-stopping rapids, long peaceful floats between soaring canyon walls, and hikes into enchanting side canyons where ancient Indian ruins are sheltered by rocky alcoves, waterfalls plunge into aqua pools, and seeping springs sustain gardens of maidenhair fern and crimson monkeyflower.

The real beauty of the experience is that just about anyone can do it. Outfitters authorized by the Park Service handle all provisioning, navigation, rowing and cooking. About all you have to do – aside from paying the (very substantial) bill – is show up.

River running elsewhere in the state can be quite good depending on the season and ranges from boat-bashing whitewater to long stretches of calm water that can be floated in an inner tube. Kayaking can give you a sense of freedom not afforded by hitching a ride on a crowded rubber boat, and a morning of instruction is often all you need before tackling Class 1 or 2 rapids on your own. The Verde, Salt, and Gila rivers promise solitude, scenery and glimpses of desert wildlife, though water levels are often too low to boat. Flatwater enthusiasts can explore the countless red-rock gorges and coves that line the edges of artificial lakes Powell and Mead, the watery caves and canyons of the lower Colorado River near Lake Havasu City and, farther south, the rich bird habitats of the wetlands and floodplains at Imperial and Cibola National Wildlife Refuges.

Climbing the walls

The learning curve is far more precipitous for rock climbing, although even in this sport, in which technical skill and strength are paramount, the opportunities for beginners are expanding. Not too many years ago, the only practical way to learn rock climbing was to tag along with experienced climbers. Today, it's much more common for newcomers to hone their skills at climbing gyms before they actually put flesh to rock. In as little as 20–30 minutes, instructors can have you up on an artificial wall, though after the basics are learned, there is no substitute for the real thing. For that, contact organizations like the Arizona Mountaineering Club (www.amcaz. org), which runs a two-week course for novices that covers the fundamentals of climbing techniques, equipment and, above all, safety. Before long, you will be clinging the sandstone at Camelback just north of Phoenix, grabbing the granite and gneiss of Mount Lemmon outside of Tucson, and gripping the basalt cracks of Paradise Forks near Flagstaff.

Climbing skills are also being used by a new breed of adventurers known as canyoneers, who combine hiking, rappelling, rock climbing, and swimming to explore some of the least accessible canyons in the Southwest. Outfitters and adventure clubs throughout the state organize regular expeditions for adventurers of all experience levels. If extreme heights are too much for you to bear, then you may be interested in the increasingly popular style of climbing known as bouldering, which involves quick scrambles sans ropes and anchors but with strategically placed foam pads to break short falls. The great thing about bouldering is that it can be done almost anywhere you can find a rock that's taller than you. That's almost everywhere in Arizona.

Much less technical but still challenging are the hundreds of peaks that rise from desert ranges scattered throughout the state. The degree of difficulty varies considerably from one mountain to another, but most require no special skills or equipment and can be climbed in a single day. Those with little or no experience may want to set their sights on a modest goal – say, the 2,610ft (795-meter) summit of Squaw Peak in Phoenix, one of the most popular hikes in the state. Mid-range summits include 8,417ft (2,566-meter) Hualapai Peak near Kingman and 9,453ft (2,881-meter) Mount Wrightson in the Santa Ritas south of Tucson. On the far end of the scale is the lung-searing trek to the top of 12,637ft (3,852-meter) Humphreys Peak north of Flagstaff.

Powder to the people

Arizona isn't particularly well known for skiing. In fact, most people – including quite a few Arizonans – are surprised to learn that a place known for its eyebrow-singeing temperatures has skiing at all. Thanks largely to its "basin and range" geography, Arizona is one of the rare places where you can spend the morning schussing through fresh powder and the afternoon sunbathing at poolside.

Arizona has four ski areas – the Arizona Snowbowl, and Elk Ridge outside Flagstaff, the Mount Lemmon Ski Valley in the Santa Catalina Mountains near Tucson (the southernmost ski resort in the United States), and the Sunrise Park Ski Resort in the White Mountains. Currently, only Snowbowl is developing snowmaking capabilities. The rest are entirely dependent on the whims of weather which, when generous, deliver mounds of dry, fluffy powder – as much as 250ins (635cm) or more a year.

All that white stuff means the possibilities for cross-country skiing and snowshoeing are even more extensive, with miles of trails at such facilities as the Flagstaff Nordic Ski Center and Mormon Lake Ski Touring Center, both in northern Arizona. For those who want to break their own trails, there are countless acres of snow-covered backcountry in Apache-Sitgreaves, Coconino, and Kaibab National Forests, including wilderness treks to the North Rim of the Grand Canyon for those with sufficient stamina and logistical know-how to make the 45-mile (72km) journey from Jacob Lake, the nearest town with year-round access. Some lodges even lead snowmobile trips for guests. It's enough to make you think you have ended up in New England, or at least hopped over into Colorado.

In the end, the deepest rewards of adventuring come not from mastering a particular

activity but from simply being outdoors in places where, as Colin Fletcher wrote of the Grand Canyon, people can move "closer to rock and sky, to light and shadow, to space and silence". Thanks to farsighted citizens and locally-elected politicians, Arizona has more than 5 million acres (2 million hectares) of legally protected wilderness, which exists for future generations to enjoy.

What that means in practical terms is that, no matter how far you hike, there will always be another canyon to explore, another hill to climb, another trail to follow. As a river guide said of her many journeys through the Grand Canyon, "the place is so huge, every trip feels like the first time".

Left: cooling off in a waterfall.
Right: meditating in Paria Canyon.

EXPLORING ANCIENT ARIZONA

You can tour prehistoric sites, visit some of the West's finest collections of artifacts, or join an actual dig supervised by a professional archaeologist

L and and people are deeply entwined in Arizona. Hike desert trails throughout the state and you'll soon come upon crumbling adobe dwellings, painted and pecked rock art, arrowheads, potsherds, and other reminders that people have been living here for thousands of years. Drive the highways and you'll pass ancient stone cities built into hills and cliffs. Float the Colorado River through the Grand Canyon and almost every side canyon will reveal sealed granaries and mud-walled dwellings that seem to have been abandoned only yesterday.

Arizona's wealth of prehistoric sites is one of its main attractions, and for many travelers the highlight of visiting the state is not only touring its many archaeological parks but getting involved in an actual dig. Not sure where to start? Four superb museums offer an overview of Arizona's ancient cultures and an easy way to get up to speed on the state's prehistory before hitting the road and visiting individual sites.

It's illegal to remove or disturb archaeological remains on public land. If you stumble across rock art, potsherds, or other artifacts, note the location and report them to the managing agency.

Getting started

Arizona State Museum, founded in 1915 at the University of Arizona in Tucson, is the oldest anthropological institution in the Southwest.

LEFT: Betatakin, occupied by Ancestral Puebloans in the 13th century, is set in the safety of Tsegi Canyon.
RIGHT: the exact meaning of some rock art is a mystery.

The museum's signature exhibit, Paths of Life, interprets 10 contemporary Indian tribes in Arizona and northern Mexico. Another gallery highlights famed university archaeologist Emil Haury's excavations at the Hohokam site, Snaketown, in the 1930s. Not to be missed is a breathtaking display of some of the 20,000 prehistoric Southwest pots in the museum collection. On display 2010 through 2012, the museum celebrates the bicentennial of Mexico's independence from Spain and the centennial of the Mexican Revolution with a traveling exhibit featuring 300 objects revealing 3,000 years of Mexican culture and the original Treaty of Guadalupe Hidalgo, the treaty ending the US War with Mexico in 1848.

The Heard Museum in Phoenix is, quite simply, the finest cultural institution in Arizona. It was founded in 1929 to display Dwight B. and Maie Bartlett Heard's large collection of Southwest artifacts and has in recent years doubled its exhibit space to nine to trace the prehistoric roots of present-day tribes. The Barry Goldwater Kachina Doll Collection, which displays the country's largest collection of painted Hopi and Navajo religious carvings, is now seamlessly woven into the spectacular Home: Native People in the Southwest permanent exhibit, a must-see for every visitor. Other exhibits include a look at all 21 of Arizona's tribes from their perspective in the We Are! Gallery and revolving exhibits featuring contemporary Indian artists.

Research is also the focus of the Amerind Foundation in Dragoon, southeast of Tucson, founded by archaeology enthusiast William S. Fulton in 1937. A large archive of ethnographic materials is available for scholars; casual visitors will be fascinated by the foundation's huge museum, which offers an excellent introduction to the cultures of the Southwest and northern Mexico, with an extensive collection of artifacts from the America-sponsored excavation of Casas Grandes, Mexico.

FOOD FOR THOUGHT

The Southwest's most controversial archaeological debate rages around that most taboo of subjects – cannibalism. At the center of the debate is physical anthropologist Dr. Christy Turner, who, with his late wife Jacqueline, spent 30 years researching cannibalism at Ancestral Pueblo sites after finding signs of butchering and cooking in human bones excavated in northern Arizona. In 1999, the Turners published their findings in Man Corn, an allusion to an Aztec word for a ritual meal of human flesh.

Though praised for its scholarship, the book's conclusions have been criticized even by supporters of the authors' work. The Turners suggest that an Aztec warrior cult from Mexico infiltrated Chaco Canyon in New Mexico about AD 900 and used ritual sacrifice to terrorize the local population into submission. The discovery of fossilized excrement (coprolite) containing human remains seems to offer more evidence of the Turners' theory.

Violence is an understandably sensitive issue for the Hopi and other descendants of the Ancestral Pueblo people, and two other studies only added fuel to the fire. A survey of Pueblo excavations conducted by archaeologist Stephen Le Blanc catalogued numerous examples of violence. Similarly, Polly Schaafsma published the results of her study of rock art depicting warfare, which makes clear that conflict was escalating in late Pueblo times.

Can you dig it?

Ever wanted to don an archaeologist's battered hat and help dig up an important piece of the past? The romance of archaeology seems to infect everyone. Unfortunately, far more people want to take part in a professionally supervised archaeological dig than there are opportunities for them to do so. But a number of programs are available, with a limited number of slots open to volunteers.

The US Forest Service operates the popular Passport in Time program (PIT), which gives anyone over the age of 18 the chance to participate in an archaeological excavation in one

Elden Pueblo Archaeological Project, one of the best participatory experiences in Arizona. Educational programs include site tours, lab work, and excavation techniques and are offered to school groups and institutions between April and September each year at Elden Pueblo, a 60–80-room Sinagua ruin within Flagstaff city limits. The site is open for public participation during Archeology Month in March and the Festival of Science in September and Public Field Days in summer, when visitors get a chance to take part in a supervised dig.

Not far from Flagstaff, the White Mountains are another good bet for anyone inter-

of the state's national forests. In recent years, PIT programs have included digs at Mogollon pueblos in Apache-Sitgreaves National Forest, fieldwork in Tonto National Forest to map an Apache settlement from the historic period, and fieldwork on the Kaibab Plateau to document archeological sites.

The Deer Valley Rock Art Center, run by Arizona State University, offers programs throughout the year that focus on rock art created by the Hohokam. Coconino National Forest, Arizona Natural History Association, and Arizona Archeological Society sponsor the

LEFT: Lomaki Pueblo in the Wupatki Pueblo National Monument. **ABOVE:** rock art, Kaibab National Forest.

ested in archaeology. The White Mountain Archaeological Center, located on a working ranch near St. Johns, offers tours of rock art sites, the chance to assist on a dig at the large Mogollon Raven Site Ruin, moonlit hikes in the surrounding area, and overnight ranch accommodations. Just east of Greer, the X Diamond Ranch also offers the chance to take part in a supervised excavation of a Mogollon ruin with a large kiva. Since 1983, Dr. E. Charles Adams and Dr. Richard Lange of the Arizona State Museum have operated a summer excavation program at Homolovi Ruins State Park near Winslow. The program relies heavily on college students, though volunteers 16 years or older are welcome. If you're interested, contact

Earthwatch, a global environmental program. The Smithsonian Institution and National Geographic Society in Washington, D.C. also offer tours of Southwest archaeological sites and are worth contacting.

For a somewhat more formal experience, the Arizona Archaeological Society offers Professional Crew Member certification during summer programs at Elden Pueblo and Q Ranch, a large Mogollon ruin on a private cattle ranch in the White Mountains. Slots are few, there is a modest fee for the weeklong digs, and you must be a society member.

Arizona State Parks organizes Archaeology Awareness and Heritage Month, a program of events and activities involving more than 60 different government and private organizations, which takes place in March of each year. More than 100 events include prehistoric site tours, exhibits, open houses, lectures, demonstrations, and other activities throughout Arizona. This is your chance to learn to use an atlatl, or spear thrower; weave a pine-needle basket; attend a lecture on the latest theories in southwestern archaeology; examine pottery rarely on public display; or take a ranger-led tour into backcountry areas that are usually off-limits.

In addition, the Museum of Northern Arizona, Heard Museum, and Arizona State Museum all sponsor lecture series, special events, cultural programs, and demonstrations as well as occasional field trips to archaeological sites accompanied by experts and working archaeologists.

Several Indian tribes now have their own archaeological resource departments and encourage culture tours led by tribal members. Entrepreneurs on the Navajo reservation, for example, offer bed and breakfast in traditional Navajo hogans and horseback and jeep tours of nearby prehistoric sites at Canyon de Chelly and Monument Valley. Or you might stop at the Kaibab Paiute Tribal Headquarters next to Pipe Spring National Monument in the Arizona Strip and take a guided tour of rock art sites left behind by Virgin Anasazi and early Paiutes.

Serve and protect

A number of national parks now have Friends groups that raise funds and lobby for

increased protection of their prehistoric sites. Site stewardship programs are also catching on fast with local archaeology enthusiasts. Arizona State Parks' highly successful Site Stewardship program trains volunteers to monitor archaeological sites for vandalism, conduct educational presentations about site preservation, and function as a trusted link between nearby communities and the State Historic Preservation Office. Arizona State Museum manages the training for the state parks, working with volunteers to monitor rock art sites east of Tucson.

ABOVE: cliff houses at Montezuma Well.
RIGHT: White House Ruin, Canyon de Chelly.

ROCK ART

Rock art is found throughout Arizona, some dating back to the Archaic period, more than 2,000 years ago. Images were pecked (petroglyphs) or painted with ground minerals like red hematite (pictographs) and depict hunting scenes, geometric patterns, and fertility symbols. Some rock art marked the solstices. The most puzzling type may be the huge intaglios or "geoglyphs" that were made on the desert floor near the Gila and lower Colorado Rivers and are best viewed from above. One huge rock art site open to visitors is the V-Bar-V Heritage Site near Beaver Creek Campground in the Verde Valley, a late period Sinagua site.

GHOST TOWNS

Abandoned mining camps and forgotten outposts are frozen in time, offering insights into the lives of their long-gone inhabitants

Scores of abandoned mining camps that once housed several thousand people can be found throughout Arizona. Some are true ghost towns – mysterious names on a topographical map, completely unpopulated, with dilapidated buildings, empty schools, churches, and collapsed mine works. Most, though, have a few residents who look after the buildings, conduct tours, and keep alive these forgotten places.

A few mining towns never really died. Bisbee, Clifton, Tombstone, Prescott, and Jerome yielded billions of tons of copper, silver, gold, lead, and other precious metals. They grew into the largest and wealthiest towns in the state and became politically important as seats of local and state government. Today, they are undergoing a metamorphosis.

> *Vulture has only one tree – a hanging tree. The mine supplied the Union with bullion during the Civil War, but miners "high-graded" (stole) as much as 40 percent. Eighteen men were hanged for it.*

Whole districts of Victorian mansions, company buildings, hotels, bars, and bordellos are now on the National Register of Historic Places. Many have been restored by artists, retirees, and local historical associations and turned into quirky homegrown museums, art galleries, bed-and-breakfasts, bars, and restaurants filled

with mine memorabilia and, as is the case at the Copper Queen Hotel in Bisbee, haunted by the restless spirits of working girls, former managers, and other ghosts of the past.

Some ghost towns grew up to serve mining communities. Benson was the railhead for Bisbee and other nearby towns. The Verde Valley Railroad once carried mineral ore and passengers between Clarkdale and Perkinsville, serving mines at the hillside town of Jerome. These historic railroads are now the center of reborn communities, carrying thousands of tourists through the scenic backcountry.

Original buildings, colorful characters, and bloody histories have attracted makers

LEFT: a rusty vehicle and a ramshackle building at Gold King Mine, near Jerome.
RIGHT: Vulture Gold Mine outside of Wickenburg.

of movie westerns to ghost towns for decades. Many production companies took up permanent residence. Newly constructed "aged" buildings sit alongside original structures in an authentic boardwalk town at Old Tucson Studios, now one of the state's top tourist attractions, with staged gunfights and set tours. A movie set at Pahreah, an 1873 Mormon ghost town just over the Utah line, north of Lake Powell, was constructed for John Sturges's 1962 Western comedy *Sergeants Three* and is now encompassed by Grand Staircase-Escalante National Monument.

located copper seams – the mineral that put Arizona on the map.

It's hard to believe that these dusty ghost towns were once the sites of gold and silver bonanzas that attracted swarms of fortune-seekers – miners and merchants, clergymen and saloonkeepers, lawmakers and lawbreakers, of every nationality. Prospectors followed reports of gold and silver, staked claims, and hoped for a lucky strike. If successful, they usually sold their claims and moved on, leaving the actual hard-rock mining to companies that could afford to invest in the necessary machinery, labor, and infrastructure. The bonanzas that

The Lord giveth

Residents of the Copper State are proud of their mining heritage. Arizona's motto is "God Enriches". The state seal depicts a miner with a pick and shovel, the likeness of George Warren, the first prospector to hit it big in the Bisbee mines in the 1860s. Even the state's name is said to be derived from the abandoned silver mining town of Arizonac, just south of the Mexican border. Indian tribes were the first to mine turquoise, malachite, and azurite deposits from marine-formed limestones. Later Spanish and Mexican miners found gold and silver near these beautiful blue minerals. In the mid-1800s, when Anglo miners reopened the Spanish diggings, they

fueled these boomtowns were dramatic, the decline often catastrophic. As mineral deposits played out and miners moved on, fortunes won turned quickly to fortunes lost, and boomtown became ghost town.

Cocktails at 30 paces

Mowry mining camp, between Patagonia and the US–Mexico border, is one of the oldest mining camps in Arizona. The Patagonia Mine was worked by Mexicans in 1857 and perhaps even earlier by Spanish Jesuits. It was renamed when mine executive Sylvester Mowry bought it in 1859. Twelve furnaces reduced the rich ore to 70lb (32kg) bars and a reported $1.5 million was shipped. Mowry is now on private land, but FR 214 bisects the townsite and two small adobe ruins can be seen. Nearby are the walls of the mine and smelter site, with a collapsed shaft, powder house, and large slag pile.

Sylvester Mowry was arrested for selling lead for bullets to the Confederates during the Civil War and lost his mine. He is also associated with the former ghost town of Tubac, the oldest European settlement in Arizona. When Edward Cross, editor of the state's oldest newspaper, the *Weekly Arizonan*, criticized Mowry for his support of splitting off Arizona territory from New Mexico,

the remains of the *presidio*, and the town has taken on new life as an art colony.

Tubac was the headquarters for Poston's Sonora Exploring and Mining Company, which reopened Spanish and Mexican silver diggings at Cerro Colorado ("red hill"), west of present-day Interstate 19, in the 1850s. The silver mine established there and named after company president Samuel P. Heitzelman was the outfit's most successful producer. Eventually, though, Apache raids, worker unrest, and the murder of Poston's brother John closed the mine. Poston's grave is all that remains.

Mowry challenged Cross to a duel with rifles. When each missed his mark, they ended up toasting each other's health.

Situated in the Santa Cruz River valley, Tubac was founded as a *presidio*, or garrison, by the Spanish in 1752, then abandoned by the Mexicans after repeated Apache raiding in 1848. It was re-established in 1855 by American Charles Poston, a politician, entrepreneur, and visionary often called the "Father of Arizona." Today, Tubac is no longer a ghost town. A state historic park preserves

LEFT: Vulture Gold Mine has many buildings still standing and in disrepair. **ABOVE:** Two Guns, a ghost town between Flagstaff and Holbrook.

Bloody murder

Another ghost town with a violent history is Ruby, 30 miles (48km) northwest of Nogales. A lead, zinc, and silver mining town that died in 1941, Ruby has more than two dozen roofed buildings, including a jail, a school (with its basketball backboards still in place), mine offices, mill foundations, mine officials' residences, and a miners' dormitory. Bandits from across the Mexican border killed four people during robberies in 1920 and 1921 in the now crumbling adobe store. Only one of the killers was captured.

The most famous murders of all were those that took place in the 30-second gunfight at the OK Corral in Tombstone in October 1881, killing Tom and Frank McLaury and Billy Clanton, known cattle rustlers, and wounding Virgil and Morgan Earp, brothers of U.S. Marshal Wyatt Earp. Clanton and the McLaurys now lie beneath gravestones in the Boothill Cemetery and the infamous contretemps is commemorated daily in staged gunfights and exhibits at the red-brick 1882 Tombstone Courthouse State Historic Park.

Buildings like the courthouse are evidence that Tombstone's history is not all blood and guts, despite the obvious truth of its claim to being "the town too tough to die". It grew from the Tombstone and Graveyard mining claims

filed by prospector Ed Schieffelin in 1877 into one of the largest and wealthiest towns in the West. Schieffelin is buried in a little-known grave west of town under a pyramid-like stone cairn that marks the spot where he spent two nights hiding from the Apache before making his famous strike.

The ghost town trail

East of Tombstone is one of the best concentrations of ghost towns in Arizona. The old copper mining town of Gleeson has the ruins of a jail, school, and hospital. Farther up the road, in the Dragoon Mountains (the stronghold of Apache warrior Cochise), all that remains of Courtland is its jail, but before World War I the town had its own auto dealership and a population of 2,000. Neighboring Pearce, the site of an 1894 gold rush in the flat Sulphur Springs Valley, has several ruins from its heyday, including the 1884 post office, a school, a jail, a few ruins and foundations, and the Old Store, a large adobe mercantile building with a high false front and an elaborate tin facade. Just to the north, the almost deserted community of Cochise was founded in the early 1880s as a water and fuel stop along the Southern Pacific Railroad. Today, all that's left is the Cochise Country Store, a school, a boarded-up church, and the 1882 Cochise Hotel.

Mining in the Verde and Prescott Valleys brought fortune hunters to central Arizona in the late 1800s, leading to the choice of Prescott as the first territorial capital in 1912. Gold deposits in the Bradshaw Mountains, southeast of Prescott, yielded

THINGS THAT GO BUMP IN THE NIGHT

Arizona's colorful history has sparked its share of ghost stories. The specters of Bisbee's Copper Queen Hotel are well known. A manager from the early 1900s still strolls the lobby and accompanies visitors in the old elevator. The ghost of Julia, one of many prostitutes who entertained men in the tiny "cribs" in neighboring Brewery Gulch, makes amorous advances toward male guests in a third-floor room that's come to be known as the Ghost Room.

"Soiled doves" and their clients also still seem to be having fun at Tombstone's Bird Cage Theatre. The theater sometimes smells of cigar smoke, and piano music is heard. When it opened as a tourist attraction, a mannequin of Wyatt Earp was mistakenly placed in the Clanton family's favorite crib. Day after day, Earp's hat sailed mysteriously to the floor, knocked off by some unseen force, until he was moved to a crib of his own.

Guests at the 1917 Vendome Hotel in Prescott report sudden temperature drops, whispered conversations, moving objects, and the appearance of Abby Byr, an owner who died in Room 16. The old hospital in nearby Jerome, now a hotel, also has a female ghost, perhaps a former nurse. "We hear voices," says the night clerk. "Feelings of cold air. Sometimes people have heard a name spoken, have turned around, and nobody's there."

$390,000 annually. By 1904, the Crown King mine had enriched its investors with $1.5 million in gold. Problems in reaching the smelter in Humboldt inspired entrepreneur George Murphy to construct what was dubbed "Murphy's Impossible Railroad", linking mining towns in the Bradshaw Mountains over impossibly steep terrain. Trestles, switchbacks, and a tunnel were required in order to lay the tracks for the 51-mile (82km) standard-gauge railroad. During its 23 years of operation, the railroad transported $1.1 million in gold and silver.

The former tracks now allow visitors to visit Humboldt, Mayer, Cordes, Bumble Bee, Cleator, and Crown King, an easy loop west of Interstate 17. The latter is a popular getaway for Phoenicians, with cabins, camping areas, the century-old Crown King General Store, and a saloon-restaurant that was packed in piece by piece from the mining camp of Oro Belle, 5 miles (8km) to the southwest, in 1910.

Colorado River ghosts

Among the earliest Anglo settlements along the Colorado River were Forts Yuma and Mohave, which were built to safeguard gold seekers traveling to mining camps on steamboats that plied the river from 1852 to 1907.

The best-preserved ghost town along the Colorado River is actually on the California side. Picacho Mine has been worked intermittently since placer deposits were discovered in 1862 beneath 1,300ft (400-meter) Picacho Peak. By 1907, the site was an "oasis of bustle," according to the Los Angeles Times, with a peak population of about 2,500. River damming in 1909 ended cheap transportation of ore and put paid to many mining towns, including Ehrenberg, La Paz, Castle Dome Landing, Hardyville, Aubrey Landing, and Polhamus Landing. Much of Picacho was submerged behind Laguna Dam. Today, it is a state recreation area, with a relocated historic graveyard and a 2-mile (3km) hiking tour that takes in the Picacho cave jail and remnants of two mills.

LEFT: the Douglas mansion at Jerome State Historic Park. **RIGHT:** Oatman, where wild donkeys are welcome on Main Street in the old mining town.

Away from the river, other Mohave Desert ghosts still cling to life. The gold-mining town of Oatman, just south of Kingman, boomed to 10,000 people in 1913. The United Eastern Mine was one of the major producers in the area; the others, Goldroad and Tom Reed, sparked short-lived communities and no longer exist. Today, Oatman has just 128 residents and is a popular stop for tourists traveling historic Route 66. Several original buildings still stand, including the renovated Oatman Hotel, Mohave County's only two-story adobe building, famous as the spot where

Clark Gable and Carole Lombard spent their honeymoon.

Three other ghosts can be found nearby, in the rugged Cerbat Mountains northwest of Kingman. Chloride, named for the silver chloride ore found there in the Silver Hill strike of the 1860s, is one of the earliest Arizona Territory mining camps. The town features a post office and false-front general store, built in 1928. Mineral Park was the seat of Mohave County in the mid-1870s but lost out to Kingman when the railroad arrived in 1887. Nearby Cerbat was settled in the early 1860s, not long after Chloride. Of its three mines – Golden Gem, Esmeralda, and Vanderbilt – only the Golden Gem mill and headframe still stand.

THE ARIZONA COWBOY

His mystique lives on at rodeos and dude
ranches and in the lives of working buckaroos

On a crystal-clear spring morning, the Sonoran Desert outside Scottsdale is carpeted with drifts of Mexican gold poppies, lupines, owl's clover, and other wildflowers. In the distance, the 7,000ft (2,000-meter) peaks of the Mazatzal Mountains are dusted with snow.

But three men and three women at the Arizona Cowboy College are oblivious to the scenery. They're hunched around the hind leg of a patient gray quarter horse as Rusty, a farrier, gives them a detailed, three-hour, hands-on lesson on the art and science of horse shoes. The group is transfixed.

The six students have spent a day learning the basics, including saddling, riding, and grooming; they've also learned the fundamentals of roping. Tomorrow, under the supervision of the cowboy college's instructor, they'll pack up supplies and horses and head to a ranch, where, for four days, they'll be at the beck and call of the rancher, doing everything from rounding up and branding cattle to mending fences, sweeping barns, and shoveling manure.

Live the legend

For a few days at least, these people will be real, working cowboys. And like real cowboys, their working conditions are pretty rough. At the college, they sleep together in an open, concrete-floored bunkhouse and share one bathroom; on the range, they sleep on the ground, eschew showers, and answer nature's call in the brush. And while real cowboys get paid for their efforts (though not much), this group of people – and many like them – pays good money for

LEFT AND RIGHT: "Cowboys", wrote Walt Whitman, "are a strangely interesting class ... with their swarthy complexions and broad-brimmed hats."

the experience. After a week of training, "graduates" could, ostensibly, work on a cattle ranch. Few do. Most come merely to fulfill a lifelong dream of cowboying.

Modern-day economics may not support many authentic ranches or cowboys, but in Arizona, at least, the cowboy dream lives on. It's a rare visitor to this state who doesn't want to experience some form of cowboy culture, be it folk art or fashion, trail rides or steak fries, dude ranches, rodeos, or even something as advanced as the no-holds-barred program at the Cowboy College.

The Spanish connection

Cowboy heritage – both real and legendary – runs deep in Arizona. The state's first cowboy was, arguably, Jesuit missionary Eusebio Francisco Kino, the "Padre on Horseback" who, in the late 17th century, planted the seeds of Spanish cattle ranching and farming throughout southern Arizona.

Cattle ranching during the Spanish colonial period was sporadic. Spain considered the region remote at best, and the missions were beset by disease, drought, and Apache raids. After Mexico's independence in 1821, southern Arizona was home to numerous Mexican families who ranched on large land grants, with herds of cattle, horses, and mules that numbered in the thousands.

vaqueros to pursue a living; *los ranchos grandes* and the resident cattle were abandoned, while owners and workers moved into town.

Ranching takes root

After the Gadsden Purchase of 1853, Americans began to trickle into Arizona. Large herds of Texas cattle were driven across the state to supply military and mining concerns in California. After the drives, Texas cowboys brought back tales of southern Arizona's mild winter climate and stirrup-high grasslands.

In 1857, Bill Kirkland became the first American rancher in the state, bringing some

An old cowboy song sums up the difficulties of adjusting to life on a dude ranch: "I'm a tough, hard-boiled cowhand with a weather-beaten hide, but herdin' cows is nuthin' to teachin' dudes to ride."

The influence of early Mexican *vaqueros* on American cowboys is still felt in ranching techniques, lingo, and equipment. Arizona historian Marshall Trimble notes that a *vaquero* could "ride a horse through steep terrain, rope a cow, roll a smoke, sing a song and do it all with a smile on his lips".

By the 1830s, however, the Apaches had made it impossible for Mexican ranchers and their

200 head of cattle to what was once a Mexican ranch south of Tucson. But between the outbreak of the Civil War and the continued hostilities of the Apaches, ranching remained in its infancy until Geronimo's surrender in 1886.

With the suppression of the Apaches, ranching flourished in both southern and northern Arizona, spurred on by the arrival of the transcontinental railroad in 1883. It wasn't unusual for large spreads to stretch for miles and support up to 60,000 head of cattle and hundreds of hired hands. Many early ranchers were from Texas and imported their own US-born cowboys. Most of these "buckaroos" (a term derived from the Spanish vaquero) fit the same profile: they were young, unmarried, and without family or educational prospects. They worked from dawn to well after dusk in a dangerous profession, all for little more compensation than room and board.

Technically, early Arizona ranches didn't have cowboys at all. The term "cowboy" was a derogatory phrase reserved for cattle rustlers and outlaws. The early ranch hands who tended cattle were referred to as "herdsmen" or "cowpunchers", because they poked at cattle with prods to move them into corrals or railcars. The cowboy moniker didn't take on its present connotation until the turn of the 20th century.

Cowboys were hired hands and tended to move from one job to another as demand or whimsy moved them. Ranchers, on the other hand, often kept their business in the family for generations. Even today, old-time Arizona ranch families are regarded as a sort of royalty, whether or not they're still in the cattle business. Despite economic ups and downs and recurrent droughts, the industry became one of the "four Cs" at the cornerstone of Arizona's economy – cattle, cotton, copper, and citrus.

Cowboys and Indians

It was about this time that rodeos became more prevalent statewide. What started out as a friendly test of cowboy skill became an organized event, complete with prize money. Both Prescott and Payson began having summer rodeos that continue today; Scottsdale's Parada del Sol Rodeo and Tucson's Fiesta de los Vaqueros are large winter events. Major rodeos also developed on Arizona's Indian reservations, particularly in the latter half of the 20th century. In an ironic twist, some of the state's best cowboys are Indians, particularly members of the Navajo and Apache nations.

By the 1920s cattle ranching changed forever. The state's southern grasslands had been overgrazed, droughts had taken a heavy toll, prices dropped, and feedlots began to replace the open range. Where once fortunes could be made by ranchers, and a hard-working cowboy could always find work, there was now only hardship and broken dreams. Today, traditional ranches are few and far between, save for the most remote parts of the state and on some Indian reservations.

Left: John Wayne takes a swing at Montgomery Clift in 1948's *Red River*, shot in Arizona. **Above:** a ranch hand at Rancho de los Caballeros dude ranch.

Fortunately, conservationists are now stepping in to rescue a few of the most vulnerable old spreads. The historic Slaughter Ranch, adjoining the Mexican border, for example, was saved from oblivion by preserving the 1890s ranch buildings as a museum. The San Rafael Ranch, also near the border, recently became a state park.

Birth of an icon

But despite the ranching industry's precipitous slide after World War I, the cowboy mystique never lost its appeal. The image was polished early on by popular entertainers like Buffalo

Bill, who romanticized the Western lifestyle and took it on the road. Countless dime novels fired up the imaginations of city slickers, as did the Western novels of Zane Grey (1872–1939), who lived in Arizona and set many of his stories here.

It wasn't long before Arizona attracted the attention of Hollywood. Westerns were big business, and a great many of them were filmed in the state. Tom Mix, star of many a silent cowboy epic, made several movies in Arizona. He died when his car flipped on State Highway 79, south of Florence. There's a roadside memorial at the crash site – a metal statue of a riderless horse, which was one of the most-stolen "souvenirs" on Arizona's highways until it was permanently installed.

John Ford came to Arizona in 1938 to film the John Wayne classic, *Stagecoach*, in Monument Valley and returned for more than half a dozen other films. Old Tucson, a "frontier town," was built in 1939 as the set for the epic *Arizona*, starring William Holden and Jean Arthur. The set remained as a desert film location, which, later, counted John Wayne as one of its business partners. Countless movies such as *Rio Bravo* and *The Outlaw Josey Wales* and television series such as *High Chaparral* and *Gunsmoke* were filmed there. The facility, still used as a movie location, is now a popular theme park.

Cash cows

Just as Hollywood was discovering the merits of Arizona as a movie set, tourism began to boom. Before long, ranchers discovered that accommodating guests could be as profitable as raising cattle, and the Arizona dude ranch was born. At first, they were primarily working ranches that took in guests as a way to supplement their income, but by the 1920s facilities that catered strictly to tourists sprang up in and around Tucson, Wickenburg, and, to a lesser degree, Phoenix. These guest ranches always kept a herd of quiet horses and plenty of steak and beans.

HOW TO CHOOSE A DUDE RANCH

Arizona has scores of dude ranches, ranging from spartan, working cattle ranches to elaborate "resorts with horses." Choosing one that suits your interests and budget can save your dude ranch vacation from turning into one giant dud.

A personal recommendation is the best way to make a selection, but in the absence of firsthand information try searching the Web or calling the ranches directly (*see Travel Tips section for information*). Be sure to ask about accommodations. Does the ranch have cabins, a bunkhouse, a lodge? Are meals included? How about the riding program? Do guests need to know how to ride or are lessons available? Does the ranch have a children's program? Is accessibility an issue? Also, check the ranch's location. Tucson and Wickenburg, both in the Sonoran Desert, are dude ranch hot spots, but if you like mountains and pine trees you won't be happy there. Consider destinations in the White Mountains or in the mountains around Flagstaff.

A few websites are useful. The Arizona Dude Ranch Association (www.azdra.com) lists comparisons of amenities and programs at their member ranches; Guest Ranches of North America (www.guestranches.com) offers profiles of more than 20 Arizona ranches; and DudeRanches.com (www.duderanches.com) lets you match activities to more than a dozen Arizona ranches. Happy trails.

As they grew more competitive, many offered Western-style entertainment, held "dudeos" (rodeos in which guests and staff compete against other guest ranches) and hay rides, and even added swimming pools and golf courses. Many of the old-time dude ranches are still open for the fall-to-spring season. In southern Arizona, these include the Tanque Verde Guest Ranch in Tucson and Rancho de la Osa in Sasabe, while in Wickenburg, it's the Flying E Ranch, Kay El Bar Guest Ranch, and the swanky Rancho de los Caballeros.

Developing at the same time were boarding schools that sprang up in central and southern Arizona, where the scions of New York and Philadelphia society were shipped West to learn the three Rs: reading, riding, and 'rithmatic. In addition to teachers who specialized in the usual subjects, the schools recruited local wranglers to instruct the young whippersnappers on cowboy basics. A few schools still exist – though, sadly, the Judson School, opened in Paradise Valley in the 1920s, was razed to make way for an upscale subdivision.

Lore and literature

But those in search of a bit of the Arizona cowboy mystique don't have to stay at guest ranches, enroll in a boarding school, follow the rodeo circuit or, for that matter, endure the rigors of the Arizona Cowboy College. There are other, less time-consuming ways to soak up snippets of cowboy lore.

The Arizona Historical Society Museum on the grounds of the University of Arizona in Tucson has numerous exhibits that chronicle the state's ranching past. For art, the Desert Caballeros Western Museum in Wickenburg exhibits work by such celebrated cowboy artists as Frederic Remington and Charles Russell, as well as period rooms with furnishings that reflect the style of the desert frontier. In Prescott, the Phippen Museum specializes in the art of the American West.

For the literary-minded, cowboy poetry festivals abound throughout the state. Prescott hosts a major cowboy poetry gathering at the Sharlot Hall Museum in summer. Many Western writers have set their books in Arizona, most notably Zane Grey (a former resident), author of

Call of the Canyon and other novels, and Louis L'Amour, whose *Hondo* takes place here.

> Retired Supreme Court Justice Sandra Day O'Connor, the first female appointed to the US Supreme Court, grew up on an isolated ranch in southeastern Arizona. She is an honorary member of the Cowgirl Hall of Fame in Fort Worth, Texas.

For cowboy duds you need only visit Stockman's Western Wear in Phoenix or Saba's, which offers jeans, shirts, hats, and cowboy

boots. For something ultra-luxurious, a pair of custom-made boots may be in order, although a real cowboy wouldn't be caught dead in them. Paul Bond's boot company in Nogales has been making boots for decades, ranging from the utilitarian to the flashy. Customers include dudes, ranchers, and movie stars (ask to see the company's attic, where wooden lasts are kept for the shop's celebrity clients). Stewart Boots in Tucson also offers a range of custom footwear.

The romance lives on at dude ranches, at poetry gatherings, on trail rides, and at every bar in which a cowboy yodels a plaintive lament. The real cowboy may be scarce in Arizona, but cowboy culture lives on.

LEFT: guests at the White Stallion Dude Ranch near Tucson try their hands at a cattle drive. **RIGHT:** a trail ride through the Sonoran Desert.

PLACES

A detailed guide to the entire state, with
principal sites clearly cross-referenced by
number to the maps

They came, they saw ... they went home. That sums up the experience of the first Europeans to see the Grand Canyon – a contingent of soldiers from Coronado's 1540 expedition seeking the fabled Seven Cities of Gold. The Colorado River, seemingly so small yet mighty enough to have carved the Canyon, proved a daunting obstacle. Unlike today's river runners, these conquistadors never even got their feet wet.

Today, the Grand Canyon is Arizona's top attraction, the destination for millions of tourists, who mostly congregate at the busy South Rim, leaving the remote North Rim blessedly free of crowds. The "Big Ditch" (as locals call it) lives up to its billing. You won't believe your eyes – nor should you – because the vision that sprawls before you is simply too vast to comprehend. It's a common problem in scenic Arizona, where stunning landscapes crop up around every bend.

The Grand Canyon is the main destination for visitors to Flagstaff, the mountainous home to Northern Arizona University, sweeping pine forests, prehistoric Indian pueblos, ranches, and outdoor activities in the San Francisco Peaks and the nearby White Mountains and Mogollon Rim country.

For a taste of Mexico – and the Sonoran Desert – head to southern Arizona's border country. Here you can kick back and sample superb local wine and food near Sonoita, enjoy internationally renowned birding in a secluded "sky island" mountain canyon, and visit dusty mining ghost towns and charming art towns like Bisbee and Patagonia. The kids can relive the gunfight at the OK Corral in Tombstone, while historians will want to visit one of Father Kino's graceful Spanish missions near historic Tubac.

The state's two largest cities – Tucson and Phoenix – home to the University of Arizona and Arizona State University, respectively, offer world-class delights. Arizonans are a diverse, opinionated bunch – a fiery salsa of Indian, Hispanic, and Anglo cultures – not afraid to make headlines. That only makes a visit here interesting. Come see for yourself.

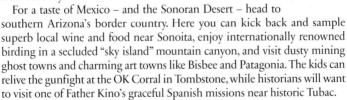

PRECEDING PAGES: the Grand Canyon; Monument Valley; a kitschy motel.
LEFT: red rocks soar above the Arizona desert. **ABOVE LEFT:** a young cowgirl at the Carrel White Stallion Dude Ranch. **ABOVE RIGHT:** Route 66 near Oatman.

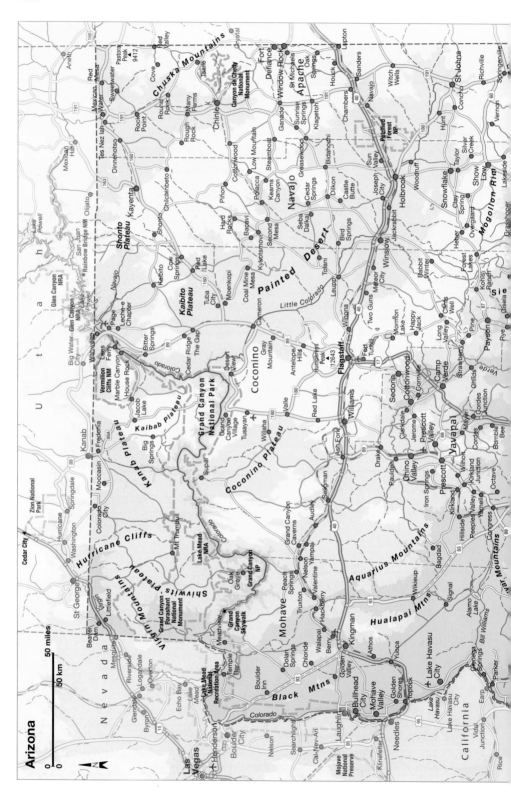

Arizona

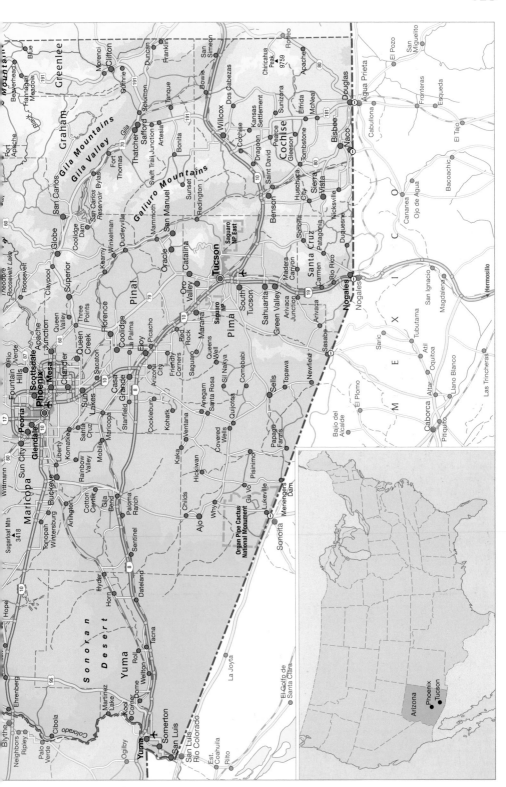

NORTHERN ARIZONA

Monumental landscapes, Indian cultures, and a
scrappy frontier spirit lure travelers to the
canyon country of the north

The Colorado Plateau – a spectacular monolithic hunk of continental crust that sprawls across 130,000 sq miles (337,000 sq km) dominates northern Arizona. Its sandstone whorls and sinuous canyons give the landscape an animate quality not found elsewhere in the state.

According to Navajo mythology, the land is indeed alive – *shimah*, mother – and the gargantuan stone formations that stand upon it are the petrified corpses of gods and monsters who preceded humans on Earth. To the Hopi, descendants of the Ancestral Pueblo people whose abandoned villages are scattered across the plateau, every aspect of the natural world is infused with spiritual life. They regard the Grand Canyon as a place of emergence – *sipapu* – where their ancestors entered the present world before migrating to their mesa-top homes to the east in the Painted Desert.

The Grand Canyon is, of course, the most popular destination in the state of Arizona. Just over 4 million tourists visit the park every year, though few venture far from the main overlooks, which is a pity. Below the rim, the canyon unfolds like an inverted mountain, passing through several ecosystems as you descend into ever more ancient rock, transected by side canyons that lead into hidden worlds of waterfalls, hanging gardens, and narrow corridors of sculpted rock. Only the intrepid backpacker or river runner ever see this intimate side of the Grand Canyon, or get a close-up view of the mighty river that carved it out from the surrounding rock.

Beyond the canyon are other wondrous places ripe for discovery. Pedal a mountain bike through the aspen groves of the San Francisco Peaks immediately north of Flagstaff. Paddle a kayak into the tortuous canyons that feed into Lake Powell. Hike around the base of Sunset Crater, a 1,000ft (305-meter) -high cinder cone in the country's largest volcanic field. Shop for silver and turquoise jewelry at an Indian trading post. Explore ancient stone pueblos built into alcoves beneath soaring cliffs. Ride horseback with a Navajo guide beneath the mineral-streaked walls of Canyon de Chelly. Or take a leisurely drive along the back roads of the Arizona Strip, the "high, wide, lonesome country" to be found north of the Grand Canyon.

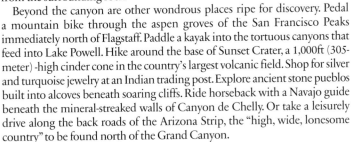

LEFT: the light penetrates Antelope canton in Navajo Monument National Park.
ABOVE LEFT: kayaking Watson Lake, near Prescott. **ABOVE RIGHT:** Sedona's red rocks.

GRAND CANYON NATIONAL PARK

Humbling, exalting, beautiful beyond words –
the canyon is undeniably one of the world's
great sights and grows only more fascinating
when you venture below the rim

The ancients spoke of the four basic elements of earth, water, wind, and fire. But at the **Grand Canyon ❶**, another element must be added – light. It is light that brings the canyon to life, bathing the buttes and highlighting the spires, infusing color and adding dimension, creating beauty that takes your breath away. Sunrise and sunset are the two biggest events of the day. In early morning and late afternoon, the oblique rays of sunlight, sometimes filtered through clouds, set red rock cliffs on fire and cast abysses into purple shadow.

The Grand Canyon in northern Arizona is rightfully one of the seven wonders of the world. Every year, visitors arrive at its edge and gaze down into this yawning gash in the earth. But the approach to the canyon gives no hint of what awaits. The highway passes a sweeping land of sagebrush and grass, through dwarf pinyon and juniper woodland, and into a forest of tall ponderosa pines. Then, suddenly, the earth falls away at your feet. Before you stretches an immensity that is almost incomprehensible.

The canyon is negative space – it's composed as much by what's not there as what is. After taking time to soak in the scene, one's eyes rove down to the bottom, where there appears to be a tiny stream. Though it looks small from this distance, 7,000ft (2,100 meters) above sea level, it is in fact the **Colorado River**, one of the great rivers of the West. And unbelievable though it may seem, the river is the chisel that has carved the Grand Canyon. The Colorado rushes through the canyon for 277 miles (446km), wild and undammed. Over several million years, it's been doing what rivers do – slowly but surely eroding the canyon to its present depth of one mile (1.6km).

Main attractions
CANYON VIEW INFORMATION PLAZA
HERMITS ROAD
BRIGHT ANGEL TRAIL
HERMIT TRAIL
SOUTH KAIBAB TRAIL
DESERT VIEW DRIVE
THE NORTH RIM
THE INNER CANYON
HAVASU CANYON
GRAND CANYON RAILWAY

LEFT: Desert View overlook.
RIGHT: Grandview Point on the South Rim.

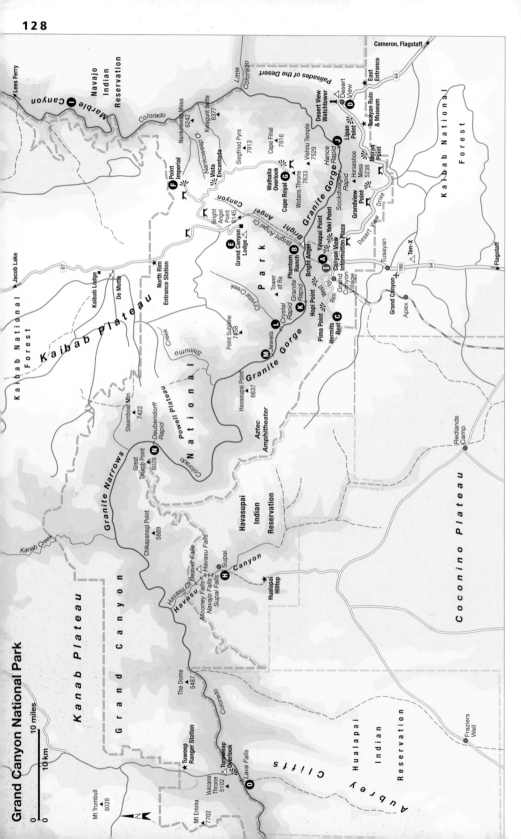

Grand Canyon National Park

Lees Ferry
Jacob Lake

Navajo Indian Reservation

Marble Canyon

Colorado

Cameron, Flagstaff

Palisades of the Desert

Little Colorado

Desert View Watchtower

Lipan Point

Tusayan Ruin & Museum

East Entrance

D Desert View

Nankoweap Mesa 6242

Kwagunt Butte 6377

Siegfried Pyre 7913

Cape Final 7916

Vishnu Temple 7529

Moran Point

Horseshoe Mesa 5238

Kaibab National Forest

Point Imperial

F

Vista Encantada

Nankoweap Cr.

Walhalla Overlook

Wotans Throne 7633

Cape Royal **G**

Hance Rapid

Grandview Point

Desert View Drive

Sockdolager Rapid

Granite Gorge Rapid

Bright Angel Point 8145

Bright Angel Canyon

Bright Angel Cr.

E Grand Canyon Lodge

North Rim Entrance Station

Kaibab Lodge

De Motte

Phantom Ranch **B**

Bright Angel

A Yaki Point

Yavapai Point

Canyon View Information Plaza

H Grand Canyon Village

Tusayan

Grand Canyon

Apex

Flagstaff

Ten-X

Kaibab National Forest

Jacob Lake

Kaibab Plateau

Tower of Ra

Crystal Creek

Crystal Rapid

Granite Rapid **K**

Hopi Point

Pima Point

Hermits Rest **C**

M Jewels

L

Point Sublime 7458

Havasupai Point 6637

Aztec Amphitheater

Granite Gorge

Coconino Plateau

Redlands Camp

Steamboat Mtn 7422

Deubendorff Rapid

N

Great Thumb Point 8028

Powell Plateau

Colorado

National

Granite Narrows

Chikapanagi Point 5889

Havasupai Indian Reservation

Kanab Creek

Kanab Plateau

Grand Canyon

The Dome 5487

Havasu Cr.

Beaver Falls

Mooney Falls

Navajo Falls

Supai Falls

Havasu Falls

H Supai

Hualapai Hilltop

Canyon

Coconino Plateau

Frazers Well

Colorado

Tuweep Ranger Station

Toroweap Overlook

O

Lava Falls

Vulcans Throne 5102

Mt Emma 7702

Mt Trumbull 8028

Aubrey Cliffs

Hualapai Indian Reservation

10 miles

10 km

N

An awful canyon

To the east, the scalloped skyline of the **Palisades of the Desert** defines the canyon rim. To the north, about 10 miles (16km) as the hawk flies, is the flat-lying forested **North Rim**. To the west, the canyon's cliffs and ledges, cusps, and curves extend as far as the eye can see, taking in the Havasupai Reservation and adjoining Hualapai Reservation, home to the famous Skywalk, with only distant indigo mountains breaking the horizon. **Grand Canyon National Park** (tel: 928-638-7888; www.nps.gov/grca; daily) is more than a million acres (400,000 hectares) of land, and this view encompasses only about a fourth of the entire canyon.

People's reactions to their first sight of the Grand Canyon can vary widely. Some are stunned, speechless. Some are brought to tears. Still others, such as early visitor Gertrude B. Stevens, have been overcome in other ways: "I fainted when I saw this awful looking cañon," she declared. "I never wanted a drink so bad in my life." Regardless of your reaction, you'll never forget your first sight.

With more than the average four-hour stay, a person can begin to explore this miraculous place, savoring different moods throughout the hours of the day, as the light constantly changes the face of the canyon.

The South Rim

Most visitors first see the Grand Canyon from the South Rim, which is open year-round and offers the bulk of lodging, food, and attractions. Start your visit just past the South Entrance at **Canyon View Plaza Ⓐ**, which has car and coach parking and free shuttle buses (open daily 8am–5pm; plaza exhibits open 24 hours). The spacious Grand Canyon Visitor Center has a large theater showing a film about the park, wall-size maps, and interpretive exhibits and books that set the canyon in a larger context and help orient visitors. Park rangers there can answer specific questions. From the plaza, it's a short stroll, or shuttle ride, out to the level Rim Trail and **Mather Point**, for that virgin glimpse of the canyon and a nice place to picnic.

TIP

Traffic at the South Entrance Gate often backs up during peak summer hours, but tends to be lighter at the East Entrance Gate.

BELOW: crowds of tourists watch the sunset from Mather Point.

Just east of the plaza is the bus terminal, where free shuttle buses run at frequent intervals all day along four routes: Grand Canyon Village (Blue Route), the Kaibab/Rim (Orange Route), Tusayan (Purple Route), and scenic Hermits Road (Red Route). By extending the public transportation system, and providing more park-and-ride opportunities, the Park Service aims to get people out of their cars, and get cars and development away from the rim, so as to restore that invigorating sense of discovery. Now, the ravens (and a good number of reintroduced condors, which congregate at Lookout Studio) are taking back their rightful place, soaring over the dizzying abyss and croaking their calls of greeting.

Hermit's Road

The historic buildings on the rim, most of them of native stone and timber, will stay, however. One is the **Yavapai Point Observation Station** (daily 8am–7pm), the next point west of Mather on the Rim Trail. One entire wall of this small museum and

bookstore is glass, affording a stupendous view into the heart of the canyon – slices of the Colorado River, a 1928 suspension bridge, and **Bright Angel Campground** and **Phantom Ranch** ❸ tucked at the very bottom.

From here, a paved path along the rim leads to Grand Canyon Village, where shuttle buses on the Red Route head out along 8-mile (13km) **Hermits Road** (also called **West Rim Drive**). Constructed in 1912 as a scenic drive, it offers several overlooks along the way. At **Trailview Point**, you can look back at the village and the steep **Bright Angel Trail**, just west of Bright Angel Lodge, one of two main trails switchbacking down to the river. **Indian Garden**, a hikers' campground shaded by cottonwoods, is visible 4.5 miles (7km) down the trail. The Bright Angel Fault has severed the otherwise continuous cliff layers that block travel in the rest of the canyon, providing a natural route for hikers into the canyon.

In the morning, mule trains plod into the canyon, bearing excited greenhorns who may wish they'd

BELOW: tourists take in views from the Visitor Center Plaza at Mather Point.

gone on foot when the day is done. The trail is also the route of a pipeline that pumps water from springs on the north side up to the South Rim. The benefit of that reliable water supply makes the Bright Angel Trail favored among canyon hikers, especially in the heat of summer. The other main trail into the canyon, the South Kaibab, has almost no shade.

Buttes and temples

Other recommended points along Hermits Road are **Hopi**, **Mohave**, and **Pima**. From each vista different isolated buttes and "temples" present themselves. There is the massive formation called the **Battleship**, best seen from **Maricopa Point**. There's **Isis** and **Osiris**, **Shiva** and **Brahma**. These overblown names were bestowed by Clarence Dutton, an erudite geologist with the early US Geological Survey and protégé of Major John Wesley Powell. Dutton's classical education inspired names with this Far East flavor. He wrote that all the canyon's attributes, "the nobility of its architecture, its colossal buttes, its wealth of ornamentation, the splendor of its colors, and its wonderful atmosphere … combine with infinite complexity to produce a whole which at first bewilders and at length overpowers."

At **Mohave Point** on a still day, you can hear the muffled roar of crashing waves in **Granite** and **Hermit Rapids** on the Colorado. With binoculars, it may be possible to spy boaters bobbing downriver in rubber rafts. The road ends at **Hermits Rest** ⊙, an historic building with a gift shop, concession stand, and restrooms. This is also where hikers head down the **Hermit Trail**, one of the more accessible backcountry trails beyond the two main corridors of Bright Angel and South Kaibab. It's about 8 miles (13km) down **Hermit Canyon** to a lovely streamside camp for overnight hikers.

The Santa Fe Railway built the camp as a destination for tourists who arrived on mules, while supplies were shuttled 3,000ft (900 meters) down a cable from the rim. In those days, according to author George Wharton James, the camp furnished accommodations "to meet the most fastidious demands."

Junior Rangers help to preserve National Parks; they learn about the Grand Canyon, have fun, and take knowledge back to their friends, families, and schoolmates back home.

On a clear day, visibility at the Grand Canyon can exceed 150 miles (240km).

The "hermit" was a Canadian prospector named Louis D. Boucher, who settled at an idyllic spot called Dripping Springs, off the Hermit Trail. Known for his flowing white beard and a white mule named Calamity Jane, Louis kept mostly to himself. He prospected a few mining claims, escorted tourists now and then, and by all accounts grew amazing fruits and vegetables down in the canyon.

Desert View Drive

Returning to the village, another road, **Desert View Drive**, follows the canyon rim for 25 miles (40km) to the east. Overlooks along the way display still more spectacular canyon scenery. From **Yaki Point**, the panorama includes the massive beveled surface of **Wotans Throne**, and beside it graceful, pointed **Vishnu Temple**. The other main hiking route, the 7-mile (11km) **South Kaibab Trail**, departs from near Yaki Point, snaking down the side of **O'Neill Butte** through a break in the Redwall Limestone, down to Bright Angel Campground and Phantom Ranch.

BELOW: hiking at beautiful Havasu Falls.

Tall tales

Farther east, **Grandview Point** looks down on **Horseshoe Mesa**, site of early copper mines. The **Grandview Trail** starts here, built by miners to reach the ore. But even a short walk will reveal that no matter how pure the ore, hauling it out was not a profitable enterprise.

Grandview was among the first destinations for early tourists to the canyon, who stayed at Pete Berry's Grandview Hotel. One of the regulars there was old John Hance. He arrived at the canyon in the 1880s and built a cabin near Grandview. For a time, John worked an asbestos mine on the north side of the river but quickly realized that working the pockets of "dude" visitors was more lucrative. "Captain" Hance regaled rapt listeners with tales of how he dug the Grand Canyon, how he snowshoed across to the North Rim on the clouds, and other fanciful yarns.

His stamp remains on the canyon – there is a Hance Creek and Hance Rapid, and the Old and New Hance

Trails, rugged routes that drop down into the canyon from Desert View Drive.

In addition to great views and good stories, the drive in this area also gives a look at stands of splendid old ponderosa pines. These cinnamon-barked giants grow back from the rim, here benefiting from slightly higher elevation and increased moisture. Their long silky needles glisten in the sunlight, and a picnic beneath their boughs is a delight. Grazing mule deer and boisterous Steller's jays may be your companions, along with busy rock squirrels looking for handouts. (Resist the temptation; feeding wildlife is strictly prohibited.) The trees growing on the very brink of the rim are Utah junipers and pinyon pines. Sculpted by the wind, they cling to the shallow, rocky soil, never attaining great heights though they can be very old. The warm, dry air rising up from the canyon explains their presence.

In certain good years, pinyon pines produce delicious, edible brown-shelled nuts. People gather them, but so do many small mammals and birds. One bird – the dusky-blue pinyon jay – shares an intimate relationship with the tree. The jays glean nuts from the sticky cones, eating some and caching others. Inevitably, some of the nuts are forgotten and grow into young pinyon pines.

The eastern tip

Just to the east of Grandview is the entrance to the **Tusayan Ruin and Museum** (daily 9am–5pm), which preserves the remains of masonry structures constructed some 800 years ago by Ancestral Puebloans. These early farmers were by no means the first humans to inhabit the canyon. Archaeologists have found a tantalizing stone point nearly 13,000 years old left by big-game hunters in the waning days of the Ice Age. For another several thousand years, hunter-gatherers made a living on canyon resources. About 4,000 years ago, they split willow twigs and wound them into small animal figures. They left the figures in caves in the canyon, where modern-day archaeologists have discovered them.

Lipan Point, farther east, provides one of the most expensive views of the

BELOW: sunrise illuminates the canyon rim.

A golden-mantled ground squirrel perches on the North Rim.

canyon and Colorado River from anywhere along the rim. The river makes a big S-turn, with **Unkar Rapid** visible below. A little farther downstream is Hance Rapid, punctuating the entry of the Colorado River into the Inner Gorge.

In autumn, hundreds of hawks – Cooper's, sharpshins, redtails, and others – migrate over Lipan Point on their way south. Nearby, in 1540, a detachment of Francisco Vásquez de Coronado's Spanish *entrada* expedition tried but failed to reach the river. They are believed to be the first Europeans to enter the canyon proper, though Native Americans had long preceded them.

The final destination on this drive is **Desert View** itself. Here the canyon opens out into the wide Marble Platform and east to the huge Navajo Reservation. The **Little Colorado** meets the main Colorado a few miles upstream. And an interesting circular tower stands out on the edge. Mary Jane Colter, architect for the Fred Harvey Company and Santa Fe Railway, designed it. (She also designed Bright Angel Lodge, Hopi House,

BELOW: the scale of the canyon is invigorating.

Lookout Studio, Hermits Rest, and Phantom Ranch.) Colter was heavily influenced by Ancestral Pueblo architecture, and **Desert View Watchtower** is modeled after structures she had seen in the Four Corners area. It was built in 1932 of native stone, and on the interior walls are murals painted by Hopi artist Fred Kabotie.

The North Rim

At times, especially during the summer, the concentration of people on the South Rim can get to feel a little crowded. The place to turn is the **North Rim**, the peaceful side of the Grand Canyon.

From the South Rim, it doesn't look very far, but the North Rim is 220 miles (346km) away by road. Leaving Desert View, join Highway 89 and head north across the **Navajo Nation** and part of the **Painted Desert**. Take Highway 89A, cross the bridge over the Colorado River at **Marble Canyon,** and allow time for the 5-mile (8km) detour to **Lees Ferry**, the put-in for Grand Canyon river trips and itself a vortex of Southwest history. This is

the only place for nearly 300 miles (480km) where you can get down to the river, sit on the shore, and marvel that this is the same insignificant-looking stream you saw from the rim.

Back on Highway 89A, drive west across the wide-open, lonesome stretch of **House Rock Valley**, where keen-eyed travelers may glimpse a giant California condor soaring over the **Vermilion Cliffs**. The road then climbs up the east flank of the **Kaibab Plateau**, re-entering pinyon-juniper forest and ponderosa pine. At **Jacob Lake**, Highway 67 winds 45 miles (72km) through the forest to the rim.

To the Kaibab Paiute Indians, who live on this side of the canyon, Kaibab means "mountain lying down." The North Rim's elevation does qualify as a mountain. It averages 8,000ft (2,400 meters), 1,000ft (300 meters) higher than the South Rim, making for a very different forest environment. Here grow dense stands of spiky dark spruce and fir, along with quaking aspen and big grass-filled "parks," or meadows, where coyotes spend their days "mousing." The limestone caprock also holds a few small sinkhole lakes. This forest supports a different variety of wildlife too – the handsome Kaibab squirrel, a tassel-eared tree squirrel of the ponderosa pines, is found only here; there's also blue grouse; a larger population of mule deer; and a consequently larger number of mountain lions, the main predators of the deer. The North Rim is buried in snow in winter, and the entrance road is closed from the end of October through mid-May.

Because of the short season and isolation, the North Rim has never been as fully developed as the South Rim. There is a campground, small cabins, a visitor center, cafeteria, and **Grand Canyon Lodge ❸**, which perches on the canyon's edge. One of the prime activities is to nab a rocking chair on the veranda of the lodge and engage in serious canyon watching.

The road to transcendence

From the lodge, a short trail goes to **Bright Angel Point**. Though you're still looking at the same canyon, the

Heading up the steep Kaibab Trail, 1910.

BELOW: Desert View Watchtower, built in 1902 by the Fred Harvey Company, rises from the edge of the canyon.

The Canyon in Winter

Winter weaves a magic spell over the Grand Canyon. In this season the rim is softened by a mantle of ermine snow, and the chilled air bristles with crystals. Pine needles are glazed with frost, and gossamer clouds snag the tops of pointed buttes. Sounds are muffled, and hectic summer days are a memory.

During the holidays, the fireplace in the lobby of El Tovar Hotel is surrounded with poinsettias. It's tempting to spend the day indoors by the fire, sipping hot chocolate. That's certainly an option, especially if the winds are buffeting the rim. But the outdoors beckons, and with proper clothing and footwear you can walk along the rim path and find yourself nearly alone with the canyon.

Juncos, nuthatches and finches flit in the tree branches. Ravens two-step out on improbable promontories, oblivious to the gaping abyss below. Tracks in the snow hint at dramatic encounters between hawk and rabbit.

Diligence is needed near the rim, though, for snow can hide a slippery drop off and trails may be icy. A ski pole or boots with instep crampons can be helpful. Beware of hypothermia, too. It can strike suddenly in wet, cold, windy weather when you're tired from exertion. Dress in layers, keep a supply of dry clothes, and drink plenty of water.

Day use rest area under shady trees at Cottonwood Campground on the North Kaibab Trail.

north side's greater depth and intricacy are immediately apparent. This is due partly to the Grand Canyon's asymmetry: the Colorado River did not cut directly through the middle of the Kaibab Plateau but slightly off-center to the south. Also because of its greater height and southward tilt, more water flows *into* the canyon here than *away* from it as on the South Rim. Thus the northern side canyons are longer and more highly eroded. The **North Kaibab Trail** along **Bright Angel Creek**, for example, is 14 miles (23km) long, twice the distance of the corresponding trail on the south side.

While many people take the North Kaibab, the only maintained trail into the canyon, all the way down to the river for overnight stays, this trail also lends itself to wonderful day hikes. Even a short hike to Coconino Overlook (1.5 miles/2.4km round-trip) or Supai Tunnel (4 miles/6.5km round-trip) reveals the canyon's natural beauty and size. Ambitious day hikers may want to continue to Roaring Springs (9.5 miles/15km round-trip). The hike there and back is extremely

BELOW: the view from the North Rim.

strenuous and takes 7–8 hours (be sure to start by 7am). Roaring Springs lies 3,050ft (930 metres) below the canyon rim. Do not attempt to hike all the way to the river in one day. Other shorter walks on the rim include the **Transept**, **Widforss**, and **Ken Patrick Trails**, which combine forest and canyon scenery.

A drive out to **Point Imperial ➊** and **Cape Royal ➋**, on the only other paved road, is well worth the time. At 8,800ft (2,700 meters), Point Imperial is the highest prominence on either rim of the canyon. Its eastward-facing view showcases **Mount Hayden**, **Kwagunt Butte**, and **Nankoweap Mesa** in the Marble Canyon portion of Grand Canyon.

From there, the road goes out to Cape Royal, where it ends. Clarence Dutton also named this promontory; his description of sunset there strains even his exuberant prose: "What was grand before has become majestic, the majestic becomes sublime, and ever expanding and developing, the sublime passes beyond the reach of our faculties and becomes transcendent."

Go vertical

With the first step down into the Grand Canyon, the horizontal world of the rims turns decidedly vertical. A walk down a trail, even for a short distance, is the only way to begin to appreciate the canyon's great antiquity and sheer magnitude.

A word to the wise, though. Adequate preparation for this back-country experience is essential. A Grand Canyon trek is the reverse of hiking in mountains: the descent comes first, followed by the ascent, when muscles are tired and blisters are starting to burn. And no matter what trail you follow, the climb out is always a long haul against gravity – putting one foot in front of the other and setting mind against matter. Never try to hike to the river and back in one day. For first-time hikers, the maintained corridor trails are recommended: the Bright Angel, or the South or North Kaibab. Also note that all overnight hikes require permits, available from the **Backcountry Information Center** (tel: 928-638-7875; www.nps.gov/ grca) in Grand Canyon Village; day hikes do not.

There are two other critical considerations – heat and water. As you descend into the canyon, you pass from a high-elevation, forested environment into desert. Temperatures in the inner canyon are routinely 20 degrees warmer than the rim – from June to September that means upwards of 110–120°F (43–49°C) down below. That kind of unrelenting, energy-sapping heat, coupled with a shortage of water, can spell disaster for the unprepared. In summer, each person should carry – and drink – a minimum of a gallon (4 liters) of water apiece. Along with water, a hiker should eat plenty of nutritious, high-energy foods to avoid hyponatremia (low sodium levels caused by overconsumption of water and not enough food) and take frequent rest stops. A hat, sunscreen, and sunglasses are necessary items. To avoid the extreme heat, hike in early morning and early evening. Or avoid summer altogether and go in spring or fall, which are the best times for an extended canyon hike.

TIP

Want to learn more? The Grand Canyon Field Institute (tel: 928-638-2485) offers 1- to 10-day trips covering a wide range of topics, including geology, ecology, photography, and cultural history.

BELOW: the view from the patio of Grand Canyon Lodge on the North Rim of Grand Canyon National Park.

The Inner Canyon

Dropping below the rims into the canyon's profound silence, you enter the world of geologic time. Recorded in the colorful rock layers is a succession of oceans, deserts, rivers, and mountains, along with hordes of ancient life forms that have come and gone. The caprock of the rims, the Kaibab Limestone, is 250 million years old. It is the youngest layer of rock in the Grand Canyon; every layer beneath it is progressively older, down to the deepest, darkest inner sanctum of black schist that rings in at close to 2 billion years.

As you put your nose up against the outcrop, you'll notice that this creamy-white limestone is chockablock with sponges, shells, and other marine fossils that reveal its origin in a warm, shallow sea. The next obvious thick layer is the Coconino Sandstone. Its sweeping crossbeds document the direction of the wind across what were once dunes as extensive as those in today's Sahara Desert. It isn't hard to imagine, because already, even in this first mile of the trail, the canyon begins to look and smell like the desert – dusty and sun-drenched. Beneath the Coconino is the Hermit Shale, soft, red mudstone that formed in a lagoon environment. Underlying the Hermit is the massive Supai Formation, 600ft (180 meters) thick in places, the compressed remains of mucky swamp bottom 300 million years past. The Redwall Limestone is always a milestone on a Grand Canyon hike, passable only where a break has eroded in the 500ft (150-meter) -high cliffs. Beneath the Redwall are the Muav Limestone, Bright Angel Shale, and Tapeats Sandstone – a suite of strata that indicate the presence of, respectively, yet another ocean, its nearshore, and its beach. Throughout most of the canyon, the tan Tapeats reclines atop the shining iron-black Vishnu Schist, the basement of the Grand Canyon and arguably its most provocative rock.

At the bottom, embraced in the walls of schist, are the tumbling, swirling waters of the Colorado River, the maker of this, its greatest canyon. The river, aided by slurries of rock and water sluicing down tributary canyons, has taken only a few million years to gnaw down into the plateau to expose almost 2 billion years of earth history.

Soak hot feet in the cool water. Listen to boulders grinding into gravel on their way to the sea. Consider these old rocks in this young canyon. Ponder our ephemeral existence in the face of deep time.

Havasu Canyon

Havasu , a side canyon in the western Grand Canyon, has been called a "gorge within a gorge." Within it flow the waters of **Havasu Creek**, lined with emerald cottonwood trees and grapevines and punctuated by travertine falls and deep turquoise pools, paradise in the midst of the sere desert of the Grand Canyon. A visit is an unforgettable experience, a gentle introduction to the Grand Canyon

BELOW: the Colorado River flows between the sheer limestone walls of the Inner Canyon.

and to the Havasupai Indians, the "people of the blue-green water," who have made their home here for at least seven centuries.

Getting there is no easy matter. The journey requires a 62-mile (100km) drive north of Route 66 (about 190 miles/300km from the South Rim) to a remote trailhead, then an 8-mile (13km) hike or horseback ride to the small village of **Supai** on the canyon bottom. In past times, the Havasupai partook of what the land offered. Evidence is seen along the trail in large rock piles, the pits used year after year for roasting the sweet stalks of agave. In their rocky homeland are distinctive natural features that hold great significance for the Havasupai. Rising high above the village is a pair of sandstone pillars known as Wigleeva. To the Havasupai, these are their guardian spirits; as long as they are standing, the people are safe.

Note that Supai is subject to severe flashflooding. In 2008, a major flashflood, compounded by the collapse of a dam, caused widespread damage and required the evacuation of residents and tourists by helicopter. The canyon reopened to visitors in 2011, but facilities are currently limited to a trading post, post office, school, tourist lodge, and tribal museum. Mail and supplies arrive by mule or horse, helicopter, and internet. For more information on visiting, contact the **Havasupai Tourist Office** (tel: 928-448-2121/2141/2180).

Waterfalls

About 1.5 miles (2.5km) beyond the village is the first of the famous waterfalls – **Navajo Falls**. A short distance beyond is 100ft (30-meter) -high **Havasu Falls** and the campground. The trail continues on to **Mooney Falls**, known as the Mother of the Waters to the Havasupai. To go farther down canyon requires a steep descent next to the falls on a water-slickened cliff face, with the aid of a chain railing. It's another 3 miles (5km) to **Beaver Falls**, a popular day hike for boaters coming up from the river to frolic in the beautiful pools. Those who make the journey know why Havasu is often called the Shangri-la of the Grand Canyon.

The lookout plaza at Desert View.

BELOW: hikers on the South Kaibab Trail.

Return of the Railroad

Locomotives began beating a path to the Grand Canyon early in the 20th century. It was the end of the trail for the old stagecoach

I n 1883, cowman William Wallace Bass was out chasing doggies south of the Grand Canyon, when he found himself on the brink of the chasm "scared to death." Two years later, he set up cabins on the rim at Havasupai Point, where tourists came to see the great sight. From the small town of Williams, they boarded stagecoaches and bounced along the 72 miles (116km) to the camp, where Bass escorted them into his "dear old Canyon home."

His competition in those days was Pete Berry's Grandview Hotel out at Grandview Point. There, tourists arrived after an 11-hour trip from Flagstaff aboard the Grand Canyon Stage and stayed at Berry's hotel or at John Hance's cabins nearby.

But things changed. On September 18, 1901, the Grand Canyon Railway's Locomotive 282 pulled up to the budding Grand Canyon Village on the South Rim. Passengers found the three-hour train ride from Williams far preferable to the dusty daylong stage trips. The arrival of the railway spelled the end of Bass's and Berry's tourist

headquarters. With construction of the Bright Angel Lodge and Fred Harvey's five-star El Tovar Hotel, Grand Canyon Village became (and has remained) the center for visitors to the South Rim. El Tovar's patrons were treated to fresh meals, prepared and served by Harvey girls dressed in white starched aprons. Accommodations were luxurious, and rocking chairs on the spacious porch permitted a classic canyon view with little exertion.

Despite the Harvey Company's dominance on the rim, other entrepreneurs came on the scene. Ralph and Niles Cameron staked mining claims and ran the Bright Angel Trail as a toll route for a time. In 1904, brothers Emory and Ellsworth Kolb built their photographic studio at the trailhead. They took pictures of people departing on mule trips in the morning, ran 4 miles (6km) down to a water source at Indian Garden to develop the film, and were ready with prints when the tourists returned. In 1911, the Kolb brothers made a film of their wild trip down the Colorado River, which visitors watched in their studio for 65 years.

Again things changed as Americans embraced the automobile, ending the era of rail service to the Grand Canyon in 1968. But another entrepreneur stepped in, restored the tracks, cars and locomotives, and relaunched the Grand Canyon Railway in 1989. Once again, locomotives chug out of the Williams station each morning, making the 135-minute, 65-mile (105km) run to the canyon. Passengers have a choice of restored coaches or the more opulent club or parlor cars. The three-hour canyon layover allows plenty of time for lunch, a bus tour, or a stroll along the rim.

Spending a night in the canyon is also an option. It's a relaxing ride back, complete with crooning cowboy troubadours and mean hombres who stage a hilarious mock holdup.

Contact the Grand Canyon Railway at 800-843-8724 or www.grandcanyonrailway.com.

ABOVE: actors dressed in Western wear perform for the crowds waiting for the Grand Canyon Railroad.
LEFT: the first run of the Grand Canyon Railway.

RESTAURANTS

Prices for a three-course dinner per person, excluding tax, tip, and beverages:
$ = under $20
$$ = $20–45
$$$ = $45–60
$$$$ = over $60

Arizona Room
Bright Angel Lodge
Tel: 928-638-2631
$–$$
A logical second choice if El Tovar is full, this steakhouse has wonderful sunset views of the canyon. Steaks, barbecue, and wild salmon are popular. Fast for lunch (seasonal only) but very slow at dinner, as there are no reservations.

Bright Angel Coffee
Bright Angel Lodge
Tel: 928-638-2631
$
Located inside the lounge of the lodge, this is a good place for morning java and pastries.

Bright Angel Restaurant
Bright Angel Lodge
Tel: 928-638-2631
$
A coffee shop serving diner-style food that should fuel you up for a day of hiking. Lots of kids' choices, including breakfast eggs, burgers, steaks, patty melts, spaghetti, and chili.

Canyon Star Restaurant and Saloon
The Grand Hotel, Tusayan
Tel: 928-638-3333
$–$$
The cavernous cowboy-themed dining room in this rustic newbuild hotel offers twice-nightly dinner shows with Indian dancing. The waitstaff is indifferent, but a few dishes show surprising flair. The seared elk tenderloin with berry reduction puts you in the mood for the Native American entertainment. There's a buffet breakfast and lunch, and a bar with cowboy saddle seats.

Coronado Room
Best Western Grand Canyon Squire Inn, Tusayan
Tel: 928-638-2681
$$
This is an excellent alternative if all the South Rim restaurants have long lines. American and Continental fare is done well and includes filet mignon, salmon, bison, and spare ribs.

Delicatessen at the Marketplace
Market Plaza
$
This deli in the South Rim's main grocery store serves surprisingly decent food and is a good choice for a quick bite. Try meat chilli served in a sourdough bread bowl, roasted chicken and turkey sandwiches, salads, fruit, yogurt, and other healthy choices. The coffee here is superior.

El Tovar Restaurant
El Tovar Lodge
Tel: 928-638-2631
$$–$$$
The views are spectacular at the tables near the windows in this rustic dining room, which has dark-paneled walls and Indian murals, crisp white linen, silver on the tables, and an attentive staff. The cuisine is Continental with Southwest flourishes and leans heavily toward steak, seafood, and pasta. It's by far the best on the South Rim, but you shouldn't expect miracles: it's nearly impossible to produce gourmet fare in such a busy dining room. Make dinner reservations weeks ahead, or plan on eating very late. Ask for a table near the huge picture window at sunset. If you can't get a reservation for dinner here, at least have a drink in the bar at sunset; it's worth it.

Grand Canyon Lodge Dining Room
Grand Canyon Lodge
Bright Angel Point
Tel: 928-638-2611
$$
The only full-fledged restaurant on the North Rim is set in a grand window-wrapped room on the edge of the canyon. The menu is dominated by American and Continental dishes – prime rib, rosemary chicken, pasta with pesto sauce and asparagus. The food is mediocre, and the service is inconsistent, but the setting – the reason people come – is magnificent. If possible, make dinner reservations weeks in advance.

Grand Canyon Quality Inn & Suites
Tusayan
Tel: 928-638-2673
$$
This light, bright, modern dining room in the Quality Inn at the far end of Tusayan is a popular choice with locals, who enjoy the large buffet at breakfast, lunch, and dinner. There is also an à la carte menu. Entrees are the typical steak and seafood at lunch and dinner with some interesting additions, such as wienerschnitzel and Navajo tacos. Vegetarians will find plenty of salads and fruit.

Happy Trails
Tusayan
Tel: 928-638-0400
$
This coffee shop offers specialty coffee, gifts, and internet access in Tusayan.

Maswik and Yavapai cafeterias
Maswik and Yavapai Lodges
Tel: 928-638-2632
$
You'll find no frills here, just cheap, fast, filling food. If you're famished after a day of hiking and the Delicatessen at Marketplace is closed, this is a good choice.

Pine Country Restaurant
107 N. Grand Canyon Boulevard, Williams
Tel: 928-635-9718
$
This homestyle restaurant offers inexpensive family fare and is a good choice if you're in Williams to take the Grand Canyon Railway. The pie's the thing. Selections include double chocolate, coconut, chocolate peanut butter, and cherry, among others.

COLORADO RIVER RAFTING

The West's mightiest waterway transports boaters on a breathtaking journey through the heart of the Grand Canyon

O n a hot July day, a flotilla of rubber rafts floats down a serene stretch of the **Colorado River** in the **Grand Canyon**. A high-pitched buzz echoes off the sun-drenched cliffs. It's a peregrine falcon sounding an intruder alarm as it swoops down to the water, then soars up into the blue sky.

For boaters, the sight of this majestic raptor is an awesome spectacle, and one of many reasons a journey through the canyon is a singular adventure. Here boaters enter the heart of the Southwest's remaining wilderness and one of the planet's deepest gorges. They encounter wild creatures, pass in wonder through stunning desert canyons, and ride some of the biggest whitewater in the West.

The Rio Colorado courses wild and free through the 1,218,375 acres (493,076 hectares) of **Grand Canyon National Park** (see page 127) in northern Arizona. From the launch point at **Lees Ferry**, the only way out in the next 277 miles (446km) is by foot on long, steep trails up to the canyon's rims.

Summer is prime season for running the "Grand," and while private individuals with the proper gear and experience may make private trips, a Park Service permit can take years to obtain. That's why most of the 22,000 people who boat the canyon each year

go as paying passengers with one of the river concessionaires licensed by the Park Service. On these trips, experienced guides row the boats, and the company furnishes all the food and gear. The guides know the river, the best places to hike and camp, and the canyon's stories. It's a tough job – part navigator, part tour guide, part entertainment director. They're up before dawn to make the coffee, they rig and row the boats, they lead hikes and side trips, and they strum their guitars under the stars.

Main attractions
MARBLE CANYON
PHANTOM RANCH
HANCE RAPID
GRANITE RAPID
CRYSTAL RAPID
REDWALL CAVERN
THE JEWELS
LAVA FALLS

LEFT AND RIGHT: kayaks and rafts on the Colorado River pass through the inner canyon.

Rafters frequently punch through rapids with a splash.

Rules and risks

Even with seasoned guides, passengers need to know a few rules and risks. The rules: wear shoes on shore, don't use soap in the water, drink plenty of fluids, never litter, and most important, wear life jackets at all times on the river. Helping in camp and kitchen is welcome but certainly not mandatory.

The chief risks: boats can flip, and sometimes they do. Should this happen, the best advice is to keep your feet up and point them downstream. The reason is twofold: first, to ward off rocks with your feet rather than your head and, second, to prevent your feet from getting trapped on the bottom, which can cause you to be dragged under by the current. Get back into the boat if possible; if not, swim to shore and wait for your party to pick you up. The water temperature hovers around 50°F (10°C), and even a short dip can be a numbing experience.

BELOW: life vests should always be worn on the water.

The Grand Canyon is a remote and wild place; emergency help is more than a phone call or a short drive away.

But if you're armed with proper information and take sensible precautions, the journey can be safe and pleasurable for everyone.

Canyon time

Canyon trips start at Lees Ferry, a desert outpost where a road goes down to the river's edge. It's a busy place on summer days, with several parties rigging at the same time. Tanned, muscled guides lash bags, coolers and metal ammo cans onto boat frames and laugh and joke with their pals. Then, a big bus or van pulls up, disgorging passengers, many of whom have never met before but who will be sharing perhaps the most intense two weeks of their lives together. It's hard to imagine, standing by the gentle, gurgling water, just what the Colorado has in store for them.

With everything neatly stowed and ready, the passengers buckle on life jackets and climb aboard. The boats push off from shore and bounce through the Paria riffle. Everyone stares up at **Navajo Bridge**, 300ft (90 meters) overhead, the last bit of

Quick River Trips

If you're short on time, consider a half-day or one-day river trip instead of a longer week or 10-day trip. **Hualapai River Runners** (tel: 888-868-9378; http://grandcanyonwest.com/rafting.php), a concession of the Hualapai Tribe, offers all-day trips in the western end of the canyon on the Hualapai Reservation. Trips begin at Diamond Creek, north of Peach Springs, a drive of about 160 miles (258km), or 4–5 hours, from the South Rim.

Half-day and all-day smooth-water trips on the Colorado River from Glen Canyon Dam to Lees Ferry are provided by **Colorado River Discovery** (tel: 888-522-6644; www.raftthecanyon.com). Trips begin at Page, Arizona, a drive of 140 miles (225km) from the South Rim.

civilization they'll see for many, many miles.

Around lunchtime, **Badger Rapid** bellows its presence. Boats slide easily down the shining tongue at the top, and passengers squeal with shock and delight at their baptism in the river's chilly water. The trip continues down through **Marble Canyon ❶**, past canyon walls rising ever higher.

The river routine sets in – eat breakfast, pack boats, travel downriver for a few miles, walk up to an ancient Pueblo granary or stop to view a historic inscription on a boulder, lunch under a shady tamarisk, boat a few more miles, then pull up onto a sandy beach for the night. Change into dry clothes, enjoy social hour and dinner, then hit the sleeping bag under a starry sky.

By the third or fourth day of a trip, the sense of being in and of the earth is palpable. Skin toughens in the sun and dry air, people start to talk more about what they're observing rather than what the stock market is doing back home. Wristwatches and worries are shed as canyon time takes over.

Past the scalloped cliffs of the **Desert Palisades**, the stone tower at **Desert View** punctuates the rim skyline. Soon, the aquamarine waters of the **Little Colorado River** interweave with the main Colorado. Guides often pause here to let their passengers enjoy a swim in the Little Colorado's relatively warm, turquoise waters, slather themselves with mineral-rich mud, or hike to the remains of a hermit's cabin.

A little farther on, at Mile 77, the canyon walls change from colorful sandstones and limestones to the ominous dark black schist of the **Inner Gorge**. Here is **Hance Rapid ❶**, the first big drop on the river. Its predecessors were only teasers. Hance is a long jumble of rocks and waves, featuring a nasty hole midway through called the **Mixmaster**. At low water it earns a rating of 10.

As the canyon closes in, boaters gear up for another series of rambunctious rapids including **Sockdolager**, translated as "the knock-out punch." A taste of rustic civilization rears its head briefly at **Phantom Ranch**, where

BELOW: the larger boats can carry a number of people, as well as supplies for a multiple day trip.

people can sip an ice-cold lemonade, watch backpackers toiling into camp, and send home a postcard that will be carried out of the canyon on the back of a mule.

This is the point at which an interchange of passengers may occur. Some hike out of the canyon, while others join the trip. They have no idea what's in store for them below Phantom Ranch, because rapids that heretofore inspired awe and fear will soon pale in comparison to those ahead.

Whitewater quartet

At lunch, the usually garrulous guides get a little serious. Furrowed brows, furtive conversations, gear tied down a little tighter. Then it's **Horn Creek**, a short, sweet jolt. At lower water levels, when the vicious rocks, or "horns," are showing, this rapid requires a precise entry and one or two strategic oar strokes.

A few miles downstream, the roar of **Granite Rapid** Ⓚ drowns out jokes and laughter. Formed by boulders washed in from **Monument Creek**, Granite is a chaotic flume of monstrous waves issuing off the right wall, along with a few crushers coming in from the left, not to mention dreaded **King Edward**, a major eddy at the bottom. A left entry into Granite is desirable, but the river often has other ideas, as all the current piles into the right. Granite's been known to flip a few boats, so everybody's happy to be right side up at the bottom and beyond the clutches of King Edward.

Hermit Rapid awaits – a series of five beautiful, standing waves – approached head on, right down the middle. The fifth wave, the granddaddy of them all, can grab a raft and hold it in a watery grip for a few seconds – though it feels like an eternity – as it decides whether to permit passage or to capsize the prisoner.

With adrenaline nearly exhausted, some guides elect to stop for the night on a pleasant little beach before attempting the last of the quartet – infamous **Crystal Rapid** Ⓛ. Crystal – the name is pronounced with reverential dread – deserves its 10-plus rating and is generally regarded as one

BELOW: guides can control the direction of the boat to a large extent, but you should still be prepared to get wet.

of the most dangerous rapids on the Colorado. Before 1966, Crystal was a mere riffle. But during a storm that winter, a flash flood deposited a mass of boulders in the riverbed, transforming Crystal into one of the two toughest runs on the river.

A far-right entry in this rapid is almost mandatory. A faulty start can send a boat into the frightening maw at center-left, which may result in a trip through the strainer known as the **Rock Garden** down below.

Heart of the earth

Once all the excitement is over, passengers can enjoy the beauty of the Inner Gorge, surrounded by walls of fluted, blue-black Vishnu schist gleaming like forged iron. The Vishnu, nearly 2 billion years old, is the oldest rock in the canyon. All the rock on top, and all the rock since leaving Lees Ferry, is younger. The Grand Canyon lays out in textbook fashion a neat chronology of the Earth's history, one of the most complete records anywhere, from 2 billion through about 250 million years ago, with only a few gaps.

The rock is old, but the canyon is young. It took the Colorado River less than 6 million years, and maybe as few as 1–2 million, to carve the mile-deep Grand Canyon. It wasn't merely flowing water that did the work, however. The Colorado once carried millions of tons of sediments in its waters. That heavy load of sand, gravel, and boulders acted like a giant rasp, grinding against the streambed, abrading the rock, and carrying it bit by bit to the delta at the Gulf of California. The river is still trying to cut deeper, but the old, hard, crystalline schist is resisting mightily.

Altered environment

Another major impediment has slowed the work of the river. **Glen Canyon Dam**, 15 miles (24km) above Lees Ferry, was completed in 1963. This 710ft (216-meter) -high, 10-million-ton concrete plug now holds back the waters of the Colorado in **Lake Powell**. The hydroelectric power generated at the dam electrifies cities all over the West. The water that goes through the turbines

BELOW: passengers on an oar-powered boat work together to get down the river.

Choosing a Boat

Many companies run both oar-powered and motorized boats. Oar boats are smaller, holding only four or five people, and trips usually last two weeks (though shorter or partial trips are an option). Motor trips typically last a week or less, and each boat carries many more passengers. Purists eschew the motors because they disturb the canyon's sublime silence. Others who go by motorized boat swear their journey could not have been more profound.

Yet another option is a dory – an elegant, wooden, oar-powered boat that is reminiscent of (though much more river-worthy than) the vessels used by such early explorers as Major John Wesley Powell, who first ran the Colorado River in 1869.

As one riverman put it, you could go down the Colorado in a bathtub and still have a peak experience.

No matter what kind of boat or outfit you choose, you're guaranteed a white-knuckle ride unlike any river you may have paddled elsewhere in the West. Though most of the Colorado's rapids aren't technical in the sense that they require a rapid-fire succession of precise maneuvers, the sheer size of the waves means the river packs a mighty wallop and should never be underestimated.

"The Colorado is the soul of the desert… Brave boatmen come, they go, they die, the river flows on forever."
– Edward Abbey

is pulled out of the lake about 200ft (60 meters) below the surface. For boaters downstream, that means cold, clear, green water. In the old days, the Rio Colorado was choked thick with mud and silt, but no more. Electricity demand now determines water levels on the Colorado and daily fluctuations can be dramatic. In some cases boats are left high and dry on beaches when the water level drops precipitously overnight.

Glen Canyon Dam has also been the single most important influence on the river ecosystem in modern times. Native fish and plants, like humpback chubs and willow trees, have given way to introduced trout and tamarisk. Altered though it may be, the river corridor still harbors a wealth of wildlife – bighorn sheep perched on impossibly sheer cliffs, coyotes coming down to the river to drink, great blue herons standing stock-still on a mudflat, Bell's vireos calling from the thickets, bats fluttering overhead at dusk, collared lizards scampering from boulder to boulder in search of shade, and

canyon wrens warbling their distinctive liquid trill.

While the river remains the focus, each day brings new places and new discoveries. Boaters frequently stop and walk up side canyons, paradises in the desert with year-round flowing streams, pools reflecting canyon colors, waterfalls where hummingbirds hide, and freshwater springs lush with maidenhair ferns and crimson monkeyflowers. The names of these places are legendary among river rats. **Redwall Cavern**, where a sandy beach is sheltered by an enormous rock alcove, frames glorious views of the canyon; spring water pours hundreds of feet down the mineral-stained walls of **Vasey's Paradise; Nankoweap** is known for ancient Pueblo granaries tucked into the canyon 600ft (180 meters) above the river; **Shinumo Creek** is favored for its inviting swimming hole and the ruins of an old mining camp; **Elves Chasm** and **Matkatamiba Canyon** have trickling streams, beautifully eroded rock formations, and lush hanging gardens of water-loving plants.

BELOW: Redwall Cavern, created by river erosion in a layer of limestone, is a favorite place to stop and rest.

Lava and beyond

Moving ever downstream, boaters soon come to a stretch of the river below Crystal Rapid known as the **Jewels** : Agate, Sapphire, Turquoise, Ruby, Serpentine, Garnet. Boats swirl peacefully past the colonnade of **Conquistador Aisle**, down to Mile 130 and **Bedrock Rapid**, and below it to **Deubendorff**, a long rapid to be run before camping for the night. **Tapeats** and **Deer Creeks** are fine places to linger before facing **Upset Rapid** with its sharp surprises.

On to Mile 157 and **Havasu Canyon**, "place of the blue-green waters," home of the Havasupai Indians, where river trips often spend the better part of a day exploring the canyon's travertine ledges and splashing in the plunge pool at the base of **Beaver Falls**.

Farther on, the rocks assume a new form. Black volcanic rocks fill side canyons and form etched pillars. **Vulcan's Anvil**, a remnant of basalt standing in the middle of the river, is an ominous marker of what lies just ahead. **Lava Falls** is yet another Grand Canyon legend, the one the guides have been talking about ever since the trip began. It's a frightful maelstrom of foaming, seething turbulence stretching the width of the river, and it's rated a 10 at all water levels.

After a scouting session that seems to last forever, everyone walks back down the hot, dusty trail to the boats, hushed and sobered. Life jackets are buckled tight, the guides check every loose line, cameras and binoculars are securely stowed. This one's for real, and everyone seems to know it.

Untied, the boats swing into the current. The guide stands up for a better view, searches for the proverbial "bubble line" that marks the entry. "Hang on," he says, and the passengers clutch whatever handhold they can find. The boat slips down the tongue. Slam. A wave hits the bow like a two-ton truck. Then the boat drops down into a trough of air and climbs up the front of another wave. In a brief second, people stare over into the gargantuan hole formed by Lava's famous V-wave. The boat just kisses it, and the guide shouts, "Get ready!" Another slam of water engulfs boat and passengers. Seconds later, the boatman whoops and orders: "Bail! Bail!" The passengers oblige, tossing bucket after bucket of water back into the Colorado.

Camp below Lava is always a big celebration; but this is only Mile 179.6; there are still another 50 miles (80km) to go. The terrain changes once again as the canyon widens and the river drops into an even more austere desert landscape. Finally, **Diamond Peak** spears the horizon. The trucks wait at the **Diamond Creek** take-out. Boats are unpacked one last time, the fine canyon sand sloshed away. It will be a while, though, before all the sand and all the memories are washed clean. Dreams of diving falcons and the sweet songs of canyon wrens will fill many nights to come, while memories of the canyon and river will last forever.

A number of animals call the Grand Canyon home, including mule deer, mountain lion, elk, bald eagle, bighorn sheep, and the black widow spider.

BELOW: the rigid frame and long oars of an oar raft give pilots powers and maneuverability.

FLAGSTAFF AND ENVIRONS

Ancient Indian ruins, a historic observatory, and one of the state's most beautiful mountain ranges are just a few of the attractions in and around this former frontier outpost

O n the road up **Mars Hill**, there's a pull-off where you can look out over **Flagstaff ❷**. The railroad tracks weave a steel ribbon through the middle of town. Famed **Route 66** parallels the tracks, and sturdy brick and stone buildings line the road. From this vantage point, Flagstaff looks for all the world like a toy railroad town, just like those miniature cardboard villages that came with your model train set.

And so it should, for the railroad made Flagstaff and has been its beating heart for more than a century. Freight trains rumble through like clockwork all day long, their whistles echoing through town, and Amtrak's passenger train, the **Southwest Chief**, stops twice a day, eastbound in the morning, westbound at night.

In the 1850s, government surveyors plotted a railroad route along the 35th Parallel. By the early 1880s, loggers rolled their big wheels into the ponderosa pine forests of northern Arizona, felled the tall trees, then sawed and stockpiled nearly a half million ties for the rails, as they blazed west. A spring at the base of Mars Hill furnished precious water for advance crews, and in 1882 the Santa Fe Railway arrived there at the first depot, a boxcar. The steep uphill grade soon mandated a move back to flatter

terrain a half mile east, from Old Town to what soon became known as New Town. Across the street, a thirsty man could find not only a cup of water but stronger brew as well in this wild and woolly newborn burg.

Crossroad town

A few Anglo-Americans had preceded the railroad. The Boston Party, a group of colonists who undertook an arduous westward journey in response to claims of good, cheap farmland, celebrated the nation's centennial in 1876

Main attractions

LOWELL OBSERVATORY
MUSEUM OF NORTHERN ARIZONA
SAN FRANCISCO PEAKS
ARIZONA SNOWBOWL
SUNSET CRATER VOLCANO NATIONAL
  MONUMENT
WUPATKI NATIONAL MONUMENT
WALNUT CANYON NATIONAL MONUMENT
METEOR CRATER

LEFT: the Clark Telescope at Lowell Observatory. **RIGHT:** a street mural in Flagstaff.

The Babbitt Building in downtown Flagstaff.

by hoisting the flag up a pine tree on the Fourth of July. Though their patriotic act gave Flagstaff its name, few of the immigrants stayed. Disillusioned, they discovered that the glowing promises of agricultural possibilities were so much promotional puffery.

Stockmen found the grasslands fine, though. A handful of them, such as Thomas McMillan and John Clark, settled in. Another pioneer, merchant P.J. Brannen, had faith in the railroad. He erected his store across from the New Town depot. Soon thereafter came five brothers from Cincinnati, Ohio, by the name of Babbitt. Through their efforts, and others, Flagstaff was on its way to becoming an established town.

Now a small and growing city of nearly 66,000 residents, Flagstaff hosts a lively, eclectic mix of small business owners, students, writers and artists, travelers, cowboys, river runners and Rastafarians, and of old-timers and newcomers. It's been characterized as a crossroads and a destination. Millions from all over the world pass through on their way to the Grand Canyon each summer. Big-city folks wander up on weekends, sampling the small-town feeling. Students stay for a few years to obtain an education at **Northern Arizona University A**. The rest – hearts captured by the town's friendliness and the surrounding beauty of forests, mountains, and canyons – find themselves permanent Flagstaffians.

Art and history

Downtown Flagstaff is a good place to start a visit. At its center is **Heritage Square A**. This outdoor plaza features a small amphitheater where concerts are presented nearly every weekend through summer and fall. Diagonal to the square is the landmark **Weatherford Hotel**. Judge John Weatherford opened this elegant establishment on New Year's Day in 1900. Like many downtown structures, the hotel is built of locally quarried sandstone called Arizona Red. The present owners have faithfully restored the hotel's original face, including a restored balcony that wraps around the second story; it's a perfect place to sip a cold drink and

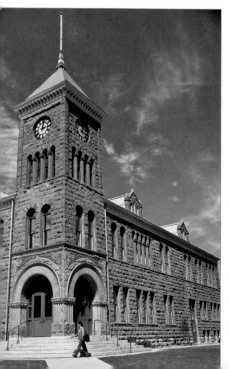

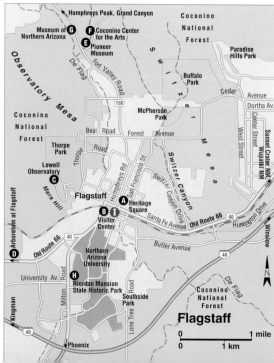

view the parade of humanity on the sidewalk below.

For a more in-depth look at downtown's many other turn-of-the-century stone buildings, two publications will help: **Flagstaff Historic Walk** and **Stone Landmarks**, both available at the **Visitor Center** ❷ (tel: 800-842-7293 or 928-774-9541; Mon–Sat 7am–6pm, Sun 7am–5pm) in the train station a block from the Weatherford Hotel or at local bookstores.

Flagstaff is no Santa Fe, but in recent years a slew of galleries has opened downtown. On the first Friday of each month, several stay open between 6pm and 8pm for the **First Friday Art Walk**. Visitors have a chance to meet the artists, many of them local, who produce fine art and crafts in glass, wood, cloth, and other media.

Lowell's legacy

A trip up to **Lowell Observatory** ❸ (tel: 928-774-3358; www.lowell.edu; June–Aug daily 9am–10pm, days and hours vary rest of the year; charge) just west of downtown affords that toy-town view of Flagstaff from Mars Hill. Wealthy Bostonian Percival Lowell chose the hill as the site for his observatory, where he ordered a telescope erected to view the planet Mars. Lowell arrived in 1894 in time to make those observations and lived part-time there for the rest of his life. The planet Pluto was discovered at the observatory in 1930, and astronomers continue to make significant contributions in their various specialties. The **Steele Visitor Center** and the **Slipher Building** contain fascinating interactive exhibits on the work of astronomers and the history of the observatory. With the clear, dark sky bursting with stars, it is a distinct treat to attend a night-time viewing through Percival's original Clark telescope.

Flagstaff is also a center of other scientific pursuits. A branch office of the US Geological Survey is located in town and is the place where the late Eugene Shoemaker founded the discipline of astrogeology. A 10-day **Festival of Science** is held each fall, with a constant round of public events. Recognizing the area's botanical diversity, the **Arboretum at Flagstaff** ❹ (tel: 928-774-1442; Apr–Oct daily 9am–5pm; charge) features native plant gardens, nature walks, and other activities on the grounds on Woody Mountain Road, 4 miles (6.4km) from town.

The Arizona Historical Society's **Pioneer Museum** ❺ (tel: 928-774-6272; Mon–Sat 9am–5pm; charge) displays interesting artifacts from Flagstaff's past. To visit, follow Highway 180 (Fort Valley Road) north until you reach a white stone building, originally the county hospital, that locals once called "the poor farm." Along with housing the small staff, the hospital had room for about a dozen patients. In 1908, the local newspaper described the new building as "a substantial one of stone, fitted up with hot and cold water in each of the airy rooms, situated among the pines on a small hill

Petroglyphs in Coconino National Forest.

Southside

South of the tracks, along South San Francisco and South Beaver Streets in Flagstaff, is what's known as Southside – a funky neighborhood of ethnic restaurants, coffee shops, dance studios, sport shops, youth hostels, historic churches, and modest homes.

Southside has always been the working-class side of town. Its residents claim a mixture of Mexican, Basque, and African-American heritage. Their ancestors moved here between the 1870s and 1930s to escape revolution in Mexico and to find jobs, mostly as shepherds and mill workers. They built modest stone cottages and frame bungalows and gathered at Zaragosa Hall on South San Francisco for dances and boxing matches. Billiards and handball played at a traditional Basque pelota court (which still stands on South San Francisco Street) provided other pastimes.

Today, the grandchildren of those early pioneers still live in the same houses and run family businesses. The streets are filled with the scent of fresh tortillas and roasted coffee. Diners can enjoy every kind of cuisine from Chicago-style hot dogs to hemp burgers. On most days, some of the 15,000 students at Northern Arizona University pedal and skateboard through this down-home neighborhood that relishes its individuality and history.

The old administration building at the University of Northern Arizona.

BELOW: Old Number 12 sits idle outside the Arizona Historical Society's Pioneer Museum.

overlooking the rich little valley to the south."

Outside the museum stands old **Number 12**, a shiny black steam locomotive put into service in the Northwest woods in 1929 and used in the Flagstaff area in the 1950s. Inside, individual rooms contain artifacts of early medicine, logging, and transportation in northern Arizona. A display of old dolls, games, children's books, tea sets, quilts, and more – called Playthings of the Past is held each holiday season. The museum's two big events each year are the **Wool/Fiber Festival** on the first weekend in June, and the **Independence Day Festival** marking the Fourth of July, with live demonstrations at each.

Immediately behind the Pioneer Museum is the **Coconino Center for the Arts G** (tel: 928-779-2300; Tue–Sat 11am–5pm;), exhibiting the work of local artists and providing a venue for live music and other programs. Next door is the **Art Barn**, location for classes and opportunities for resident artists.

Family treasures

A mile farther along Highway 180 is the **Museum of Northern Arizona G** (tel: 928-774-5213; daily 9am–5pm; charge). Dr Harold Colton, his wife Mary-Russell Ferrell Colton, and other community members founded this institution in 1928. This gem of a museum, standing amid ponderosa pines beside the Rio de Flag, shares the wealth of geology, biology, and culture of the Colorado Plateau, the geologic province in which Flagstaff is located. Rotating exhibits showcase some of the museum's extensive collections of basketry, pottery, paintings, and kachina carvings. Mrs Colton, an accomplished artist in her own right, encouraged Native American artists. Her legacy continues at the museum to this day, with a series of shows and marketplaces in summer and early fall featuring some of the best arts and crafts produced in the region.

Back in town near Northern Arizona University, another piece of Flagstaff's history has been preserved in a state park. **Riordan Mansion State Historic Park H** (tel: 928-779-4395;

May–Oct 9.30am–5pm, Nov–Apr 10.30am–5pm; hourly tours start at 10am, reservations recommended) was the home of businessmen and brothers Michael and Timothy Riordan.

The 40-room, 13,000 sq ft (1,200 sq meter) house, designed by Charles Whittlesey, architect of the Grand Canyon's El Tovar Hotel, was built in 1904. Stone, plank, and shake construction was used; some of the wood was scrap ponderosa pine from the nearby Arizona Lumber and Timber Company mill, which the Riordans owned. The two brothers married the Metz sisters, and each family had separate living areas in the mansion, connected by a common space called the "cabin room." The Steinway piano, Tiffany stained-glass windows, velvet upholstered seats, and six-car garage show what life was like for the "upper crust" in Flagstaff in the early years. But the Riordans weren't immune to grief. In daughter Anna's bedroom is her hoop dress, which she wore as a young woman. On the night of her engagement party in 1927, she was stricken with polio and her life was cut short.

Sacred peaks

The **San Francisco Peaks** ❸ sweep up behind Flagstaff, a small range as far as mountains go but an extremely captivating one. The Peaks are sacred mountains to nearly everyone who has felt their attraction, in particular the Hopi, Navajo, and many other Native Americans. The Peaks are the highest mountains in Arizona – 12,643ft (3,854 meters) at the windswept tundra atop **Humphreys Peak.** A trio of separate summits complete their impressive profile: **Agassiz, Doyle, and Fremont.**

Franciscan friars who saw the mountains from the Hopi Mesas in 1629 named them in honor of their founder, St. Francis. Early travelers headed for the springs that issue from them, and a fledgling Flagstaff relied on those water sources for the town's sustenance. Now people flock to the mountains for recreation and inspiration. They hike the trails in summer, gawk at golden aspens in the fall, sled

TIP

Amateur archaeologists can help excavate Elden Pueblo, a Sinaguan ruin in Flagstaff. Educational programs include site tours, lab work, and excavation techniques. Call 928-527-3452 for information.

BELOW: Museum of Northern Arizona.

One of several telescope domes at Lowell Observatory.

and ski in winter, and watch for the first candytuft to bloom in spring. Botanists search the alpine tundra for rare plants, hunters scan the ridges for elk, and woodcutters load up logs for their stoves.

Geologists classify the Peaks as a "stratovolcano." Numerous explosions piled layer upon layer of lava, cinders, and ash to an elevation of nearly 16,000ft (4,800 meters) about 400,000 years ago; on the north side, the mountain collapsed into a huge bowl called the Inner Basin.

Mountain wilderness

The uppermost reaches of the San Francisco Peaks are protected as the **Kachina Peaks Wilderness Area**. While no motorized or wheeled vehicles are allowed, hikers walking the wilderness may be rewarded with the sights and sounds of gray fox, Mexican owls, and bugling elk. Two popular trails, the Humphreys and Kachina, can be reached by driving to the **Arizona Snowbowl** (tel: 928-779-1951; daily 9am–4pm) 17 miles (27km) from town, off Highway

180. The **Humphreys Trail** ascends steeply through dense evergreen forest to the rocky tundra of the highest summit. The **Kachina Trail** is a gentler path that follows the lower slope. Northward stretches the grassy expanse of **Hart Prairie**, home to a Nature Conservancy preserve with rental cabins. Forest Road 151, accessible from Highway 180, is a scenic unpaved drive that gives unending views of the Peaks.

Ski country

With the first dusting of snow on the Peaks in early winter, Flagstaffians rejoice at the prospect of downhill skiing. The sport arrived here in 1915. That winter, with 6ft (2 meters) of snow on the ground, Ole and Pete Solberg strapped on homemade wooden skis and swooshed down Mars Hill. Townsfolk gathered to watch, and the local paper exclaimed, "They call it 'skiing!'" In the 1930s a local ski club was formed to foster the sport, and the first lodge was built at what is now the Arizona Snowbowl. It's music to skiers' ears when the snow report reads "67

Flagstaff Arts and Crafts

Flagstaff's community spirit extends to its rich cultural offerings, which reflect this university town's pioneer past, scenic mountain location, seasonal tourism, and multicultural makeup.

Northern Arizona University has an exciting program of dance performances, readings, lectures, plays, and concerts by the Flagstaff Symphony, as well as art shows in the NAU Art Museum. The Coconino Center for the Arts, next to the Pioneer Museum (see page 153), showcases local and regional artists and musicians. It has intimate concerts and the annual Recycled Art Show in April and the *It's Elemental Fine Crafts* exhibit in December.

The First Friday Art Walk is hugely popular. It offers a chance to mingle with residents and enjoy late opening of local shops, independent art galleries, and dining in downtown's restaurants and wine bars. Heritage Square is a good place to meet. Live music concerts are offered every Thursday in summer, and almost nightly in the nearby historic Orpheum Theater.

Flagstaff is famous for its festivals. March's Arizona Archeology Month and September's Festival of Science bring archeology enthusiasts and science lovers of all ages to dig at Elden Pueblo; view Mars, Jupiter, and other planets at Lowell Observatory; and attend talks and lectures at the Museum of Northern Arizona, Northern Arizona University, and the United States Geological Survey.

Snow sports dominate the chilly WinterFest in late winter, and include Nordic and Alpine skiing. A series of concerts, lectures and cultural happenings round out the calendar of activities in WinterFest.

Summer in the mountains is peak season for outdoor festivals. A Labor Day county fair and several horse races bring lots of folks to town, and many different types of arts and crafts festivals are held at the huge Fort Tuthill County Park, south of town, while the Zuni, Hopi, and Navajo juried shows at Museum of Northern Arizona attract international connoisseurs and collectors of Indian arts and crafts.

inches of packed powder at Midway, all runs open." The Snowbowl's five lifts serve beginner to advanced skiers. (In summer, one lift operates as a scenic skyride, taking riders to an elevation of 11,500ft/3,500 meters.)

Without snow-making equipment, the Snowbowl depends on mother nature. In dry years the season can be short; but in average years, with 260 inches (660cm) of snow possible, the slopes are open from mid-December through March.

For a more low-tech experience, the **Flagstaff Nordic Center** (tel: 928-220-0550; daily 9am–4pm winter only) is the place to go. On Highway 180, 8 miles (13km) past Snowbowl Road, the center offers a variety of groomed cross-country and snowshoe trails through the forest and meadows. Cross-country skiers will also find a nearly endless supply of backroads, most of them closed in winter, in **Coconino** and **Kaibab National Forests** that provide a wealth of possibilities for winter trekking.

During the entire month of February, a kind of cold-weather mania grips Flagstaff during **Winterfest**. All manner of snow-related activities are scheduled, including skiing, dogsledding, snowshoeing, ice skating, and skijoring (a cross between cross-country skiing and dogsledding), not to mention the Snowball Slide and Icicle Walk and Gawk. An array of music, food, and dance events complements the more vigorous endeavors.

Volcanic origins

The San Francisco Peaks are part of the 1,152,000-acre (466,200-hectare) San Francisco Volcanic Field, a young, still active volcanic field that has shaped the landscape. Some 600 cinder cones are scattered throughout the grassy plains surrounding Flagstaff. And though some of the cones date back several million years, the **Sunset Crater Volcano National Monument** ❹ (tel: 928-526-0502; daily May–Oct 8am–5pm, Nov–Apr 9am–5pm) is less than 1,000 years old. This black 1,000ft (300-meter) -high cone was formed when hot ash and lava exploded from a vent around AD 1064–65. It continued

Artist James Turrell has spent decades sculpting the interior of Roden Crater near Flagstaff into a celestial landscape art installation. He plans to open it for public viewing in 2011.

BELOW: a shop in downtown Flagstaff.

Percival Lowell, founder of Lowell Observatory, believed that 'canals' on Mars were built by intelligent life.

BELOW: snowshoeing at the base of the San Francisco peaks.

erupting for 150 years or so, pouring out fiery lava and other volcanic debris that has frozen into a black, jagged moonscape.

To see Sunset Crater up close, travel 12 miles (19km) north of Flagstaff on Highway 89 and turn at the national monument sign. After a stop at the visitor center, continue on the loop road at the base of Sunset Crater. Though the crater itself is now off-limits to hikers due to erosion, you can walk around it on the mile-long **Lava Flow Trail**. Along the way you'll see the many byproducts of the eruption – football-shaped volcanic bombs, upturned slabs of lava descriptively called squeeze-ups, and the entrance to an ice-filled lava tube.

After the eruption

When the volcano first erupted, the people living in the vicinity must have thought the world was coming to an end. But the fine cinder mulch the volcano deposited, along with a favorable period of precipitation after the eruption, lured them back. Harold Colton, founder of the Museum of Northern Arizona, named these people the Sinagua, which means "without water," for their arid homeland. He and other archaeologists believed the "new" volcanic farmland lured thousands of settlers into northern Arizona.

Ancestral Pueblo people were probably among them. Their stunning architectural stonework is on display at **Wupatki National Monument ❺** (tel: 928-679-2365; daily sunrise to sunset), 22 miles (35km) beyond Sunset Crater on the loop road. Several beautiful pueblos have been excavated and are open to visitors. The largest is namesake **Wupatki Pueblo**. From the visitor center, a half-mile self-guiding path leads through this four-story dwelling built of sandstone slabs set in mud mortar. Some of the masonry resembles that of Chaco Canyon in New Mexico. Wupatki Pueblo's more than 100 rooms ramble without any apparent plan, and recent work suggests it was built in several phases from the mid- to late 1130s through the early 1200s. Cached in several rooms were remains of such tropical birds as scarlet macaws and thick-billed parrots. These and other finds have led archaeologists to suggest that Wupatki was a site of high political or spiritual significance. Other intriguing sites in the park – **Wukoki**, the **Citadel**, and **Lomaki** – certainly support this theory.

Wupatki is located in the high-desert valley of the **Little Colorado River**. For a real backroad trip, take a ride to the **Grand Falls ❻** of the Little Colorado. The river's muddy brown waters tumble over a 185ft (56-meter) ledge, a virtual Niagara in the desert. Keep in mind, however, that Grand Falls flows only seasonally, when the river is running with springtime snowmelt or summer storm water, and requires quite an undertaking to reach.

Take Highway 89 just north of Flagstaff, turn right onto the

Townsend–Winona Road, go 8 miles (13km) to Leupp Road, turn left and go another 15 miles (24km) to the boundary of the Navajo Nation. Turn left (north) onto Navajo Route 70, a good gravel road when dry, but impassable when wet. In another 9 miles (15km), you'll spot picnic ramadas and find yourself at Grand Falls.

Relics of the past

Returning to Flagstaff, head east on Interstate 40 for 10 miles (16km) to the area's third national monument – **Walnut Canyon** ❼ (tel: 928-526-3367; daily May–Oct 8am–5pm, Nov–Apr 9am–5pm). The Sinagua lived here too, though in a totally different setting than Wupatki. They tucked their living quarters beneath limestone ledges in a deep canyon. Descend the **Island Trail** to the small rooms and smoke-blackened walls of their abodes. A host of plants along the streamcourse, on the drier hillsides, and on the forested rim sustained them with wild foods and material for clothing and other utilitarian items. By building small rock dams across gullies, the Sinagua gathered pockets of soil where they grew corn, beans, and squash. Some of these are visible along the **Rim Walk**, a fine place to gaze into Walnut Canyon or up into the sky for soaring hawks and eagles.

Continuing on Interstate 40 another 25 miles (40km), there's a big hole in the ground about 6 miles (10km) south of the highway that interests many people. And well it should. About 50,000 years ago, a chunk of iron traveling at about 40,000 mph (65,000 kph) hit the Earth. With the force of about 20 million tons of TNT, it blew out a depression known as **Meteor Crater** ❽ (tel: 928-289-2362; daily May–Sept 7am–7pm, Oct–Apr 8am–5pm; charge). This natural landmark – 4,000ft (1,200 meters) across and 560ft (170 meters) deep – is open for guided tours, or the crater can be viewed through windows at the fine museum on the rim.

Another 25 miles (40km) beyond Meteor Crater is the railroad town of **Winslow** ❾. Beside the tracks stands **La Posada**, a grand hotel designed by Mary Jane Colter, which dates to the heyday of American passenger trains in the 1930s. Private owners have superbly restored the huge mission-style structure, and it is well worth a visit.

A few miles north of town is **Homolovi Ruins State Park** ❿ (tel: 928-289-4106; daily 8am–5pm; charge). Situated atop high mounds overlooking the **Painted Desert** are 14th-century pueblos. Certain Hopi clans claim Homolovi as the home of their ancestors, the Hisatsinom, who made this their last stop before arriving at present homes on the mesas about 60 miles (100km) to the north. Homolovi sites I and II are accessible to visitors. Hiking trails, a campground, picnic areas, and a chance to watch archaeologists at work are features of the park. Check at the visitor center for the latest information.

Cracked and dry earth, with the San Francisco Peaks in the background, as seen from route 89A north of Flagstaff.

BELOW: the Wupatki Pueblo National Monument.

RESTAURANTS

Prices for a three-course dinner per person, excluding tax, tip, and beverages:
$ = under $20
$$ = $20–45
$$$ = $45–60
$$$$ = over $60

Beaver Street Brewery and Whistle Stop Café
11 S. Beaver Street, Flagstaff
Tel: 928-779-0079
$
This popular microbrewery, south of the tracks near the university, pairs delicious wood-fired pizza, hefty salads, fresh steaks and seafood, fondue, and an assortment of bar food with an interesting selection of suds, from a robust stout to a light berry ale. Expect a spirited college crowd.

Black Bean Burrito Bar and Salsa Company
12 E. Route 66, Flagstaff
Tel: 928-779-9905
$
A tasty variety of rib-sticking Mexican burritos are the specialty here, served in foil and plastic and eaten at the counter. Just the thing for a cheap filling feast.

Brandy's Bakery and Restaurant
1500 E. Cedar Avenue, Flagstaff
Tel: 928-779-2187
$–$$
This sister restaurant to downtown's La Bellavia (see below) is hidden in a shopping center on the east side of town but is worth searching out. It's larger and airier than La Bellavia but has similar menu items and Flag's best brunch. They stage art openings monthly.

Brix Restaurant and Wine Bar
413 N. San Francisco Street, Flagstaff
Tel: 928-213-1021
$$
Located in an old carriage house, Brix offers a New American menu that focuses on light Mediterranean-style cuisine made with local and organic foods. An artisanal cheese plate paired with poached apricots and homemade lavosh crackers features creamy goat cheese from Black Mesa Ranch in the White Mountains. Entrées include pan-seared seasonal fish served with polenta and corn soufflé, an authentic bistro steak-frites using hormone-free beef, and pork, lamb, and chicken dishes from similarly cosseted livestock. Vegetarians may swoon over the Black Mesa chevre tortellini, fava beans, sautéed beet greens, and caramelized fennel with tomato vinaigrette. Soups, salads, sandwiches, and burgers round out the lunch menu. Closed Sun.

Charly's Pub and Grille
23 N. Leroux Street, Flagstaff
Tel: 928-779-1919
$–$$
Housed on the ground floor of the historic Weatherford Hotel, Charly's has one of the best locations in town. Food here is reliably good southwestern fare, and the wine list offers many selections. There are sidewalk tables to watch the people go by.

Cottage Place Restaurant
126 W. Cottage Avenue, Flagstaff
Tel: 928-774-8431
$$
This unassuming 1909 bungalow, next door to a New Age bookstore, harbors an elegant little dining room where customers feast on rich Continental dishes such as châteaubriand, gorgonzola-crusted filet, Dijon-crusted salmon, veal chops, and seafood ravioli, presented with silver-platter fanfare – snooty to some, a delight to others.

Delhi Palace
2700 S. Woodlands Village Boulevard, Flagstaff
Tel: 928-556-0019
$–$$
This excellent north Indian restaurant is in the Woodlands Plaza shopping center on the south end of town and offers authentic Asian food. You can't go wrong with the lunch buffet, a great option if you're on a budget. White-tablecloth service from family members make this a good dinner option, too.

Diablo Burger
Old Town Shops
120 North Leroux Street, Flagstaff
Tel: 928-774-3274
$
Named Best Burger in Arizona by USA Today, this eatery near Heritage Square serves out-of-this-world burgers made from local range-fed, hormone- and antibiotic-free beef from Diablo Trust ranches in northern Arizona. A delicious home-made veggie burger gives the carnivores a run for their money. The Belgian-style frites, with their dusting of Herbes de Provence, have their own fan club. You can also get soup, salad, and sandwiches. Closed Sun.

Downtown Diner
7 E. Aspen Avenue, Flagstaff
Tel: 928-774-3492
$
A classic greasy spoon with typical diner fare and historic photos of Flagstaff on the walls.

Jackson's Grill at the Springs
Highway 89A, Flagstaff
Tel: 928-213-9332
$$–$$$
En route to Sedona, at the edge of a meadow in the national forest, Jackson's is a popular special-occasion restaurant. Continental cuisine is done well and includes choice steaks, free-range chicken, fresh seafood (including lobster) flown in regularly, wood-fired pizzas, and salads. The award-winning wine list is long, and the views are spectacular. Dinner daily and lunch Fri, Sat, Sun.

Josephine's Modern American Bistro
503 N. Humphreys, Flagstaff
Tel: 928-779-3400
$$

Following on from the long-time success of Chez Marc in the cozy 1911 Craftsman bungalow at this location, Josephine's serves appealing New American bistro food. The menu is globally inspired and includes Mediterranean lamb loaf, tequila-lime roasted half-chicken, wok-charred salmon with cranberry-citrus sauce, as well as pork osso bucco, crab cakes, and steak. Vegetarian fare includes roasted butternut squash and oven-roasted tomato risotto. The wine list is extensive. Dinner daily and lunch during the week.

La Bellavia
18 S. Beaver Street, Flagstaff
Tel: 928-774-8301
$

Bellavia is a great little breakfast spot. The breakfast trout, Swedish oat pancakes, and build-your-own omelets are Flagstaff classics. There's often a line; get here early.

Late for the Train Coffeehouse
107 N. San Francisco Street, Flagstaff
Tel: 928-779-5975
$

Located downtown, on the ground floor of the historic Babbitt Building, this superb little coffeehouse roasts its own delicious joe and serves cleverly monikered coffee drinks, pastries, and sandwiches.

Macy's European Coffeehouse and Bakery
14 S. Beaver Street, Flagstaff
Tel: 928-774-2243
$

When Californian Tim Macy opened his eponymous café south of the tracks in 1980, his was the first coffeehouse in Arizona to roast its own beans. Today, the java is still rich and dark and the fresh pastries healthy yet sinful at this classic college-town hangout. Sandwiches, pasta, and an all-vegetarian menu round out the offerings.

Monsoon on the Rim
6 E. Aspen Avenue, Flagstaff
Tel: 928-226-8844
$

Located in a large, attractive building on Heritage Square, which once housed the late-lamented Down Under New Zealand restaurant, this combo Asian restaurant and sushi bar is in a cavernous space. You can sit in the main dining room, at a sidewalk table, or in the Martini Bar, a hip spot among Flagstaff's sophisticates.

Mormon Lake Lodge Steak House and Saloon
Mormon Lake Road, Mormon Lake Village
Tel: 928-354-2227
$$–$$$$

In business since 1924, this steak house in the White Mountains, 28 miles (45km) southeast of Flagstaff, is a real ranch country experience. Locally raised mesquite-grilled ribs, chicken, and trout are the centerpieces of the menu. The dining room has Arizona brands seared into the wood paneling. Just the thing after a day on the trail. Only open for dinner on weekends.

Morning Glory Café
115 S. San Francisco Street, Flagstaff
Tel: 928-774-3705
$

A staple of the university district for years, Morning Glory is your typical college-town, crunchy-granola, happy-vibe café. The tasty food is organic and vegetarian and all freshly sourced and made. The menu runs the gamut from blue corn tamales and pancakes to soups and salads. Lunch Tue–Sat, breakfast on Sat only.

Mountain Oasis International Restaurant
11 E. Aspen Avenue, Flagstaff
Tel: 928-214-9270
$–$$

Fresh, globally inspired cuisine; an airy, plant-filled dining room in a historic building across from Heritage Square; and remarkably reasonable prices are among the selling points of this friendly and often overlooked restaurant. The menu includes appetizers like sushi, spring rolls, dolmas, and hummus and entrées, such as coconut curry salmon, Thai plate, prime rib, or pasta. Crisp, creative salads include one at lunchtime with grilled ahi (yellowfin) tuna or organic chicken.

Pasto
19 E. Aspen Street, Flagstaff
Tel: 928-779-1937
$–$$

Located next door to Mountain Oasis, Pasto gets the lion's share of press for its creative Italian fare and imaginative dining room. The menu includes a few local twists, such as the southwestern black-bean ravioli. The atmosphere is casual, and there's nearly always a line. Closed Sun.

Racha Thai
Monte Vista Hotel, 104 N. San Francisco Street, Flagstaff
Tel: 928-774-3003
$

The best Thai restaurant in the Northland, Racha specializes in Pad Thai but has many unusual offerings, including a curry pot pie. It occupies an old hotel coffee shop, so there's lots of retro atmosphere.

Sakura Sushi and Teppanyaki Restaurant
1175 W. Route 66, Flagstaff
Tel: 928-773-9118
$–$$

This Japanese restaurant is in the elegant Radisson Woodlands Hotel on the west end of town. Menu highlights are teppanyaki steak, chicken, and seafood, but it's also a favorite for sushi.

Tinderbox Kitchen
34 S. San Francisco Street, Flagstaff
Tel: 928-226-8400
$–$$

"American Comfort Food Redefined" is the tagline for this south-of-the-tracks trendy food haven, co-owned by NAU culinary graduate and seasoned chef Scott Heinonen and his cousin Kevin Heinonen. As promised, gourmet comfort food is in abundance, from halibut cheeks and chicken livers to sausage links, but you'll also find pheasant pâté and venison on the large menu. Both the dining room and the bar in the Annex attract a lively college crowd.

Reach for the Stars

Dry air and dark skies produce what astronomers call "good seeing," attracting both professional and amateur skywatchers to Arizona

Three major observatories are located in southern Arizona, each atop a mountain peak far from the glare of city lights and the dust and moisture that tend to settle at lower elevations. A fourth and much older facility, Lowell Observatory, is in Flagstaff and has been engaged in fundamental research for more than a century.

Kitt Peak, the best known of the state's observatories, stands at an elevation of about 6,900ft (2,100 meters) in the Quinlan Mountains 56 miles (90km) southwest of Tucson. The ridge bristles with the largest array of telescopes in the world, including three major night-time telescopes and the facilities of consortia that operate 19 optical telescopes and two radio dishes on this site. The largest is the 13ft (4-meter) Mayall reflector, which is housed in an 18-story dome. About half a mile away, the white angular housing of the McMath Solar Telescope rises from the mountain's south end, looking more like a modern sculpture than an astronomical instrument. At the top of the structure is a 6.5ft (2-meter) mirror that collects the sun's rays and reflects the light down a 530ft (162-meter) -long diagonal shaft into an underground laboratory.

Stop at the visitor center (*see page 303 for opening times*) for either guided tours or self-guided tours that offer a look at the workings of the observatory. Nightly viewings give amateurs a chance to probe the heavens with a 16-inch reflector under the guidance of a graduate student. An advanced program limited to two participants per night lets you work side by side with professionals. Reserve well ahead.

To the east, in the Pinaleño Mountains outside Safford, Mount Graham International Observatory is operated by Steward Observatory, the research arm for the Department of Astronomy at The University of Arizona. Tours depart from Discovery Park, a visitor center at the base of the mountain, followed by stargazing through the 20-inch telescope in the evening.

Fred Lawrence Whipple Observatory, in the Santa Rita Mountains 35 miles (56km) south of Tucson, offers a visitor center (Mon–Fri 8.30am–4.30pm) and 6-hour bus tours (tel: 520-670-5707; mid-Mar–Nov; charge). The highlight is a close-up look at the Multiple Mirror Telescope which combines

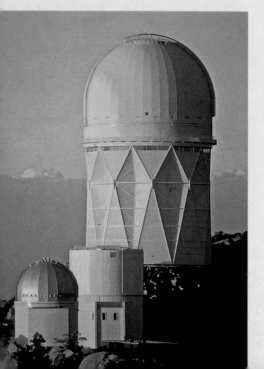

LEFT AND RIGHT: the Kitt Peak Observatory.
TOP: star trails streak across the sky in a time-lapse photo of Monument Valley. **ABOVE RIGHT:** spiral galaxy photographed from Kitt Peak.

the light from six 6ft (1.8-meter) mirrors constantly realigned by laser sensors.

Lowell Observatory (*see page 153*) welcomes visitors with numerous interactive exhibits, informative tours, viewing programs and special workshops. Best known for Percival Lowell's obsessive search for Martian life, the observatory is also credited with Clyde Tombaugh's discovery of Pluto and observations that led to the discovery of the expanding universe.

Lowell's belief in Martian life was based on observations of lines radiating from the planet's surface, which he thought was a network of canals. Assuming Mars was arid, he believed an irrigation system would have been necessary to channel water from melting polar ice caps, dew, or frost. He also suggested that Mars had an atmosphere, thin and cloudless but adequate to support life.

Today, astronomers at Lowell conduct research on the planets, stars, galaxies, comets, and asteroids. One project locates and tracks objects that could collide with Earth, causing the same ecological catastrophe believed to have wiped out the dinosaurs.

The stargazing tour continues at Tucson's Flandrau Science Center and Planetarium, where visitors can see a 200-pound (90kg) chunk of the Barringer iron that blasted out Meteor Crater, take in a planetarium show, and gaze through a 16-inch telescope in a rooftop observatory. Nearby is the Steward Observatory's Mirror Laboratory, which produces optics for some of the world's biggest telescopes.

Star parties are a great way for travelers and amateur astronomers to mingle and enjoy stargazing through several telescopes specially set up for the occasion. One of the best star parties is the annual Grand Canyon Star Party in June, which takes place over several nights at the edge of the abyss.

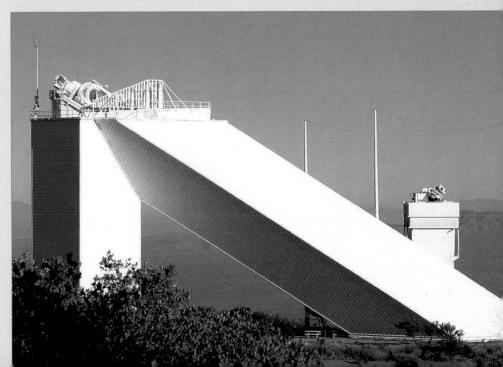

PAGE AND THE ARIZONA STRIP

A modern town built to harness the power of the Colorado River is a gateway to the lean and lonesome country north of the Grand Canyon

"**H**igh, wide, lonesome country" is what cowboys called the **Arizona Strip**. Even many Arizonans have never heard of this quiet stretch of high desert on the Arizona–Utah border, sandwiched between the **North Rim of the Grand Canyon** and the **Vermilion Cliffs**. For most visitors, it's the Highway 89A Grand Canyon corridor, connecting the communities of northern Arizona with those of southern Utah via the only road bridge over the **Colorado River** in 600 miles (970km).

To the Kaibab Paiute, the Arizona Strip was once a bountiful homeland of tallgrass prairie, sunflowers, and hundreds of other food plants. Their ancestors roamed long distances seasonally, living in wickiup brush shelters and weaving beautiful baskets to gather pinyon nuts, seeds, and other foods. In summer, they hunted deer and elk on the Kaibab Plateau, then returned to stone houses beside springs to harvest corn and squash like their predecessors, the Virgin River Anasazi. Springs "belonged" to individual families, who acted as caretakers on behalf of the natural world, learning the songs of each rock and tree.

The road to recovery

The Kaibab Paiute were almost wiped out by 18th-century Spanish diseases and 19th-century Navajo and Ute slave trading. Then, in the 1860s, Mormon colonists took over water sources and traditional hunting and gathering lands for farms, ranches, and settlements, and the Kaibab Paiutes quickly lost their self-sufficiency and became poverty-stricken. The situation has changed, due largely to education, legal challenges over self-determination and access to water, and modest

PRECEDING PAGES: Arches National Monument. **LEFT:** on Lake Powell. **RIGHT:** a mountain goat in Grand Canyon National Park.

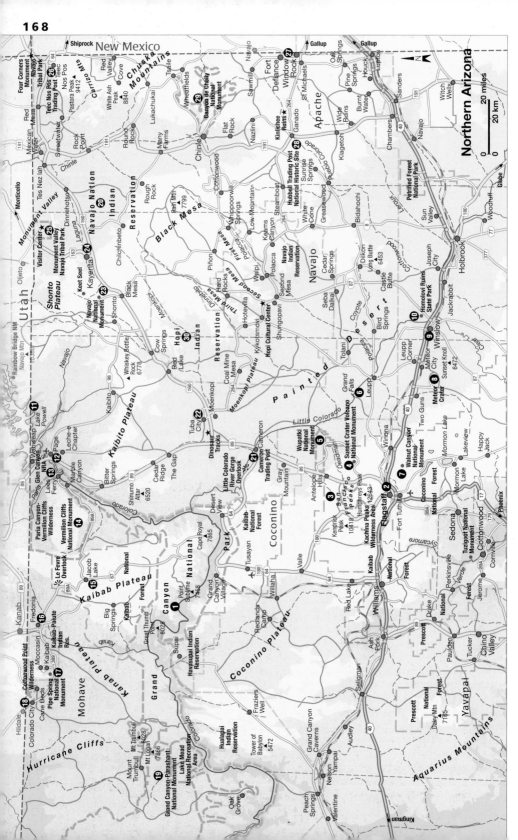

Northern Arizona

20 miles

0   20 km

New Mexico

Shiprock

Gallup

Gallup

Utah

Four Corners Monument Navajo Tribal Park

Teec Nos Pos Trading Post

Monument Valley

Navajo Nation Indian Reservation

Black Mesa

Shonto Plateau

Kaibito Plateau

Grand Canyon National Park

Kaibab Plateau

Kaibab National Forest

Coconino Plateau

Hurricane Cliffs

Mohave

Kanab Plateau

Navajo Indian Reservation

Hopi Indian Reservation

Painted Desert

Coconino National Forest

Yavapai

Aquarius Mountains

Apache

Kingman

Chuska Mountains

Carrizo Mts

Monument Valley

commercial development on the tiny reservation surrounding Pipe Spring National Monument.

Things look less rosy for the land itself. The huge cattle drives of the 1870s and 1880s badly overgrazed the Strip. Lush grasslands have been replaced by sagebrush and erosion of deep arroyos, and despite better stewardship of the land under the Bureau of Land Management, it struggles to recover. Although ranching, logging, and mining are still evident, tourism and outdoor recreation are becoming more important economically. Four-wheel-drivers, river runners, hikers, and other outdoor-lovers can explore some of the most beautiful and little-traveled backcountry in the state in **Grand Canyon National Park**, four national monuments, and eight wilderness areas.

Unnatural beauty

Given this abundant natural beauty, it's ironic that the area's most popular attraction is unnatural. Some 130 miles (210km) north of Flagstaff, on Highway 89, is 180-mile (290km)

-long **Lake Powell ⑪**, the second largest man-made lake in the Western Hemisphere. The lake is formed by 710ft (220-meter) -high **Glen Canyon Dam**, downstream at **Page ⑫**, which generates 1,200 megawatts of hydro-electricity for the megalopolises of Phoenix and environs – and ample controversy.

When it was begun in 1956, the dam had the blessing of almost everyone concerned. By the time it was finished in 1963, conservationists like the Sierra Club's David Brower and writer Wallace Stegner had belatedly recognized that Glen Canyon was comparable in grandeur to anything – including the nearby Grand Canyon – on the Colorado Plateau.

That said, Lake Powell, administered by the National Park Service as part of 1.2-million-acre (486,000-hectare) **Glen Canyon National Recreation Area** (tel: 928-608-6200; www.nps. gov/glca; Mon–Fri 7am–4pm), is a stunning place to waterski, fish, and explore the shoreline. Miles of blue water and a 1,961-mile (3,156km) shoreline of carved sandstone cliffs

The Glen Canyon National Recreation Area provides the opportunity for water recreation.

BELOW: the Glen Canyon Dam impounds the waters of Lake Powell.

make the lake a photographer's dream. Houseboats, popular with vacationers, may be rented at **Bullfrog Marina** (tel: 435-684-7423), one of four marinas, along with fishing tackle and powerboats.

Carl Hayden Visitor Center (tel: 928-608-6404; daily May–Oct 8am–6pm, Nov–Feb 8.30am–4.30pm, Mar–Apr 8am–5pm with exceptions; charge), next to the dam in Page, has exhibits, interpretive presentations, and information on hiking side canyons and river trips. It offers frequent self-guided and guided tours of the dam and powerplant, which is operated by the US Bureau of Reclamation. Expect tight security measures at Glen Canyon Dam. No bags, purses, knives, weapons, or food are allowed inside the visitor center. You may only bring in wallets, cameras, and clear water bottles.

The Park Service operates a developed campground at Lees Ferry and primitive campgrounds at Lone Rock Beach, Stanton Creek, Hite, Dirty Devil, and Farley. A concessionaire operates well-developed campgrounds at Wahweap and Bullfrog inside the park.

Also on Navajo land is 290ft (90-meter) -high **Rainbow Bridge National Monument** (tel: 928-608-6200; daily), the world's tallest known natural bridge. The bridge can only be reached by hiking overland across the Navajo Nation or by boat, followed by a 1-mile (2km) hike into a side canyon directly from Lake Powell. The site is sacred to the Navajo, who control overland access to the two rugged access trails. For hiking and camping permission, contact Navajo Parks and Recreation (tel: 928-871-6647; www.navajonationparks.org). You can only enter **Antelope Canyon Tribal Park**, one of the area's most beautiful slot canyons, east of Page, with a tour guide. Authorized tour companies are listed at www.discovernavajo.com.

You'll find equally stunning vistas at the **Horseshoe Bend** viewpoint, which is set on the cliffs over a hairpin loop in the Colorado River. It's roughly a half mile (800 meters) to the overlook from the trailhead, which is about 5 miles (8km) south

of the Carl Hayden Visitor Center on Highway 89.

Lake Powell was named for explorer John Wesley Powell, whose 1869 and 1871–72 river-running trips were the first to explore the Green and Colorado River gorges. **John Wesley Powell Memorial Museum** (tel: 928-645-9496; Mon–Fri 9am–5pm; charge) has old drawings and photos about Powell's life and voyages, geological displays, and Indian artifacts. The museum is located in downtown Page, which has grown from a makeshift shantytown for dam workers into far northern Arizona's largest community, with a variety of mainstream lodgings, restaurants, and gas options.

Into the Strip

To enter the Arizona Strip itself, head back south to the junction of Highway 89 and 89A, at **Bitter Springs**, and drive west on Highway 89A via **Marble Canyon**. When it opened in 1929, the narrow, 467ft (142-meter) -high **Navajo Bridge** over the Colorado River was the highest steel structure in the world. A wider bridge was opened in 1997, and you can walk across the old structure. The small **Navajo Bridge Visitor Center** (tel: 928-355-2319; Mar–Oct 9am–5pm) is an impressive piece of desert architecture, with pueblo-style sandstone walls and a fine little bookstore. This is a popular spot to look for one of the reintroduced California condors now living in and around the Grand Canyon. Birds can be seen circling Marble Canyon looking for food in the cliffs below.

Behind the dramatic Vermilion Cliffs is **Lees Ferry** ⓭, once a ferry crossing operated by John D. Lee, a prominent Mormon elder. He was sent here by Mormon leader Brigham Young after the 1857 Mountain Meadow Massacre in Utah of a wagon train bound for California, for which he would be executed. At the mouth of the **Paria River**, Lee's old homestead, **Lonely Dell Ranch**, is a pretty spot with a log cabin, a blacksmith shop, ranch house, and shady orchards, a good place to stop and watch the river runners putting in on the Colorado River.

Canyons and crossings

The 293,000-acre (119,000-hectare) **Vermilion Cliffs National Monument** ⓮ incorporates **Paria Canyon–Vermilion Cliffs Wilderness**, which has no fewer than three spectacular slot canyon hikes. The most popular is the 38-mile (61km) hike through the narrow, 2,000ft (600-meter) -deep **Paria River Canyon to Paria, Utah**, a trip of four to six days. The southern trailhead is at Lees Ferry. Day users must register before setting out; all overnight trips are by permit only, with daily quotas in force. The best time to do this river hike (which requires wading in places) is mid-March to June. This is not a place you want to be during a flash flood in the summer monsoon season.

Monument hiking tips, permits, and up-to-date weather information can be obtained from the **Paria**

TIP

There are numerous undeveloped sites along the shoreline and camping on the southern shore of Lake Powell with permission from the Navajo Nation.

Buffalo Jones

Jesse "Buffalo" Jones was an aging buffalo hunter who had participated in the mass slaughter of the shaggy beasts on the Great Plains in the 1870s. In 1906, realizing that the buffalo were close to extinction, he drove a herd of survivors to the Arizona Strip, where he set up a buffalo preserve and tried unsuccessfully to breed "cattalo," a cross between buffalo and cattle.

Celebrated western writer Zane Grey was introduced to Jones in 1907, while the colorful frontiersman was on a fund-raising tour of the East Coast. Jones, clad in fringed buckskin, held audiences spellbound with stories of lassoing wild mountain lions in the Grand Canyon and other tales of life on the western frontier. Grey, who had honeymooned in northern Arizona the year before, was intrigued. He traveled to Arizona and witnessed Jones's lion-hunting skills firsthand, which became a key inspiration for *Last of the Plainsmen* and other stories.

Although Grey admired Jones, he was dismayed by Jones's ruthless pursuit of his prey. "He shore can make animals do what he wants," wrote Grey in *Don, the Story of a Lion Dog*. "But I never seen the dog or horse that cared two bits for him." Descendants of Jones's original buffalo herd may still be seen in House Rock Valley today.

Swirling sandstone and dramatic lighting make Antelope Canyon a favorite of photographers.

BELOW: although the landscape can appear harsh, a number of animals make the desert their home.

Contact Station (Mar–Nov daily 8.30am–4.15pm), located 41 miles (66km) east on Highway 89 from Kanab, or from the **BLM Arizona Strip Field Office** in St. George, Utah (345 E. Riverside Dr; tel: 435-688-3200; Mon–Fri 7.45am–5pm, Sat 10am–3pm).

The first white men to see the mouth of the Paria River were Spanish Padres Dominguez and Escalante whose expedition left Santa Fe, New Mexico, in 1776, hoping to forge an overland route to Monterey, California. They were forced to turn back near St. George, then tried, unsuccessfully, to cross the Colorado River at Lees Ferry. Eventually, they found a good ford, 40 miles (64km) upriver, at a spot known as the Crossing of the Fathers (it has since been flooded by Lake Powell). The **San Bartolome Historic Site** marker on the north side of Highway 89A, marks one of their campsites. You'll find it west of the 1890 **Cliff Dwellers Lodge**, a tiny redstone oasis built beneath a boulder, with lodging, restaurant, gas station, store, and stunning views.

The Vermilion Cliffs support desert bighorn sheep, pronghorn, mountain lion and, since 1996, California condors, which were reintroduced at **House Rock Valley**, a grassy break in the cliffs. House Rock Valley was home to Mormon pioneer Jim Emett, who operated Lees Ferry in the early 1900s. Emett and his neighbor, frontiersman Jesse "Buffalo" Jones (*see page 171*), guided Zane Grey on his first mountain lion hunting trip to Arizona in 1907, when they spent time at both ranchers' homesteads on the Strip and explored **Surprise Valley**, near the Grand Canyon. Grey later wrote that Emett was "the man who influenced [me] most," noting Emett's love of the West and all living things despite "so few of the joys commonly yearned for by men." The frontier spirit embodied in men like Emett became recurrent themes in such classic Grey novels as *Riders of the Purple Sage* and *Last of the Frontiersmen*.

The Kaibab Plateau

The road winds onto the 8,000ft (2,400-meter) **Kaibab Plateau** through old-growth ponderosa pine forest. The turnoff for the North Rim of the Grand Canyon is at **Jacob Lake** ⓲, named for Mormon missionary Jacob Hamblin, whose exploring party came through in the 1860s. Starting in 1866, Franklin Woolley, followed by his brother Edwin "Dee" Woolley, explored the plateau's potential for lumber, grazing, and Mormon settlements and hatched numerous schemes for development.

Woolley's most extravagant caper came in 1892, when he and Brigham Young's son John, on a mission in England, hired Buffalo Bill, whose famous Wild West Show was currently in London, to escort a party of wealthy English nobles interested in game hunting and ranching in the region. None of the Brits decided to purchase ranches, but they stopped at Jacob Lake, where Buffalo Bill reputedly said grace at one meal, offering

thanks for many blessings, specifically "Emma Bentley's custard pie."

Excellent homemade pies and milkshakes are still served at historic **Jacob Lake Inn**, operated by descendants of Edwin Woolley Tiny **Jacob Lake Visitor Center** has exhibits and information on visiting the rough backcountry of **Kaibab National Forest**. One of the best hikes here is in **Snake Gulch**, where you'll see remarkable Virgin River Anasazi rock art.

From Jacob Lake, Highway 89A spirals 3,000ft (900 meters) off the plateau, descending from ponderosa pine into pinyon-juniper dwarf forest. Views of the western Arizona Strip and southwestern Utah's Color Country are breathtaking. It's hard to drive and goggle at the scenery, so pull off at **Le Fevre Overlook**. From here, you can see the geological formation known as the **Grand Staircase**, including the **White Cliffs** of Navajo Sandstone in **Zion National Park**.

At the base of the Kaibab Plateau, the small Mormon community of **Fredonia** ⑯ (a contraction of the English word "Free" and the Spanish word "Doña" to signify a free woman – a reference to the town's polygamous past) is a good place to spend the night, with small motels, Mexican restaurants, gas stations, and convenience stores. If you're heading south, you can also pick up information on Kaibab National Forest at the US Forest Service headquarters.

Mormon outpost

Turn west on Highway 389 and continue to **Pipe Spring National Monument** ⑰ (tel: 928-643-7105; daily Jun–Aug 7am–5pm, Sept–May 8am–5pm; tours on the hour and half-hour up to 4.30pm; charge), a small 1870 fortified ranch where the Mormon-owned Canaan Cattle Company ran the Church's large tithe cattle herd. The two-story fort was ostensibly built to enclose springs from the nearby Sevier Cliffs and to keep out Navajo raiders; in reality, there was more to fear from government officials hounding polygamous families (including Dee Woolley and his young wife Flora). The women were kept busy making pies, bread,

Map on page 168

TIP

Designed around natural sandstone formations, Lake Powell National Golf Course (tel: 928-645-2023) is one of the most scenic in Arizona.

BELOW: Horseshoe Bend is a dramatic U-shaped meander in the Colorado River.

TIP

The Bureau of Land Management's excellent Arizona Strip map offers an overview of the region and is essential for navigating backcountry roads.

and stews for travelers, explorers, miners and, after the St. George Temple had been completed, Mormon newlyweds who had been "sealed" and were returning home on the Honeymoon Trail. John Wesley Powell used the West Cabin as a headquarters during his 1872 survey, which ascertained that lands originally thought to be in Utah were actually in Arizona, creating the area we know today as the Arizona Strip.

In summer, rangers in period costume offer fascinating living-history demonstrations of pioneer life. Year-round tours leave from the visitor center and pass through the heavy wooden doors of the fort into two buildings joined by a catwalk. Spring water was piped into a ground-floor spring room where milk was kept cool, then processed into butter and cheese. Milk, meat, butter, and cheese were sent by the wagonload to St. George, Utah, every two weeks to feed workers constructing the new St. George Temple. A second-floor room housed Arizona's first telegraph. A self-guided tour through the orchards

has a push-button oral history by Maggie Heaton, a hired hand at Pipe Spring in 1898.

The Kaibab Paiute Tribe, whose reservation surrounds the monument, jointly operates the monument and the attractive on-site museum, the only facility documenting Kaibab Paiute history and culture, with the National Park Service. The tribe runs a campground, offers guided tours of rock-art sites, hikes, and cultural activities, and holds a powwow every October. Many tribal members work at the tribe's convenience store or at tribal headquarters opposite the visitor center, and live in nearby Kaibab and Moccasin.

All in the family

The Arizona Strip tends to attract nonconformists. **Colorado City** ⑱, on the Arizona–Utah border, is one such town. Its massive, half-finished houses with more than one door, bonneted wives, and young girls in quaint leggings and floral shifts are just a few outward signs of the secretive polygamous lifestyle still practiced

BELOW: watch your step carefully when near the edge.

The Return of Glen Canyon

Since 2000, ongoing drought in the Southwest has severely affected the Colorado River and brought Lake Powell reservoir levels down to 118ft (36 meters) below capacity. As the water levels drop, marinas are drying up but hiking and primitive camping on new beaches and side canyons in the northern reaches of the lake are improving. Archaeological remains are now reappearing like the mythical lost city of Atlantis. Some are reachable via day hikes, such as Defiance House, an Ancestral Pueblo dwelling with granaries and rock art, located 3 miles (5km) up Forgotten Canyon. Once mourned as "The Place No One Knew," Glen Canyon is beginning to reemerge of its own volition, even as the dam faces an uncertain future.

by members of the Fundamentalist Church of Jesus Christ of Latter Day Saints (FLDS), a breakaway sect of the Mormon church. Residents of Colorado City are tolerated by the authorities, but the recent trial of the sect's leader Warren Jeffs for coercing underage girls into forced marriages has thrust an unwelcome spotlight back on the community and caused residents to shun outsiders. It's probably best to avoid stopping here.

Views to the south take in an area of spare beauty that includes the **Shivwits Plateau**, **Mount Trumbull Wilderness** and **Mount Logan Wilderness**, **Grand Wash Cliffs Wilderness** and **Paiute Wilderness** in the **Virgin Mountains**. All of these are now part of the 1.1-million-acre (450,000-hectare) **Grand Canyon–Parashant National Monument** ❶❾ (tel: 435-688-3200; Mon–Fri 7.45am– 5pm, Sat 10am–3pm), managed by the Bureau of Land Management. The very remote monument expands the geological story of the Grand Canyon by including volcanic landmarks like 8,028ft (2,447-meter) **Mount**

Trumbull (which provided the wood for the St. George Temple). It is also an ecologically unique area where the Sonoran, Great Basin, and Mohave Deserts intersect, providing critical habitat for endangered California condors, desert tortoises, Southwest willow flycatchers, desert bighorn sheep, and pronghorn antelope.

Remote outpost

Dirt roads are the norm in this undeveloped monument. Avoid them during the summer, and don't travel without several gallons of gas and water, food, and spare tires. The monument's size and the long distances required to reach its features are intimidating, but travelers will enjoy the 60-mile (100km) drive to 6,393ft (1,947-meter) **Toroweap Overlook**, where the Grand Canyon drops away 3,000ft (900 meters). **Tuweep Ranger Station**, about 6 miles (10km) before the overlook, is open year-round and has information on hiking, camping, and road conditions.

Curious rock formations are found throughout the Glen Canyon National Recreation Area.

BELOW: the Glen Canyon Bridge spans the chasm just below the dam.

RESTAURANTS

Prices for a three-course dinner per person, excluding tax, tip, and beverages:
$ = under $20
$$ = $20–45
$$$ = $45–60
$$$$ = over $60

Anasazi Restaurant
100 Lakeshore Drive, Page
Tel: 888-896-3829
$–$$
This bright, airy restaurant at the Lake Powell Resort offers good casual dining of the steak, seafood, and pasta variety, but the big draw, of course, is the gorgeous lake view.

Blue Buddha Sushi Lounge

644 N. Navajo, Page
Tel: 928-645-0007
$–$$
Its zen-like atmosphere, cool name, and hand-made Japanese food announce that this hip eatery is something new for staid Page. The sushi plates have enticing names like Now and Zen, Volcano Roll, and Buddha Roll (half off during the daily happy hours 5-6pm and 8-10pm). A separate menu features Asian crab cakes, tempura coconut shrimp, teriyaki chicken, macadamia coconut mahi-mahi, and Phat bowls for larger appetites featuring chicken, tofu, and veggies.

Butterfield Steakhouse
704 Rimview Drive, Page
Tel: 928-645-2467
$–$$
Set on a bluff overlooking Lake Powell, this family-friendly restaurant serves satisfying portions of straightforward American and Southwestern food. This restaurant has been in Page a long time and is a popular rendezvous.

Dam Bar and Grille
644 N. Navajo Drive, Page
Tel: 928-645-2161
$–$$
Upscale and hip, this restaurant is a surprise in Page. It works the dam theme hard, including a transformer at the entrance that shoots off neon sparks and a wall of concrete sculpted like the dam, but the food can keep up. Steak and seafood are the main stars, along with pasta, chicken, sandwiches, burgers, and salads. Closed for lunch Sun.

Fiesta Mexicana Family
125 S. Lake Powell Boulevard, Page
Tel: 928-645-4082
$
Reliably good but pretty mainstream Mexican food in Page. Try the Fiesta Salad.

Jacob Lake Inn
Highway 67 and 89A, Jacob Lake
Tel: 928-643-7232
$
This inn's chummy coffee shop is a welcome break during a long, lonesome traverse of the Arizona Strip and the perfect place to eat homestyle food and mingle with locals. There's a cozy dining room with regular table service, but the old-fashioned counter is more fun. The menu features Mormon family recipes such as Southwest-baked chicken, jagerschnitzel, and baked trout. In the late 1800s, Buffalo Bill was enamored of the pies at this historic place ("I kiss the hand that made the pie," he exclaimed.) The famous milkshakes are a meal in themselves. Expect lots of hunters fueling up at breakfast in the fall. A good place for a hearty meal before pressing on to the North Rim of the Grand Canyon or into the Arizona Strip.

Ja'di' Tooh Restaurant
Antelope Point Marina, Navajo Nation
Tel: 928-645-5900
$
A vision in glass and timber, the very attractive new Antelope Point Marina entirely floats on Lake Powell, on Navajo Nation land within Glen Canyon NRA. It's worth a trip out here to enjoy the lovely setting right on the lake, east of Page. The chef offers some creative,

inexpensive wood-fired pizzas, wraps, sandwiches, and salads. A good place to watch the sunset and relax to the sound of lapping waves.

Kaibab Lodge Restaurant
Kaibab Lodge, US 67
Tel: 928-638-2389
$–$$
This cabin resort in the woods, near the entrance to Grand Canyon's North Rim, offers reasonably priced down-home breakfasts and dinners. Breakfast might include your choice of omelets and egg dishes, fresh fruit smoothies, French toast, huevos rancheros, and biscuits and gravy. At dinner, there are hot sandwiches and American steaks and seafood options, such as salmon, Kaibab chicken (basted in beer), mesquite-grilled chicken on salad greens, and St. Louis ribs. Light soup and salad options and kids' menu are available. Dessert is a major draw. Try their homemade cheesecakes, pies, and cobblers, the Mountain Lion triple-chocolate cake, and ice cream. Closed in winter.

Parry Lodge
89 E. Center Street, Kanab, UT
Tel: 435-644-2601
$–$$
The lodging of choice for Hollywood's stars filming westerns in the area, the 1931 Parry Lodge is worth a look if you're passing through Kanab. The walls have many autographed

photos of stars. A very reasonably priced breakfast buffet, half price for guests, is available April through October (free continental breakfast for guests the rest of the year). It offers many items, from croissants and fruit to eggs. The hotel is under new local ownership and has been remodeled. Open Thur–Sat.

Rainbow Room
100 Lakeshore Drive, Page
Tel: 928-645-2433
$–$$$
The dining focal point of the large Lake Powell Resort at Wahweap Marina, this two-story window-wrapped dining room dishes up above-average fare in its lovely waterside location. There's a buffet for breakfast, and soups, sandwiches, and salads at lunchtime. At dinner, prime rib, seafood, chicken, salads, and American Indian dishes are well done. Four-course special Chef's Table dinners, served in a section of the adjoining Driftwood Lounge, are offered June through September, highlighting the chef's use of sustainable foods, such as wild salmon, grass-fed beef, organic greens, and wild mushrooms.

Ranch House Grille
819 N. Navajo Drive, Page
Tel: 928-645-1420
$
The kind of local hangout to know about in any

American town, this reliable diner serves up good, solid breakfasts like huevos rancheros with green chilli and a host of other popular egg dishes and rib-sticking burgers, steaks, Caesar salad, and other fare for lunch. Huge portions, good value, and excellent service. The owner is a local teacher.

Rewind Diner
18 E. Center Street, Kanab, UT
Tel: 435-644-3200
$
Don't be fooled by this 1950s diner. It looks like a soda fountain, but the menu is surprisingly sophisticated, with unusual offerings such as faux gyros, falafel, and other vegetarian items alongside classic diner food such as burgers and milkshakes. Locals highly recommend it.

Rocking V Café
97 W. Center Street, Kanab, UT
Tel: 435-644-8001
$–$$
Kanab's best restaurant is an unexpected Slow Food haven, where you'll enjoy real food, freshly prepared, cooked to order, and beautifully presented in a fun atmosphere. The dining room is eye-poppingly colorful and has art on the walls, cool music on the stereo, and a laid-back atmosphere. Choose from a variety of salads made from organic greens, grass-fed beef and bison, locally raised trout, and wild Alaskan salmon, flown in four times weekly

in season. There are many vegetarian and vegan items. For dessert, try the house specialty: crème brulée. Dining with pets and smoking allowed on outside patio; full liquor license. Open daily for dinner in season, Mon and Tue in Mar; closed Jan and Feb.

Stromboli's Restaurant and Pizzeria
711 N. Navajo Drive, Page
Tel: 928-645-2605
$–$$
This sister restaurant to the hugely popular pizza spot in Flagstaff serves up large thin-crust pizzas and lots of traditional Italian dishes and calzones, as well as salads. A popular boaters' gathering place. Closed Nov–Feb.

Vermilion Cliffs Bar and Grill
Lees Ferry Lodge, US 89A, Marble Canyon
Tel: 928-355-2231
$–$$
American fare like steaks, burgers, and baby back ribs served in a rustic, wood-paneled dining room makes this attractive, rock-built Western lodge popular with rafters preparing to take on "the Grand" at nearby Lees Ferry. The lodge knows exactly how to create a good sendoff for river runners (and others lucky enough to pass through and happen on this little place in the middle of nowhere). There are 80 kinds of beer on the menu, and the wine list is an unexpected pleasure.

LEFT: tacos, burritos, and other Southwestern dishes are usually a good choice for an inexpensive and filling meal.

Desert Blooms

Engaged in a competition to attract pollinators, wildflowers bring a splash of vibrant color to even the harshest environments

Arizona has two main wildflower seasons – the result of steady winter rains and violent summer "monsoons" that awaken first delicate annuals and later hardy perennials. As a result, flowers are blooming somewhere in Arizona from late January all the way to October, starting with low-elevation deserts and ending with the high country of the White Mountains and San Francisco Peaks near Flagstaff.

But it is the brilliant March displays of brightly colored annuals below an elevation of 6,000ft (1,830 meters) that catch the headlines and send photographers scrambling for their cameras. With the right balance of r ain and sunshine between October and January – an event that occurs only every five years . or so – expect a wildflower extravaganza the following February to May. Displays of annuals are unpredictable. To find out what is blooming and where, check in with wildflower reports on the Web and at local parks, in newspapers like the Arizona Daily Star,

and the 602-754-8134 Arizona Wildflower Hotline set up each spring.

In February, Organ Pipe Cactus National Monument and other low-elevation spots in the west deserts are the first to bloom, in delicate waves of desert chicory, bladderpod, desert marigolds, and verbena. They are followed by showy displays of sulfur yellow brittlebush, a shrub that, like creosote, appears to die in summer heat, only to releaf a few days after consistent rains.

In late March and early April, trails along hillsides in Catalina State Park and Picacho Peak, north of Tucson, are carpeted with Mexican and California poppies in shades of gold, yellow, and peach, interwoven with bunches of white-purple Coulter's lupine, blue toadflax, pink owl clover, white desert phlox, and yellow evening primrose.

By May, pricklypear, hedgehog, claret cup, and cholla cactus begin wearing topknots of neon red, purple haze, and acid yellow to attract birds for pollination and to spread their seeds through juicy fruits, while saguaros are crowned with white blossoms that lure nocturnal Mexican long-nosed bats and hawkmoths to pollinate them. Green-barked paloverde trees are decked out in a golden rain of blossoms; long-lived ironwood trees erupt into a

LEFT: the century plant blooms only once in its lifetime. **ABOVE:** pricklypear cactus blossom.
TOP RIGHT: fissures in sandstone channel moisture and support a lush growth of vegetation. **RIGHT:** ocotillo flowers attract hummingbirds, whose long, thin bills are the right shape to feed on the tubular blossoms.

riot of lilac blooms. Living fences of ocotillo branches are tipped with red blooms in villages all over Sonora, Mexico.

Just as low-elevation wildflowers start to wilt under triple-digit temperatures in the deserts, the race to reproduce is heating up in the reawakening high country. After wet winters, look for outrageous displays of penstemons atop the rocky limestone and volcanic soils around Flagstaff, including one species that grows only at Sunset Crater Volcano National Monument.

Monsoons saturate the soil, and by August, wildflowers are drinking up moisture greedily. Flame-colored Indian paintbrush, a parasitic beauty, roots atop other plants. Five-fingered purple lupines "wolf" down nitrogen. Red skyrocket gilia and a variety of salvias, or sages, attract hummingbirds. Along shady streams and washes, bog iris, Rocky Mountain columbines, nodding bluebells, pink shooting stars, and jolly yellow and red monkeyflowers keep their feet wet, while in open sandy areas, like those on the Navajo Reservation, vetches and princes plume occupy sandy ridges rich in selenium.

Yellow sunflowers and purple asters are the summer stars of the high country. They line roadsides and form joyful throngs in meadows, allowing tits and finches to stock their larders with seeds before the first snows of October once more blanket the mountains.

Surrounded by such beauty, it's easy to forget that wildflowers are engaged in a competition to reproduce. Their shape and color are designed to attract the animals they rely on for pollination and seed dispersal. Pastel purples and pinks attract butterflies; yellow flowers lure carpenter bees; red trumpet flowers advertise for hummingbirds. It's all part of an evolutionary scheme that links one living thing to another. As is always the case in nature, the survival of any one species depends on the health of the whole ecosystem.

NAVAJO AND HOPI RESERVATIONS

At home in remote and sacred valleys and mesas, the Navajo and Hopi tread a path between centuries-old rituals and modern lifestyles

Travel anywhere in Indian Country, in the Four Corners region where Arizona, Colorado, Utah, and New Mexico join, and you will encounter beauty. It haunts the eerie rock formations of places like Monument Valley, deeply etched canyons such as Canyon de Chelly, sacred peaks, and serpentine rivers that give form and meaning to the Navajo and Hopi homelands. Life in such huge, empty, dry country seems ephemeral – a question of chance. What is really required is adaptation and a deep understanding of the land, the seasons, and the rituals that help humans remember their place in the cosmos.

Both the Hopi and Navajo understand this. The Hopi say that, after being expelled from three lower worlds because they fell out of harmony with the Creator Spirit, the people entered this Fourth World and encountered Masaw, the caretaker of the Earth. Masaw offered them a short ear of blue corn, from which they realized that life would be difficult, and, in order to cultivate the corn, they would have to learn humility, cooperation, respect, and earth stewardship. The Hopi clans migrated for countless generations, traveling in all four directions in search of the Center of the Earth. They finally settled on this arid plateau between the Rio Grande and the Colorado River, a place so barren they would be forced to depend on prayer for rain and food. Never again would they forget to be thankful to the Creator.

Indian country gateway

Begin your explorations of the 29,817-sq-mile (77,225-sq-km) **Navajo Nation ⑳** and much smaller adjoining **Hopi Reservation** north of Flagstaff, on Highway 89. In about 30 miles (50km), the elevation drops

Main attractions
CAMERON TRADING POST
NAVAJO NATIONAL MONUMENT
MONUMENT VALLEY
WINDOW ROCK
HUBBELL TRADING POST NATIONAL HISTORIC SITE
CANYON DE CHELLY NATIONAL MONUMENT
HOPI CULTURAL CENTER

LEFT: a Navajo girl in traditional clothing.
RIGHT: sandstone pillars, known as the Elephant Feet, off US 160.

from 7,000 to 6,000ft (2,100–1,800 meters), with a corresponding change in scenery from ponderosa pine forest to sagebrush rangeland dotted with pinyon and juniper. The road passes through the large volcanic field that gave birth to **Sunset Crater Volcano** and the 12,000ft (3,600-meter) **San Francisco Peaks**, revered by both the Navajo and Hopi. To the east are the pastel-hued badlands of the **Painted Desert** and the distant **Hopi Mesas**.

Trading post and dino tracks

Ahead is the **Little Colorado River**, which rises on Mount Baldy in the White Mountains and flows northwest to its confluence with the Colorado River in the Grand Canyon. A good view of the river can be had from the historic **Cameron Trading Post ㉑** (tel: 800-338-7385) left of the highway bridge, established by Mabel and Hubert Richardson in 1916. Still in the Richardson family, there's now a 65-room motel, an RV park, a gas station, a post office, and an art gallery. The original trading post retains

its authentic atmosphere, with creaky wood floors and dry and canned goods traded for rugs, jewelry, and the other Indian arts and crafts sold here. Skip the cheap souvenirs in the front rooms and head for the stone gallery, where big-ticket, museum-quality artifacts are sold. The dining room serves a tasty Navajo frybread taco (voted Arizona's state dish in a 1995 **Arizona Republic** poll). It's a good idea to get here early to avoid the tour bus lunch crowd and to obtain a room, if you wish to spend the night.

Drive east on Highway 160 through a spectacular landscape of rocks laid down during the time of the dinosaurs, 200 million years ago. Handmade signs lead north of the highway to the famous **Dinosaur Tracks** in the red Kayenta Formation, where, for a few dollars, a young Navajo guide will show you the three-toed tracks of dilophosaurus, a "running dinosaur." This dinosaur weighed 1,000 pounds (450kg), stood 8–10ft (2.4–3 meters) tall, and ran on its powerful hind legs. It used short forearms

BELOW: *kachina* dolls for sale at the Cameron Trading Post.

and clawed fingers for grasping and tearing apart its prey. Claw marks can be seen in the tracks.

Mormon way station

To the north is **Hamblin Ridge**, named for Mormon missionary Jacob Hamblin, who was sent by Church President Brigham Young to make contact with the Hopi and Navajo and assess the area's potential for colonization in 1858. Hamblin farmed here for several years, after befriending Hopi Chief Tuuvi, who subsequently converted to Mormonism. **Tuba City** ㉒, founded by Mormons in 1877, honors this chief. The town was used as a way station for Mormons traveling south from Utah to develop communities on the Colorado River and still displays the Lombardy poplars that typically mark such settlements.

Even before the Mormons arrived, Charles Algert had opened the **Tuba Trading Post** in 1870. This unusual octagonal trading post, built in 1906 to resemble a traditional Navajo hogan, is a good place to buy a Storm Pattern rug, the signature design of the Western Navajo Reservation, with symbols that vividly recall the landmarks and bright colors of this dramatic area.

The Mormons never obtained clear title to the land on which Tuba City was built, and in 1903 it was withdrawn by the US government and added to the Navajo reservation. In 1905, the Bureau of Indian Affairs (BIA) built the large two-story sandstone complex of Tuba City Boarding School. Schools like this one aimed to assimilate Indian children by taking them from their families, cutting their hair, forbidding them to speak their language, and enforcing military-style discipline.

Today, despite 50 years of educational reform and a renaissance in Indian culture, only half of the 300,000 tribal members speak Navajo, although reservation schools have been required to teach the language since 1984. Sixty percent of the Navajo Nation is now between the ages of 19 and 38 and exposed every day to the more materialistic Anglo

A mechanized coal line runs from the mines on Black Mesa.

BELOW: herding sheep across the dunes.

The Navajo tribe has finally embraced Indian gaming. Fire Rock Casino near Gallup, New Mexico, opened in 2008, and five more casinos are being fast-tracked, with Twin Arrows Casino and Resort, near Flagstaff, Arizona, opening in 2012. They are the first Indian casinos to be smoke free.

culture. Many, though by no means all, see little value in the old land-based traditions.

South of the highway, between Red Lake Trading Post and Kayenta is 8,210ft (2,500-meter) **Black Mesa**, the largest single landform in northern Arizona. Peabody Western Coal Company once operated two of the largest open pit strip mines in the country here, paying royalties to both the Navajo and Hopi tribes. Coal from the Black Mesa Mine went to the Mohave Generating Station on the Nevada–Arizona border through the Black Mesa Pipeline, which used a billion gallons of pristine aquifer water a year to slurry the coal more than 273 miles (440km) around the Grand Canyon.

In 2010, Peabody's mining permit was withdrawn by a federal judge after residents and environmental groups sued the Office of Surface Mining, citing inadequate permit documentation on environmental impacts to local springs. The Black Mesa Mine and other coal mines are now closed, taking with them 240 jobs and $20

million in revenues. To replace lost jobs and revenue, the Navajo Tribe has finally decided to embrace Indian gaming on the reservation, with two of four casinos opened in New Mexico and Arizona.

The ancient ones

North of Black Mesa, a 10-mile (16km) drive on Highway 564 leads through swirling pink slick-rock country to **Navajo National Monument** ㉓ (tel: 928-672-2700; daily May–Sept 8am–6pm, Oct–Apr 8am–5pm; free), which protects some of the largest and best preserved prehistoric cliff dwellings in the nation. Snugged into a 450ft (140-meter) -high alcove above **Tsegi Canyon**, the 135-room pueblo of **Betatakin** ("Ledge House") was built in AD 1250 and housed about 135 people for 50 years. It harmonizes so perfectly with its surroundings, visitors standing at the overlook at the end of the short Sandal Trail may overlook it at first. Free 5-mile (8km) ranger-led hikes to Betatakin are offered each morning in summer (weekends in

BELOW: Monument Valley Navajo Tribal Park.

winter) and are limited to 25 hikers. To avoid disappointment, stay in the monument's delightful 47-site campground and high-tail it to the visitor center first thing in the morning to pick up a ticket.

A second, larger pueblo, **Keet Seel**, lies 8 miles (13km) in the backcountry and requires a permit and challenging overnight hike to view. A limit of 20 visitors per day is strictly enforced; make reservations far ahead of your trip and be sure you're up to it. Elevation loss and regain is 1,000ft (300 meters) and the hike is very hot, dry, and exposed the whole way. Temperatures reach 100°F (38°C) in summer. Wear a hat, sunscreen, sunglasses, and sturdy boots, and carry high-energy food and at least a gallon (4 liters) of water. A ranger guides hikers through the ruins.

Monument Valley

Kayenta ㉔ is a large prosperous town with good food and lodging. It has benefited from its proximity to the Black Mesa Mine and **Monument Valley Navajo Tribal Park** ㉕ (tel:

435-727-5870; www.navajonation-parks.org; daily May–Sept 6am–8pm, Oct–Apr 8am–5pm; charge), the crown jewel of the Navajo tribal park system. Begin your tour at the newly remodeled visitor center, 20 miles (32km) north of Kayenta on Highway 163, which has exhibits about the Navajo, or Diné, way of life, a gift shop, restrooms, and water.

Monument Valley is the place to watch the world's most awe-inspiring sunrise illuminate the Owl, Mittens, Totem Pole, and other fiery sandstone landmarks familiar from such John Ford Westerns as *Stagecoach*, *She Wore a Yellow Ribbon*, and *Cheyenne*. Local Navajo pose for photos in traditional dress, but always ask first and offer payment. Families rely on tourism income.

A tour booklet has information on 11 scenic overlooks along the 17-mile (27km) unpaved scenic drive, including John Ford Point, the most famous view in the valley. You'll need to hire a Navajo guide to go into the backcountry. Horseback, van, and open Jeep tours usually include a visit to

Kachina dolls are a popular souvenir item, but remember that to the Hopi, they are sacred objects.

BELOW LEFT: enjoying the desert views in Monument Valley.

The Navajo–Hopi Land Dispute

The Hopi, whose mesa-top homes are surrounded by the larger Navajo Nation, have long claimed that the expansion of the Navajo reservation during the 19th and 20th centuries was made at the expense of Hopi land.

Tensions ran over in 1974, when the US Congress passed the Navajo–Hopi Relocation Act. The law, which divided nearly 2 million acres (800,000 hectares) between the tribes, was supposed to compel 11,000 Navajo and about 100 Hopi to leave homes they had known for generations. Many of the Navajo moved to new government housing; others resisted relocation.

In May 2009, President Obama repealed the Bennett Freeze, an order by BIA director Robert Bennett, following a lawsuit brought by the Hopi in 1966, preventing Navajos living on contested land from building new homes or making substantial repairs to old ones. For the next 40 years, the Bennett Freeze affected 8,000 Navajo living on a 1.5-million-acre (607,00-hectare) disputed area, only 10 percent of whom have running water and 3 percent have electricity.

By 2000, both tribes were directed by the federal district court to settle the dispute, resulting eventually in the removal of portions of the area from the freeze. In 2006, the courts returned most of the 1.5 million acres to the Navajo.

TIP

Shopping for Hopi
crafts? Try McGee's
Indian Art Gallery
(Highway 264; tel: 928-
738-2295; www.
hopiart.com) in Keams
Canyon or Monongya
Gallery (Highway 264;
tel: 928-734-2344)
near Oraibi.

the hogan of famed Navajo weaver Susie Yazzie and her family, and the chance to view some of the more than 200 Ancestral Pueblo ruins and petroglyphs in the valley. Bring your own food and water and cash to pay tour guides and tips for Navajos who pose for pictures. Tour arrangements can be made at the visitor center and local hotels inside and just outside the park.

Monument Valley isn't a valley at all but the Monument Upwarp, a geological uplift, or monocline, riddled with faults. It stretches from Comb Ridge and the San Juan River on the Arizona–Utah border to the north and Black Mesa to the south. Restless earth movements have created all kinds of strangely tilted cliffs (long mined for valuable minerals) and major landmarks. Looming on the northern horizon is 10,416ft (3,175-meter) **Navajo Mountain**, sacred to the Navajo and Hopi, and the twin buttes called the **Bear's Ears**. At the valley's southern perimeter is craggy **Agathla Peak**, a dark basaltic volcanic neck bared by erosion that once

marked the southern boundary of Ute territory. The only camping in the park is in Mitten View Campground, which has 100 sites. Gouldings Lodge runs a developed campground next to Oljato Mesa on the opposite side of the valley.

Four Corners

Highway 160 continues east from Kayenta on the south side of **Comb Ridge** (try to do this drive at dusk when the oblique rays of the sun turn the sandstone blood red). In 64 miles (103km), you'll reach historic **Teec Nos Pos Trading Post ㉖** (tel: 928-656-3224), a good place to view superb examples of large, intricately patterned Teec Nos Pos rugs. Many say the design is reminiscent of Persian rugs – with a price tag to match. A brief detour north takes you to the recently reconstructed **Four Corners Monument Navajo Tribal Park** (daily May–Sept 7am–8pm, Oct–Apr 8am–5pm; charge), the only place in the United States where you can stand simultaneously in four states – Utah, Arizona, New Mexico, and Colorado.

BELOW: the Hopi are known for crafting exquisite handmade pottery.

The monument is remote. It has a modest vistors center, native vendors, but no water or electricity.

Highway 191 heads south on the west side of the **Carrizo, Lukachukai,** and **Chuska Mountains**. So many of the reservation's overscaled, fantastically shaped rocks seem alive. Indeed, Navajo legends state that many of these formations were once fearsome, human-devouring monsters, slain by the mythic Hero Twins – Monster Slayer and Born for Water – thereby freeing the Navajo to pursue *hozho*, the Beauty Path in the Fourth World. The Chuskas, Lukachukais, and Carrizos are said to be the head, torso, and feet of the male god Yootzill.

Navajo capital

Northwest of **Window Rock ㉗** is **Fort Defiance**, the site of an 1851 fort built by the US Government to calm tensions between Navajo and newly arrived Anglo residents. By 1863, things had deteriorated to the degree that US Army Captain Kit Carson, under the orders of General James Carleton to "solve the problem,"

instigated a five-year scorched-earth campaign to drive out the Navajo. Homes and possessions were burned, fruit trees cut down, and livestock slaughtered. As many as 8,000 Navajo were sent on a 300-mile (480km) forced march to Bosque Redondo (Fort Sumner) on the Pecos River in New Mexico, while several thousand others hid in remote Canyon de Chelly, the Grand Canyon, and Monument Valley.

Although many Diné starved or died of disease in confinement, survivors of the Long Walk were eventually allowed to return to a fraction of their original homeland in 1868. They quickly rebounded in numbers and livestock holdings and began to thrive. The federal government built a Bureau of Indian Affairs (BIA) agency at Fort Defiance in 1868, followed by the first reservation boarding school.

A few miles to the south is **Window Rock**, the capital of the Navajo Nation. In 1923, after vast oil reserves were found underneath the Navajo Reservation, the federal government created the Navajo Tribal

A butte in the northern Navajo Reservation rises above bands of sedimentary rock.

BELOW: the Sandal Trail at Navajo National Monument leads to a dramatic view of the Betatakin cliff dwelling.

Council to facilitate negotiations of lease agreements with oil companies. Later discoveries of oil, gas, and uranium further concentrated the power of the tribal council, and eventually widespread corruption necessitated a complete reorganization in 1991 and again in 2010. It now has 24 delegates representing 110 chapter houses, or local councils, across the reservation, which meet four times a year (and on many special sessions) in the beautiful Navajo Nation Council Chambers. Delegates speak in Navajo while the council is in session, and visitors are welcome to observe the proceedings.

Navajos fought bravely in World War II, Korea, Vietnam, and other recent conflicts. Their finest hour may have been when Navajo Code Talkers foiled Japanese codebreakers by transmitting important communications among allies in Navajo. Commemorating the tribe's distinguished military service is the **Navajo Nation Veterans Memorial Park** in **Window Rock Tribal Park**, a pleasant spot for a picnic and a closer look at Window Rock itself, a geological opening in the Cow Springs Sandstone.

Stop at the Navajo Nation Parks and Recreation Department (tel: 928-871-6647, www.navajonationparks.org; daily) off Highway 264 to pick up information on Navajo tribal parks and visitor permits for hiking, camping, and fishing. Next door is the delightful **Navajo Nation Zoo and Botanical Garden** (tel: 928-871-6574; Mon–Sat 10am–5pm; free), which exhibits mountain lions, coyotes, Mexican wolves, churro sheep, and other native animals, interpreting them from the Navajo point of view. Well worth a look, too, is the adjoining **Navajo Nation Museum** (tel: 928-871-7941; Tue–Fri 8am–8pm, Mon 8am–5pm, Sat 9am–5pm; free) a gorgeous, oversize, hogan-style building with permanent and revolving exhibits

Historic trading post

Highway 264 leads west to **Ganado**, named for Navajo leader Ganado Mucho, a friend of trader Lorenzo Hubbell, who, in 1876, opened a trading post here. The still operational

BELOW: Navajo sheep herders in Monument Valley.

Hubbell Trading Post National Historic Site ㉘ Tel: 928-755-3475; daily Apr–Sept 8am–6pm, Oct–Mar 8am–5pm; charge) is a fine place to learn about the important role of trading posts in the late 1800s.

Hubbell became a powerful political figure in Arizona, hosting Theodore Roosevelt and other dignitaries. He is best remembered, though, as a loyal friend and mentor to the Navajo, whom he encouraged to make heavier, better designed rugs and to eschew new artificial dyes from back east in favor of natural dyes. The trading post is known for the Ganado Red blanket, a bright-red design with a diamond or cross in the center. Pottery, baskets, and renderings of rug designs by famous artists hang in the Hubbell Home next door. Daily tours are limited to 15 people. Navajo rug weavers and silversmiths demonstrate in the visitor center. There is an excellent gift shop. Arts and crafts auctions, held in May and October at the trading post, should not be missed if you are in the area. Rugs, katsinas, and other items can be purchased at reasonable prices.

Sacred canyons

About 30 miles (50km) north of Ganado, off Highway 191, is **Chinle**, headquarters of 130-sq-mile (340-sq-km) **Canyon de Chelly National Monument** ㉙ (tel: 928-674-5500; daily 8am–5pm; free), where the Rio de Chelly has carved 1,000ft (300-meter) -deep **Canyon de Chelly** and **Canyon del Muerto** into the Defiance Plateau. Two 35-mile-long (56km) scenic drives along the North and South Rims offer heart-stirring views into inner canyons and historic overlooks, such as the one above **Massacre Cave**, where 90 men and 25 women and children were massacred by Spanish Lieutenant Antonio de Narbona in 1805. The 2.5-mile (4km) **White House Trail** down Chinle Wash is the only route accessible without a Navajo guide. It leads to the multilevel pueblo cliff dwelling called **White House**. These canyons were home to Ancestral Pueblo farmers for centuries before the arrival of the Navajo. The trail is a wonderful introduction to this most beautiful of Southwest canyons. Swallows swoop

The Cameron Trading Post is a good place to shop for textiles, arts, and crafts.

BELOW: Spider Rock in Canyon de Chelly.

A Navajo girl, c.1910, in traditional skirt and velveteen blouse.

down to the wash from the clifftops. Raven caws rend the silence. And in summer, you'll encounter Navajo residents tending corn near hogans on the canyon floor.

If you have a four-wheel-drive vehicle, consider hiring a Navajo guide who can accompany you deeper into the canyons to see cliff dwellings like **Antelope Ruin**, **First Ruin**, and **Junction Ruin**, remarkable rock art on canyon walls from the Ancestral Pueblo, Spanish, and Navajo eras, and stunning formations like **Spider Rock**, a sandstone spire that rises 800ft (240 meters) from the canyon floor. Guides are available at the 1902 Thunderbird Lodge, a beautiful historic building with lodgings, reasonably priced rugs and other artworks, and a popular cafeteria. Half- and whole-day tours in large, jostling open-air vehicles (jokingly referred to as "shake-and-bakes") also depart from here.

Hopi homeland

BELOW: Navajo National Monument.

Highway 264 continues west to the 1.5 million-acre (607,028-hectare) **Hopi Reservation** ㉚, a series of 12 compact, autonomous stone villages atop windswept **First**, **Second**, and **Third Mesas**, and **Moenkopi**, several miles to the west, near Tuba City. The Hopitu, the "peaceful people," are the descendants of the Ancestral Puebloan culture, which they call Hisatsinom. A proud, private people, the Hopi live a very different kind of life than their Navajo neighbors, whose larger reservation surrounds theirs. Their east-facing villages, which house about 10,000 Hopi, have changed little since late Pueblo times. Hopi men dry-farm untilled plots of corn, melons, squash, and other crops at the base of the cliffs and in terraces that catch the scant 10 inches (25cm) of rain that falls here each year. Women make pottery and baskets. Children play in dusty streets. Visiting the villages is about as close to stopping time as you may ever experience – which is, of course, its greatest attraction to travelers and, ironically, one of the biggest threats to the Hopi way of life.

It is believed that the Bear Clan was the first to arrive on the mesas. In time, other clans arrived from their

migrations, and each was asked to contribute a different skill or ceremony to ensure the well-being of people on earth. From this, a complex seasonal ceremonial calendar was devised, with sun priests in each village determining the timing of ceremonies based on the positions of the sun, moon, and planets.

The most important ceremony of the year is the Niman, or Home Dance, in July, when the *kachinas*, serving as supernatural intermediaries between the Creator Spirit and the people of Earth, return to their winter home in the San Francisco Peaks after blessing the crops and bringing rain. The hypnotic singing and dancing of the *kachinas* symbolize the harmony of good thought and deed necessary for a balanced life and to bring the blessing of rain.

Sacred dances

Hopi dances are deeply spiritual and should be accorded the same respect as any other religious event. Dancers are required to undergo extensive preparations for their roles. Spectators have a role, too: they contribute their prayers to the successful completion of the dance's mission. Disrespect by outsiders means that some dances have been closed to non-Hopis. If you are lucky enough to attend a dance, both men and women should dress modestly; refrain from talking, asking questions, or following the *kachinas*; and never photograph, sketch, videotape or record the dances in any other way. Information on current dances is available at the **Hopi Cultural Center** (tel: 928-734-2401; Mon–Fri 8am–5pm, Sat–Sun 9am–3pm, closed weekends in winter; charge for museum) on Second Mesa, the best place to orient yourself with the reservation.

Artistic specialties

Inside the cultural center is the **Hopi Museum**, which has modest but effective displays on Hopi art and culture. Each mesa specializes in a particular craft. First Mesa is known for its pottery, which women coil by hand, smooth with a polishing stone, and fire outdoors, usually with dung. The pots are then hand-painted with

White House Ruin, at the bottom of Canyon de Chelly, can be reached via a steep trail from the rim.

BELOW: Hopi women grinding corn in 1906.

Blue corn is a stable of traditional Hopi cooking.

intricate designs using fine yucca-fiber brushes and natural paints. Second and Third Mesas are renowned for basketry, one variety made of woven wicker, the other of coiled yucca. Kachina dolls, perhaps the best known of the Hopi crafts, are made by craftsmen on all the mesas and carved from cottonwood roots. Hopi silversmiths specialize in the distinctive overlay style, although a number of talented jewelers are now branching off into inlay and channel work with turquoise, jet, coral, shell, and other semiprecious stones, and a few jewelers work with gold settings. Many craftspeople work out of their homes and sell directly to the public.

The cultural center offers tours that include workshops, craft stores, villages, and other places of interest. The villages of **Shungopavi** (home of artist Fred Kabotie, who painted the mural inside the Grand Canyon's Desert View Tower), **Shipaulovi**, and **Mishongnovi** all feature dances.

The 33-room motel next to the Hopi Cultural Center (tel: 928-734-2401) fills up quickly in summer. A restaurant serves all-American fare as well as Hopi specialties, such as paper-thin blue-corn *piki* bread and traditional stews, though these will seem bland to most palates. The blue-corn pancakes are the best bet. You can also stay at **Keams Canyon**, an administrative town east of the Hopi Mesas. Before 1860, it was known to the Hopi as Peach Orchard Springs. It was renamed in honor of English trader Thomas Keam, who established a trading post there in 1875 and defended the Hopi from repressive government practices.

Ancient villages

Behind Keams Canyon is the abandoned 12th-century village of **Awatovi** on Antelope Mesa. Awatovi was the only Hopi village to be converted by Spanish missionaries, who built a church here in 1629. In 1680, the Hopi joined their New Mexican Pueblo neighbors and killed or exiled the Spanish. When the mission was re-established in 1700, the Hopi grew so angry over the continued Christian influence, they destroyed Awatovi,

BELOW: Hopi cornfields sprawl around the village of Moenkopi.
BELOW RIGHT: Navajo riders gallop through Canyon de Chelly.

massacred all the men of the village, and removed the women and children to other villages. You'll need a permit and a Hopi guide to visit.

Of all the Hopi villages, be sure not to miss **Walpi**, atop First Mesa. A traditional village, with no running water or electricity, residents live much as they have since prehistoric times. The village may be entered only with a Hopi guide on free 40-minute walking tours that leave from Ponsi Hall in **Sichomovi** or from the tourist booth at the Walpi parking lot. Interestingly, **Hano**, the first village you reach, is not Hopi; it's a Tewa village built by people from the Rio Grande region of New Mexico, who sought refuge here during an unsuccessful revolt against the Spanish in 1696. The village at the base of the mesa is **Polacca** – also a latecomer – made up of residents of the three villages on First Mesa.

Old Oraibi, on Third Mesa, constructed in 1125, is often dubbed the oldest continuously inhabited community in the United States. The ruins of a Spanish mission built in 1629 are visible north of the village. In 1900, Old Oraibi had one of the reservation's largest populations (800), but disputes between chiefs caused many to leave. In the first major dispute, in 1906, two leaders staged a "push-of-war" contest, where two groups pushed against each other until one side crossed a line marked in the dust.

The loser, You-ke-oma, left with his followers and established **Hotevilla**, 4 miles (6.5km) away. Eventually, some tried to return to Old Oraibi, but were ousted again in 1909. They settled at a new site called **Bacavi**, opposite Hotevilla. Other residents moved to join New Oraibi, at the foot of the mesa, otherwise known as **Kykotsmovi**.

Today, Kykotsmovi is the location of the modern Hopi tribal government, which has itself been the source of a continuing conflict among the traditionally self-determined villages ever since it was created by the federal government in the 1930s. "One is not born Hopi," explains one tribal member, when asked what it means to be Hopi. "One becomes Hopi."

"We walk in our moccasins upon the Earth and beneath the sky. As we travel on life's path of beauty, we will live a good life and reach old age."

– Navajo Blessing

RESTAURANTS

Prices for a three-course dinner per person, excluding tax, tip, and beverages:
$ = under $20
$$ = $20–45
$$$ = $45–60
$$$$ = over $60

Blue Coffee Pot
US 160/US 163, Kayenta
Tel: 928-697-3396 $
The food is nothing special at this diner, although you'll find Navajo tacos and mutton stew. The building has more character than most establishments in town, and it's a good place to meet locals.

Garcia's Restaurant
Holiday Inn – Canyon de Chelly, Indian Route 7, Chinle
Tel: 928-674-2511 $
There's Southwestern and American food and a few Navajo specialties at this well-maintained restaurant near Canyon de Chelly National Monument.

Hopi Cultural Center Restaurant
Second Mesa
Tel: 928-734-2401 $
The most interesting items here are Hopi piki bread (paper thin and cooked on a griddle), lamb stew, and blue-corn pancakes.

Quality Inn Navajo Nation Capital
48 Highway 264, Window Rock
Tel: 928-871-4108 $
A favorite meeting place for locals. Navajo tacos and local specialties, and standard American diner food.

Stagecoach Dining Room
Goulding's Lodge, Monument Valley
Tel: 435-727-3231 $
The lodge's dining room, about 5 miles (8km) west of Monument Valley, has gorgeous views of the park and a collection of movie memorabilia. Solid American fare and Navajo tacos.

Thunderbird Lodge
Chinle
Tel: 928-674-5841 $
This old stone trading post now serves as a hotel and cafeteria. The food is cheap and tends to be greasy.

The View Restaurant
The View Hotel, Monument Valley
Tel: 435-727-5555 $–$$
If only you could eat the scenery at this stunningly located restaurant. Don't expect too much from the food and you won't be disappointed. Try local dishes like the Navajo taco sampler and New Mexico red chilli posole and pork dish.

American Indian Art: a Buyer's Guide

Jewelry, pottery, and other artworks made by Arizona's native people are things of beauty, and, in some cases, good investments

The quality of Indian craftsmanship varies from artist to artist and from piece to piece. Obviously, the finer the workmanship, design, and materials, the more a piece is worth. And Indian arts and crafts can be very expensive indeed, priced in the tens of thousands of dollars. While it's true that beauty is in the eye of the beholder – and that it is sometimes the imperfections of a work that make it most endearing – keep in mind a few points when judging arts and crafts.

Jewelry

Most Navajo and Hopi jewelry is made with silver and semiprecious stones. The Hopi are known for the "overlay" style in which a design is cut out of a sheet of silver and welded onto a blackened layer below. The Navajo are best known for their work with silver and turquoise and such distinctive forms as "squash blossom" necklaces and concha belts.

Ask what kind of silver you are buying. If it is sterling, there should be a stamp on the back. Nickel silver, a lower grade alloy, is also sometimes used.

Ask the seller to identify the types of stones that are used. Be especially careful of turquoise; various forms of mock turquoise can fool an inexperienced eye. Jewelry should look clean and finished. Check the piece for file marks, sloppy soldering, and other irregularities. Check the stones for cracks, pits or discoloration, and make sure the settings are adequate to hold the stones.

Pottery

Traditional Indian pottery is made by hand without a potter's wheel, painted with natural dyes, and fired over an open flame. The first thing you should ask about pottery is whether it is handmade or manufactured and made from local or commercial clay. Because the price of handmade pottery is so high, manufactured pots have become quite common. They are often handpainted in the traditional way and – so long as you know what you're buying – can be quite beautiful. Most Indian vendors make a point of distinguishing between handmade and manufactured pottery. Gift shops may not always be so scrupulous. Manufactured pots and pots made from commercial clay tend to be lighter in color and weight and uniform in size and shape.

If you're shopping for handmade pottery, look for a graceful, symmetrical form, fairly thin walls, and precise, neatly applied decoration. As always, watch out for irregularities: cracks, discoloration, bumps, or pits in the clay, lopsidedness, slanted or uneven decorations. Keep in mind that firing clouds, which usually appear as dark smudges, are sometimes quite desirable, even though many potters consider them a problem.

LEFT: Navajo sandpainting. **RIGHT:** a pictorial-style Navajo rug. **ABOVE:** bracelet by Hopi artist Charles Loloma. **ABOVE RIGHT:** the Heard Museum in Phoenix has one of the country's best collections of Native American art.

Basketry

Fine, handmade baskets are quite rare these days, but a few Indian people still produce exquisite traditional work. First of all, make sure you are buying an American Indian basket. Imports have found their way into the Southwest and occasionally crop up next to genuine American Indian work.

There are basically two types of basketry: coiled and woven. In both cases, look for tight, even, and sturdy construction, a pleasing shape, and clear and even designs. To test the tightness of the weave, hold the basket up to the light. You should also check how the basket was started; the first coil should not stick out or be loose.

Weaving

Again, be absolutely sure you are buying Indian work. The popularity of Navajo rugs has created an entire industry of imitations. A few Navajo weavers still do their own washing, carding, dyeing, and spinning, but most buy prepared wool. Some use a mixture of commercial products and traditional techniques. In any case, the finished product should be tightly woven, with a "balanced tension" of design and color.

The rug or blanket should have a smooth texture and the corners should not curl. It should also have fairly even edges (all four corners should meet when folded). Ask if the rug is 100 percent wool. Some weavers will use cotton or synthetic fibers in the warp. You should also know if the dyes are vegetal, commercial, or both. Commercial dyes tend to give brighter, more saturated colors. Vegetal dyes are subtler and made by hand.

Kachina carving

Although most often associated with the Hopi, *kachina* dolls are also made by other Pueblo people as well as by the Navajo. The most valuable *kachina* dolls are carved from a single piece of cottonwood root. Less expensive pieces may have separate arms or legs and possibly leather, feather, or other adornments attached to the figure. Most reputable dealers will tell you if the figure is Hopi-made. Many people feel that Navajo *kachinas* are less authentic, but considering the high price of Hopi work, Navajo work may be a reasonable option. As with any purchase, let your eyes, conscience, and wallet be your guide.

CENTRAL ARIZONA

Phoenix, the state's urban heart, anchors a
region of varied charms

Phoenix and its suburbs, known collectively as the
Valley of the Sun, form the nucleus of central Arizona.
Built upon the bones of an ancient Hohokam settlement, the city has grown from a drowsy, rough-and-ready
low-desert outpost to a booming metropolis of nearly 1.45
million souls.

Phoenix's reputation as a cultural lightweight is
most assuredly changing, and the city is becoming a
vibrant center for arts, culture, education, and restaurants and accommodations with a strong local character and world-class chops. The metro area now has a
well-used light rail system connecting far-flung areas of
the valley, two major sports venues, several architecturally acclaimed performing arts centers, and a cluster
of new and expanding renowned museums, theaters, parks, shops. Gourmet restaurants in the restored
downtown area have also given the city a much-needed
center of gravity.

Beyond the Valley of the Sun is a region that too many
travelers overlook in their dash to the Grand Canyon. In
the White Mountains, for example, you may hardly suspect
you're in Arizona at all. Ponderosa pine and Douglas fir
tower above you, cool breezes tousle your hair, and cold
streams feed the headwaters of the Salt River.

To the northwestare the red-rock formations of Sedona, whose reputation for "spiritual hot spots," known as vortexes, and trendy shopping
have made it a popular weekend getaway. It's about 50 miles (80km) and
yet another distinct set change to historic Jerome, a former rough-and-
tumble mining town.

Far to the west is Arizona's "West Coast," a 350-mile (560km) -long
water world with resort towns, wildlife refuges, and an abundance of
boating and fishing. There's also the state's second most popular tourist
attraction, the London Bridge, which, as an extravagant marketing gim-
mick, was shipped to the desert brick by brick and rebuilt on the banks
of Lake Havasu.

PRECEDING PAGES: Old Route 66, near Oatman. **ABOVE LEFT:** London Bridge, relocated
to Havasu City. **ABOVE RIGHT:** Robson House on Heritage Square.

ARIZONA'S WEST COAST

The Colorado River forms a 350-mile (560km) coastline on the state's western border, with palm-shaded beaches, excellent boating and fishing, wildlife refuges, and, improbably, London Bridge

It seems a misnomer at first. After all, Arizona's "west coast" is far from any ocean, in a desert so hot and dry that rain often evaporates before it can reach the ground. In the eyes of newcomers, this harsh landscape may seem completely devoid of life. Yet first impressions can be deceptive. There are, in fact, many life-forms that thrive here, including humans, along the all-important coastline of the **Colorado River**.

The Hualapai, Yavapai, Mohave, Quechan, Chemehuevi, Cocopa, and Maricopa cultures flourished here for millennia, hunting and gathering wild foods as well as cultivating gardens. Descendants of some of these early residents remain, commingling with Hopi and Navajo who have migrated from northeastern Arizona. The secret of their survival is the Colorado's delivery of the region's most precious commodity – water.

In 1540, Hernando de Alarcón became the first European to sail the Colorado. The Spaniard navigated its broad delta and, near present-day Yuma, met Quechan Indians with facial tattoos "covering their faces almost entirely" and ear piercings "in which they placed beads and shells." Juan de Oñate pushed farther upstream 64 years later, encountering the Mohave and other tribes. In 1699,

the peripatetic Father Eusebio Kino crossed the river and paused to name it. *Colorado* means "red" in Spanish, a reference to the iron-laden silt the waterway historically carried from the north.

Troubled crossing

Over the next two centuries, the Spanish developed trails that linked their settlements in California and New Mexico. Following their official exit from the area in the early 1800s, western Arizona drew Mexican farmers and American adventurers. In

Main attractions

LAKE MEAD NATIONAL
    RECREATION AREA
CHLORIDE
KINGMAN
OATMAN
ROUTE 66
SKYWALK
LAKE HAVASU CITY
LONDON BRIDGE
KOFA NATIONAL WILDLIFE REFUGE
YUMA

LEFT: the beach at Lake Havasu City.
RIGHT: a gift shop on Route 66.

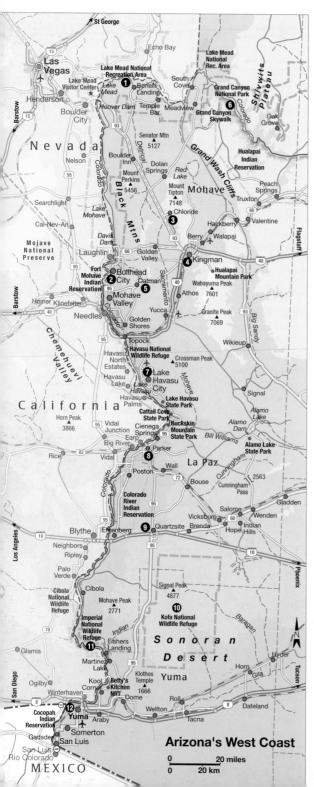

Arizona's West Coast

0   20 miles
0   20 km

1849, thousands of fortune-seekers used Yuma Crossing, where the Gila Trail met the Colorado, en route to California's goldfields. This had a devastating effect on the Quechans, who had historically controlled the ford and gathered food nearby. Americans took over the crossing, established a fort, and allowed their livestock to eat most of the mesquite beans that Quechans depended on for sustenance. Similar incursions to the north routed the Mohave people from their homelands.

Eventually, the mighty Colorado was tamed and the remaining indigenous people were granted reservations along the river: Fort Mohave, Chemehuevi, Colorado River, and Yuma. Now that the Colorado is the most harnessed river in the United States, thousands of acres of farmland have been developed along its course with the use of elaborate irrigation systems.

The lure of water

Today, Arizona's West Coast is an aquatic playground in a land that averages a mere 3 inches (8cm) of rain annually. Snowbirds and retirees are attracted by the year-round sunshine, carefree lifestyle, easy access to casinos, and endless outdoor recreation. Thousands of vacationers converge from Las Vegas, Phoenix, and Los Angeles, most heading for the reservoirs formed by a series of dams along what is now a tame stretch of the once-unpredictable Colorado.

Fortunately, at least a small percentage of the river's extraordinary biodiversity is protected at several wildlife preserves, which maintain vital wetland habitats used by migrating birds as well as resident flora and fauna.

Three east–west interstate highways traverse western Arizona and connect it with the Southwest's major cities. Interstate 40 bisects the state via Kingman as it connects central California with Flagstaff and points east; Interstate 10 links Phoenix and Los Angeles through Quartzsite;

Interstate 8 flows through Yuma, half-way between San Diego and Phoenix. In the northwest, US Highway 93 links Kingman with Las Vegas, Nevada. State Route 95 follows a north–south axis, roughly parallel to the Colorado, from Davis Dam (straddling the border with Nevada) through Parker and Yuma to Mexico.

Recreational oasis

Start your drive in Arizona's northwest corner, along US Highway 93 at **Lake Mead National Recreation Area ❶**, which encompasses the largest reservoir in the United States (twice the size of Rhode Island). Created by the impoundment of the Colorado River at **Hoover Dam**, Lake Mead extends more than 100 miles (160km), nearly into the Grand Canyon. The reservoir, which straddles the Arizona–Nevada line and is stocked with gamefish, has four marinas and more than 500 miles (800km) of shoreline that have made it a sun-drenched mecca for those keen on boating, water-skiing, fishing, sunbathing, picnicking, and RV or tent camping. Boats and sports equipment can be rented in many locations, and you'll also find numerous tackle shops, restaurants, motels, and groceries.

Popular scenic boat tours of Lake Mead and Hoover Dam are offered by park concessionaire Lake Mead Cruises (tel: 702-293-6180). Tours leave from **Boulder Beach**, 2 miles (3km) north of Highway 93 on Nevada State Route 166. The three-deck steamboat *Desert Princess* makes two-hour brunch, midday, and dinner cruises from the main **Lake Mead Cruises Landing** on Route 166. From the Arizona side, the reservoir is accessible from Highway 93 at **Temple Bar** (via Temple Bar Road) and **Meadview** (via Dolan Springs-Meadview Road).

In 2011, the **Lake Mead Visitor Center** closed for a year-long renovation. Visit the temporary visitor center (601 Nevada Way, Boulder City; tel: 702-293-8990; daily 8am–4.30pm) for maps, brochures, and information on desert ecosystems and dam construction.

Due to an extended drought, water levels in the Colorado River and

From March to September is the peak boating season on Lake Havasu.

BELOW: the Lake Mead National Recreation Area.

Golf is a popular sport in Arizona because of the consistently warm weather.

Lake Mead continue to fall, jeopardizing marinas. Lake Mead Marina, the main marina, has now been moved to Hemenway Harbor and has become part of Las Vegas Boat Harbor.

Without Hoover Dam's water and power, not only would Lake Mead not exist but the neon-lit oasis of Las Vegas (30 miles/48km northwest) would have remained a tiny settlement. The structure is the keystone of the Colorado River Reclamation Project, which serves millions of users in Nevada, Arizona, and California. US Highway 93 passes over this edifice, at 726ft (221 meters) the highest concrete arch dam in the Western Hemisphere. Hoover was completed in 1935 (by 5,000 men working in 24-hour shifts) and can retain some 30 million acre-feet of water. The spectacular new Mike O'Callahan-Pat Tillman Memorial Bridge opened in 2010 and re-routes traffic off the dam, allowing you a great view of the structure as you cross.

Hoover Dam Visitor Center (tel: 702-494-2517; daily 9am–6pm; charge) has a parking garage (daily 8am–6pm; charge), exhibits, and a viewing area. Powerplant tours last 30 minutes, dam tours last an hour. Both are offered several times each day except Thanksgiving and Christmas. Motorized raft trips can be taken from a dock below the dam to and from Willow Beach, about 20 miles (32km) downstream. Due to heightened security, visitors must pass through a security checkpoint at the visitor center. Cameras, purses, and small-size backpacks are permitted.

Services are available in nearby **Boulder City**, the Nevada town created by the US Bureau of Reclamation for those who built and continue to manage the dam. (Boulder is the dam's original name, changed in 1947 to honor former President Herbert Hoover.) About 50 miles (80km) below Hoover is **Davis Dam**, one of three smaller dams that control the river's flow along the rest of Arizona's West Coast. Davis creates **Lake Mohave**, a part of Lake Mead National Recreation Area accessible from both banks but relatively undeveloped.

Boom and bust

Below Davis Dam are the twin cities of **Bullhead City** ❷, Arizona, and **Laughlin**, Nevada, about 20 miles (32km) east of US Highway 95. As recently as the 1980s, these communities barely existed. They have since morphed into a bridge-connected metropolis with more than 11,000 hotel rooms, scores of restaurants, and, in Laughlin, 11 major casino-resorts, including a few on old-fashioned river-boats. These cities provide gaming and other amenities (notably golf) to those who don't want to drive another 100 miles (160km) to Las Vegas or who simply prefer a less glitzy atmosphere.

Switching from the modern to the historic, the colorful mining legacy of western Arizona is well preserved in **Chloride** ❸, 20 miles (32km) north of Kingman on US Highway 93 and another 4 miles (6.5km) east via Chloride Road. Home to 2,000 people during its 1860s boom, Chloride's name derives from the silver-chloride ore extracted from mines in the nearby **Cerbat Mountains**. Only 250 residents remain in the rustic, frontier-style buildings, but at the end of June each year the town comes alive during Old Miners Day. Festivities are marked by burro (donkey) rides, a swap meet, a crafts fair, and a parade. Gunfights are held every Saturday at noon (every other Saturday in summer). For more information, contact the Chloride Chamber of Commerce (tel: 928-565-4251).

Honeymoon suite

The sprawling city of **Kingman** ❹ extends from the intersection of Interstate 40 and US Highway 93, 48 miles (77km) east of the California border in the brown plain of the **Hualapai Valley**. Established as a turquoise-mining center and railroad stop, the town now mainly serves highway travelers and retirees. Learn about the region's history at the worthwhile **Mohave Museum of History and Arts** (400 W. Beale St; tel: 928-753-3195; Mon–Fri 9am–5pm, Sat–Sun 1–5pm; charge). See a detailed replica of a Mohave village, an impressive collection of carved turquoise, and an entire room dedicated to the

> **TIP**
>
> Look for colorful murals painted by artist Roy Purcell on boulders outside Chloride. Follow Tennessee Avenue into the hills about a mile from town.

BELOW LEFT: an iconic star for an iconic road.

Route 66: The Mother Road

For generations, US Route 66 drew hundreds of thousands of travelers to the Southwest, providing a concrete trail between Los Angeles and Chicago for those in search of a better life. Most of Route 66 was destroyed to create Interstate 40, and many communities along the highway nearly died. But nostalgia and shrewd promotion revived interest in "the Mother Road," now commemorated in places like Kingman and Flagstaff, where Route 66 is still the main thoroughfare.

The longest remaining stretch of the highway is open between Topock (east of the Colorado River) and Ash Fork. Besides spectacular desert scenery, Route 66 provides access to the Hualapai Indian Reservation on the edge of the Grand Canyon. Near Peach Springs is Grand Canyon Caverns, where you can take an elevator 21 stories into the earth for a 45-minute tour (tel: 928-422-3223). You can also spend the night underground here, in the newly opened Cavern Suite, the deepest motel room in the world. A fun stop in Seligman is the Snow Cap Drive-In, a popular hamburger joint for some 40 years.

The Route 66 museum celebrating this stretch of highway is located at the Kingman Visitor Center (tel: 928-753-9889). Nearby is Mr. D's Route 66 Diner (106 Andy Devine), a 1950s-era eatery filled with memorabilia from the road's glory days.

Water Issues

The greatest challenge for the Colorado River in modern times is quenching the thirst for power of a burgeoning populace in the desert Southwest

"Too thick to drink, too thin to plow." That's what they used to say about the Colorado River. Not anymore. The 1,450-mile (2,330km) –long Colorado, rising in the Rocky Mountains and draining an area the size of France, has been tamed – dammed, diverted for irrigation and power, and so heavily used by the states it flows through that it is no longer a river by the time it passes over the Mexican border. The river once known as the Grand is now a managed resource, not the wild, churning, seasonally flooding Great Unknown that so intimidated John Wesley Powell's 1869 and 1871 river expeditions.

Historically, the Colorado was a warm river that swelled into a red, silty, roaring froth when snow in the high country melted. Two-thirds of its volume comes from the Green River, which confluences with the Colorado in what is now Canyonlands National Park in Utah. The Colorado then rages in a

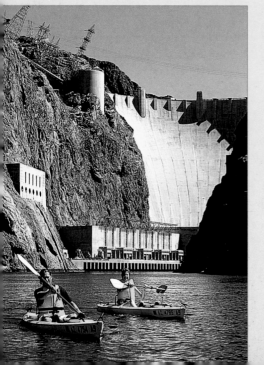

series of whitewater rapids through the narrow confines of Cataract Canyon.

Plants and animals in the Grand Canyon, carved by the Colorado, evolved to deal with seasonal surges in the river. Humpback chub appeared in the warm waters of the Colorado some 3–5 million years ago, when the river first cut through the layer-cake strata of the uplifted Colorado Plateau. Now, warm-water fish like the chub and razorback sucker struggle to survive in the colder waters exiting Glen Canyon Dam, which has created Lake Powell. In the words of environmental analyst Stephen Corothers, the Grand Canyon is now a "naturalized" environment rather than a natural one, meaning that the ecosystem has changed to suit man-made conditions.

The greatest challenge today is to provide for the needs of a burgeoning Southwest population in the nation's fastest-growing region while conserving its natural habitats, such as those of the Grand Canyon and the lower Colorado. Daily surges in demand for power in large metropolitan centers like Phoenix once drove dam releases, creating damaging high and low river levels. This has been improved by the passage of the 1992 Grand Canyon Protection Act, which requires the dam's operators to smooth out flows to ensure that the natural habitat downstream is not subjected to extreme fluctuations.

On the other hand, infrequent great floods were once a feature of the Colorado and may have a place in the downstream environment. In 1996, the floodgates at Glen Canyon were opened to allow the river to run unchecked through the Grand Canyon. Beaches were renewed, old vegetation whisked away, and habitat improved in the week-long flood.

As former Secretary of the Interior Bruce Babbitt put it: "When the dam was going up in the 1950s, it never occurred to anybody that they needed to think about what would happen a hundred miles downstream because we tended to see the landscape as fragments and each one of them independent. What we've learned ... is that nature doesn't operate that way."

LEFT AND ABOVE: the Glen Canyon National Recreation Area on Lake Mead is a popular attraction.

memory of Kingman's most famous native son: "good guy" actor Andy Devine, who died in 1977. Nearby is the **Powerhouse Visitor Center** (120 W. Beale St; tel: 928-753-6106; daily 8am–5pm). The center has information about historic sites in the area and a Route 66 museum. Fourteen miles (23km) southeast is **Hualapai Mountain Park** (daily 5am–3pm; tel: 928-681-5700; charge), a pine-forested enclave that rises to 8,500ft (2,600 meters) above sea level, with scenic hiking trails, a campground, and picnic areas.

A scenic detour from Kingman takes you to the old mining town of **Oatman** ❺, 25 miles (40km) southwest on Historic Route 66 (Oatman Road). Oatman's single dusty street is lined with tourist-oriented curio shops, saloons, cafés, and hotels. Among the more venerable institutions is the ramshackle **Oatman Hotel** (Route 66, Oatman; tel: 928-768-4408), a virtual museum of century-old memorabilia where Hollywood legends Clark Gable and Carole Lombard spent their wedding night in 1939,

after getting hitched in Kingman. Wandering throughout the town are good-natured burros (a prospector's favorite helper), eager for hand-outs of carrots and similar goodies. Fake shoot-outs are staged on the main drag on weekends and holidays.

Skywalk

Kingman is a good base for visiting Grand Canyon West on the Hualapai Indian Reservation. The western end of the Grand Canyon, east of Hoover Dam (just before the Colorado River turns south along the state border to form the West Coast), offers a very different experience from the main Grand Canyon.

Grand Canyon West (tel: 888-868-9378; www.grandcanyonwest.com; daily, Apr–Sept 7am–7pm, Oct–Mar 8am–5pm) is aimed at tourists arriving from the West who want a quick visit to the Grand Canyon. Las Vegas in Nevada to the northwest, and Kingman and Peach Springs, both in Arizona off old Route 66, are all 2.5 hours away. Small commuter airlines offer day trips directly to Grand

Burros roam freely in the old mining town of Oatman; they are descendants of the animals once used by the miners.

BELOW: London Bridge is the second most popular tourist attraction in Arizona, after the Grand Canyon.

Canyon West Airport from Flagstaff
and Las Vegas. Scenic helicopter rides
are offered daily from the airport.

Hualapai Lodge (tel: 888-255-9550),
in the small tribal headquarters community of Peach Springs, is the only
lodging available on the reservation.
To see Grand Canyon West sights, you
will need to purchase a package tour,
available online or from the concierge
desk at the lodge. Packages include
entrance to Grand Canyon West, and
shuttle rides to Eagle Point, Guano
Point, and Hualapai Ranch. Diamond
Creek Road, the only road into the
canyon, is the main river takeout for
Grand Canyon river trips and may be
driven for a small fee. It is also used
by Hualapai river outfitter **The River
Runners** (tel: 888-868-9378), which
offers day-long whitewater trips that
include ground transportation, lunch,
and a helicopter tour (Mar–Oct only).

The main attraction at Grand
Canyon West is, of course, **Skywalk
❻**, a unique observation deck at
Eagle Point. Jutting 75ft (23 meters)
out from the canyon, the platform
is mostly made of 4-inch (10cm)
thick Plexiglass, allowing visitors a
clear (and vertiginous) view of the
Colorado River 4,000ft (1,200 meters)
below. The sleek structure has been
designed to withstand earthquakes
and 100mph (160kph) winds.

London Bridge

Follow Interstate 40 and State Route
95 for about 60 miles (95km) to the
south of Kingman to arrive at the
improbable "instant city" of **Lake
Havasu City ❼**, developed on the
Colorado River during the early
1960s by the late tycoon Robert
McCullough. McCullough's chain-saw
factory moved from here to Tucson
years ago but not before his town
acquired its greatest single attraction: **London Bridge**. Yes, the same
graceful, arched structure of granite
– quarried at Dartmoor in southwest
England – built in 1824 across the
River Thames in London, England.
When it was replaced in 1971, it was
sold for $2.5 million and shipped
in numbered pieces to the Arizona
desert, where it was reassembled on a
peninsula jutting into the lake.

Despite its unlikely relocation, this is an authentic piece of history: note the strafing scars left on the stones by German bombers during World War II. Next to the 900ft (275-meter) span, **English Village**, a tourist-oriented promenade of shops and restaurants decked out in an "old London" theme, has closed but three other shopping areas are open: Island Fashion Mall, just across from London Bridge; Historic Main Street on McCulloch Boulevard, the heart of Lake Havasu; and the Shops at Lake Havasu City on the north end of town.

Lake Havasu is home to more than 50,000 year-round residents, including many retirees. A full spectrum of water recreation, golf courses, tennis courts, and related services is available. Although you can hike up nearby **Crossman Peak**, most of the action is on Lake Havasu, a 45-mile (72km) -long artificial lake. Be advised that, like others on Arizona's West Coast, this reservoir is extremely popular with the spring-break crowd during March and April, when thousands of party-hungry college students arrive.

Those who favor somewhat more sedate pursuits may wish to visit nearby **Buckskin Mountain State Park**, **Bill Williams National Wildlife Refuge**, or **Lake Havasu National Wildlife Refuge**, each of which protect scenic areas and key ecosystems along this particular stretch of the river. The parks provide a mix of boat-launch ramps, campgrounds, swimming beaches, picnic areas, and hiking trails.

Parker Dam, which impounds the Colorado about 20 miles (32km) south of Lake Havasu City, is not as stunning as Hoover, although workers were required to dig an amazing 230ft (70 meters) into bedrock below the river in order to make the structure secure. Self-guided tours are no longer available at Parker Dam. However, visitors are welcome to park in the turnout on the California side of the dam and view the features and interpretive panels around the site. For more information, call 760-663-3712.

Another 15 miles (24km) downstream is the small town of **Parker 8**, headquarters of the **Colorado**

When London Bridge was moved from the United Kingdom to Arizona, it was disassembled stone by stone, shipped across the Atlantic Ocean, and then reassembled, at a cost of $7million.

BELOW: the Dixie Belle waits for passengers at a dock near the London Bridge.

Mohave Girl, by Edward Curtis, 1932. The tribe numbered about 6,000 people at the arrival of the first Europeans.

BELOW: canoeing is a popular activity on Lake Havasu.

River Indian Reservation, which extends about 40 miles (64km) south to **Ehrenberg** and across the border into California. The reservation is unusual in that it is open not only to those whose ancestors (mainly the Mohave and Chemehuevi) lived here traditionally but to members of other tribes whose homelands are hundreds of miles away. A complicated legal history has also resulted in a number of non-Indians owning land and living on the reservation. Residents derive much of their income either from farming or by catering to tourists attracted to **Lake Moovalya**, a reservoir below Parker Dam. Crowds here are smaller than those at Lake Havasu and Lake Mead but increase dramatically during spring break.

Parker is home to the **Colorado River Indian Tribes Museum** (Second and Mohave streets; tel: 928-669-9211, ext. 1335; Mon–Fri 8am–5pm, Sat 10am–3pm; voluntary donation), a terrific place to learn about the indigenous people who have made this part of Arizona their home.

The museum displays an impressive collection of baskets, pottery, jewelry, and historical artifacts. There's a craft shop, and a casino dominates the adjacent shopping center.

State Route 95 veers east of the river south of Parker and, 35 miles (56km) later, intersects Interstate 10 at **Quartzsite** ❾. This scruffy, unincorporated hamlet is home to about 3,300 year-round residents and 200,000 snowbirds, who migrate from the cold north in their RVs and mobile homes during the winter months. Most of these sun-worshippers alight in the surrounding desert, which is public land.

Rock show

Throughout the winter, Quartzsite's single main street is an amazing flea market, where a motley crew of vendors hawks everything from anvils to zithers. The season's biggest events, however, are the week-long **Quartzsite Powwow Rock and Mineral Show** (tel: 928-927-6325; free) and a series of smaller gem fairs which draw as many as a million visitors during January

and February. Sellers offer precious or collectible stones of every size, shape, and description. Concurrent events include a rodeo, parade, and camel and ostrich races. Despite their quirky independence, the encamped snowbirds organize themselves well enough to hold dances, hoedowns, and potluck dinners to which the public is invited.

Continuing south on State Route 95, the remote **Kofa** and **Castle Dome** ranges loom as jagged escarpments to the east. Much of this pristine desert is protected by 665,400-acre (269,000-hectare) **Kofa National Wildlife Refuge** ⑩ (tel: 928-783-7861), accessible via dirt roads and unimproved trails. Campers and backcountry hikers face primitive conditions and rough, waterless terrain but may be rewarded with a glimpse of some of the state's few remaining desert bighorn sheep. Rare California palm trees – the only palms native to Arizona – are found in the refuge's rugged, secluded canyons. Some botanists speculate that the palms were stranded here at the end of the last Ice Age.

Bordering the refuge is the military's **Yuma Proving Ground**. Secondary roads cross through this restricted area into **Cíbola** (tel: 928-857-3253) and **Imperial National Wildlife Refuges** ⑪ tel: 928-783-3371), which protect wetlands along the Colorado River north of Imperial Dam and Martínez Lake, offering birding, hiking, boating, fishing, hunting, and camping.

A sense of Yuma

State Route 95 returns to the Colorado at **Yuma** ⑫, a farming and military community with a population of just over 91,000 where an important ford has existed since long before Europeans first visited. The Spanish presence here was brief, terminated by an uprising of the native Quechan in 1781. A riverside fort on the California bank, now run as **Fort Yuma Quechan Museum** (tel: 760-572-0661; daily 8am–5pm; nominal charge) by the Quechan Tribe, was built to protect travelers five years before the area fell under United States control under the terms of the 1854 Gadsden Purchase.

"The thermometer failed to show the true heat because the mercury dried up. Everything dries; wagons dry; men dry; chickens dry; there is no juice left in anything, living or dead."

– J. R. Browne, 1864, on summer in Yuma

BELOW: Route 66 winds through the desert.

Hikers need to keep an eye open for snakes and scorpions.

This was followed by construction of the penitentiary that is now **Yuma Territorial Prison State Historic Park** (Prison Hill Road; tel: 928-783-4771; Thur–Mon May–Sept 9am–5pm, Oct–Apr 8am–3pm; charge). Known as the Hell Hole, the prison housed 3,069 convicts before its closure in 1909. Its best-known resident was Pearl Hart, the prison's only female inmate, sentenced to five years for robbery. She was released two years early when it was learned that she was pregnant, presumably by one of her guards.

Other attractions include **Yuma Quartermaster Depot State Historic Park** (201 N. 4th Avenue, Yuma; tel: 928-329-0471; Sept–May daily 9am–5pm, closed June–Aug Sun; charge), which preserves the original river ford and the quartermaster depot. Living-history demonstrations are offered by docents, recalling the bygone era when paddlewheel steamers plied the Colorado.

More information on Yuma Crossing National Historic Landmark can be found at outdoor exhibits in the newly opened **Pivot Point Interpretive Plaza** (daily 6am–11pm) in the restored historic riverfront area at the location where the first railroad train entered Arizona in 1877.

Ride the rails

Besides the state parks, day-trip options include boat rides, date farm and camel ranch tours, and the **Yuma Valley Railway** excursion train (tel: 928-782-9629; Jan–Mar Sat–Sun 1pm; Apr–May and Oct–Dec Sun 1pm; charge), a narrated, two-hour excursion in a 1922 Pullman coach featured in the film *Judge Roy Bean* that follows a 22-mile (35km) route downriver. Not a restaurant but a recreation site, **Betty's Kitchen** (past Laguna Dam, 14 miles/23km north of Yuma) offers hiking, birding, picnicking, and fishing in a lush, shady spot. A word of warning: this part of the Sonoran Desert is uncomfortably hot in summer, and many tourist businesses close – wisely – until relatively cooler weather returns in fall.

BELOW: Yuma City Hall has an imposing edifice.

RESTAURANTS

Prices for a three-course dinner per person, excluding tax, tip, and beverages:
$ = under $20
$$ = $20–45
$$$ = $45–60
$$$$ = over $60

Beale Street Brews
418 E. Beale Street, Kingman
$
The Beale Street Brews coffeehouse is a lovely, airy space, just perfect for a quick pick-me-up when you're passing through. They serve specialty coffee drinks, healthy fruit smoothies, teas, and home-made pastries from 6am to 6pm. Enjoy live music on Friday nights and an open-mic evening. On either side is an art gallery and the Cellar Door Wine Bar (see below), Kingman's first wine bar.

Big John's Steak 'n' Pub
717 N. Lake Havasu Avenue, Lake Havasu City
Tel: 928-453-5858
$
A long-time local favorite for its certified Angus beef burgers and lively sports-bar atmosphere. Try the burgers or surf 'n' turf specials.

Cellar Door Wine Bar
414 E. Beale Street, Kingman
Tel: 928-753-3885
$
Owned by the superbly bearded Scott Rhoades and his wife Nancy, both longtime teachers (hence the limited opening hours), the Cellar Door occupies an attractive space in historic downtown

Kingman. The food is strictly nibbles, but the gourmet cheeses and locally made bread are winners. The wine list showcases 140 reasonably priced, mostly Californian, wines, several premium beers, and non-alcoholic wines. They may also be purchased in the bottle shop. Entertainment includes live folk and bluegrass music, Saturday afternoon chess sessions, and wine tastings. Open Wed–Sat only.

Chretin's Mexican Food
505 E. 16th Street, Yuma
Tel: 928-782-1291
$
Filling, home-made Mexican specialties are the attraction at this no-frills restaurant, a big favorite with locals and visitors for more than five decades.

Garden Café
250 Madison Avenue, Yuma
Tel: 928-783-1491
$
Birdsong and the scent of lemon trees delight customers at this leafy oasis, which serves a delectable assortment of pancakes, quiches, salads, and tempting desserts.

Javelina Cantina
1420 McCulloch Boulevard, Lake Havasu City
Tel: 928-855-8226
$–$$
Expect a party atmosphere at this lively Mexican eatery, located near the London Bridge. Its spacious bar and patio are open year-round and popular for drinks.

Margaritas are the main draw, along with an extensive tequila menu. Soak it all up with fish tacos or a cool salad featuring exotic fruits and seafood.

Market Wine Bar Bistro
1501 S. Redondo Center Drive, Yuma
Tel: 928-373-6574
$$–$$$
Located in the Radisson Hotel, this popular bistro offers elegant dining with an emphasis on local and fresh. Former sous chef at the Arizona Biltmore in Phoenix, Matt Alleshouse offers his spin on gourmet comfort food, from beef tenderloin and roast lamb to halibut and free-range chicken pot pie. There are daily specials, weekly home-made Sunday dinners, occasional wine dinners, and local dates also make an appearance on the changing menu.

Mr D'Z Route 66 Diner
105 E. Andy Devine Avenue, Kingman
Tel: 928-718-0066
$
Flamboyant colors, doo-wop tunes, and lots of formica and chrome give this diner lots of kitsch appeal that perfectly suits the location on Route 66. The atmosphere is strictly cornball, but it's a good place for root beer, burgers, and fries.

OK Saloon and Road Kill Café
502 Route 66, Seligman
Tel: 928-422-3554
$
Friendly local café with added personality: there's a carved naked lady bar post, and they

collect dollar bills. The name is misleading: all the meat is fresh here. They make a mean barbecue sandwich.

River City Grill
600 W. Third Street, Yuma
Tel: 928-782-7988
$$–$$$
Global fusion cuisine using natural and grass-fed meat, wild seafood, and organic produce are hardly mainstream in Yuma, but this neighborhood bistro has made converts from far and wide. The menu offers great seafood specials, such as crab cakes, tequila snapper, seafood gumbo, and sushi; you'll also find burgers, steaks, salads and pastas. Open for lunch during the week and dinner nightly.

Shugrue's
1425 McCulloch Boulevard, Lake Havasu City
Tel: 928-453-1400
$$
Diners enjoy a view of London Bridge as they chow down on pasta, seafood, steak, and sandwiches. Food and service are consistently satisfying, and families appreciate the special children's menu.

Westside Lilo's Café
415 W. Chino, Seligman
Tel: 928-422-5456
$
Reliably good American fare and some German classics like schnitzel. Try the buffalo chicken sandwich or a huge burger. Popular with locals. Friendly service and live entertainment.

PHOENIX AND ENVIRONS

Summer heat can purge the mind of lucidity, but air-conditioning – and a strong economy – made the Valley of the Sun one of America's fastest-growing metropolitan areas

Widespread irrigation and post-World War II air-conditioning were primarily responsible for the growth of the modern metropolis of **Phoenix** ❶, which is now home to nearly 4.2 million people. With the arrival of the 57-mile (92km) metro light rail service, connecting communities in the Valley of the Sun, inroads are being made into Phoenix's near-total dependence on automobiles and its accompanying traffic headaches and smog.

Solar power, alternative fuels, and green building have become a *cause célèbre* for the city and some private developers. A citywide water conservation education program has reduced water usage by 20 percent in the past 20 years. Today, Phoenix uses just 3 percent groundwater from its aquifers – down from a high of 35 percent in the profligate 1980s; 90 percent of water greening up Phoenix's 200-plus golf courses, irrigating crops, and used in award-winning riparian habitat restoration projects is reclaimed. Drought-tolerant xeriscaping and water-catchment devices are, finally, the height of fashion.

Risen from the ashes

Long before modern Phoenix burst onto the scene, the Valley of the Sun was home to a prehistoric civilization well adapted to the harsh conditions of the Salt River Valley. As early as 500 BC, these people, the Hohokam, developed an intricate system of canals for irrigating fields of corn, beans, squash, and cotton. Remains of that ancient system were absorbed and expanded in 1868 by the Swilling Irrigation Canal Co., the first Anglo organization to stake claims in the long-deserted valley. The following year, their settlement was named Phoenix by an Englishman who saw a new civilization rising like the mythical bird from the ashes of the vanished Hohokam.

Main attractions
HERITAGE SQUARE
PHOENIX ART MUSEUM
HEARD MUSEUM
ARIZONA BILTMORE HOTEL
PUEBLO GRANDE
MUSEUM OF MUSICAL INSTRUMENTS
TALIESIN WEST
COSANTI
APACHE TRAIL

PRECEDING PAGES: the Superstition Mountains.
LEFT: golfing at the Pheonician Resort in Scottsdale. **RIGHT:** a young mariachi musician.

Frank Lloyd Wright left an indelible mark on the Phoenix cityscape.

What rose from the ashes was an aggressive ranching community that catered to miners and military outposts. Canals were extended through the alluvial valley, watering fields of cotton and alfalfa, pastures for cattle, and rows of citrus to the horizon's edge. Water storage began on a grand scale with construction of Roosevelt Dam, dedicated in 1911 and still the world's largest masonry dam, on the Salt River some 90 miles (145km) upstream from Phoenix. Three more dams on the Salt, and two on its major tributary, the Verde, allowed agriculturalists to send water where they liked. The Salt River itself became the driest place in the region.

Residents with long memories recall the 1930s as a Phoenician golden age. Those who couldn't afford the Arizona Biltmore Hotel found it too snobbish anyway and frequented a lively downtown that still retained a Spanish-American flavor. In summer, when temperatures often exceeded 110°F (43°C) and daytime highs did not dip below the hundreds for months, locals complained less about the heat than they boasted of tricks to stay cool. It was common sport to be pulled on an aquaplane along the canals, holding a rope from a car.

Phoenix was transformed forever by World War II. The open desert was ideal for aviation training, and much of Phoenix became something of an extension of nearby Luke Air Force Base. Aviation equipment companies moved into the valley and even the cotton fields turned out silk for parachutes. It is less known that Phoenix had internment camps for German prisoners of war, and many of the prisoners, as susceptible to the desert's allure as anyone else, remained in the area after the war to become a part of the community.

The military revolutionized Phoenician life with a device called air-conditioning. The city had previously seen use of the evaporative or "swamp" cooler, but now there was genuine refrigeration. Suddenly Phoenix was a year-round possibility for those who couldn't stand the heat. The great migration was on. Camelback Mountain, at whose feet

lay the most elegant dude ranches, was engulfed by suburbia. To the east, greater Phoenix swallowed up the once-isolated communities of Scottsdale, Tempe, Mesa, and Apache Junction. Golf courses replaced dude ranches, and resorts sprouted like desert flowers after a thunderstorm.

An era of rapid development hit Phoenix when **Sun City**, America's first fully planned retirement community, was pitched by the Del Webb Corporation in 1960. More recently, cactus forests to the north of Phoenix have been bulldozed for a realty bonanza. Homeowners in Phoenix were severely impacted by the global financial crisis of 2008, which has led to an epidemic of foreclosures as a result of the collapse of big banks and real estate investment packages that proved anything but a good deal for homeowners.

The recent influx of career-oriented young people in high-tech industries has radically altered the demographic in Phoenix, and the average resident, contrary to popular belief, is younger than the national average. With them has come a push for a more cohesive community, sustainable lifestyles, a better urban infrastructure, and restaurants, hotels, shops, and cultural offerings on a par with any major American city. Phoenix is growing up. It's getting to be fun to visit there these days.

Downtown Phoenix

Whether you fly in or drive in, you'll notice right away: the geographical setting of Phoenix is impressive. To the east soar the massive Four Peaks and the flanks of the Superstition Mountains, while the Sierra Estrella, sacred to the Gila and Salt River Indian tribes, rides the southwest horizon in dorsales of blue silk. Hemming in the city north and south are lower ranges of Precambrian gneiss and schist, framing the Phoenix trademark peak of Camelback Mountain, a free-standing, rosy, recumbent dromedary with a sedimentary head and granitic hump, and recently renamed Piestewa Peak, a landmark that now honors fallen Iraq war hero Lori Piestewa, the

"Desert rains are usually so definitely demarked that the story of the man who washed his hands in the edge of an Arizona thunder shower without wetting his cuffs seems almost credible."
– Administration in the State of Arizona, U.S. public relief program, 1935–1943

BELOW:
Mark Reynolds of the Arizona Diamondbacks charges to field a bunt.

The Cactus League

Tolerable desert temperatures and wildflower blooms are two excellent reasons to travel to southern Arizona in February, March, and April. Another is to get an advance preview of the upcoming major league baseball season during spring training – an annual ritual that offers fans a chance to see teams like the Arizona Diamondbacks and Chicago White Sox compete in the Cactus League.

Most teams begin their workouts in mid-February, then play around 15 games in March and the first week of April. Games are held at popular venues like Bank One Ballpark and Salt River Fields at Talking Stick Resort on the Salt River Maricopa-Pima Indian Reservation in Phoenix. Venues also offer special events, such as fireworks nights, bat and T-shirt giveaways, and visiting sports mascots.

The athletes often come over and meet fans after the games – an extra thrill for autograph-seeking kids. Tickets go on sale as early as December and range from $5 for bleacher seats to $15 for reserved seats. Lawn seating is available at most venues, making picnics a popular option for those not enamored of hot dogs, barbecue, and other stadium fare. Ticket information and game schedules can be obtained by calling the team's Arizona venue or by visiting www.arizonaguide.com or www.cactusleague.com.

TIP

James Beard award-winning chefs Matt Bianco and Nobuo Fukada both have restaurants in historic Heritage Square in downtown Phoenix that have received critical acclaim.

first Indian woman to die in a United States conflict.

Downtown Phoenix has blossomed into an impressive cultural center, with an array of performing arts venues, including the Museum of Musical Instruments in Scottsdale, and the recently expanded Heard Museum and Phoenix Art Museum, reflecting a new self-assurance and maturity in this young city.

What remains of the city's Victorian heritage can be seen at **Heritage Square Ⓐ** (115 N. Sixth St; tel: 602-262-5029; free), a block east of the **Civic Plaza** and part of downtown's Copper Square and **Heritage and Science Park**. Most striking of Heritage Square's 11 buildings – some of them, like the Lath House Pavilion, quite modern – is the **Rosson House** (tel: 602-262-5029; Wed–Sat 10am–3.30pm, Sun noon–3.30pm; closed mid-Aug through Labor Day; special tours available; charge), built in 1895 and once one of the most prominent homes in Phoenix. Some of the other houses here, dating from the early 1900s, were moved from other

locations to save them from demolition. Also part of downtown's Copper Square and Heritage and Science Park is the **Arizona Science Center** (tel: 602-716-2000; daily 10am–5pm; charge), housed in a beautiful $50 million building designed by famed architect Antoine Predock. Heritage Square is easily reached by the METRO light rail, which stops here.

Several multimillion-dollar expansions – the most recent to reconstruct the lobby area for better access and gallery improvements in 2011 – have created a funhouse of hands-on science. The center has 300 exhibits in five themed galleries on four floors, where kids can explore inside the human body, understand networks and the digital world, experiment with solar power, and otherwise be "blinded by science." There is an immersion theater that offers a thrilling virtual experience of different weather conditions and a flight simulator in an exhibit on aviation. Arizona's dominance as a center for astronomy is highlighted in the planetarium, and an IMAX theater has been a hit with kids.

Previous featured exhibitions in the Sybil B. Harrington Galleries include the internationally renowned Gunther Von Hagen's Body Worlds & the Brain.

Seat of government

Arizona's modest state capitol building lies 1.5 miles (2.5km) to the west of downtown, along Washington Street. The **Arizona State Capitol Museum Ⓑ** (tel: 602-926-3620; Mon–Fri 9am–4pm; tours 10am and 2pm; free) uncovers some of the building's secrets. The capitol was constructed in 1899 to house the territorial government; its dome was covered in 1976 with 15 tons of copper donated by the state's mining interests. Atop the dome is Winged Victory, a quarter-ton statue dating from 1899 that turns with the wind. Much of today's governing is done in adjacent modern structures, but the restored Senate and

BELOW:
Robson House in Heritage Square.

House of Representatives chambers are open to visitors. Furnishings and ornamentation throughout the building date from 1912, when Arizona became a state.

The classy **Phoenix Art Museum** Ⓒ (tel: 602-257-1880; www.phx-art.org; Wed 10am-9pm, Thurs-Sat 10am-5pm, Sun 12pm-5pm, first Friday of the month 6-10pm, closed Mon, Tues) is located at Central Avenue and McDowell Road, a mile (1.6km) north of Heritage Park, and easily reached by METRO light rail (McDowell & Central station). It underwent a huge $50 million expansion in 2007 that created an entirely new four-level wing to accommodate international shows, a new lobby, and a sculpture garden. Galleries display some 17,000 individual art works by American and Asian artists, Southwest painters from the Taos School, and recent Mexican artworks. Art of the American West includes works of Thomas Moran and Frederic Remington. PAM's on-site restaurant, Arcadian Farms, offers casual dining and organic dishes for a moderate price and is a popular place to eat downtown.

The **Heard Museum** Ⓓ (tel: 602-252-8848; www.heard.org; Mon–Sat 9.30am–5pm, Sun 11am–5pm; charge) is one of the must-sees in Phoenix, even for those travelers who aren't particularly fond of museums. It was founded in 1929 to house the Heard family's collection of American Indian art and artifacts, and it remains an exceptional collection. Several huge expansions since 1999 have enhanced the visitor experience. The museum occupies 13,000 sq ft (33,670 sq km) with 11 exhibit galleries, and is a major presence on Central Avenue, a few blocks north of the Phoenix Art Museum. Aside from its famed museum store, which sells authentic Indian art of the highest caliber, a new bookstore, cantina, and coffee bar opened in 2011, along with the 11th gallery, the Nichols Sculpture Garden, with a groundbreaking exhibition by Creek artist Retha Walden Gambaro.

The museum's signature exhibit, *Home: Native People in the Southwest,*

BELOW: the Apache Trail leads into the Superstition Mountains outside Apache Junction.

Phoenix Spa Resorts

For those who prefer humanity untrammeled by nature, there are numerous sumptuous resorts in the Phoenix area, including the luxurious Boulders resort in Carefree, north of Scottsdale; three mountainside Pointe resorts on the north and south edges of Phoenix; and the elegant Sheraton Wild Horse Pass Resort on the Gila River Indian Reservation adjoining Chandler, southwest of Tempe, and Talking Stick, on the east side of town on Salt River Maricopa-Pima Indian Reservation land. Gone is any pretense of the dude-ranch culture common before World War II, and the only reference to cactus may be worked into the macrame in the lobby. Offering golf, tennis, spas, pools with underwater bar stools, gourmet restaurants, nightclubs, discos, refrigerated suites, and a clientele armored in platinum credit cards, these are not desert hideaways but total-concept luxury resort complexes.

Roman Widow, *by Dante Gabriel Rossetti, is on display at the Phoenix Art Museum.*

is immediately to your right as you enter the museum. It tells the story of Arizona's Indian tribes, then and now, through multimedia, and includes 250 historic *kachina* dolls from the famous Barry Goldwater Collection. This is a very handsome exhibit room, which features blond bentwood exhibit cases that give the space a feeling of light and space. The central Crossroads Gallery and adjoining Sandra Day O'Connor Gallery display recent acquisitions from the Heard Museum Collection. To the left is the other permanent signature exhibit We Are! Arizona's First People in the Ullman Learning Center. Other permanent exhibits are located in the Lovena Ohl Gallery, the Freeman Gallery, on the second floor, and the Jack Steele Parker Gallery on the upper level. Also on the upper level is the East Gallery, which has a moving permanent exhibit on Indian boarding schools and pottery.

Phoenix feels positively European as sidewalk cafés, such as the Courtyard Café at the Heard Museum, take advantage of the warm weather and

Spanish courtyard ambiance and more and more visitors choose to ride the METRO, which runs down the center median of Central Avenue. Just east of Central Avenue, on 16th Street, in the increasingly popular and vibrant barrio, are some of Phoenix's hottest Mexican restaurants for an easy bite at the end of the day.

Smaller branches of the Heard can be found in two far-flung locations in Greater Phoenix. The **Heard North** (tel: 480-488-9817) is located in an attractive building in a small shopping center, just south of Carefree. The permanent exhibit *Choices and Change: American Indian Artists in the Southwest* is well worth the drive north of downtown Scottsdale; an adjoining gallery has revolving exhibits. There is a restaurant on site, a large gift shop, and a Sculpture and Native Plants Garden. The **Heard West** (tel: 623-344-2200), affiliated with the City of Surprise, is more of an educational facility but it, too, has 400 items from the Heard's permanent collections and is worth a look if you are in this neck of the woods.

A great monument to another period is the **Arizona Biltmore Hotel Resort and Spa** Ⓔ (tel: 602-955-6600), 5 miles (8km) northeast of downtown and Heritage Park. With a slack economy to begin with, Phoenix hardly noticed the Great Depression of the early 1930s, living off its own agriculture and catering in fine style to those tourists who managed to keep their money. Built just before the crash of 1929, the Biltmore sailed in splendor through the bleakest of times. It is to the Biltmore that Phoenix owes the arrival of famed architect Frank Lloyd Wright. The hotel was originally designed by Albert Chase McArthur, a former student of Wright, who summoned the master for help. Wright came, and then stayed to create his home and architectural school Taliesin West in Scottsdale.

Wright probably gave more help than required, for the result was a

BELOW: Allan Houser's *Earth Song*, 1978, at the Heard Museum.

masterpiece of textile block construction and is a delight for the eye – geometrically tidy, quietly whimsical, and aesthetically inspiring. Gutted by fire in 1973, the interior was refurnished with furniture and textile designs from all periods of Wright's career. The visitor who enters no other building in Phoenix should make it to 24th Street and Missouri to inspect the Arizona Biltmore.

Tempe is home to **Arizona State University** F This vibrant university community anchors the south side of Phoenix, with its lively downtown and postmodern buildings along the river. Of these, don't miss the beautifully designed **Tempe Center for the Arts**, a state-of-the-art community center housing two theaters, an art gallery, a restaurant with a view of **Tempe Town Lake**, an artificial lake impounded from the Salt River, and adjoining riverwalk and sculpture garden. The university campus is home to **ASU Gammage Auditorium**, designed by Frank Lloyd Wright, and renowned for its excellent acoustics, and **Tempe**

Diablo Stadium, used as a base for spring training by the Angels baseball team.

Nearby is **Pueblo Grande Museum and Archaeological Park** G (tel: 602-495-0901; Mon–Sat 9am–4.45pm, Sun 1–4.45pm, closed May–Sept Sun, Mon; charge) is sited just outside the central city, wedged in between an interstate highway and the international airport. It is a confounding juxtaposition, but this ancient pueblo site is worth a look. A wheelchair-accessible trail, just over half a mile long, encircles the ruins and has numerous, wellwritten interpretive displays. The visitor center has a museum displaying artifacts from the Hohokam culture and this pueblo site, and a film about the Hohokam.

The Hohokam people lived in southern Arizona until around AD 1450. Experts at cultivation, the Hohokam developed a complex system of irrigation canals extending hundreds of miles; some of these canals remain today. It is conjectured that bad weather, internal conflicts,

"A grand garden, the like of which in sheer beauty of space and pattern does not exist, I think, in the world. "

–Frank Lloyd Wright, about the desert

BELOW: a Wright mosaic design at the Arizona Biltmore.

Frank Lloyd Wright

When Frank Lloyd Wright (1869–1959) was in his sixties, an age when other men are retiring, he was designing buildings that continued to revolutionize architecture, dismissing the stagnation found in much architectural design. Indeed, the older he got, the more innovative and revolutionary his designs became. His unique Guggenheim Museum in New York City, for example, was completed in 1959, the year he died at the age of 90. From his earliest days as an architectural student in the Chicago area in the 1890s, Wright remained true to his philosophy of "organic architecture," which stated that a building should be an integral part of its natural surroundings.

The historian Lewis Mumford wrote in 1929: "Wright has embodied in his work two qualities which will never permanently leave it – a sense of place and a rich feeling for materials." Wright's works in Phoenix, including Taliesin West and the Arizona Biltmore Hotel, on which he served as a consultant, revealed his belief that architecture should enhance both person and environment. Taliesin West, Wright's winter home and studio from 1937 to 1959, remains a school that encourages experimentation.

Contemporary art at a Scottsdale gallery.

BELOW: guests at the Arizona Biltmore relax in the pool.

and salinization of farmland from over-irrigation may have contributed to the abandonment of the Salt River Valley in the 1400s.

The Pueblo Grande mound is actually two smaller mounds dating from around AD 1150. Less than 200 years later, the two mounds were combined into a mound the size of a football field and about 30ft (9 meters) high. Many of the buildings once on top of the mound were probably used for other purposes, including ceremonial. Immediately north of the mound, accessible by a walkway, is an excavated ball court similar to those found at ancient Mayan sites in Mexico.

Beyond downtown

To the east of downtown, increasingly surrounded by the expansion of greater metropolitan Phoenix, the **Desert Botanical Garden ❶** (tel: 480-941-1225; daily 7am–8pm; charge) is located on 50 acres (20 hectares) within Papago Park. It is home to 139 rare, threatened, and endangered species of plants from around the world as well as the Sonoran Desert

and is said to be the world's largest collection of desert plants living in a natural environment. Several trails lead through the plants, displays, and balmy air. The garden emphasizes, as one might expect, the Sonoran Desert of southern Arizona.

Not far away on the same road, the **Phoenix Zoo ❶** (tel: 602-273-1341; daily June–Aug 7am–2pm, Sept–Nov and Jan–May 9am–5pm, Nov–Jan 9am–4pm; charge) was voted one of the nation's top five zoos. It has 1,200 animals housed on 125 acres (50 hectares) and 2.5 miles (4km) of walking trails. The Arizona Trail features the flora and fauna of the Southwest.

The attractive and fast-growing community of Scottsdale lies to the northeast of Phoenix itself and is a center of elegant boutique and modern hotels, sprawling resorts, ritzy shops, excellent restaurants, and some of Phoenix's most enjoyable museums. The historic Old Town of Scottsdale has a number of galleries selling cowboy and Indian art, while the **Scottsdale Museum of Contemporary Art ❶** (7374 East

Second St; tel: 480-874-4766; Wed, Fri, Sat 10am–5pm, Thur 10am–8pm; charge, free Thur) features an installation by light artist James Turrell.

The ambitious new **Musical Instruments Museum O** (4725 East Mayo Boulevard; tel: 480-478-6000; Mon–Wed, Sat 9am–5pm, Thur, Fri 9am–9pm, Sun 10am–5pm; charge) is located in far northern Scottsdale. Dreamed up by the energetic retired CEO of Target Stores, MIM seeks to tell the story of music throughout the world in a dizzying array of exhibits featuring musical instruments and videos of live performances (visitors wear headphones that are activated by sensors on each display). This place makes the Hard Rock Café's displays of rock musicians' instruments and paraphernalia look tame! Eric Clapton's guitar Brownie and the piano on which John Lennon composed "Imagine" are both on display here.

Taliesin West O (tel: 480-627-5340; daily for guided tours 9am–4pm, gift shop and grounds close at 6pm, special evening tours available at certain times of year; charge), in the foothills of northeastern Scottsdale, was Frank Lloyd Wright's personal residence and architectural school, and most of the buildings and facilities continue to be an ongoing, hands-on educational exercise for architectural students.

New techniques in the use of natural materials were developed here, often after the many failures that Wright considered part of the educational process. Rocks from the desert and sand from dry washes were melded into foundations, walls, and walkways, all the while following geometrical proportions that stayed constant from the smallest ornamental detail to the dimensions of the buildings themselves.

Some of Wright's trademark techniques, such as the squeeze-and-release of a cramped entranceway opening into an expansive room, are apparent here. But from a distance, the buildings merge so beautifully with the landscape, they almost disappear.

One of today's best-known architects is Paolo Soleri, an Italian who has lived in Arizona since 1956. In Scottsdale, Soleri's **Cosanti M** (tel: 480-948-6145; Mon–Sat 9am–5pm, Sun 11am–5pm; voluntary donation) offers a broad-brush overview of Soleri's architectural philosophy and of a grander site 65 miles (105km) north of Phoenix, Arcosanti. Cactus and olive trees are scattered amid Cosanti's earth-formed concrete structures, designed to maximize both ecological efficiency and use of space.

Apache Trail

East of Phoenix is the spectacular desert drive known as the **Apache Trail ❷**. As an Arizona initiation rite, locals like to take visiting friends out for a drive along the curvy route. During this desert ritual, in-the-know motorists will turn to passengers just before a series of steep, hairpin turns and hoarsely whisper something to

At the Desert Botanical Gardens in Scottsdale.

BELOW: Taliesin West was Frank Lloyd Wright's winter home and school in the Arizona desert.

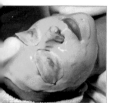

Scottsdale is known for its high-end spas and resorts.

the effect that the brakes are out. If you can avoid having a local jokester at the wheel, a drive along the Apache Trail is a day well spent. Most of the chills and thrills come from the spectacular scenery along the way, including mountains, sheer cliffs, canyons, and a series of large lakes. The 45-mile (72km) -long trail – actually a section of State Highway 88 – snakes its way past the **Superstition Mountains** and along the edge of the **Four Peaks Wilderness** in **Tonto National Forest**, just east of metro Phoenix.

The Apache Trail's moniker reflects its Native American history. Attracted by the availability of water from the Salt River and Tonto Creek, the Salado people inhabited the area as early as AD 1150. Many farmed along the flat land on the water's edge and built cliff dwellings in the mountainous terrain. Later, nomadic Apache and Yavapai Indians found sanctuary in the canyon lands.

By the 1860s, Anglo-European traders and prospectors drifted into the mountains. One such entrepreneur was German-born Jacob Waltz, who periodically came into the fledgling community of Phoenix with sacks of gold nuggets that he claimed were from his secret mine in the Superstition Mountains. Waltz died without revealing the location of his mine, and the enduring legend of the Lost Dutchman Mine worked its way into local folklore. (Back then, apparently, nobody knew the difference between Dutch and Deutsch).

By the early 20th century, Phoenix's influential farmers and ranchers saw gold in the form of a steady water supply at the confluence of the Salt River and Tonto Creek. The federal government agreed, and the site was chosen to be one of the first major reclamation projects in the West. Funds for **Theodore Roosevelt Dam** ❸ were approved in 1903 – as was money for the construction of a roadway linking the outskirts of Phoenix to the dam site. The roadway, of course, was the Apache Trail, which followed portions of the old Indian pathway. By the time the dam was completed in 1911 (and dedicated by its namesake), millions

Phoenix Environs

of pounds of freight had been hauled up the road by mule teams and wagons, and tourists, too, had gotten their first glimpses of the wild and beautiful landscape of the Superstition Mountains.

No need to worry about encountering mule teams today, although you might pass some grazing cattle or wildlife, including coyotes, rattlesnakes, various bird species, and even elusive bighorn sheep. The plant life includes the usual suspects of the upper Sonoran Desert – saguaro, prickly pear, and cholla cactus – as well as striking century plants. Look for pockets of deciduous trees along the washes and creek beds; in spring, after a rainy winter, roadsides are ablaze with lupines, Mexican gold poppies, owl's clover, and other wildflowers.

Coming from Phoenix, most visitors drive the Apache Trail south to north, picking up State Highway 88 off US 60 in **Apache Junction**, a suburban community (this is a good place to get gas – there aren't any service stations along the scenic part of the road). The scenery starts just outside Apache Junction, where the road is flanked on one side by **Goldfield Ghost Town** (tel: 480-983-0333; daily 10am–5pm, saloon until 8pm; charge) and on the other by **Lost Dutchman State Park** (tel: 480-982-4485; daily sunrise–10pm; charge). The ghost town – once a mining hamlet – has been re-created as an Old West town, complete with shootouts, a narrow-gauge railroad, shops, and a restaurant, while the park offers hiking and trails, ranger-led programs, picnic areas, and campsites.

About 7 miles (11km) from the park is an overlook for **Canyon Lake**, the first of the three lakes created by the Roosevelt and other dams. The lake is visually striking but often crowded on warm weekends. You can rent a boat from the marina, cruise the lake aboard a steamboat, or hike one of several trails.

Tortilla Flat and beyond

A few miles beyond Canyon Lake is **Tortilla Flat**, once a rest stop for freight operators and construction workers traveling to Roosevelt Dam. Today, it's a series of false-front buildings that lures tourists with burgers and chilli, drinks served in mason jars, and a gift shop stuffed with souvenirs. For good luck, pin a dollar bill to the wall of the restaurant or gift shop (the walls sport thousands) and buy a T-shirt that begs the question, "Where the hell is Tortilla Flat?"

At this point, many travelers turn back, but the most beautiful scenery begins beyond Tortilla Flat. A few miles up, the pavement ends, but the gravel road is well maintained (watch for flash flooding during heavy rains) and suitable for all vehicles except RVs and cars pulling trailers. Here, the road begins its precipitous descent into **Fish Creek Canyon**, the scenic high point of the drive and the spot where the no-brakes story usually unfolds. As the road twists downward, cliffs, mountains, and the creekbed (usually dry) become visible. Parking

A "sheriff" lays down the law in Goldfield Ghost Town.

BELOW: the Pueblo style building at the Phoenician resort in Scottsdale.

areas and hiking trails are at the bottom of the hill.

About 5 miles (8km) farther, you will get your first glimpse of **Apache Lake**, the most remote of the man-made lakes, hence the quietest and, some say, the loveliest. Against painted cliffs, the lake is 17 miles (27km) long and rather narrow. You can take a boat almost to the foot of Roosevelt Dam at the lake's eastern end. A small marina offers boat rentals, bait, supplies, and light meals.

At the end of the Apache Trail is the mighty Roosevelt Dam, which, at 280ft (85 meters), is the highest masonry dam in the world. There are several points from which to view the dam and **Roosevelt Lake**, the largest artificial lake in central Arizona; a visitor center (daily 7.45am–4.30pm; free), boat ramps, and campgrounds are on the lakeshore.

Closing the circle

At this point, you have several choices. You can either return the same way you came, or you can head back to Phoenix via Highways 188

BELOW: Casa Grande Ruins National Monument.

and 87, or, you can always make a full loop around the Superstition Mountains by continuing southeast on Highway 88 and then west on US 60. The latter option offers the most attractions, including **Tonto National Monument ❹** (tel: 928-467-2241; daily 8am–5pm; charge), site of wellpreserved cliff dwellings occupied by the Salado people from the 13th to early 15th century. Set in natural limestone alcoves, the apartment-like structures were built of rough quartzite crudely mortared with mud. These were topped with mud-and-wood roofs, many of which can still be seen, as can the ghostly handprints of the some of the construction workers in the mud. Examples of fine Salado pottery and woven textiles are exhibited in the visitor center.

It's a scenic drive around the eastern side of the mountains through the little mining towns of **Miami** and **Superior** to the **Boyce Thompson Arboretum ❺** (tel: 520-689-2811; Sept–Apr 8am–4pm; May–Aug 6am–4pm; charge), a showplace for desert plants and wildlife founded in the 1920s by mining magnate William Boyce Thompson and now run by the University of Arizona. Self-guided trails wind through 35 acres (14 hectares) of beautifully landscaped grounds. A stone house listed on the National Register of Historic Places serves as an interpretive center.

A 25-mile (40km) detour on highways 79 and 287 leads to **Casa Grande Ruins National Monument ❻** (tel: 520-723-3172; daily 8am–5pm; charge), a prehistoric village occupied by the Hohokam until about AD 1450. The central structure is a four-story "great house" (now protected by a modern roof). Though its function remains a mystery, the presence of holes aligned with the sun on the equinox and solstices suggests that it may have been used as an observatory.

RESTAURANTS

Prices for a three-course dinner per person, excluding tax, tip, and beverages:
$ = under $20
$$ = $20–45
$$$ = $45–60
$$$$ = over $60

Arcadia Farms at the Phoenix Art Museum
1625 N. Central Avenue, Phoenix
Tel: 602-257-2191 **$–$$**
Arcadia Farms at the Phoenix Art Museum (look also for the popular stand-alone Arcadia Farms Café in Old Town Scottsdale) marries sophisticated, European-style museum dining with locally raised, organic ingredients inspired by the indigenous foods of the Southwest. Reasonably priced and carefully presented artisanal salads, sandwiches, and hot specials lure both local businesspeople and museum visitors. Try the cheese plate featuring local Fossil Creek goat cheese, wild salmon salad with cactus-pear glaze, sweet corn succotash on local greens with prickly-pear vinaigrette, chicken tamale tart, or rosemary-roasted ham baguette.

Barrio Café
2814 N. 16th Street, Phoenix
Tel: 602-636-0240 **$$**
Nominated for James Beard awards in 2010 and 2011, chef-owner Silvana Salcido Esparza is going for it at this raucous, upscale Mexican eatery in the upcoming Mexican foodie area of Phoenix, where the food is as loud as the ambiance. Packed every night with appreciative fans, the menu offers dishes that are primarily associated with southern Mexico; they are spicy (and quite salty) but not overly hot. This is your chance to try Cochinito Pibil, rarely glimpsed outside the Yucatan peninsula where it is the specialty, a moist mélange of marinated pulled pork cooked in a banana leaf until succulent (also available as a tilapia dish). The mole here is complex and authentic. Be sure to save room for rich desserts like flan and churros.

Cowboy Ciao
7133 E. Stetson Drive, Scottsdale
Tel: 480-946-3111 **$$–$$$**
This quirky contemporary eatery brings new meaning to the term "spaghetti Western," with playful culinary pairings such as porcini-mushroom-crusted ribeye steak, pesto-crusted elk loin, and smoked pork in chipotle balsamic barbecue sauce atop soft polenta. Sounds odd, perhaps, but the chefs manage to pull it off with an infectious sense of fun and daring.

Ed Debevic's Short Order Deluxe
2102 E. Highland Avenue, Phoenix
Tel: 602-956-2760 **$**
This frenetic, old-fashioned diner has a mini-jukebox in every booth, loads of retro charm (harassed waitresses notwithstanding) and a choice of familiar, almost-like-mom's fare – burgers, fries, meatloaf, malteds, and much more.

Hap's Real Pit BBQ
101 S. 24th Street, Phoenix
Tel: 602-267-0181 **$**
Forget the low-rent atmosphere and dig into some of the best barbecued spare ribs in the Phoenix area.

House of Tricks
114 E. Seventh Street, Tempe
Tel: 480-968-1114 **$$**
Ask for a table on the leafy covered patio, order a round from the open-air bar, then prepare to enjoy such tasty and creative dishes as pork rack with jalapeño-orange marmalade, grilled Middle Eastern spiced salmon, or grilled Angus sirloin with mashed potatoes and shiitake mushroom gravy. A fireplace keeps patrons toasty on the rare chilly nights in winter. A winning marriage of cuisine and atmosphere.

Joe's Farm Grill
3000 E. Ray Road, Gilbert
Tel: 480-563-4745 **$**
The Johnston family who have created this New American restaurant in their old farmhouse have a winner here. From pesto-topped burgers and sweet potato fries to salads made with organic greens grown just a few feet away, there's something here for the whole family at lunch and dinner. Find a picnic table under the trees and kick back. There's also a coffee shop and farm stand. Closed Fri and Sat.

Kai
Sheraton Wild Horse Pass Resort and Spa, Gila Indian Reservation, 5994 W. Wild Horse Pass Boulevard, Chandler
Tel: 602-225-0100 **$$$–$$$$**
The heart and soul of Indian country beat strongly at Kai, frequently voted one of Phoenix's most lauded and reliably excellent restaurants. Executive chef Michael O'Dowd, along with consulting chef Janos Wilder, have concocted a unique menu that pays homage to indigenous foods of the desert and beyond. Hearty Western dishes showcase produce raised by reservation school children, Sea of Cortez shrimp, tepary beans and rare seeds from the Sonoran Desert; buffalo raised by the Cheyenne Tribe; and Colorado lamb. Reserve a table on the balcony overlooking the Estrella Mountains at sunset for the most breathtaking setting for dinner of anywhere in Phoenix. Closed Sun and Mon.

La Hacienda
Scottsdale Princess Resort, 7575 E. Princess Drive, Scottsdale
Tel: 480-585-4848 **$$–$$$**
Fabulous gourmet Mexican

Prices for a three-course dinner per person, excluding tax, tip, and beverages:
$ = under $20
$$ = $20–45
$$$ = $45–60
$$$$ = over $60

food shines at this resort restaurant once again, after it fell victim to the recession, then found the wherewithal to open again. Try the Mexican corn delicacy huitlacoche in various guises, including in a tamale made with goat cheese, zucchini, and chilli guajillo sauce; or costillas de cordero, a charbroiled rack of lamb with pumpkin-seed crust and chilli plum sauce. And don't forget the margaritas!

Lon's at the Hermosa Inn
5532 N. Palo Cristi Road, Paradise Valley
Tel: 602-955-7878 **$$$–$$$$**
This gorgeous art-filled Southwest restaurant, housed in Western artist Lon Megargee's old home (the cosy bar is also a favorite local watering hole), this is a truly special place for a romantic night out. The award-winning New American menu includes beautifully conceived meat, seafood, and pasta dishes such as pecan-crusted pork, free-range chicken with goat cheese gnocchi, and grilled fillet of salmon with blackberry shellac, baby cabbages, marbled potatoes, corn, and fire-roasted tomatillo sauce. Everything on the menu is natural, organic, or sustainably sourced, and many of the greens and grains are

grown by the chef on the grounds. There's a multi-course prix-fixe dinner monthly to highlight what's in season. The Sunday brunch is a popular treat among locals, but breakfast any day is delicious, and includes light farmhouse frittatas with free-range eggs, smoked bacon, mesquite-flour pancakes, and the chef's popular monkey-puzzle sweet bread.

Matt's Big Breakfast
801 North First Street, Phoenix
Tel: 602-254-1074 **$**
Fresh local food has created a big buzz at this sweet little retro diner in a historic brick building on the corner of First and McKinley in downtown Phoenix. Chef Matt Pool uses organic produce, honey, cage-free eggs, and hormone-free meats to create healthy comfort food, such as eggs and thick-sliced bacon, stacked pancakes, cobb salad, salami scramble, omelets, chilli, burgers, juicy chicken sandwiches, and rosemary fries. Get here early to snag a seat as it closes at 2.30pm. Closed Sun.

Nobuo at the Teeter House
Heritage Square, 622 E. Adams Street, Phoenix
Tel: 602-254-0600 **$$–$$$**
Inspired Japanese chef Nobuo Fukada gained legions of fans and a James Bear Award at his Scottsdale restaurant Sea Saw for his inventive fine dining. His new restaurant in a historic house in Heritage Square brings his culinary brilliance to the masses with a casual, accessible menu that

checks all the right boxes for a fun night out. This is not your mother's sushi restaurant. The Japanese tapas (izakaya, or tavern food) are still here, and there are warm and cold dishes – all simply and imaginatively prepared. The lunch menu includes a warm duck salad, panko-fried soft-shell crab on foccacia sandwich, and short rib steamed buns. At dinner, try Teeter tots (flash-fried tofu with soy dipping sauce), sea bass and mushrooms baked in parchment with sake and soy, or the daily fish special flown in fresh from Japan. Japanese microbrewed beer and craft cocktails are available, and the restaurant will occasionally do *omakase* (chef's choice) five-course tasting menus. No reservations. Closed Mon.

Pane Bianco
4404 N. Central Avenue, Phoenix
Tel: 602-234-2100 **$**
When local foods booster Chris Bianco is not cooking pizza in his popular dinner pizzeria in Heritage Square in downtown Phoenix, you'll find him over at his bakery on Central, selling locally sourced market salads and rustic sandwiches made on his own hearty bread highlighting Chris's favorite food: local organic tomatoes and homemade mozzarella. Take-out only. Closed Mon.

Pho Dinh Restaurant
2025 N. Dobson Road, Chandler
Tel: 480-812-1877 **$**
Set in a corner of a large Asian marketplace known as Lee Lee, this casual Vietnamese restaurant

serves authentic and reasonably priced food. Sample such specialties as barbecued pork with char-broiled ground shrimp; spicy salt-and-pepper squid; rice noodles tossed with shrimp, beef, pork, and chicken; and sizzling clay hot pots loaded with meat, shrimp, and veggies atop rice.

Pizzeria Bianco
623 E. Adams Street, Phoenix
Tel: 602-258-8300 **$$**
Chef-owner Chris Bianco helped found the Phoenix branch of Slow Food. In his charming but very tiny pizzeria, in an old brick home in historic Heritage Square, he conjures Phoenix's most authentic Neapolitan pizza, such as the margherita, using fresh-tasting sauces made from heirloom organic tomatoes, home-made mozzarella, and other local organic ingredients. Only reservations for large groups are taken, but Bianco has a method in his madness. He owns a wine bar next door, where patrons relax with a glass of wine and get to know their neighbors, thereby building community in this sprawling metropolis. No takeout. Closed Sun and Mon.

Quiessence Restaurant and Wine Bar
The Farm at South Mountain, 6106 S. 32nd Street, Phoenix
Tel: 602-276-6360 **$$–$$$**
The lovely rural setting – on a 12-acre (5-hectare) organic farm south of Phoenix – makes this wonderful restaurant inside a historic farmhouse unique in bland Phoenix. But it's the amazing food – all of it

fresh, organic, and sustainably sourced – that takes Quiessence to the next level. Everything is simply prepared, with an eye to marrying flavors and textures, allowing the ingredients to step forward and shine. The menu changes daily, reflecting what's available. One signature dish is braised lamb with roasted vegetables, procured from a local sheep farmer. Six-course sampling menus are reasonably priced. Reservations are strongly suggested. If you're here between September and April, come early and enjoy visiting South Mountains organic gardens, shops, and two other cafés, including Morning Glory, a popular Phoenix breakfast spot. Closed Sun and Mon, and in summer.

RoxSand
Biltmore Fashion Park, 2594 E. Camelback Road, Phoenix Tel: 602-381-0444 **$$–$$$**
The owner of this slick contemporary restaurant is a proponent of "fusion cuisine," a cross-cultural approach to combining flavors and ingredients. It's not unusual to open the meal with a Middle Eastern braised curried chicken, rice tamale with Thai peanut sauce, or short ribs with Korean soy and honey marinade, then move to air-dried duck with buckwheat crepes and pistachio-onion marmalade, or chicken breast with Louisiana étouffée sauce. Leave the jeans at home.

San Carlos Bay Seafood Restaurant
1901 E. McDowell

Restaurant, Phoenix Tel: 602-340-0892 **$**
Mexican seafood is the bill of fare here. Highlights include a tender octopus cocktail; fiery shrimp endiablados; a rich "seven-seas" stew stocked with crab, cockles, shrimp, and squid; shrimp with tangy green-chilli sauce; and *pescado a la Veracruzana* (grilled snapper with olives, tomatoes, onions, and peppers).

St. Francis
111 E. Camelback Road, Phoenix Tel: 602-200-8111 **$–$$**
A modern-meets-rustic neighborhood bistro with lots of heart and soul, St. Francis is the brainchild of Phoenix local Aaron Chamberlin, a classically trained chef who wanted to open a restaurant to serve the community in which he was raised. The menu features fresh, inspired renditions of comfort foods sourced from local purveyors. Many dishes, from the pizza and hearth, breads to meats, are cooked in the restaurant's wood-fired ovens. Choose from among a changing variety of soups with home-made baguette bread, baked goat cheese appetizer, Caesar salads, pizzas, meatballs, hanger steak, and a salmon superfood dish featuring wild salmon and red quinoa.

The Stockyards
5001 E. Washington Street, Phoenix Tel: 602-273-7378 **$–$$**
Steakhouse with 19th-century decor and Old West specialties like Rocky Mountain oysters (the tender bits you remove to

make a bull into a steer) and hand-cut beef.

T. Cook's
Royal Palms Resort, 5200 E. Camelback Road, Phoenix Tel: 602-808-0766 **$$–$$$**
This Mediterranean-style restaurant drips romance. It's hard to go wrong here. Poultry, beef, and pork cooked in a wood-burning oven are popular, although other dishes such as paella and sautéed lobster are equally tempting. Chocoholics may want to skip dinner and move directly to the heavenly chocolate sampler.

Taggia
Fire and Sky Resort, 4925 N. Scottsdale Road, Scottsdale Tel: 480-424-6095 **$$–$$$$**
Situated inside a dramatically remodeled motel, this Italian restaurant is a foodie haven. Italian chef Claudio Urchiuoli, a proponent of Phoenix's Slow Food movement, creates authentic coastal Italian seafood using ingredients sourced locally and from sustainable fisheries worldwide. Winners include hearty sausage dishes and pasta favorites like pumpkin ravioli with sage butter. For dessert, there are sinful, authentically Italian cakes.

True Food Kitchen
Biltmore Fashion Park, 2502 E. Camelback Road, Phoenix Tel: 602-774-3488 **$$**
Healthy living guru Dr Andrew Weil is co-owner of this light, bright, modern eatery, where the Asian-Mediterranean diet is the basis for some creatively thought-out dishes using organic produce and clean

meats and fish. Try the Tuscan kale salad, a "TLT" featuring tempeh instead of bacon, miso-glazed black cod, and the grass-fed bison burger. Smoothies, elixirs, and tea drinks are served with meals. There's another branch in Scottsdale.

Wright's at the Biltmore
Arizona Biltmore Hotel, 2400 E. Missouri Avenue, Phoenix Tel: 602-954-2507 **$$–$$$$**
This fine-dining restaurant in Phoenix's historic Arizona Biltmore Hotel is a treat you'll long remember. You'll find dishes showcasing Maui goat cheese, Colorado lamb, elk from Wyoming, wild salmon from Alaska, and snails from Oregon, in addition to wild boar medallions, buffalo tenderloin, and filet mignon. A feather-light soufflé flavored with chocolate, Grand Marnier, and butterscotch is a specialty. Order them at the start of the meal due to preparation time. Dinner Mon–Sat, brunch only Sun.

Zinc Bistro
15034 N. Scottsdale Road, Suite 140, Scottsdale Tel: 480-603-0922 **$$$**
This top-rated French haute-cuisine restaurant is a perfect choice for an elegant lunch or dinner. Chef-owner Matt Carter knows how to please the most refined sensibilities. The basil chicken, creamy risotto, and filet mignon are all winners. Made-to-order chocolate soufflé with Grand Marnier-infused chocolate sauce are a specialty and must be ordered at the start of the meal.

THE HEARD MUSEUM

This remarkable museum is devoted to the heritage, living cultures, and arts and crafts of the Indian tribes of the Southwest

The museum, based in Phoenix, was founded by Maie Bartlett Heard in 1929, soon after her husband Dwight died, to house the couple's art collection. Much of the archaeological material came from La Ciudad Indian ruin, at 19th and Polk streets, which the Heards bought in 1926.

For 20 years, Mrs Heard served as director of what was then a small family museum in a dusty one-horse western town. When she died, in 1951, the Heard grew into Arizona's premier cultural museum, adding a museum store selling authenticated Indian arts and crafts and an annual Indian Market and Fair. Following a multimillion-dollar expansion, it now has 11 galleries.

The museum's signature exhibit, "HOME: Native People in the Southwest," offers the best interpretation of southwestern Indian tribes in the state. Highlights include elegant case exhibits displaying 2,000 items from the museum's permanent collection, artist quotes, video presentations, a full-size Navajo hogan, artist demonstrations, and the Barry Goldwater and the Fred Harvey Company collections of historic kachina dolls.

Other permanent exhibits include "Remembering Our Indian School Days," a poignant look at Indian boarding schools; "Around the World," featuring the Heard's global collection; and "Every Picture Tells a Story," an examination of symbols in Indian art. Changing exhibits focus on contemporary arts and crafts, such as jewelry and fashion design, and there is now a sculpture garden.

Two small satellite branches – in North Scottsdale and Surprise – have permanent exhibits displaying items from the Heard collection and interesting temporary exhibits. Like the main museum, the Scottsdale branch has a store and a café. The Surprise branch emphasizes educational workshops.

ABOVE: lectures, performances, and other special events are held at the museum's Steele Auditorium.

BELOW: a third phase chief's blanket by Navajo weaver Rene Begay. This style was developed in the early 1860s during the "classical" period of Navajo weaving before the Long Walk.

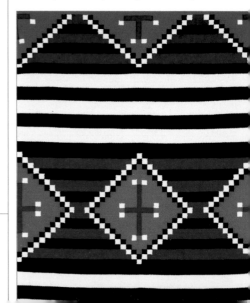

LEFT: *Niman katsina*, 1983, by Hopi artist Tino Youvella. Kachina dolls – religious icons originally made for children – depict the ceremonial dancers who represent Hopi spirits.

THE INDIAN FAIR AND MARKET

Rivaling July's Santa Fe Indian Market in size and prestige, the Heard Guild's annual Indian Fair and Market, held every March on the beautiful grounds of the museum, attracts Indian vendors and art collectors from around the country and is Arizona's biggest Indian arts and crafts gathering. A total of 650 outstanding Indian artists display and sell their work at this juried show, which highlights exceptional pottery, basketry, sculpture, jewelry, paintings, weavings, and other arts by America's best Indian artists. Among the scheduled events are Indian dancing and storytelling in the amphitheater. Traditional Indian foods like Navajo fry bread and Hopi piki bread are on sale in the food booths. Every year, one outstanding Southwest artist is honored at the market.

Museum members gain early admission and purchasing privileges the first morning of the show. The Phoenix METRO light rail stops at the Heard Museum, which is located at 2301 N. Central Avenue, Phoenix, a block away from the Phoenix Art Museum. The Heard is also host to a Spanish Market, held each November, devoted to the Southwest's Hispanic art and culture. For information about opening hours, exhibits, and special events, call the Heard Museum general line at 602-252-8848 or log on to www. heard.org.

Above: visitors can browse and purchase fine works by contemporary Native artists at the museum's Berlin Gallery.

Right: a Hopi dancer performs at the Heard Guild Indian Fair and Market. The annual event attracts nearly 20,000 visitors and 650 artists.

SEDONA AND THE VERDE VALLEY

Spectacular red-rock formations surround this
popular getaway town, known for its dining,
shopping, and New Age vibrations

Although its reputation has taken a beating, due to the deaths, in 2009, of three people taking part in a Native American-style sweat lodge at a New Age retreat run by famed self-help guru James Ray, **Sedona ❶**, a picturesque town in Arizona's Red Rock Country, is still a destination on almost every New Ager's wish list. You can take Jeep tours to male and female "vortexes," unusual power points in the earth where energy flows freely, affecting living things with their vibrations; read all about the latest local UFO sightings and abductions; and have your aura tuned, your chakras aligned, crystals placed on your body, be rebirthed, immerse yourself in sacred healing mud, and even buy a T-shirt hand-dyed with Sedona Red Dirt "believed to bring good luck to the wearer"; and still have time to shop at Sedona's faux Mexican marketplace, *Tlaquepaque*, before sunset sets the rocks afire.

It would be easy to write off Sedona as Arizona's answer to Santa Fe. But what both places have in common, beyond their sometimes wacky offerings, is a stunning natural setting and a quality sought after by all the weary urban refugees, wealthy retirees, artists, and spiritual seekers who have moved here since the 1980s: inspiration. They

seem to find it. The Cowboy Artists of America was established in Sedona, and today, more than 40 galleries offer some of the most sophisticated art in the Southwest. The town is home to an array of world-class artists, writers, photographers, musicians, and others who ensure that Sedona maintains a jam-packed cultural calendar.

Natural splendor

But the main reason to visit Sedona is to get outdoors and enjoy the scenery. At this 4,000ft (1,200-meter)

LEFT: swimming and subbathing are popular activities at Slide Rock State Park.
RIGHT: meditating near Court House Rock.

The iconic profile of Cathedral Rock peaks over the treeline.

BELOW: yucca blossoms amid red-rock formations outside Sedona.

elevation, temperatures stay above freezing year-round. Summer months see 90°F (32°C) days at low elevations, but relief is always just a hike away in thousands of acres of cool, high-elevation national forest. Spring arrives early, with newly leafed cottonwoods and wave after wave of poppies, lupines, and other wildflowers on the desert floor. Summer brings drenching monsoon rains and ephemeral waterfalls in the canyons. By October, fall leaves in **Oak Creek Canyon ❷** are peaking. In January, the **Mogollon Rim** is dusted with snow, but down in the valley the crowds have evaporated and locals have taken back the trails. The best remedy for cabin fever, say residents of Flagstaff, 30 miles (48km) to the north, is a drive to Sedona.

The route of choice from Flagstaff is spectacular **Highway 89A**, which spirals down off the ponderosa-pine-clad Colorado Plateau into Oak Creek Canyon. The road descends stratum by stratum from pale Kaibab Limestone into the variegated Supai Group, the Hermit Formation, and the Schnebly

Hill Formation. Differential erosion has carved a fantasyland of rock formations here: alcoves, arches, hoodoos, buttes, and mesas with anthropomorphic names such as Cathedral Rock, Coffee Pot Rock, Bell Rock, and Vultee Arch.

Oak Creek Vista is a good place to stop and get a first look at the canyon described by Zane Grey in **The Call of the Canyon** as "a gigantic burrow for beasts, perhaps for outlawed men – not for a civilized person." Civilization, for better or worse, finds its way into the canyon regularly now: an astounding 4 million visitors a year make the drive. But before Arizona's first designated scenic highway was built in the 1940s, early residents remember Oak Creek Canyon as a gloomy, isolated place, home to deer, elk, bobcats, black bear, and at one time grizzlies.

The first permanent homesteader in the canyon was Irishman Jim Thompson who, in 1876, built a log cabin at Indian Gardens, where Tonto Apaches had only recently been raising corn, squash, and beans.

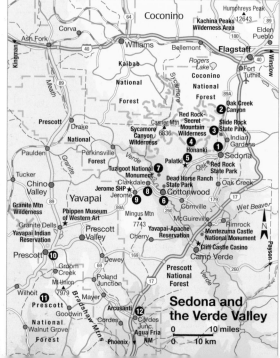

Homegrown produce is still one of the main attractions at **Garland's Oak Creek Lodge** (tel: 928-282-3343; Apr–mid-Nov), a 1930s cabin resort located 7.5 miles (12km) north of Sedona. It's almost impossible to get a room reservation here, but don't miss a stroll in the gardens (a popular wedding venue) and one of the lodge's famous dinners, a chef's choice of whatever is fresh that day, served family style, in a warm, friendly atmosphere.

Two miles (3km) south of Garlands, is 55-acre (22-hectare) **Slide Rock State Park ③** (tel: 928-282-3034; daily 8am–7pm; charge). In 1907, Frank Pendley built a home and planted an apple orchard in the meadow above Slide Rock that is still producing today. *Life* magazine named Slide Rock one of the top 10 swimming holes in the United States, and the park attracts some 1,600 bathers on a typical hot July day.

But even if you don't want to whoosh down the natural rock chute (it's hard on the rear), stop here for a stroll along the creek, which is home to more than 20 species of fish.

Red-rock trails

Slide Rock may also be your best bet for trailhead parking during peak seasons. Several spectacular hikes – including the 3-mile (5km) **West Fork of Oak Creek Trail**, which follows the creek through a narrow slot canyon – take off near here into the 44,000-acre (17,800-hectare) **Red Rock-Secret Mountain Wilderness ④**. It's easier to find solitude in the backcountry. Better still, connecting trails allow you to begin in Oak Creek Canyon and end up in **West Sedona**. One possibility is **Sterling Pass Trail**, which connects with **Vultee Arch Trail** for a 4-mile (6km) one-way hike. Inexpensive daily and weekly **Sedona Redrock Passes** are required to park and hike in the area and are available from area businesses, at trailheads, and from the Red Rock Ranger District

of Coconino National Forest (tel: 928-203-7500, 928-203-2900; Mon–Fri 8am–4.30pm), on Highway 179, just south of the Village of Oak Creek. Five small campgrounds line Highway 89A in Oak Creek Canyon (one is closed seasonally); they fill quickly and reservations are essential.

Sedona has suffered from a very visible, unregulated real-estate boom, which, to its present regret, allowed runaway development and overscaled homes to blight its famous red-rock vistas. Since then, new zoning has led to environmentally sensitive, smaller-scale public buildings like the attractive little Sedona Library. Outside the library is an engaging bronze statue of Sedona's founder, Sedona Schnebly, a Missouri pioneer, who with her husband T. C., began farming 80 acres (32 hectares) on the west bank of Oak Creek in 1902. Some of the most spectacular vistas in Sedona lie along **Schnebly Hill Road**, a dirt road that winds onto **Munds Mountain**. It's closed in winter, but for careful drivers this makes a scenic alternative to Interstate 17.

TIP

Sedona's dramatic setting and artsy atmosphere lend themselves to a schedule of special events, including the Sedona International Film Festival in March, the Chamber Music Festival in May, and Jazz on the Rocks in September.

BELOW: the main street of Sedona.

Oak Creek.

BELOW: Tuzigoot
National Historic
Monument.

House of worship

For many spiritual seekers, Sedona's breathtaking setting is all the proof they need that God exists. In 1932, architect and sculptor Marguerite Bruswig Staude, a student of Frank Lloyd Wright, conceived the idea for a Catholic church literally rising up from the symbolic cross at the center of the Christian faith. She went around the world searching for the right location and found it in Sedona. Built on one of Sedona's famous vortexes, or power centers, on forest service land outside downtown Sedona, the **Chapel of the Holy Cross** (Chapel Road, off US 179; tel: 928-282-4069; Mon–Sat 9am–5pm, Sun 10am–5pm; free) was a remarkable achievement in 1956, when it was completed. Its soaring angled glass facade framing an over-sized cross is snugged between two 250ft (76-meter) redrock pinnacles with a 1,000ft (300-meter) cliff for a backdrop and seems to have arisen spontaneously from the redrocks themselves. One of the main attractions in Sedona, it was voted one of Arizona's Seven Man-Made Wonders in 2007.

For lessons in how to live harmoniously with the environment, look no farther than the Sinagua Indians who lived in Sedona a thousand years ago. They farmed along Oak Creek and built warm, south-facing cliff-side pueblos in the red rocks that blend seamlessly with their surroundings.

Hundreds of ruins are secreted away in the red rocks, but the easiest to visit are **Palatki** and **Honanki** ❺ on the north side of the valley. To reach them, drive Highway 89A west 9.5 miles (15km) from the Y intersection with Highway 179. Turn right on FR 525, drive 6 miles (10km) to where FR 795 branches to the right, and take FR 795 2 miles (3km) to a dead end. For Honanki, continue on FR 525 another 3 miles (5km) beyond the intersection with FR 795. Forest Service rangers offer tours daily.

Reservations are required to visit Palatki. Call Palatki (tel: 928-282-3854). Honanki is open daily 10am–6pm. No reservations required, but please

call Palatki or the Red Rock Ranger District (928-282-4119) before going.

Ancient crossroads

The Verde River Valley is increasingly a bedroom community for those who'd rather live in Sedona but can't afford the rent. One such town is **Cottonwood** ❻, 17 miles (27km) southwest of Sedona. Picnicking, camping, canoeing, and fishing for trout, bass, and catfish are available at 320-acre (130-hectare) **Dead Horse Ranch State Park** (tel: 928-634-5283; daily 8am–5pm; charge). Nearby is **Tuzigoot National Monument** ❼ (tel: 928-634-5564; daily May–Sept 8am–6pm, Oct–Apr 5pm; charge), a large Sinagua pueblo built on a high ridge above the **Verde River**. Begun as a small pueblo in AD 1000, Tuzigoot grew to 110 rooms in the 1200s, as Sinagua refugees from drought-stricken northern areas moved south. The fertile, well-watered Verde Valley became an important prehistoric crossroads for traders, but eventually overpopulation, diminishing natural resources, and epidemics seem to have taken a toll. The pueblo took on a defensive appearance and began to store more food. By 1425, all the residents had moved away.

Tuzigoot is a Tonto Apache word meaning "crooked water," a reference to a crescent-shaped lake near the monument. The Apache are still a strong presence in the Verde Valley, where they have intermarried with Yavapai Indians to such a degree that the two groups have merged into the Yavapai-Apache Nation. They live together on three separate tracts of land on the 560-acre (225-hectare) **Yavapai-Apache Reservation** and operate **Cliff Castle Casino** (Montezuma Castle exit 289, off Interstate 17; tel: 800-381-slot) in **Camp Verde**, now the Verde Valley's main employer and the state's most popular casino. Even if you don't gamble, stop at this casino for a look at the tribe's administrative offices, which were designed by Hopi architect Dennis Mumkena in the shape of a kiva. The interior (not open to the public) is decorated with symbols connected to Hopi legends.

Sedona is a center of New Age culture.

BELOW: Chapel of the Holy Cross.

The First Lady of Arizona Letters

The rancher and writer Sharlot M. Hall was "a genuine young frontierswoman," wrote Charles F. Lummis, her editor and friend. "Not of the cheap drama and Sunday-edition counterfeits, but a fine, quiet, loveable woman made strong and wise and sweet by life in the unbuilded spaces."

This love of "unbuilded spaces" began early. The first white child born in Kansas, in 1870, Sharlot and her family traveled west along the Santa Fe Trail in 1882 and built up a ranch on Lynx Creek near Prescott, which Sharlot continued to run until 1928, when she began her museum. She retained a love of adventure, the outdoors, and free-spirited living until her death in 1943.

In 1906, she helped defeat a congressional bill to make New Mexico and Arizona a single state by using her epic poem *Arizona* to sway the US Congress. In July 1911, while serving as territorial historian (the first woman to serve in the territorial government), she and famed guide Al Doyle spent 10 weeks journeying by wagon through the remote Arizona Strip. Her glowing accounts of the trip led Congress to include the area when statehood was granted in 1912. She wrote 10 books and more than 500 articles, stories, and poems and was the first woman to be inducted into Arizona's Hall of Fame. Prescott's Sharlot Hall Museum is one of northern Arizona's best-loved history museums.

Arcosanti

The focus here is on putting into practice the communitarian ideas of one visionary on how we should live with nature and each other

"Unless we reinvent the American dream in terms of the physiology of it, then it's not going to be a dream, it's going to be doomsday," Italian-born architect Paolo Soleri told an interviewer in 1995. Soleri was talking about the pollution, congestion, social isolation, and enormous waste of resources caused by Americans' pursuit of the good life at the expense of the rest of the planet. Furthermore, states Soleri, "We would be in need of 40 planets by the year 2050, if the American dream becomes the planetary dream."

Soleri's solution? Arcosanti, an experimental city on 25 acres in the high country of Cordes Junction, 70 miles (115km) north of Phoenix. Since 1970, Soleri's Cosanti Foundation has been building the new community, which incorporates large, siltcast, concrete structures, and solar greenhouses. It is a strange vision in the midst of sweeping grasslands surrounded by mountains, prompting everything from praise for its far-reaching vision to horror from one critic who labeled it "a social experiment that has more to do with totalitarianism than harmonious living."

When complete, Arcosanti will soar 25 stories high, house 7,000 people, and include apartments, businesses, studios, and performance venues in an urban setting that emphasizes privacy linked to accessible public spaces. The complex is designed in accordance with the concept of "arcology" (architecture+ecology) developed by Soleri. In such a system, artificial structures and living things interact as organs do in the human body, with efficient circulation of people and resources, and solar orientation for lighting, heating, and cooling.

Soleri began developing his arcological concepts after spending 18 months studying with renowned architect Frank Lloyd Wright at Taliesen West in Scottsdale and Taliesen East in Wisconsin. Taking to heart the famous edict, "Form ever follows function," he returned to Italy and began building large ceramics, using processes that led to the award-winning windbells of ceramic and bronze that are sold to support his experimental work, as well as the siltcast architectural structures at Arcosanti. Soleri returned to Arizona and began constructing his first experimental village, Cosanti, in Paradise Valley in 1956, which remains his permanent home today.

Volunteers and students from around the world, many with no previous design experience, undertake a five-week workshop that teaches building techniques and arcological philosophy, while continuing the city's construction. Residents are workshop alumni who continue the work of planning, construction, and teaching. They produce the world-famous Soleri Bells as well as host 50,000 tourists each year. Daily tours (voluntary donation) introduce visitors to the site, and concerts and other events are held regularly in the Colly Soleri Music Center, named for Soleri's late wife. Shows include dinner and are often followed by a light show on the opposite mesa. Tours of Cosanti in Paradise Valley are also available.

For more information, contact Arcosanti at 928-632-7135 or visit www.arcosanti.org.

LEFT AND ABOVE: Arcosanti reflects the "arcological" philosophy of its founder, architect Paolo Soleri.

Before Tuzigoot National Monument was deeded to the National Park Service in 1939, it was the property of the United Verde Copper Company, the Verde Valley's primary industry from 1882 to 1953. Two miles (3km) northwest of Cottonwood is the old smelter town of **Clarkdale ❽**, which is sputtering back to life with the revival of the historic **Verde Canyon Railroad** (tel: 800-582-7245; Wed–Sun excursions 1–5pm, reservations required).

The Verde Valley Railroad carried ore and passengers – the Verde Mix, it was called. Today, it's strictly tourists, with about 60,000 passengers a year boarding the old locomotive for the four-hour, 40-mile (64km) round-trip from **Clarkdale** to **Perkinsville**. With its bright blue engines and obvious family appeal, the railroad is a pleasant way to spend an afternoon. It also offers one of the easiest ways to view **Sycamore Canyon Wilderness**, a 21-mile (34km) -long gash in the earth, with 700ft (215-meter) -high red cliffs, huge cottonwoods, endangered wildlife, and bald and golden eagles in winter.

Sin City

The Verde Valley Railroad was financed by Senator William A. Clark, owner of the United Verde Mine in **Jerome ❾**. Jerome began life as a mining camp in 1876 and eventually yielded $1 billion of copper, gold, silver, zinc, and lead during its 77 years of operation. Seeming to defy gravity as it clings to the side of 7,743ft (2,360-meter) **Mingus Mountain**, quaint little Jerome could be a miniature Bisbee, with its stacked Victorian "painted ladies," narrow streets, and innovative art galleries. But it beats it hands down for breathtaking scenery, with vertiginous views of the Verde Valley all the way north to the San Francisco Peaks.

Entranced by such beauty, it's easy to forget the reality. Between 1895 and 1935, 150 miners lost their lives in the 4,650ft (1,420-meter) -deep shaft. Even in the 1940s, the son of a mine executive recalls, "the miners were in rubber boots, working in water about a foot deep. It was humid, and very, very hot … They could work only 20 minutes without rest."

Remnants of the Verde Valley's mining boom clutter a yard near Cottonwood.

BELOW: a view of Jerome from the site of the former Little Daisy Mine.

Bull riding at the Prescott Frontier Days rodeo.

BELOW:
the Spirit Room saloon in Jerome.

Despite this sad history, by 1900 Jerome had 2,681 residents, making it the fifth-largest town in Arizona Territory. Americans and immigrants from Mexico, Spain, Italy, Austria, Ireland, and Eastern Europe vied for lodging, often having to bunk in shifts. Prostitution was so common it was intermittently legalized. Saloons, opium dens, and gambling houses did a roaring trade, leading the *New York Sun*, in 1903, to dub Jerome "the Wickedest Town in the West" and to express the opinion that "the best thing that could happen to Jerome would be a nice, big, citywide fire."

Mud slides, floods, and devastating blazes did destroy much of the town between 1894 and 1925, but somehow it has never given up the ghost. A handful of artists, retirees, and others looking for cheap digs began restoring individual buildings in the 1960s, and now the whole town is listed on the National Register of Historic Places. Jerome's interesting art galleries are its best feature today. **Jerome State Historic Park** (tel: 928-634-5381; daily 8am–5pm; charge), located in the 8,000-sq-ft (750-sq-meter) 1916 home of "Rawhide Jimmy" Douglas above his Little Daisy Mine, has a model of the mines, an assay office, old photos, mining tools, and mineral displays.

Capital idea

By contrast, upstanding Victorian values seem to ooze out of **Prescott** ❿ (pronounced PRESS-cut), a little town cradled in a forested basin beneath the **Bradshaw Mountains**, south of Jerome. Historic Prescott has a population of over 43,000, but mushrooming subdivisions have pushed the Prescott area population much higher, and the total Yavapai County population, of which Metro Prescott is the center, is now nearly 230,000, the third largest in the state after Phoenix and Tucson. Tree-shaded streets, solid Victorian buildings, and an elegant courthouse make historic Prescott's town center a delightful place to linger on a sleepy summer afternoon. Several historic hotels offer lodging, including the 1927 **Hassayampa Inn**, a gorgeous grande dame in the old style, recently renovated and featuring antiques, painted ceilings, and plush furnishings.

Prescott had noble aspirations from the get-go. When President Lincoln made Arizona a territory in 1863, Governor John Goodwin and other appointed officials toured the territory for three months, looking for a site for the new capital that had lands rich in mineral wealth and grazing but was relatively free of Confederate sympathies. The party based itself at Fort Whipple and chose gold-rich Granite Creek for the new settlement, which they named Prescott, after the historian noted for his work on Mexico. Government buildings were built in 1864, at the height of the campaign against the Tonto Apache and Yavapai Indians. As with the Verde Valley, the shoe is on the other foot these days. **Bucky's Casino**, operated by the small Yavapai Indian tribe, is one of Prescott's booming businesses.

Prescott lost the capital to Tucson in 1867 (it eventually ended up in Phoenix), but quickly consoled itself with gold mining and cattle-ranching operations. The town became legendary as a hard-drinking haven for cowboys spending their pay on a Saturday night. By the early 1900s, 40 saloons lined Montezuma Street, or **Whiskey Row**, as it was known. Working cowboys are still very much in evidence and have been known to down a whiskey or two at the **Palace Saloon**. What's billed as "the world's oldest rodeo" takes place in early July and the popular **Arizona Cowboy Poets Gathering** (www.azcowboypoets.org) attracts saddlestruck bards to the town in September

Western visions

Six miles (10km) north of Prescott, just north of Highway 89A, the **Phippen Museum of Western Art** (tel: 928-778-1385; Tue–Sat 10am–4pm, Sun 1–4pm; charge) honors western artist George Phippen, founder of the Cowboy Artists of America. The museum has a good selection of paintings, sketches, and bronzes. Arizona's

territorial history is beautifully told at the **Sharlot Hall Museum** (tel: 928-445-3122; Mon–Sat 10am–5pm, Sun noon–4pm; charge), housed in the 1864 Governor's Mansion and 11 other buildings. It was founded in 1928 by former territorial historian Sharlot Hall, a pioneer Prescott rancher, travel writer and, not incidentally, cowgirl poet.

Trails lace **Prescott National Forest** ⓫. One of the most popular is 1.7-mile (2.7km) Thumb Butte Loop Trail, which winds through the surrounding countryside. Granite Mountain Wilderness is also popular with hikers and rock climbers. For information, contact Prescott National Forest (tel: 928-443-8000). A beautiful drive north through the grasslands of Chino Valley takes you to Ash Fork and Interstate 40. Highway 69 heads south past dirt roads leading to old mines and historic ranches before connecting with Interstate 17 at Cordes Junction, the turnoff for **Arcosanti** ⓬, the futuristic concrete city founded by visionary architect Paolo Soleri (*see mini-feature on page 240*).

The Gold King mine and ghost town maintains colorful details from the town's historic past.

BELOW: houses cling to Jerome's Cleopatra Hill.

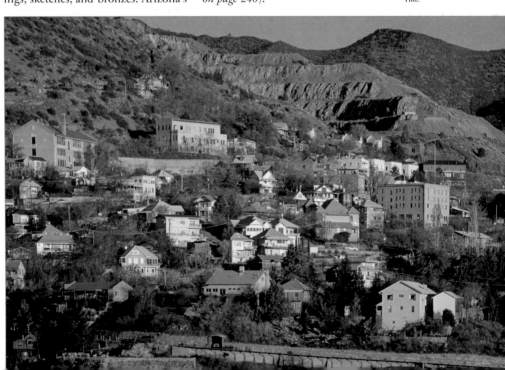

RESTAURANTS

Prices for a three-course dinner per person, excluding tax, tip, and beverages:
$ = under $20
$$ = $20–40
$$$ = $40–60
$$$$ = over $60

The Asylum Restaurant
Jerome Grand Hotel, 200 Hill Street, Jerome
Tel: 928-639-3197 **$$–$$$**
Don't miss this restaurant in a former hospital atop Cleopatra Hill in Jerome. At dinner, choose among lobster tail, shrimp skewers, Sonoran spiced chicken pasta, achiote-rubbed pork tenderloin, mesquite-bacon-wrapped filet mignon, and veggie specials.

Café Elote
771 State Route 179, Sedona
Tel: 928-203-0105 **$–$$**
This modern Mexican café offers seductive fare that will fill the belly and snap the taste buds. The eponymous Elote corn appetizer is a must-taste. Mains include carnitas, stuffed pork cheeks, and a number of veggie options. Expect a line!

ChocolaTree Organic Bakery
1595 W. Highway 89A, Sedona
Tel: 928-282-2997 **$–$$**
This bakery, on the same premises as a chocolatier, is the best place in Sedona to sample raw chocolate. Voted one of the US's most healthy restaurants, ChocolaTree also serves a plethora of delicious globally inspired organic raw and cooked vegetarian dishes, such as soups, salads, sandwiches, tamales, and noodles.

Coffee Pot Restaurant
2050 W. Highway 89A, Sedona
Tel: 928-282-6626 **$**
A legend since the 1950s, the Coffee Pot is a down-home diner famous for its 101 omelets.

Cowboy Club
241 Highway 89A, Sedona
Tel: 928-282-4200 **$$**
Cowboy cuisine takes a Sedona twist at this stylish eatery adorned with spurs, boots, lariats, and other buckaroo gear. Ribs, meat loaf, and beef are given gourmet treatment. Don't pass up Southwest specialties like fried cactus, rattlesnake, and bison.

Garland's Oak Creek Lodge
Highway 89A, Sedona
Tel: 928-282-3343 **$$**
Four-course prix-fixe dinners are served in a relaxed dining room, family style, at this resort in Oak Creek Canyon. Guests have first preference, but there are sometimes reservations available for non-guests, so check for cancellations. It's well worth the effort because the country-style cuisine leans heavily on the resort's organic produce.

Heartline Café
1610 Highway 89A, Sedona
Tel: 928-282-0785 **$$**
An eclectic mix of flavors emanates seductively from the kitchen of Charlie Kline, a classically trained chef with creativity to burn. Among the signature entrees are smoked mozzarella ravioli with red-pepper pesto, local farm-raised trout with a pecan crust, and pistachio-crusted chicken with pomegranate demi-glace.

Oak Creek Pub and Grill
336 Route 179, Sedona
Tel: 928-282-3300 **$–$$**
This popular microbrewery in the Tlaquepaque Marketplace is a good place to sample seriously good ale, such as the gold-medal Oak Creek Hefeweisen, in a relaxed atmosphere. The grill offers pub food

The Palace
120 S. Montezuma, Prescott
Tel: 928-541-1996 **$$**
A historic saloon on Prescott's infamous Whiskey Row, the Palace has been restored to its former splendor. It now serves up a meat-heavy menu of ribs, steaks, chops, and a memorable corn chowder.

Pietro's Italian Restaurant
2445 Highway 89A, Sedona
Tel: 928-282-2525 **$$**
Pietro's brings style and imagination to traditional offerings. Options include grilled eggplant rolled with goat cheese and sweet-pepper sauce, red-pepper ravioli filled with smoked mozzarella, and filet mignon grilled in a wine-shiitake mushroom sauce.

Prescott Brewing Company
130 W. Gurley Street, Prescott
Tel: 928-771-2795 **$**
The beer is good, the crowd is spirited, and the food is cheap and filling at this popular brewpub, housed in an old mercantile building in downtown Prescott.

Reds Restaurant
Sedona Rouge Hotel and Spa, 2250 W. Highway 89A
Tel: 928-203-4111 **$$–$$$$**
This resort restaurant offers relaxed dining and updated comfort-food classics. Many dishes are cooked in the wood-fired oven, a central feature of the open-plan kitchen.

Rene at Tlaquepaque
Highway 179, Sedona
Tel: 928-282-9225 **$$$–$$$$**
One of Sedona's favorite special-occasion restaurants, René's offers a beautiful French Provincial dining room in the midst of the Mexican marketplace of Tlaquepaque.

Wildflower Bread Company
The Shops at Piñon Pointe, Highways 179 and 89A, Sedona
Tel: 928-204-2223 **$**
All the bread and pastries are home-baked at this fragrant little bakery in the back of an upscale shopping center. At breakfast, there are lemon-ricotta pancakes. At lunch, there's a variety of sandwiches on healthy whole-wheat and other breads. Free Wi-fi.

Bird Watching

Varied biogeographical regions allow birders to experience a wide range of species, including subtropical birds not seen elsewhere in the US

Of the 23 documented species of hummingbirds in the US, 18 visit southern Arizona. Add to that the 10,000 sandhill cranes, snow geese, and other waterfowl that descend on flooded Willcox Playa in winter and the 4–10 million birds that migrate along the San Pedro River flyway, and it's clear why Arizona is one of the nation's top birding spots.

Hummers enchant visitors at bed-and-breakfasts in Ramsey and Miller canyons in the Huachucas, Patagonia in the Patagonia Mountains, Madera Canyon in the Santa Ritas, and Cave Creek Canyon in the Chiricahuas. The latter is also popular for its summer populations of rare elegant trogons, a relative of Mexico's immortal quetzal bird, and other subtropical species such as sulphur-bellied flycatchers, red-faced warblers, and painted redstarts.

The densely vegetated banks of the Colorado River in the Grand Canyon are used by endangered Southwest willow flycatchers, a drab bird whose numbers are dwindling as native willows are replaced by exotic tamarisk. Bald and golden eagles are seen at Nankoweap Canyon in the Grand Canyon in winter and along the Verde River in Sycamore Canyon in central Arizona. California condors are also seen soaring over the Grand Canyon alongside other carrion-eaters like turkey vultures and enormous desert ravens.

In the low desert, birds thrive in inventive ways. White-winged doves and cactus wrens feed on the nectar and succulent fruit of the saguaro. This signature cactus of the Sonoran Desert provides food, shelter, and moisture for many birds, including cute elf owls, which breed in nests pecked into saguaro trunks by Gila woodpeckers and declining populations of gilded flickers, while red-tailed and Harris hawks, and curve-billed thrashers build nests cradled by the cactus's spiny arms.

Left: commonly seen throughout the West, the Swainson's hawk migrates some 6,000 miles (10,000km) from Alaska to South America.

Above: a Gila woodpecker perches on a giant saguaro blossom. The birds have distinctive coloring – black and white stripes on the back and flashing white wing patches. Adult males have a red cap.

Above: an elf owl nests in a saguaro cactus. Among the smallest owl species, the elf is found in Mexico and adjoining areas of the US. They feed on crickets, beetles, and other invertebrates and can be identified by a series of yipping, doglike calls.

Top Birding Activities

Birders will want to remember two important southern Arizona birding events: the Southeast Wings Birding Festival in mid-August and the Wings Over Willcox Sandhill Crane Celebration in January, when more than 10,000 cranes overwinter on the marshes and fields around Willcox Plaza.

Southeastern Arizona Bird Observatory (tel: 520-432-1388; www.sabo.org) has information on local birding events. In spring and summer, participate in banding hummingbirds at San Pedro House, the visitor center and gift shop at San Pedro Riparian Area; guided river and canyon walks; owl excursions; and workshops on neotropical migrants like trogons and parrots. In fall and winter, SABO offers tours of top migratory waterfowl areas such as Sulphur Springs Valley and Whitewater Draw.

Tucson Audubon Society (tel: 520-629-0510; www.tucsonaudubon.org) has free guided birding hikes, talks, and workshops and allows you to participate in local Christmas bird counts. Seven Audubon chapters throughout Arizona offer regional programs, including Yuma, where the California black rail, a small bird that lives among the marshes of the lower Colorado and Gila rivers, is one of five Arizona birds on Audubon's Watchlist of birds in peril. The others are California condors, Southwest willow flycatchers, Mexican spotted owls, and gilded flickers.

Grand Canyon National Park Condor Ranger Talk: Wings Over the Canyon. Learn about the important condor reintroduction program at the Grand Canyon and Vermilion Cliffs, one of three breeding populations in the world, through daily talks in front of Kolb Studio at the South Rim's Grand Canyon Village. 1.30pm, summer only.

Above: a bird photographer waits for a shot at the Arizona-Sonora Desert Museum. Bird-watchers will find an abundance of guided tours, workshops, festivals, and organizations devoted to Arizona birds.

Below: hummingbirds use slender beaks and long, flicking tongues to sip nectar from flowers. Arizona has 18 species of hummingbirds; they are especially attracted to red blossoms.

Top: a Mexican jay at the northernmost extent of its range in Arizona. **Right:** a cactus wren alights on a cholla cactus; the birds often nest in cactus, using the needles to protect themselves from predators.

MOGOLLON RIM AND TONTO BASIN

Once roamed by the Apache, this land of rugged beauty encompasses ancient pueblos, historic forts, and reminders of a violent past

C aptain John G. Bourke, an Apache fighter under the command of General George Crook in the 1880s, described the **Mogollon Rim** as "a strange upheaval, a strange freak of nature, a mountain canted up on one side. One rides along the edge and looks down two and three thousand feet into what is termed the 'Tonto Basin,' a scene of grandeur and rugged beauty."

Bourke was equally impressed by the way the Apache lived so harmoniously with this rugged terrain. "The Apache was a hard foe to subdue, not because he was full of wiles and tricks and experienced in all that pertains to the art of war, but because he had so few artificial wants and depended almost absolutely upon what his great mother – Nature – stood ready to supply."

But the lessons of the Apache, brave fighters whom Bourke and Crook admired, were mostly lost on the white settlers whose lands they were charged with defending. Attracted initially by gold, then by timber, rivers, and rich lands that could sustain ranches and farms, those who came to the Mogollon Rim and **Tonto Basin** found themselves locked in an epic struggle of possession – with nature and their fellow men. Nowhere in Arizona saw more bloody battles between Indians and white men,

ranchers and rustlers, homesteaders and rogue wild animals.

It was this authentic Wild West quality that led western novelist Zane Grey to fall in love with the area in the early 1900s. "For wild, rugged beauty, I had not seen its equal," he wrote. Grey built a hunting lodge near Payson and returned year after year to hunt bear and mountain lion with local guides like Babe Haught and Al Doyle. More than half of Grey's novels are set in the Tonto Basin, earning the area the official moniker Zane Grey Country.

Main attractions

MONTEZUMA WELL
MONTEZUMA CASTLE NATIONAL
  MONUMENT
FORT VERDE STATE HISTORIC PARK
WET BEAVER WILDERNESS
TONTO NATIONAL FOREST
PAYSON
TONTO NATURAL BRIDGE STATE PARK
MAZATZAL DIVIDE TRAIL

LEFT: hikers on the Mogollon Rim. **RIGHT:** *Opuntia chlorotica*, or Dollarjoint Pricklypear.

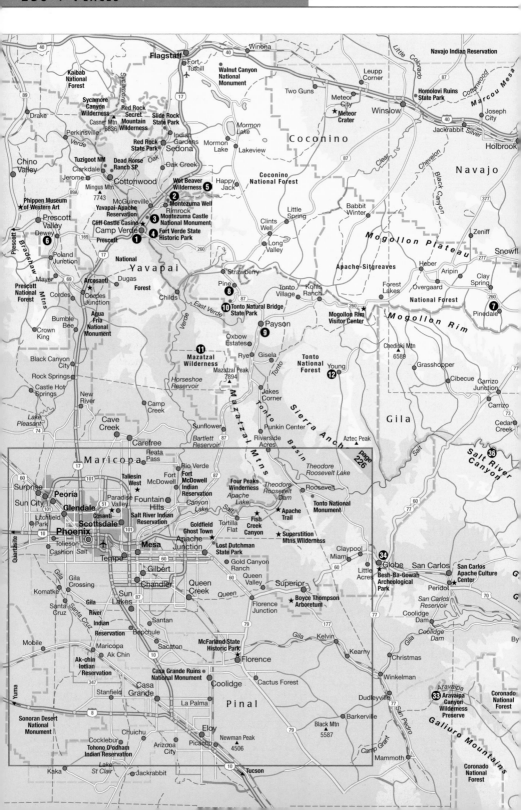

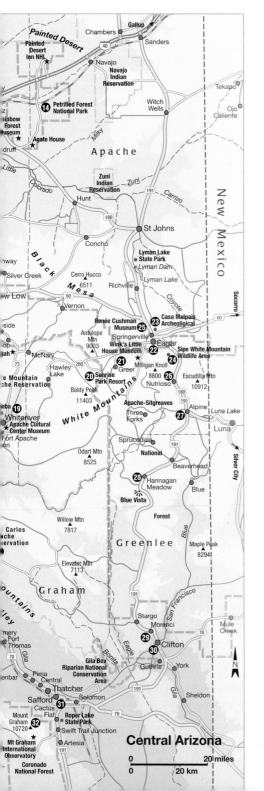

Early inhabitants

Start your drive at **Camp Verde ❶**, off Interstate 17, where the **Verde River** meanders through the stark Verde Valley basin. Farmers from the Prescott area founded the first Anglo settlement here in 1865, but 1,000 years earlier prehistoric farmers were raising corn, beans, squash, cotton, and other crops on these riverbanks, using technology perfected by the Hohokam to the south. A rare 12th-century Hohokam-style pithouse can be viewed at **Montezuma Well ❷**, 11 miles (18km) north of Camp Verde, along with irrigation ditches and pueblos built by the northern Sinagua culture. The Sinagua were adept dry-land farmers who moved into the Verde Valley from the Flagstaff area in the 1100s, following the eruptions of Sunset Crater Volcano.

Montezuma Well is a detached unit of **Montezuma Castle National Monument ❸** (tel: 928-567-3322; daily May–Sept 8am–6pm, Oct–Apr 8am–5pm; charge). The "castle" is really a beautifully preserved five-story, 13th-century Sinagua cliff dwelling above Beaver Creek. It so impressed early settlers they erroneously thought it the palace of Aztec leader Montezuma. An adjoining pueblo, Castle A, has collapsed, but most of Montezuma Castle's limestone walls and 20 rooms have survived, protected in an alcove high in the cliffs. Visitors may view the dwelling from a trail below but aren't permitted to enter.

By the time Spaniard Antonio de Espejo rode through the Verde Valley in 1583, these early farming cultures had disappeared. Strong but inconclusive evidence indicates the Sinagua may have moved back north into the Hopi and Zuñi pueblos in the 1400s. In their place were hunter-gatherer Yavapai Indians, related to the Havasupai and Hualapai of the Grand Canyon, and small bands of Tonto Apache. The latter proved so troublesome during an 1863 gold rush on the Hassayampa River and the subsequent settlement of the Verde Valley that the US Army was dispatched to build Fort Lincoln, later called Fort Verde

Apache campaign

The fort became a staging area for General Crook (known as "Gray Eyes" by the Apache) and his army's successful Tonto campaign, which resulted in the defeat of Chief Chalipan and 2,300 Tonto Apache in the winter of 1872–73. As part of the peace agreement with the Tonto Apache, the honorable Crook promised to provide jobs, farmland, and a police force and immediately had the Indian workers dig a 5-mile (8km) -long irrigation

Reavis Trail.

BELOW: re-enactors
use authentic clothing
and weaponry.

ditch, planting 57 acres (23 hectares) of crops. **Fort Verde State Historic Park** ❹ (tel: 928-567-3275; daily 8am–5pm; charge) preserves four surviving fort buildings, including General Crook's adobe headquarters. Exhibits include 1880s-era furnishings, old saddles, Indian crafts, letters, and uniforms belonging to cavalry, infantry, and the Apache scouts Crook used to understand and outmaneuver his opponents.

Forest trails

North of Camp Verde, hiking and swimming are popular activities at 6,700-acre (2,700-hectare) **Wet Beaver Wilderness** ❺, a lush oasis with sycamore-, cottonwood-, and ash-lined riverbanks. Trails follow the river and climb the 2,000ft (610-meter) -high Mogollon Rim. This is a popular area in summer, with swimming holes that provide respite from temperatures in the 90s°F (30s°C). The Red Rock Ranger District of the Coconino National Forest (Highway 179, just south of the village of Oak Creek, near Sedona; tel: 928-282-4119 or 928-203-7500) has information on trails throughout the area.

The **General George Crook Trail**, which starts in **Dewey** ❻, near Prescott, proceeds east through Camp Verde, up along the Mogollon Rim, and finally ends at Cottonwood Wash near **Pinedale** ❼, is an Arizona State Historic Trail that passes through three national forests – Prescott, Coconino, and Apache-Sitgreaves – over its 138-mile (222km) length. The trail was blazed in 1871 by Crook and his men and used for 22 years to patrol the northern boundary of the Apache Reservation. Connecting trails at the west end join the **Highline Trail** at the base of the Mogollon Rim in **Tonto National Forest**, allowing you to hike from desert scrub to pine-fir forest. The Crook Trail is best hiked in spring or fall; portions are open for cross-country skiing in winter.

To access the eastern section of the trail, drive east on Highway 260 from Camp Verde, turn north on Highway 87, then east on unpaved Forest Road 300, the 1928 logging road that parallels the Crook Trail for 42 miles (68km) along the forested rim. Views are breathtaking from this

perched route, with range after range of hazy mountains, emerald forest basins and valleys, and heart-stopping drops below limestone outcrops. The remains of the devastating 1990 Dude Fire, which blackened 24,000 acres (9,700 hectares) and killed six fire-fighters, can still be seen.

Along the road are monuments to the major conflicts of the Apache campaign: the Battle of Skull Cave (1872), the Battle of Turret Butte (1873), and the final showdown, the Battle of Dry Wash (1873), which resulted in the deaths of 22 Apaches and the flight of the remainder.

Rim country

Scenic Highway 87 drops down from the Mogollon Rim into the heart of the Tonto Basin. Historic homes, antique shops, and galleries line the main street of the little Mormon settlement of **Pine** ❽, while nearby **Strawberry** (named for the wild strawberries that used to grow here) preserves Arizona's oldest one-room log schoolhouse (by appointment mid-May–mid-Oct 10am–4pm, Sun noon–4pm), which was built in 1885 (call Strawberry Lodge at 928-659-7200 for information).

Busy little **Payson** ❾ started out as a gold-mining camp in 1881 but is now more popular as a shopping center, a getaway destination for Phoenicians, and a base for exploring the cliffs of the Mogollon Rim, which loom majestically over the town. Limestone deposited at the bottom of an ancient ocean forms the cliffs surrounding the Tonto Basin. Mineral springs at **Pine Creek**, northwest of Payson, have carved the rock into the world's longest natural bridge, preserved at **Tonto Natural Bridge State Park** ❿ (tel: 928-476-4202; Thur–Mon 8am–6pm; charge). At 400ft (120 meters) wide, with many limestone formations similar to those found in caves farther to the south, the bridge is a beautiful little oasis off the main highway and a bonus on any trip into the rim country.

Forest trails

What is advertised as the West's oldest rodeo (begun in 1884) takes place in Payson every August. Get in the saddle yourself or hike a trail in some of the state's most glorious forests. Tonto National Forest's **Payson Ranger District** (1009 E. Highway 260, Payson) has information on hiking, horseback riding, and camping in the surrounding forest and the 252,000-acre (102,000-hectare) **Mazatzal Wilderness** ⓫, whose highest point, 7,894ft (2,406-meter) **Mazatzal Peak**, dominates the southern skyline. You can arrange private horse-packing trips into the Mazatzals (pronounced *MAT-a-zals*) at the Forest Service office.

One of the most popular entry points into these steep, rocky mountains is the 6-mile (10km) **Barnhardt Trail**, near the little town of **Rye**. The trail joins the 29-mile (47km) **Mazatzal Divide Trail**, which runs along the crest of the Mazatzals and features stunning views of the Sierra Ancha Wilderness to the south and the San Francisco Peaks near Flagstaff to the north.

Writer of the Purple Sage

Pearl "Zane" Grey was born in Zanesville, Ohio, in 1872 and trained as a dentist before finding his calling as a self-taught Western writer and avid outdoorsman. Between 1903 and his death in 1939, Grey wrote 56 Western romances, 13 outdoor books, seven juvenile stories, three historical novels, a novel set in Ohio, one set in Tahiti, two screenplays and numerous short stories and non-fiction articles collected in some 20 anthologies.

Sales of his novels have exceeded 100 million copies, and at least 100 of his books and stories have been adapted to film. Much of their appeal lies in the portrayal of simpler times, authentic settings, and classic characters like the lone gunman Lassiter of *Riders of the Purple Sage*, a rugged individual who achieves redemption by wrestling with the ghosts of his past. Almost all of his tales reveal a West where man is engaged in an epic struggle with his environment and is either redeemed or destroyed by it.

Although Grey loved Arizona, he and his wife Dolly and their children moved to Altadena, California, in 1918. Dolly handled her husband's business deals, freeing Grey to write, scout movie locations, and take extended hunting and fishing trips every fall using as a base his cabin in Payson, Arizona.

On the western side of the range is the 28-mile (45km) **Verde River Trail**, which follows a wild and scenic stretch of the **Verde River**. Float trips are possible on the river, though water levels vary considerably depending on spring runoff and summer rains and, in some years, may not be high enough to use a boat. However you choose to explore the Mazatzals – on foot, on horseback, or by boat – be prepared for a hot, dry, rough country. Bring plenty of water, food and appropriate clothing.

Long pack trips were a mainstay of life in the Tonto Basin for Zane Grey, who made the Payson area his base. In 1921, his long-time guide Babe Haught, scion of Payson's first pioneer family, sold Grey several acres of land and built him a hunting cabin.

The Zane Grey Lodge burned to the ground in the 1990 Dude Fire, but you'll find a replica at the Northern Gila County Historical Society's sweet little **Rim Country Museum** (tel: 928-474-3483; Wed–Mon 10am–4pm; charge) on Main Street. The museum, housed in a 1907 forest ranger's house, has a marvelous display of Grey memorabilia that

Tonto National Bridge State Park.

survived the fire (including the author's tooled leather saddlebags, first editions of several of his books, and an embroidered waistcoat) as well as exhibits on the area's forests and Indians. The town has just over 15,000 residents, half of them retirees.

Family feud

Grey visited the Tonto Basin every fall, hunting and fishing and writing detailed notes about the landscape, the people, and the historic events that have given the rim country its unique character. No event has had more impact than the 1887 Pleasant Valley War, one of the most bloody and violent range wars of the frontier era, which pitted the Tewksbury family against the Graham family. Details vary, but the feud was between sheepmen and cattlemen. Adding fuel to the fire was the presence of cowboys from the Hashknife outfit who had been chased out of the Holbrook area. By the time the smoke cleared five years later, 30 people were dead, including 12 Grahams and three Tewksburys. And residents of rim country weren't talking – even to famous authors.

Grey's novel, *To the Last Man*, wove fact with fiction. To try to uncover more of the truth, history buffs won't want to miss visiting **Pleasant Valley**, located between the rim country and the remote little settlement of **Young** ⓬. Hard to reach over rough dirt roads (turn off Highway 260 at Milepost 284, about 33 miles/53km east of Payson), Young is one of Arizona's last cow towns. In keeping with a tradition of feistiness, local folks are independent types with little use for authority. The Antlers Bar, long a symbol of rowdy good cheer, sadly burned down in early 2010, leaving many locals, hunters, and other aficionados bereft.

The first victim of the Pleasant Valley War, a Navajo sheepherder, is buried 5 miles (8km) north of Young. A white cross and sign mark the spot on Forest Route 200, a mile (1.6km) west of the road.

BELOW: Montezuma Castle National Monument.

RESTAURANTS

Prices for a three-course dinner per person, excluding tax, tip, and beverages:
$ = under $20
$$ = $20–45
$$$ = $45–60
$$$$ = over $60

Beeline Café
815 S. Beeline Highway, Payson
Tel: 928-474-9960
$
This old-fashioned diner serves tasty, homestyle, all-American food and is a favorite of locals and week-enders, who drive up for breakfast then head into the forest to walk it off.

Cedar Ridge Restaurant
Mazatzal Hotel and Casino, Highway 87 (Mile Marker 251), Payson
Tel: 928-474-6044
$–$$
Inside the casino on the south edge of Payson, this fine-dining restaurant serves good food at reasonable prices. There's a buffet and early-bird special. The specialty of the house is slow-roasted prime rib.

Creekside Steakhouse and Tavern
Christopher Creek
Tel: 928-478-4389
$–$$$
East of Payson, in Christopher Creek, this steakhouse has a good selection of ranch country steaks, seafood, fresh trout, and one or two vegetarian dishes.

Fiesta Mexicana
911 S. Beeline Highway, Payson

Tel: 928-468-0709
$
Filling, inexpensive Mexican food hits the mark at this local joint, one of two great little Mexican places in Payson (see below). You'll find all the usual combinations of burritos, enchiladas, tacos, and meat and seafood dishes.

Fireside Espresso
614 N. Beeline Highway, Payson
Tel: 928-474-6200
$
A great spot to get off the highway and fill up your go-cup with excellent java.

Gerardo's Firewood Café
512 N. Beeline Highway, Payson
Tel: 928-468-6500
$–$$
This casual Italian restaurant serves some of the best food in Payson. The specialty is wood-fired pizzas, but you will find other Italian specialties such as butternut squash ravioli, eggplant Parmesan, and lasagna in epic portions. Of special note for celiacs: gluten-free pizza and sausages are available. Very popular with Phoenicians on weekends. Get there early.

La Sierra Mexicana Restaurant
800 N. Beeline Highway, Payson
Tel: 928-468-6711
$
This is a local favorite for Mexican food. The portions are large and reminiscent of what everyone's mamacita makes back in the old country. Try the sopa de albondigas (meatball soup), tamales, and fajitas, all of it accompanied

by home-made chips and salsa. Leave room for flan or churros for dessert. Service can be slow when they're busy, but always friendly.

Laura's Small Café
512 S. Beeline Highway, Payson
Tel: 928-474-9018
$
Tucked away in a shopping center near the intersection of Highways 87 and 260, this friendly family-run café is now under the ownership of the eponymous Laura, a longtime employee who bought it from the previous owner. Although they also serve lunch, breakfasts remain the big draw. Try the café's famous almond-crusted French toast with caramel sauce for something different, or any of the egg dishes.

Pine Deli
6240 Hardscrabble Mesa Road, Pine
Tel: 928-476-3536
$
Locals rave about the fresh-tasting pizza at this deli, one of the few eateries in Pine. The deli also makes sandwiches with quality Boar's Head meats and rotisserie chicken. Try the goat's milk fudge for a sweet treat. Eat in or make your own picnic to eat in the forest.

Rimside Grill
Rimside Grill and Cabins
3270 N. Highway 87 (mile marker 267), Pine
Tel: 928-476-3349
$–$$
This homey cabin resort north of Payson is owned by an

enthusiastic young couple. The restaurant has a mellow ambience and dishes up excellent food, ranging from sandwiches at lunch time to the works at dinner. Specials change daily and might include chef's pasta, a seafood dish such as ahi tuna or salmon with dill sauce, a Friday night fish fry and lunch-time fish and chips, prime rib on Saturdays, and yummy home-made desserts. Give it a try. Open Wed–Sun. Call for winter hours.

Strawberry Lodge
Highway 87, Strawberry
Tel: 928-659-7200
$
The menu at this historic lodge is mainstream and comprehensive, so there should be something for everyone. Look for daily specials, and don't miss their home-made pies.

Zane Grey Steakhouse and Saloon
Kohl's Ranch Lodge, Highway 260, Payson
Tel: 928-478-4211
$–$$
Hearty Western fare is the focus in the dining room of this mountain resort. Choices range from build-your-own burgers and chicken pot pie to filet mignon and local Tonto Creek rainbow trout. You'll find an assortment of good pastas and salads and specials such as Cajun-style catfish and hush puppies. Note: This is a tourist spot, and service can be slow. Live music Wed and Sat in summer.

WHITE MOUNTAINS AND EAST CENTRAL

Forest-clad slopes offer stunning mountain drives, an abundance of recreational opportunities, and welcome relief from desert heat

I n his classic *A Sand County Almanac*, naturalist Aldo Leopold describes the **White Mountains** in the early 1900s as "the exclusive domain of the mounted man: mounted cow-man, mounted sheepman, mounted forest officer, mounted trapper, and those unclassified mounted men of unknown origin and uncertain desti-nation always found on frontiers."

A century later, rugged individual-ism is still a way of life in the White Mountains, but ever since Arizona's oldest roadway, Route 666, linked "the palms to the pines" along the Arizona–New Mexico border in 1926, isolation has been more a matter of choice than necessity. Newer paved highways have shrunk the time it takes to reach the White Mountains. As a result, carloads of overheated city slickers now make the pilgrimage on summer weekends, and almost every sleepy town is happy to host them, offering the gamut from rustic lakeside cabins, historic inns, and home-grown museums to round-ups, rodeos, and hands-on archaeo-logical digs.

Laid-back lifestyle

Visitors are lured to these skyscrap-ing peaks, sapphire lakes, and ice-melt streams by a laid-back western lifestyle, temperatures in the 70s°F

(20s°C), and some of the Southwest's best trout fishing, winter sports, and mountain biking. Arizona's second- and third-highest mountains are found here – 11,403ft (3,476-meter) **Baldy Peak**, sacred to the White Mountain Apache on whose reserva-tion it lies, and 10,912ft (3,326-meter) **Escudilla Mountain**, on the adjoin-ing 2-million-acre (809,000-hectare) **Apache-Sitgreaves National Forest**.

Silent Indian ruins are reminders that east-central Arizona also sits on a cultural frontier – a frontier breached

Main attractions

PAINTED DESERT
PETRIFIED FOREST NATIONAL PARK
MOGOLLON RIM OVERLOOK
SUNRISE SKI AREA
CASA MALPAIS NATIONAL HISTORIC
   LANDMARK
SPRINGERVILLE TO CLIFTON HIGHWAY
MOUNT GRAHAM
SALT RIVER CANYON

LEFT: the North Fork of the White River flows through the Fort Apache Indian Reservation. **RIGHT:** White Mountain Apache.

TIP

Anglers will find lots of rainbow, brown, and brook trout as well as an occasional Apache trout and Arctic grayling in the lakes and streams of the White Mountains. A tribal fishing license is required for the White Mountain Apache Reservation.

by US Army soldiers sent to quell the Apache in the 1870s but never entirely subdued, as can be seen in the spirit of self-determination displayed on the San Carlos and White Mountain Apache Reservations today. Equally strong are the Mormon communities founded during the same period, which prospered by trading meat and vegetables with the troops at Fort Apache. Descendants of pioneer families still work the land, trade with travelers, and exert political clout from their mountain stronghold.

King cattle

Holbrook ⓭, 92 miles (148km) east of Flagstaff on Interstate 40, is a convenient place to start your explorations. Founded as a railroad town in 1881, the vast surrounding grasslands quickly attracted cattlemen, and the town became a major ranching center. The Hashknife outfit was one of the most famous cattle companies, running 60,000 cattle on a million acres (405,000 hectares) and becoming the third-largest cattle empire in the United States. Rustling and poor

management eventually shut down the ranch in 1900, but not before Hashknife cowboys had become celebrated for their whoop-'em-up Saturday-night ways in upstanding Mormon towns to the south. Situated near the Navajo, Hopi, and Apache reservations, Holbrook is a good place to pick up silver-and-turquoise jewelry, pottery, and Apache baskets at a local trading post or attend Indian dances held nightly on the lawn next to the old courthouse in summer. In January or February, you can post a letter via Hashknife Pony Express, which carries the mail on horseback from Holbrook to Scottsdale.

Trees of stone

The town is surrounded by the **Painted Desert**, a highly atmospheric backdrop of buttes, mesas, and banded pink, gray, brown, and purple badlands that have an unearthly glow at sunset or after a heavy rain. To explore this evocative landscape, drive southeast of Holbrook on Highway 180 to the south entrance of 147-sq-mile (381-sq-km) **Petrified Forest National Park** ⓮ (tel: 928-524-6228; daily May–Sept 7am–7pm, Oct–Apr times vary; charge), set aside in 1906 to protect one of the world's most abundant deposits of petrified wood. Allow about half a day to see the park. The southern section of the park contains the best examples of the highly prized petrified wood. Resist the temptation to slip a few samples into your pocket. Regulations strictly prohibit rock collecting in the park and, anyway, petrified wood is sold for pennies outside the park.

Exhibits in the **Rainbow Forest Museum** explain that petrified wood began forming 225 million years ago, when North America was about where West Africa is today. The warm tropical climate sustained enormous reptiles and amphibians (look for the fearsome crocodile-like phytosaur and "Gertie," a dinosaur found here in 1984), cycad ferns, and conifers up to 200ft (60 meters) tall.

BELOW: living wood becomes petrified when cellulose is gradually replaced with silica.

When these trees toppled into rivers, they were washed in logjams into swamps, then buried by silt and ash from volcanoes to the south. Silicates gradually mixed with groundwater and replaced woody cells with the jasper, amethyst, and smoky quartz so prized today.

A 27-mile (44km) scenic drive, accessed at either end of the park, has pullouts, interpretive trails, and picnic areas. The middle section contains a number of Ancestral Pueblo ruins, including **Agate House**, an unusual 900-year-old structure made of petrified wood, and the 100-room **Puerco Pueblo**, occupied around AD 1400. Look for the spectacular petroglyphs here, one of which marks the summer solstice. The **Painted Desert Inn** (daily 9am–5pm), built in 1924 as a lodging, is now a national historic landmark and has exhibits and a bookstore. There are no campgrounds, but you may hike and camp by permit in the park's 43,020-acre (17,410-hectare) **Painted Desert Wilderness** and 7,240-acre (2,930-hectare) **Rainbow**

Forest Wilderness. Bring a hat and plenty of water, food and sunscreen; summer is hotter than Hades in this relatively undeveloped park.

Along the rim

Highway 77, south of Holbrook, passes through a pair of oddly named Mormon towns. **Snowflake** ❶ isn't named after the winter storms that occasionally blow through town but the combined surnames of Mormon elders William J. Flake and Erastus Snow who, in the 1870s, escaped government persecution of polygamists in Utah and headed south to Arizona to settle and convert Indians. About 19 miles (31km) to the south is **Show Low** ❶, a small commercial center on the edge of the White Mountains, at the junction of Highways 77, 260, and 60. Show Low's strange name apparently dates from 1870, when the legendary Corydon Cooley, a former fur trader and Indian scout at nearby Fort Apache, challenged Marion Clark, his business partner, to a card game to settle differences over the ranch they co-owned. "Show low

Petrified Forest National Park.

BELOW: a view of the Painted Desert from Whipple Point in Petrified Forest National Park.

The Painted Desert Inn glows in the sunset.

BELOW: Equipment from the Wallow Fire, 2011

and you win," Clark reputedly said. Obligingly, Cooley pulled out an unbeatable deuce of clubs and won the ranch. Ironically, the gaming site (Cooley's kitchen) eventually became the town's Mormon Church. Its main street is called the Deuce of Clubs, where you'll find the town's motels, restaurants, and gas stations.

Stop between mileposts 347 and 348, 7 miles (11km) southeast of Show Low on Highway 260, to get your first look at the Mogollon Rim, the escarpment that sharply divides the Gila–Salt River watersheds and the mile-high Colorado Plateau. Stroll along the mile-long **Mogollon Rim Overlook** and **Nature Trail** for scenic vistas of forested peaks and shadowy valleys. Signs offer information on the ponderosa and pinyon pine, Douglas fir, three types of juniper, and Gambel and scrub oak that make up the forest.

Lakeside–Pinetop ⓱, 8 miles (13km) southeast of Show Low, is the largest resort area in the White Mountains, with a wide range of developed lodgings and restaurants. Lakeside (elevation 6,745ft/2,056 meters), founded by Mormons in 1880, was originally called Fairview but changed its name to reflect its abundance of lakes. Soldiers laboring up the Mogollon Rim from Fort Apache often stopped to rest at Pinetop (elevation 7,279ft/2,219 meters) and gave the town its name. All around are forest roads, hiking and horseback trails, and lakes and streams stocked with trout. The community was also voted the third-best mountain biking town in the country. Forest Route 300, a dirt logging road, begins here and heads west along the Mogollon Rim for nearly 200 miles (320km). It's impassable in winter.

For information on trail and road conditions, contact the **US Forest Service Lakeside Ranger District** (2022 W. White Mountain Boulevard; tel: 928-368-5111).

Apache homeland

Just south of Lakeside–Pinetop is the 1.6-million-acre (650,000-hectare) **White Mountain Apache Reservation** ⓲ (tel: 928-338-4346; www.wmat.nsn.us). An abundance of outdoor activities is available on the reservation, which offers a quiet, natural, and very spiritual setting for those wanting to get away from the all-American ambiance of adjoining areas. Permits for outdoor sports and visiting Indian ruins on tribal land are available at **Hon Dah** ("Be My Guest" in Apache) at the junction of Highways 260 and 73 about 5 miles (8km) south of Lakeside–Pinetop, an attractive roadside complex with a log motel and restaurant, casino, grocery store, and gas station. Or you can visit the Wildlife and Outdoor Recreation Department at White Mountain Apache Game and Fish Department (100 West Fatco Road; tel: 928-338-4385) at tribal headquarters in **Whiteriver** ⓳, where you'll find a motel, trading post, restaurants, a shopping center, hospital, and tribal offices.

While you're in Whiteriver, be sure to visit **Fort Apache**, the former US

Army post built in 1870 as a supply base for soldiers sent to keep an eye on the White Mountain Apache and prevent white settlers from encroaching on Indian land. The fort was later used as a staging area for campaigns against the Tonto and Chiricahua Apache. The army relied on friendly Apache scouts, of whom the most famous was Alchesay, who assisted Indian fighter par-excellence General George Crook in making peace with Geronimo in 1886. The commanding officer's quarters, adjutant's office, and officers' row still stand. Exhibits and photographs of the old fort are on display at the *Nohwike Bagowa* (House of our Footprints) **Apache Cultural Center and Museum** (tel: 928-338-4625; Mon–Fri 8am–5pm; charge), 4 miles (6.5km) southwest of Whiteriver.

Snow trails

The White Mountain Apache also own and operate the popular **Sunrise Park Resort** ⓴, 20 miles (32km) east of Hon Dah, on 10,700ft (3,260-meter) **Mount Ord**, which has three peaks – Sunrise, Apache, and Cyclone

Circle – with 11 lifts and 65 ski runs. For diehard powder bunnies, there's an onsite hotel, restaurant, marina, and sports center offering ski, snowshoe, and mountain bike rentals. A quieter option is to stay in the tiny community of **Greer** ㉑ (pop. 100), 15 miles (24km) east as the crow flies. It's hardly a straight shot for drivers: continue on Highway 260 for 10 miles (16km), then drop south on Highway 373 for 5 miles (8km) until it dead-ends in the village. But Greer, nestled at an elevation of 8,500ft (2,600 meters) in a beautiful valley at the headwaters of the Little Colorado River, is worth the trip. It's the kind of stopped-in-time place with local characters and friendly innkeepers that seems to have stepped right out of the mythical Brigadoon.

Small-town memories

Greer was originally called Lee Valley after Mormon pioneer Willard Lee, who founded the town as a farming community in 1879. The name was changed in 1898, at the request of the post office, to honor America

White Mountain Apache men pose for a picture in 1909.

BELOW: a snow-covered forest near Greer.

Father and Son Team

"Civilization? I have always avoided it whenever possible." So said explorer, naturalist, and writer James Willard Schultz, author of 37 books, who, in 1914, moved into a cabin in Greer, where he wrote, among other books, *In the Great Apache Forest: The Story of a Lone Boy Scout*, a tale inspired by the World War I adventures of Molly Butler's children, George and Hannah Crosby.

Schultz, a refugee from a wealthy East Coast family, moved out west as a young man and had lived for many years among the Blackfoot Tribe in Montana, the subject of his first book, *My Life as an Indian* (1907). He dubbed his new home Apuni Oyis (Butterfly Lodge) and was soon joined by his half-Blackfoot son, Hart Merriam, or Lone Wolf, a popular American Indian artist.

Lone Wolf found inspiration here for paintings and sculptures of Western scenes, purchased by such luminaries as Herbert Hoover and Mrs. Calvin Coolidge. Lone Wolf inherited the cabin in the mid-1920s and lived here on and off until his death in 1970. Butterfly Lodge is now on the National Register of Historic Places and has been converted into a museum (tel: 928-735-7514; May–Sept Thur–Sun 10am–5pm; charge) containing Schultz's writing desk, Lone Wolf's paintings and other memorabilia.

The White Mountains are crisscrossed with Nordic skiing and snowshoeing trails.

BELOW: a scenic road winds through Apache-Sitgreaves National Forest.

Vespucius Greer, a prominent Mormon. It was the generous hospitality and good cooking of townspeople like Molly Butler, however, that attracted famous guests like President Theodore Roosevelt and writer Zane Grey, who spent days hunting cougar and bear in the backcountry guided by Molly's husband John. True, the 1908 **Molly Butler Lodge** (*see page 269*) hasn't been quite the same since Aunt Molly died, although new owners are trying to breathe some life into the aging hostelry. But no matter. You can have a fish fry or a steak here for old times' sake and stay at one of the other lodges in the valley. Your best bet for consistently good food and lodging in Greer is the privately owned **Greer Lodge Resort** (*see page* 262), which offers a variety of rustic and elegant log cabin vacation rentals. Note: A fire burned the main historic lodge and 373 Grill and Bar to the ground in May 2011; however, the rest of the resort is still open for business.

Another good choice is the Commons at **White Mountain Lodge**. It's housed in the 1892 Lund Home, Greer's oldest residence, and offers "cottages" (guest suites in the main historic lodge) and free-standing modern log cabins on the edge of a beautiful riverside meadow. **Greer Lakes Recreation Area**, which surrounds Greer, has cross-country skiing and hiking trails, and four campgrounds with fishing.

Memories of John and Molly Butler remain strong for Wink Crigler, Molly's granddaughter, who, with her sister Sug (short for Sugar), operates the family's 1889 **X Diamond** and **MLY Ranch** over the hill from Greer. Wink is a strong Western woman and recently successfully won a lawsuit to prevent her historic ranch from falling into the hands of developers. Today, she continues to offer cabin rentals, unspoiled flyfishing, horseback riding, roundups, and an archaeological dig at a Mogollon site on her 20,000-acre (8,100-hectare) working ranch, 7 miles (11km) west of **Eagar** ㉒, off Highway 260.

Don't pass up a chance to visit **Wink's Little House Museum** (tel: 928-333-2286; tours by reservation; charge). Begun in 1990 as a memorial to her late husband Oscar, a rodeo champ, the 6,000-sq-ft (557-sq-meter) museum's collection of finely tooled saddles and trophies has swelled to include pioneer tools, the buggy used in John Wayne's 1960 movie *The Alamo*, and vintage clothing. The *pièces de résistance*, however, are the antique music machines, including nickelodeons, pianolas, and one of only 700 violin "virtuosas" in the world, which Wink plugs in and brings to toe-tapping life during her two-hour tour. If the Smithsonian is America's Attic, the Little House Museum is surely Arizona's.

Mogollon ruins

The Little House Museum is one of the undiscovered delights of the White Mountains, and so is the large number of relatively unvisited prehistoric Mogollon Indian ruins throughout

the mountains. The Mogollon culture originated in the mountains of southwestern New Mexico, where they lived on ridges and farmed corn, beans, and squash in the valleys, supplementing their diet with deer, antelope, rabbit, and other game.

They were the first people in the Southwest to make pottery, which they learned from their trading partners to the south. Beautiful black-on-white pottery decorated with images of lizards, traders, macaws, and other daily scenes characterize the Mimbres branch of the Mogollon culture and is highly prized among collectors today. After AD 1000, the Mogollon moved north to Arizona's east-central mountains, where they merged with the Ancestral Pueblo culture. Archaeologists can still identify their settlements by the presence of their signature pottery style and other cultural traits such as the construction of rectangular kivas, or ceremonial chambers.

Casa Malpais

Springerville in Round Valley is situated in the heart of Mogollon country, with one of the most important ruins, **Casa Malpais Archeological Park** ㉓, 2 miles (3km) north of downtown, perched on five basalt terraces above the Little Colorado River. The 14-acre (6-hectare), two-story **House of the Badlands**, as it was called by 19th-century Spanish-speaking residents, is one of the most complex Mogollon communities yet discovered and caused excitement in the archaeological world when excavations began there in the 1940s. The site was occupied between AD 1266 and the late 1400s by an estimated 300 people. Unusual features include a large rectangular *kiva*, evidence that sacred ceremonies and burials took place in natural fissures throughout the site, and a solar calendar.

Tours of the pueblo are conducted daily at 9am, 11am, and 2pm (weather permitting) and begin at **Casa Malpais Museum and Visitor Center** on Main Street (tel: 928-333-5375; daily 8am–4pm, call for reservations; charge), which has exhibits on Casa Malpais and Springerville, a film about excavations at the pueblo, and information on the area.

"We abuse land because we regard it as a commodity belonging to us. When we see land as a community to which we belong, we may begin to use it with love and respect."

– Aldo Leopold

BELOW: hiking with domestic llamas in Aravaipa Canyon.

The Salt River forms a natural boundary between the San Carlos and White Mountain Apache reservations.

BELOW: bold black-on-white designs are a common feature of Mogollon and Ancestral Puebloan pottery.

Wildlife lovers won't want to miss the relatively unpublicized 1,362-acre (551-hectare) **Sipe White Mountain Wildlife Area**  (tel: 928-367-4281; visitor center mid-May–Oct daily 8am–5pm; free), 2 miles (3km) south of Springerville. Administered by Arizona Game and Fish, Sipe Ranch is an old ranch homestead that was purchased to protect the threatened Little Colorado spinedace, a tiny native fish. It also provides winter range for up to 800 elk and 175 acres (70 hectares) of wetlands used by hundreds of bird species, including migratory avocets, sandpipers, white-faced ibis, and other waterfowl. Ask for information on how to reach the Mogollon petroglyph panel near the old homestead.

The source of the basalts used in construction of Casa Malpais is obvious when you stand atop the pueblo and look south. The **Springerville Volcanic Field**, the third-largest volcanic field in the continental United States, covers 1,158 sq miles (3,000 sq km) and contains 405 vents, craters, and shield volcanoes, which began erupting 3 million years ago. To the

south of Greer is the older **White Mountain Volcanic Field**, created by a different type of volcanism 8 million years ago. Baldy Peak, sacred to the Apache, is at its center. The youngest lava flows are from Twin Knolls, northwest of Springerville, a double volcano that erupted twice.

The **Renée Cushman Art Collection Museum** (150 N. Aldrice Burk, Springerville; tel: 928-333-2123; tours by appointment) can be found in the town of **Springerville**. Renee Cushman was the daughter of a prominent European artist. Her family traveled extensively around the world. After marrying for a second time, she moved to the White Mountain Hereford Ranch in Springerville. When she died in 1969, she left her entire art collection to the Church of Jesus Christ of Latter-day Saints. The museum is in one wing of the LDS Meeting House in Springerville. The building is appropriately designed to show her treasured pieces, which include three ink drawings by Tiepolo, a complete set of Austrian china, a priceless drawing by Rembrandt, and a single piece by Sir Godfrey Kneller. Many of the pieces range from the Renaissance period to the 20th century.

The roads less traveled

Two breathtaking, but white-knuckle, drives wind precipitously from the mountains to the low desert. The first, the 123-mile (198km) **Springerville to Clifton Highway** (Route 666/191), follows the eastern edge of Apache-Sitgreaves National Forest and the Arizona–New Mexico border. It reaches an elevation of 9,000ft (2,700 meters) at Hannagan Meadow, then drops into the copper mining towns of Morenci and Clifton – a plummet of 5,000ft (1,525 meters). The route, one of the country's first federal road projects, opened in 1926, with 5,000 dignitaries puttering into the high country in their Model T Fords for the ribbon-cutting festivities, which

included barbecued bear. Things have quieted down considerably since then. This is now one of the state's most beautiful but lonesome highways, driven only by a handful of motorists each day.

The road has long been promoted as the route that Spanish conquistador Francisco Vásquez de Coronado took through the mountains into New Mexico in 1540. Some historians now dispute that, including former Interior Secretary Stewart Udall, who grew up in St. Johns and is an authority on Coronado's route through the Southwest. Udall believes the Coronado expedition took a route 40 miles to the west, in the gentler topography of the Natanes Plateau.

Check road conditions before starting out. Snow may make sections of the road impassable in winter. The road leaves Springerville and heads south through **Nutrioso** ㉖, another odd local name derived from the Spanish words for beaver (*nutri*) and bear (*oso*). It was home to Arizona's first forest ranger at the turn of the century, when Apache

National Forest was part of Black Mesa Forest Reserve.

The next community is 8,050ft (2,450-meter) **Alpine** ㉗, originally known as Bush Valley, near the headwaters of the San Francisco River, where Escudilla Mountain, which features prominently in Aldo Leopold's writings, dominates the horizon. There is good camping at **Luna Lake**, a wildlife refuge where you can see bald and golden eagles and look for Luna agate. Dog sled races are held here in January.

The road's halfway point is **Hannagan Meadow** ㉘, named for Robert Hannagan, a Nevada miner who had a cattle ranch here in the 1870s. Legend has it that Hannagan racked up $1,200 in debt to some neighbors, who chained him to a tree until his son arrived from New Mexico to bail him out.

Hannagan Meadow Lodge (tel: 928-339-4370), renovated in 1996, was built at the same time as the road for travelers making the two-day trip into the high country; it's still a logical place to gas up, stop for lunch, or spend the

Corn lilies and sneezeweed grow along a brook near the headwaters of the Little Colorado River.

BELOW: a man sits at the center of the world's largest telescope, the Large Binocular Telescope, high on Mount Graham.

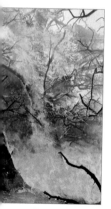

Wallow Fire, 2011.

BELOW: the Salt River Canyon Bridge.

night in one of the rustic cabins. **Hannagan Meadow Cross-Country Ski Trail** starts nearby and has 12 miles (19km) of backcountry paths.

Dangerous curves

South of Hannagan Meadow, the road begins to live up to its reputation as one of the best "serious-drivers' roads in America," with sharp hairpins that make a slalom course look straight. Step out of the car for some calming breaths at the Blue Vista overlook, on the edge of the 2,000ft (600-meter) Mogollon Rim, and look down into the pinyon-juniper forests and savannah grasslands of the upper Sonoran ecosystem, 4,000ft (1,200 meters) below.

To the east are the **Blue Range Mountains**, where, since 1997, several packs of Mexican wolves have been released. The Blues contain the last designated primitive area in the National Forest System and are a fine place to lose yourself for a while on foot. Simply turn off, park, and start walking. Perhaps you'll get lucky and hear a wolf howl, glimpse one of the resident herds of Rocky Mountain bighorn sheep, or surprise a blue heron on a creek.

Copper country

Twelve miles (19km) farther on and the road drops below the Mogollon Rim into copper country. **Morenci** ㉙ is a mining town owned by the Phelps Dodge company (free tours are given on weekdays by appointment). Arizona isn't called the Copper State for nothing, and Morenci is the leading copper producer in the USA. But at a cost. The open-pit mine, built in 1937, gradually swallowed the old town of Morenci; today's community is a modern replacement. **Clifton** ㉚ on the other hand, retains much of its historic charm. Nestled in a rugged canyon carved by the San Francisco River, the former copper-mining town still has a number of historic buildings, including the 1912 Southern Pacific Depot, Clifton Jail (which was blasted from a cliff face), and the Chase Creek Historic District with its outstanding Territorial architecture.

From Clifton, continue south to the junction with Highway 70 and head west through the cotton-growing town of **Safford** ③. Looming more than 8,000ft (2,400 meters) above Safford is 10,720ft (3,270-meter) **Mount Graham** ㉜, home of **Mount Graham International Observatory** (tel: 928-428-2739; Fri–Sat 6–10pm). This University of Arizona observatory houses several huge telescopes and has been controversial from the start because it impinges on the habitat of the Mount Graham red squirrel (tours of the observatory are limited due to permit requirements). Visitors can learn about Mount Graham by visiting Safford's science, culture, and education center, **Discovery Park** (tel: 928-428-6260; visitor center Mon–Fri 8am–5pm, Sat 4pm–9.30pm; tours of the observatory mid-May–mid-Nov Sat, Sun by reservation; free), which is on the campus of Eastern Arizona College. It has a 12-passenger spaceship simulator that gives visitors a virtual tour of the solar system, and a 20-inch telescope. The 35-mile (56km) **Swift Trail Parkway** ascends the mountain; camping, hiking, and fishing are available in Coronado National Forest until snow halts access.

North of Safford is an unpaved road leading west into **Aravaipa Canyon Wilderness Preserve** ㉝ (tel: 928-828-3443; daily). The Nature Conservancy protects 7,000 acres (2,800 hectares) of this magical 10-mile (16km) -long canyon, where author Ed Abbey wrote movingly of encountering a mountain lion along Aravaipa Creek at dusk.

You can hope for a precious encounter with one of the big cats or perhaps a less intimidating bobcat, a rare bighorn sheep or more than 200 bird species. Camping and hiking are only allowed throughout this remote canyon with a permit from the Bureau of Land Management in Safford, which manages East and West Aravaipa Canyon Wildernesses.

For information on permits, call the ranger stations on 928-828-3380 (East) and 520-357-6185 (West).

Globe and the Salt River

Highway 70 continues to **Globe** ㉞, the site of enormous silver and copper deposits, which led to boom growth between 1870 and 1920 and the success of the Old Dominion Copper Company, one of the world's largest copper-mining operations. You won't miss the enormous man-made terraces on the north side of town; they look almost extraterrestrial.

Globe's name came from the extraction of a large, orb-shaped piece of silver with what appeared to be a rough outline of the continents upon it.

Downtown Globe retains a 19th-century feel, and you can take a historic walking tour of 25 buildings ranging from the 1906 Gila County Courthouse (now the Cobre Valley Center for the Arts) to the "Oldest Woolworths in the West" (1916). Homey Globe was one of contrarian Ed Abbey's favorite Arizona towns.

The Besh-Ba-Gowah ruins have been partially restored.

BELOW: the Salt River Canyon.

TIP

Hikers and mountain bikers can hitch a ride up the mountain at Sunrise Ski Resort in the off-season. Chairlifts run on weekends from late May to mid-October.

The main reason to stop in Globe is to view the large Salado ruin known by the Apache name **Besh-Ba-Gowah Archeological Park**, or House of Metal, for the abundance of precious metals that attracted newcomers in the late 1800s. Besh-Ba-Gowah was begun in 1225 and abandoned around 1400.

The 200-room pueblo was first excavated in the 1930s, but excavation has been sporadic ever since. Now partially stabilized, the ruin is still revealing its secrets. Large quantities of beautiful polychrome pottery have been uncovered at the site and are on display in the small museum.

North of Globe, Highway 60 skirts the **San Carlos Apache Reservation** ㉟. Globe was originally part of the reservation, but when silver was found there in 1870 the boundaries were redrawn, causing prolonged bitterness with the San Carlos Apache, who allied themselves with Geronimo and other warring Apache leaders. The San Carlos Apache now hold the popular **Apache Days** in Globe in October and one of Arizona's best rodeos in November in San Carlos. **San Carlos Apache Culture Center** (US 70, milepost 272; tel: 928-475-2894; Mon–Fri 9am–5pm; free) has a special exhibit, "Window on Apache Culture," which describes the Apache's spiritual beginnings and important ceremonies such as that of Changing Woman, an ancient female puberty ritual.

Highway 60 follows a dramatic twist-and-turn route through the **Salt River Canyon** ㊱. The Jesuit missionary Padre Eusebio Francisco Kino visited this canyon in 1698, naming it Salado for the salt springs in the area (eventually that name would also be applied to the prehistoric people who once lived here).

The bridge over the Salt River and the beginning of the climb into the White Mountains marks the boundary between the San Carlos Apache Reservation and White Mountain Apache Reservation, which lies to the north. This is the second of the beautiful scenic byways on this tour and a perfect sunset drive, when lengthening shadows in the canyon deepen the drama of the colorful formations.

Rodeo-Chediski Fire

"The whole place looks like death," said a Show Low resident after surveying the charred remains of her home and land. The house was only one of more than 400 buildings that were destroyed by the 468,000-acre (189,393-hectare) Rodeo-Chediski Fire of 2002, the biggest in Arizona history.

The Rodeo-Chediski Fire actually began as two separate blazes that merged into one monster conflagration. The first was started by a part-time firefighter hoping for work, the other by a lost hiker signaling for help.

Fueled by a buildup of deadwood and fanned by warm, gusty winds, the 15-day fire consumed nearly half a million acres (200,000 hectares) in Apache-Sitgreaves National Forest and the White Mountain Apache Reservation and forced the evacuation of more than 30,000 people from 10 towns, including Show Low and Pinedale.

Among the hardest hit, in addition to those whose homes and businesses were burned, was the White Mountain Apache Tribe, which lost more than 700 million ft (200 million meters) of timber, one of the reservation's main resources. Evidence of the fire will be visible for years in the charred landscape around Cibecue, site of the tribe's principal mill, but the economic fallout will last even longer. "This devastation will affect our kids for two or three generations," said tribal president Lorin Henry.

Although Arizona has luckily not had a fire cause greater damage, residents must be ever vigilant in the battle against the flames. Wildfires are a growing hazard in the state and throughout the Southwest region, due to climate change, long-running drought, and depradations by bark beetles that weaken trees, making them more susceptible to fires. Winds can also contribute to the spread of a wildfire; fire travel significant distances because of a fierce and dry wind.

Fire prevention strategies include being extremely careful when using fireworks, building a campfire, or discharging a firearm, as all of these have been known to cause a spark that starts a wildfire.

RESTAURANTS

Prices for a three-course dinner per person, excluding tax, tip, and beverages:
$ = under $20
$$ = $20–45
$$$ = $45–60
$$$$ = over $60

Amberian Peaks Lodge and Restaurant
One Main Street, Greer
Tel: 928-735-9977
$–$$
An elegant bed-and-breakfast lodge in Greer, Amberian has a romantic bistro that's just the thing for a quiet dinner. The chef has a way with buffalo and salmon. The focus is specialty pizzas in the casual Cantina, a bar with a huge log deck. Take-out pizza is available. Open in summer only.

Amelia's Garden
305 S. Main Street, Snowflake
Tel: 928-536-2046
$
Housed in a converted historic house on the main drag in Snowflake, Amelia's, let it be said, is primarily a health foods store. But inside is a small café serving organic vegetarian fare, a blessing in Ranch Country. The light fare runs to the usual soups, salads, sandwiches, and quiches, all homemade, but the lentil salad features locally made Black Mesa goat cheese, the pride of the White Mountains, and is well worth sampling. Closed Sun.

Booga Reds
521 E. Main Street, Springerville
Tel: 928-333-2640
$

Hungry travelers stop here for comfort food – roast beef, mashed potatoes and gravy, pancakes, home-made pie – as well as a selection of Mexican dishes.

Corky's BBQ Hamburgers and Ice
580 W. Cleveland Street, St Johns
Tel: 928-337-2388
$
Under new ownership, this burger place in St Johns is popular with the locals.

El Rancho Pinetop
1523 East White Mountain Boulevard, Pinetop
Tel: 928-367-4557
$
Cheap and cheerful Mexican food for over four decades. What could be better than that, after a long day's drive? Dollar tacos on Wednesdays, and plenty of chimichangos, fish tacos, burritos, and Mexican pizzas for the whole family to dig into at any time.

Hannagan Meadow Lodge
Highway 191, 22 miles (35km) south of Alpine
Tel: 928-339-4370
$–$$
Diners can watch deer and elk browse in the meadow around this rustic lodge's restaurant, a lovely room with wood beams and linen-covered tables. The menu offers a choice of hearty steaks, burgers, and chops, as well as trout, grilled salmon, jumbo fried shrimp, and baked chicken with lime-butter sauce.

Licano's
571 W. Deuce of Clubs, Show Low

Tel: 928-537-8220
$
Generous portions of Mexican food, steak, seafood, pasta, and salad are the formula at this Western-style restaurant.

Mesa Italiana Restaurant
2318 E. Navajo Boulevard, Holbrook
Tel: 928-524-6696
$–$$
The best homestyle Italian restaurant in Holbrook offers some great entrees. Try baked ziti or the chicken Jerusalem, a delicious melange of chicken breast sautéed with butter, garlic, artichoke hearts, mushrooms, and shrimp and covered in a white-wine and lemon sauce.

Molly Butler Lodge
109 Main Street, Greer
Tel: 928-735-7226
$–$$
Mormon pioneers Molly and John Butler built their early 1900s homestead in Greer, a tiny forested community next to the Apache reservation. While John served as hunting guide to Theodore Roosevelt and writer Zane Grey, Molly was famous for her home cooking. The authentic food in the old lodge is still worth an overnight trip to Greer. Famous for its aged steaks and prime rib (you're in ranch country here), the restaurant's perfectly cooked halibut is also a contender. All dishes are accompanied by baked potato, salad, fresh veggies, and an entire miniloaf of warm home-made bread.

Save room for home-made pie. Make reservations; it gets busy here on weekends when Phoenicians come up to play. There's pub food in the adjoining Molly's Patio and Grill.

Pasta House
2188 E. White Mountain Boulevard, Pinetop
Tel: 928-367-2782
$–$$
Home-made pasta is the cornerstone of the menu, though you will also find veal, chicken, fish, and a wide selection of pizza.

Turquoise Room
La Posada Hotel, 303 E. 2nd Street, Winslow
Tel: 928-289-2888
$–$$$
Classically trained English chef John Sharpe creates food worthy of a last meal on earth at his excellent restaurant inside Winslow's restored La Posada, originally designed by architect Mary Colter for railroad concessionaire Fred Harvey. Sharpe's award-winning Southwestern food is a homage to local, sustainably produced foods and native cultures as well as the glory days of Harvey House restaurants and, not incidentally, his English roots. Among the winners are a yin-yang corn and black-bean soup, a hearty Native American cassoulet, piki bread with Hopi hummus, a classic prime rib au jus, Navajo churro lamb, and elk medallions. Save room for bread pudding, gelato, and flaky pies.

SOUTHERN ARIZONA

Successive cultures – Indian, Hispanic, Anglo – have left their mark on the region's desert landscapes and quirky small towns

Tucson, Arizona's second-largest city and the focal point of the southern tier of the state, has a maverick streak that's characteristic of the region as a whole. Tucsonans value individuality. They tend to be politically more liberal and culturally more daring than their conservative neighbors, and, as a community, identify themselves more closely with the city's Hispanic roots. They also share an awareness of the environment. Ringed by mountain peaks and bracketed by parklands, Tucson embraces its desert setting. A short drive from downtown leads into Tucson Mountain Park or Saguaro National Park. A bit farther on are the breezy heights of Mount Lemmon and the Santa Catalina Mountains.

An independent spirit is evident elsewhere in the south. In the old mining town of Bisbee, a coalition of artists and entrepreneurs have transformed decaying saloons into shops and restaurants and breathed new life into the "painted ladies" once occupied by the town's thriving middle class. A similar revival occurred in Tubac, the state's oldest European settlement, founded about 1723. Had it not been for the vision of various artists and business people, the village – now a popular arts colony – might have been left to the elements. The atmosphere in Tombstone is far more commercial but no less vital. The "town too tough to die" has capitalized on Wyatt Earp's fateful encounter at the OK Corral, with staged shootouts, stagecoach rides, and an entertaining, if hokey, Old West ambience.

But the towns of southern Arizona are merely grace notes to the landscape. The Sonoran Desert is the dominant presence. Sky islands like the Chiricahua Mountains offer relief from the sere lowlands. The lush grasslands that so enticed Spanish *rancheros* now support Arizona's small but growing scenic "wine country," and wetlands ranging from desert springs to the San Pedro River sustain a profusion of plant and animal life, including the thousands of migratory waterbirds that flock to the seasonal marshes of Willcox Playa.

PRECEDING PAGES: Superstition Mountain.
LEFT: Seven Falls in Coronado National Forest.
ABOVE LEFT: Tempe City Hall. **ABOVE RIGHT:** a Cinco de Mayo celebration.

TUCSON AND ENVIRONS

Smaller and more liberal than Phoenix, with a streak of feisty independence, Arizona's "Old Pueblo" embraces its Hispanic roots and scenic desert setting

Tucson ❶, or the Old Pueblo, as it's known locally, is a modern metropolis of some 980,000 souls that has insinuated itself across 500 sq miles (1,300 sq km) of southern Arizona's Sonoran Desert between five encircling mountain ranges. Warm winters, low year-round humidity, an unbeatable desert setting, hundred-mile vistas, and perhaps the easiest access to hiking, biking, camping, horseback riding, rock climbing, and skiing of any city in the nation have lured visitors for decades. Four-star resorts, spas, dude ranches, historic inns, and gourmet restaurants nudge up against nature parks, Wild West towns, Indian reservations, and Mexican border towns.

To get oriented and enjoy a killer sunset view, drive up **Sentinel Peak ❷**, the dark volcanic hill west of downtown Tucson with the whitewashed "A" (the work of University of Arizona students since 1915). Used as a lookout by Mexican soldiers between 1821 and 1853 (hence the name), the peak now known as "A" Mountain offers sweeping views of the burgeoning city, nearby mountains, and the basin-and-range topography all the way into Mexico, 65 miles (105km) away.

Long before Spanish, Mexican, and Anglo settlers arrived, the Sonoran Desert was home to the Hohokam culture, irrigation farmers who left behind pecked petroglyphs on basaltic boulders, such as those at Signal Hill in Saguaro National Park West. By the time of the Spanish conquest, in 1540, the Hohokam had been replaced by ancestors of today's Tohono O'odham ("People of the Desert," formerly known as Papago) and Akimel O'odham ("People of the Water," also known as Pima) tribes, whose modern reservations adjoin Tucson. O'odham people lived in a *rancheria*, a scattering of huts built from mesquite limbs,

LEFT: Mission San Xavier del Bac in Tucson.
RIGHT: an "outlaw" at Old Tucson Studios.

TIP

In October El Presidio is host to the Tucson Heritage Experience Festival, a melange of food, dance, and music. Scottish highland dancers follow old-time fiddlers; Burmese performers are sandwiched between a *mariachi* band and Polish singers.

saguaro ribs and thorny ocotillo, along the now-dry Santa Cruz River at the base of "A" Mountain.

A rough beginning

The O'odham referred to their village as Stjukshon (*stjuk* means "black"; *shon*, "hill"). This word was roughly transliterated to "Tucson" by Colonel Hugo O'Conor, an Irishman in the service of the Spanish Crown, when he was ordered to build a new garrison to protect nearby San Xavier Mission. The Tucson presidio replaced the one at Tubac in 1775, after its former commander, Juan Bautista de Anza, left to find an overland route to Alta California.

El Presidio de San Agustín del Tucson, just east of "A" Mountain, was heavily fortified with adobe walls 12ft (4 meters) high and 750ft (230 meters) long, but soldiers found little protection here and complained that they spent more time making adobes than in military pursuits. Mexican tenure did little to improve a situation where settlers were at the mercy of Apache raiders. Even after it became American

territory, Tucson remained essentially a Mexican town of miners, ranchers, and merchants. To Anglo traveler J. Ross Browne, it seemed "a city of mud boxes, dingy and delapidated, cracked and baked into a composite of dust and filth." Only with the coming of the railroad in the 1880s, linking markets across the country, did Tucson evolve from a rough Wild West outpost to a booming frontier trading center.

The old Presidio

Portions of the original Presidio wall are preserved in downtown's **Presidio Historic District ⑧**, a good place to get a feel for Tucson's Spanish, Mexican, and Anglo heritage. Begin your historic walking tour at the **Tucson Museum of Art** (tel: 520-624-2333; Tue–Sat 10am–5pm, Sun noon–5pm; charge) on the corner of Alameda and Main Streets. Noted for its Spanish colonial paintings and furnishings, pre-Columbian artifacts from Latin America, pleasant courtyard and café (often frequented by downtown office workers), the museum's most interesting feature is the five historic

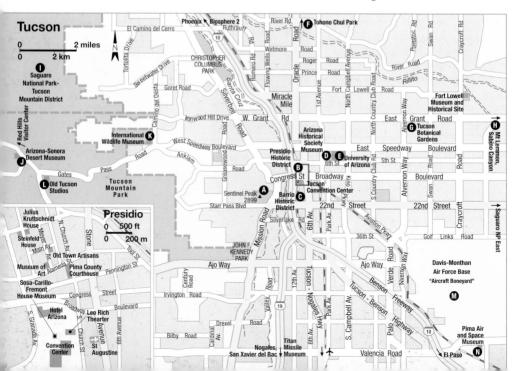

houses incorporated into its layout (all open during museum hours).

La Casa Cordova, built in 1848, is Tucson's oldest home. A classic Mexican adobe with traditional saguaro rib ceiling latillas and dirt floors, it has a central courtyard and dark interior rooms that have been restored to reflect early life in the Old Pueblo, complete with beds, cribs and furnishings. One room has exhibits that trace the Presidio's history; an adjoining room contains, from November to March, the Nacimiento, a traditional Mexican nativity installation that changes yearly and uses more than 200 hand-painted figurines to create tableaux depicting the life of Christ.

In the museum's southwestern corner, two adjoining houses – the **Stevens/Duffield House**, also known as the Palice Pavilion, and the 1868 **Edward Nye Fish House**, constructed on the site of an old Mexican barracks with 15ft (4.6-meter) ceilings and adobe walls more than 2ft (60cm) thick – were built by wealthy merchants and were the center of social life in Tucson. The Fish House is

now home to the **John K. Goodman Pavilion of Western Art.** On the other side of the museum, the 1860 **Romero House**, used by the Tucson Museum of Art School, and the **Corbett House**, a 1906 brick-and-stucco building on Main Street, incorporate the northern boundary walls of the Presidio.

Privately owned **Old Town Artisans** carries arts and crafts by more than 150 Western, Indian, and Mexican artists and occupies an adobe, parts of which date to between 1862 and 1875.

Distinguished architecture

Stroll along Main and Court streets to view other houses in **Snob Hollow**, as it was called, including the 1886 American Territorial-style **Julius Kruttschnidt House**, now El Presidio Bed and Breakfast Inn (297 N. Main); the **Owl's Club Mansion** (378 N. Main), a men's club with an ornate facade, and nearby **Steinfeld House** (300 N. Main), both designed by renowned architect Henry Trost in the Spanish Mission style at the turn of the century. **El Charro Restaurant** (311 N. Court), which claims to be

The mural "Races" by David Tineo adorns the exterior of the Tucson Museum of Art.

BELOW: Tucson's Barrio Historic District.

Restored adobes bring color and whimsy to the Barrio Historic District.

the oldest Mexican restaurant in the United States, occupies the 1900 **Jules Flein House**, built of Sentinel Peak basalt by a French stone mason who worked on St. Augustine Cathedral.

To see more of the Presidio, cross Alameda and enter 10-acre (4-hectare) **Presidio Park. Pima County Courthouse** (115 N. Church), a building that combines Spanish and Southwestern architectural styles in its columns, arches, decorated facade, tiled dome, interior courtyard, and fountain, and has a portion of the original Presidio wall inside. **St Augustine Cathedral** (192 S. Stone) was begun in 1896, though by the 1930s it had fallen on hard times and was subsequently used as a whorehouse, garage, bootlegger warehouse, and boxing arena. Completely refurbished in 1967, today it is noted for its magnificent 1922 carved sandstone facade, modeled after the Cathedral of Queretaro in Mexico, which depicts yucca, saguaros, and horned toads. The bronze statue of Tucson's patron saint, St Augustine, above the entry is dramatically floodlit at night.

BELOW: Pima County Courthouse.

El Barrio

South of the **Tucson Convention Center** (260 S. Church) is the 13-block **Barrio Historic District ❻**, where crumbling adobes with unusual metal flared roof drains, or *canales*, Territorialstyle brick homes and skinny row houses have been lovingly restored by Bohemians, architects, and business people. The *barrio libre*, "the neighborhood where anything goes," is, according to writer Lawrence Cheek, "a lesson in urban living – courtyards instead of lawns, pastel colors that seem to drink the sunlight instead of fighting it." On a forgotten street, you'll come across entwined cacti blocking the entry to an old building or glimpse a Mexican tin hand of fate over an altar in an artist's compound. A Mexican factory (corner of Simpson and S. Main) turns out fresh tortillas daily. Opposite is **El Tiradito**, the **Outcast's Wishing Shrine**, the legendary unconsecrated burial place of a young man killed in a love triangle and the only national historical landmark dedicated to a sinner.

Adjoining El Tiraditio is **La Pilita Museum** (420 S. Main Ave; tel: 520-882-7454; Aug 15–June 1 Mon–Fri 11am–2pm, weekends by appointment; voluntary donation), a charming community museum whose mission is to restore and preserve the La Pilita site. Affiliated with nearby Carrillo School, the research center and museum is run by volunteer educators well versed in the neighborhood. It has revolving art exhibits, award-winning after-school classes, and a fascinating collection of historic photos showing two popular early Tucson pleasure parks – Elysian Grove and Carrillo Gardens – which occupied the site in Victorian times.

The Arizona Historical Society offers frequent guided walking tours of the historic downtown by reservation, leaving from the **Sosa-Carrillo-Fremont House** (151 S. Granada; tel. 520-622-0956; Wed–Sat 10am–4pm; charge, free first Sat of the month), on

the grounds of the Tucson Convention Center. This historic house was rented in 1881 to the daughter of the fifth territorial governor, famed explorer John C. Frémont.

Museum row

East of downtown is a glut of worthwhile museums. The **Arizona Historical Society Museum ⓓ** (949 E. 2nd; tel: 520-628-5774; Mon–Sat 10am–4pm; charge) is the place to bone up on Arizona's colorful history, including 1870s Tucson, and transportation and mining, with a full replica of an underground copper mine.

Other museums can be found across the street on the **University of Arizona ⓔ** campus, founded by the territorial legislature in 1891 (in Old Main, the campus' oldest building) on land donated by a saloonkeeper and two gamblers. The University of Arizona was Tucson's consolation prize after it lost its bid to host the state capitol and the state insane asylum – both of which went to Phoenix – and today most Tucsonans agree they got the better deal.

First stop should be the **Arizona State Museum** (Park and University; tel: 520-621-6302; Mon–Sat 10am–5pm; charge), which occupies two buildings inside the west entrance. It was founded in 1893 to collect and preserve materials related to the native cultures of the Southwest and is the region's oldest anthropological and archaeology museum. An award-winning multimedia exhibit, *Paths of Life: American Indians of the Southwest*, traces the origins, history, and contemporary life of the Seri, Tarahumara, Yaqui, O'odham, Colorado River Yumans, Southern Paiute, Pai, Western Apache, Navajo, and Hopi cultures.

Exhibits include a video and full-scale diorama of the Pascua Yaqui Deer Dance, which is performed every Easter by residents of a Yaqui Indian village in the heart of Tucson. Displays on the long-vanished Hohokam, whose major community, Snaketown, was excavated by the university's Dr. Emil Haury, are found in the South Building.

The museum's newly opened Pottery Project displays some of the 20,000-plus Indian pots in ASM's

Outdoor art adorns the University of Arizona campus.

BELOW: hiking in Saguaro National Park

The University of Arizona is a hub of art, science, and culture.

collection, the largest and most comprehensive in the world, along with a state-of-the-art conservation laboratory and a new interpretive gallery featuring a multimedia Virtual Vault, video interviews with archaeologists and Indian potters, and hands-on experiences.

Photo feature

No one interested in photography should miss the **Center for Creative Photography** (tel: 520-621-7968; Mon–Fri 9am–5pm, Sat–Sun noon–5pm; free), a world-class exhibit and research center with more than 50,000 photographs by leading 20th-century photographers such as Paul Strand, Edward Weston, and Alfred Stieglitz. Conceived and co-founded by master landscape photographer Ansel Adams as a repository for his work, one of the best reasons to stop here is to view Adams's soul-stirring black-and-white photos of Yosemite and other western parks. Exhibitions of the center's holdings are held year-round.

BELOW: El Charro claims to be the oldest restaurant in Arizona.

On the other end of campus, **Flandrau: The UA Science Center,**

Planetarium, and Mineral Museum (tel: 520-621-star; science center and planetarium Mon–Fri 10am–3pm, Thur, Fri 6–9pm, Sat 10am–9pm, Sun 1–4pm; observatory Wed–Sat 7pm–10pm; charge) is out-of-this-world fun for kids and adults alike, with hands-on exhibits, night-sky viewing through a 16-inch telescope, star shows that include an introduction to Arizona skies, Native American skylore, and the demise of the dinosaurs, as well as evening laser light shows in the planetarium.

Look for exhibits about the Phoenix Mars Mission, which launched in 2007 to investigate water quality and habitability potential on the planet Mars. UA was the first public university to partner with NASA on this mission, which landed on Mars in May 2008 for a successful three-month mission. NASA eventually lost contact with the Phoenix Mars Lander, and photos transmitted by NASA's Mars Reconnaissance Orbiter in May 2010 showed ice damage to the solar panels on the spacecraft from the Mars winter. Those in town for Tucson's **Rock**

Phoenix Mars Lander

During its summer 2008 mission, the Phoenix Mars Lander made an important scientific reconnaissance of Mars. It confirmed and examined patches of the widespread deposits of underground water ice detected by Odyssey, which has been orbiting Mars since 2001. It identified a mineral called calcium carbonate that suggested occasional presence of thawed water, found soil chemistry with significant implications for life, and observed falling snow. The mission's biggest surprise was the discovery of perchlorate, an oxidizing chemical on Earth that is food for some microbes and potentially toxic for others. To find out more, visit the Flandreau Observatory on the University of Arizona campus or the UA-run Biosphere 2 in Oracle, which has exhibits on the mission.

and **Mineral Show** in February (the largest in the world) should check out the museum's large mineral collection and exhibit of global meteorites, one of which, the 1,400-pound (635kg) Tucson Ring, was used as an anvil in the 1860s.

Urban oases

Escape the dust and artificial hush of the indoors and head north of downtown to **Tohono Chul Park**  (7366 N. Paseo del Norte; tel: 520-742-6455; daily 8am–5pm; charge). "Desert Corner" in the Tohono O'odham language, the 49-acre (20-hectare) park was created to promote conservation of arid lands. It has nature trails and 500 plants from Sonora and the Southwest arranged by genus. Picnic here or have afternoon tea in the popular Tea Room. Closer to downtown, **Tucson Botanical Gardens**  (2150 N. Alvernon Way; tel: 520-326-9686; daily 8.30am–4.30pm; charge) is in bloom all year. Of particular interest is the Native Seeds/SEARCH Ethnobotanical Garden, which cultivates native desert crops in its

demonstration garden and has banked some 1,800 heritage seeds in an effort to preserve native foods. (Gardeners can buy these at the garden or by mail order.)

When temperatures top 100°F (38°C) in May and June, before the summer "monsoon" thunderstorms arrive, locals give up saying "but it's a dry heat" and head into the mountains surrounding the city. Trails abound in **Coronado National Forest** atop the rugged **Santa Catalina** and **Rincon Mountains**, northeast and east of town, respectively. A 40-mile (64km) scenic drive into the Santa Catalinas (named by Jesuit missionary Padre Eusebio Francisco Kino in 1697) leads to the summit of 9,157ft (2,791-meter) **Mount Lemmon** , the highest peak in the area. Motorists pass through five distinct life zones before reaching the top, where temperatures are about 20 degrees cooler than at the base. **Mount Lemmon Ski Valley** (tel: 520-576-1321; Mon–Fri 10.30am–4.30pm, Sat, Sun 9.30am–4.30pm; charge), the southernmost

A barrel cactus blooms at the Arizona-Sonora Desert Museum.

BELOW: the Arizona State Museum is on the campus of the University of Arizona.

TIP

The Tucson Festival of Books takes place each March on the University of Arizona campus and includes books signings and readings by nationally known authors.

ski resort in the United States, is a popular winter destination and offers fabulous chairlift views of the Tucson area on its Sky Ride the rest of the year; the valley's Iron Door restaurant is open Thursday through Monday. The tourist resort of Summer Haven suffered a devastating wildfire in 2003 but has since been rebuilt and offers food and lodging.

Natural treasures

At the base of Mount Lemmon in Coronado National Forest is **Sabino Canyon Recreation Area** (24 hours daily; tel: 520-749-8700; charge and concessioner fees for tram, parking, and tours), a lush canyon cut by Sabino Creek supporting cottonwood and willow bosque, deer, coyotes, javelinas, and numerous birds. One of the most heavily patronized day-use areas in Tucson, this historic canyon has seen mammoths, Hohokam irrigation ditches, and pony soldiers from the now-ruined Fort Lowell, who used to horseback ride to the "ol' swimming hole." There's a bookstore and a visitor center with exhibits on the natural and cultural history of the mountains, a butterfly and hummingbird sanctuary, a self-guided nature trail starting behind the building, and daily naturalist-led walks.

From the parking area, you must either hike, horseback ride, or take one of the regular narrated shuttle tours up the 4-mile (6.5km) road that winds through the canyon. Popular trails include 5.5-mile (9km) round-trip **Seven Falls**, which follows the flat floor of **Bear Canyon** (14 stream crossings are necessary during snowmelt periods) to a waterfall, a welcome sight in this arid land. Allow at least half a day here. No pets allowed.

For bicycle riders, it doesn't get more scenic than taking a spin through the two units of 87,000-acre (35,000-hectare) **Saguaro National Park ❶**, which bookend the city. The **Rincon Mountain District** (tel: 520-733-5153; park daily 7am–sunset, visitor center daily 9am–5pm; charge), off Old Spanish Trail in the 8,400ft (2,560-meter) Rincons, was set aside in 1933 to highlight a giant forest of mature saguaros.

BELOW: a view of Tucson from Sentinel Peak.

The **Tucson Mountain District** (tel: 520-733-5158; park daily 7am–sunset, Red Hills Visitor Center daily 9am–5pm), located west of the **Tucson Mountains**, was added in 1961 for research purposes, and contains stands of younger saguaros. Both units have excellent scenic drives and a variety of long and short hiking trails that wind among the saguaros, but if you choose only one unit to visit, choose Tucson Mountains. It is possible to enter from the north via Ina Road (exit 248 off Interstate 10), but the entry point from downtown, via narrow, winding Gates Pass, is really breathtaking as the route summits the pass and starts to descend into Tucson Mountain Park, the county park adjoining the national park.

Typical Sonoran Desert Arizona Upland vegetation of yellow-blossomed paloverde trees, flame-tipped ocotillo, mesquite, and ironwood surrounds this area which is frequented by roadrunners, Harris's hawks, gila woodpeckers and other birds (visit in late April and the whole desert will be in bloom). Rangers at **Red Hills**

Visitor Center on Kinney Road offer orientations and can tell you how to find Hohokam petroglyphs at the **Signal Hill** picnic area. The graded, 6-mile (10km) **Bajada Loop Drive** is the main scenic drive. It winds through vigorous stands of young saguaro that march across the south-facing bajadas, or slopes, in charming Jolly Green Giant armies waving spiny arms in all directions.

Desert flora and fauna

Desert animals are largely nocturnal, keeping cool in burrows or beneath rocks or shrubs during the day. Your best chance of seeing and learning about Sonoran Desert flora and fauna is to visit the world-famous **Arizona-Sonora Desert Museum** ❶ (2021 N. Kinney Road; tel: 520-883-2702; daily Mar–May 7.30am–5pm, Jun–Aug Sun–Fri 7am–4.30pm and Sat 7am–10pm, Sept 7am–4.30pm, Oct–Feb 8.30am–5pm; charge) next door in **Tucson Mountain Park**. This isn't a museum at all but a large outdoor zoo, botanical garden, and nature trail that so effectively

The Life Zones exhibit at the Arizona-Sonora Desert Museum explores ecological diversity within desert environments.

BELOW: Tucson Mountain District of Saguaro National Park.

A Titan II missile rests in its silo at the Titan Missile Museum. It's the last of more than 50 such missiles in Arizona and elsewhere in the western US.

BELOW LEFT AND RIGHT: pottery on display at the Arizona State Museum.

re-creates the Sonoran Desert, the 299 species of native animals and 1,400 species of native plants that live here are fooled into thinking they never left home.

You'll need good walking shoes, a hat, sunscreen, and at least half a day to see all the exhibits, which include wild cats such as mountain lions, bobcats and jaguarundi; bighorn sheep; Mexican wolves; coyotes; and delightful furballs known as coatis, a relative of the ringtail, which snooze in the trees. Beautifully landscaped paths wander through a wildflower and cactus garden.

In the walk-in **Hummingbird Aviary**, hummers divebomb feeders and buzz loudly in the mesquite trees. An engaging **Life Underground** exhibit allows you to observe kit foxes, kangaroo rats, tarantulas, and other nocturnal animals asleep in their underground burrows.

If you want to understand how elevation affects temperature and moisture for desert plants, check out the **Life Zones** exhibit, which takes you through five life zones – the

equivalent of journeying from Mexico to Canada in just a few short steps. A raptor presentation by naturalists, featuring free-flying hawks, is very popular; check for times at the entrance.

After visiting this museum, you'll never look at the desert with the same eyes again. There is an international food court offering excellent and interesting meals and a pleasant restaurant. An art gallery shows temporary exhibits, and a gift shop sells thoughtfully chosen books, games, desert foods, and many unique items.

Not far from the Arizona Sonora Desert Museum, the **International Wildlife Museum** Ⓚ (4800 W. Gates Pass; tel: 520-629-0100; Mon–Fri 9am–5pm, Sat–Sun until 6pm; charge) features dioramas with more than 400 mammal, bird, and insect species from all over the world, as well as interactive exhibits and wildlife films. The museum is an educational program of the Safari Club International Foundation. The displays are quite elaborate and informative, but the Safari Club's conservation message has a distinctly hollow ring considering

that the animals on display were hunted and taxidermed; there are no living creatures at this facility at all.

Strike the set

There's more fakery at the **Old Tucson Studios** ⓛ (201 S. Kinney Rd; tel: 520-883-0100; daily 10am–6pm, tours June–Sept Tue, Wed and Fri–Sun; charge), one of the most visited attractions in Arizona after the Grand Canyon. Originally constructed in 1939 as a set for the movie *Arizona* (and reconstructed after a major fire in 1995), more than 300 movies and TV shows have been filmed here, including the John Wayne movie *Rio Lobo* and *Tombstone*, starring Kurt Russell. Highlights at this family theme park include gunfights, saloon shows, barbecues, miniature train rides, musicals, Native American storytelling, games, rides, and a Town Hall Museum.

Air and space

Davis-Monthan Air Force Base "Aircraft Boneyard" ⓜ (Kolb Road; tel: 520-228-8448; tours Mon–Fri 9am–5pm; charge), east of Tucson, was dedicated by Charles Lindbergh in 1927. During World War II, it was a training ground for B-17 bombers and still trains pilots in combat aircraft. One of the base's tenants is the **Aerospace Maintenance and Regeneration Group**, where the U.S. military takes advantage of the dry climate and hard ground surface to mothball an extraordinary 5,000 planes and helicopters before they are scrapped.

Access to the Aircraft Boneyard is restricted. The only way to tour it is to take one of the bus tours through the facility offered by adjoining **Pima Air and Space Museum** ⓝ (6000 E. Valencia Rd; tel: 520-574-0462; daily 9am–5pm; charge). This huge air and space museum is just the place to take kids. It has more than 300 aircraft and spacecraft – the world's largest private collection. Exhibits include a replica of the Wright Brothers' Kitty Hawk and President John F. Kennedy's Air Force One. A Space Gallery looks at the history of space exploration. Children like the **Challenger Learning**

Despite a rocky start, Biosphere 2 is now utilized for research and recreation.

BELOW: Biosphere 2's rainforest is one of several environments contained within the 3-acre glass structure.

Center, housed in the **Aerospace Exploratorium**, which has a mission briefing room, transportation room, mission control area, and space station.

Two other museums on the outskirts of Tucson offer entirely different visions of a space-age future. The **Titan Missile Museum ❷** (1580 W. Duval Mine Rd, Sahuarita; tel: 520-625-7736; daily 8.45am–5pm; charge), 20 miles (32km) south of Tucson off Interstate 19, is a sobering reminder of Cold War politics and the only site in the United States with a disarmed US intercontinental ballistic missile (ICBM) still on its underground launch pad. One-hour tours of this declassified subterranean museum allow visitors to hear a tape of an Air Force crew preparing to launch a nuclear missile, then see the missile itself – a 110ft (34-meter) -tall, 170-ton (when fully loaded) monster contained behind 6,000-pound (2,700kg) blast doors.

A far more positive experience awaits visitors at **Biosphere 2 ❸** (tel: 520-838-6200; daily 9am–4pm; charge) in the town of **Oracle** 30 miles (48km)

north of Tucson. Basically a 3-acre (1-hectare), glass-enclosed terrarium designed to support the four men and four women who sealed themselves inside the facility for two years in 1991, Biosphere 2 was a grand, private experiment that went awry.

Amid accusations of hype, New Age cultism, poor science, and failed systems that endangered the health of the "bionauts," Biosphere 2 started down the long road to credibility in 1996, when Columbia University's Lamont-Doherty Earth Observatory assumed management. The University of Arizona took over in 2007, and Biosphere 2 now operates as a department of UA's College of Science. The agreement to pay a $100 annual fee to owners CDO Ranching and Development may extend to 10 years. A $30 million gift from the Philecology Foundation, founded by Edward P. Bass, funds Bisophere 2's operations and some research projects. Other grants and awards, primarily from the National Science Foundation, also support research activities.

BELOW: three amigos entertain an audience at Old Tucson Studios.

Fairs and Fiestas

Whatever the occasion or the season, folks in southern Arizona like to get together for food, music, and good times

The annual calendar is jam-packed with parades, rodeos, fairs, and festivals featuring everything from bird-watching to chilli tasting. Fiestas celebrating Arizona's Mexican heritage are among the most popular and are held in every community with a sizeable Mexican-American population. Cinco de Mayo commemorates Mexico's victory over the French at Puebla on May 5, 1862. Mexican Independence Day, September 16, is cause for even more celebration. Phoenix's Civic Plaza holds one of the biggest parties. Booths sell *carne asada*, or flame-broiled beef, and small Mexican flags, while mariachi bands and *ballet folklorico* take the stage, along with speakers reciting the call to arms that started the revolution in 1810.

El Día de los Muertos, the Day of the Dead, is commemorated on All Souls Day, November 1–2. Family members decorate graves with flowers, candles, and sugar skulls bearing the names of the deceased. The historic Sosa-Carillo-Fremont House in downtown Tucson exhibits traditional *nichos*, flowered wreaths, and candles.

Mariachi music, a style that traces its roots to 18th-century Spain, has become synonymous with Mexican fiestas. Some of the best bands in America can be heard every April in Tucson at the International Mariachi Conference and at the Christmas Mariachi Concert in Phoenix.

Christmas is a magical time in southern Arizona. El Centro de Las Americas in Tucson holds a month-long celebration of Mexican Christmas traditions called the Ferías Navideñas and Nacimiento Tour. Events include Las Posadas, a traditional dramatization of Jesus's birth. Tucson and Phoenix Botanical Gardens have elaborate displays of *luminarias* (lit candles in brown paper bags). The Tucson Museum of Art installs an elaborate nativity scene, or *nacimiento*, involving hundreds of figurines, in Casa Cordova, the work of a mother and daughter from a northern Mexican village.

Easter has special meaning for the Pascua Yaqui Indians of Tucson, whose Lenten ceremonies include traditional rituals like the Deer Dance. The normally private Tohono O'odham Nation throws a lively three-day celebration with a powwow and rodeo every February in Sells, southwest of Tucson. The tribe also holds the Wa:k Powwow at Mission San Xavier del Bac in March. The Waila Festival, featuring O'odham "chicken scratch" music, is held at the Arizona Historical Society in Tucson in May.

Cowboys and rodeos are the focal point of the world's longest nonmotorized parade, which takes place at Tucson's La Fiesta de los Vaqueros, a huge outdoor rodeo, in February. Winter also brings the Gem, Mineral, and Fossil Showcase at venues around Tucson. Birders won't want to miss Wings Over Willcox, *the* big birding event in southeastern Arizona. It's held in January at Willcox Playa, winter home of thousands of migratory fowl.

ABOVE AND RIGHT: performing mariachi and dance.

RESTAURANTS

Prices for a three-course dinner per person, excluding tax, tip, and beverages:
$ = under $20
$$ = $20–40
$$$ = $40–60
$$$$ = over $60

Beyond Bread
6260 Speedway Boulevard
Tel: 520-747-7477
$
What could be simpler or more delicious for breakfast than a loaf of bread still warm from the oven and a steaming cup of coffee? You'll find more than 20 varieties of bread as well as thick sandwiches, salads, pastries, and cakes at this friendly and aromatic bakery and café. There's another location at 421 W. Ina.

Blue Fin Seafood Bistro
7053 N. Oracle Road
Tel: 520-531-8500
$$–$$$
This hip restaurant has the most varied piscine menu in town. Blue Fin has a bar downstairs with live music on weekends. Upstairs there are cozy booths. Service is friendly, fast, and efficient. If you're in the mood for fish, this is the place.

Café Poca Cosa
110 E. Pennington
Tel: 520-622-6400
$
At this perennially popular restaurant, chef-owner Susana Davila works her magic with innovative

Sonoran cuisine that is truly memorable. Daily specials are listed on a chalkboard and include a variety of unique tamales, mole dishes, *carne asado*, and chicken cooked several ways, bathed in fresh herbs and sauces and served with home-made tortillas. Her daughter runs a second, smaller, cash-only restaurant nearby serving tamales with unusual nouveau Mexican fillings and sauces. Closed Sun and Mon.

Cup Café
The Hotel Congress, 311 E. Congress Street
Tel: 520-622-8848
$$
You'll find a little slice of Bohemia at this café in the historic Hotel Congress, which serves a hearty breakfast, a variety of thick lunch sandwiches, and an eclectic dinner menu with Italian and Southwestern touches.

Dakota Café
6541 E. Tanque Verde Road
Tel: 520-298-7188
$–$$
Set in a complex of faux Old West buildings known as Trail Dust Town, the restaurant has won kudos for its healthful and imaginative cooking. The menu ranges from meat loaf sandwiches, burgers, and several vegetarian dishes to specials like chicken enchiladas, braised pork

tacos, and tempura shrimp. Patio dining is available. Closed Sun.

El Charro Mexican Café
311 N. Court Avenue
Tel: 520-622-1922
$
A venerable stone building in the Presidio Historic District houses what claims to be the oldest family-operated Mexican restaurant in the United States. Tasty Sonoran-style food is the bill of fare here, including spinach enchiladas, chimichangas, tamales, and *carne seca* (dried beef), a house specialty. Satellite restaurants are located at El Mercado (Broadway and Wilmot) and Tucson International Airport.

Elle: A Wine Country Restaurant
3048 E. Broadway Boulevard
Tel: 520-327-0500
$–$$
Italian-inspired dishes are refreshing in their simplicity yet intriguingly creative. Clear, natural flavors add nuance to entrées such as risotto with butternut squash, balsamic-roasted onion and sage, or a simple capellini with tomatoes, basil, and garlic. True to its name, the restaurant offers a selection of more than 40 wines by the glass. Dinner only Sun.

Gold Room
Westward Look Resort and Spa, 245 E. Ina Road

Tel: 520-297-1151
$$$–$$$$
Fabulous food dreamed up by award-winning executive chef Jamie West and a panoramic view of Tucson from the foothills of the Catalina Mountains. Dishes include melt-in-the-mouth seared ahi tuna, vodka-infused smoked salmon, and toast points, Asian-inspired pan-seared salmon with wasabi potatoes, bok choi and ginger sauce, and a Sonoran "surf 'n' turf" featuring cowboy steak, lobster mac and cheese, and tumbleweed potatoes. West grows all his produce and herbs in an on-site organic garden. Tours are offered on Saturday mornings.

Hacienda del Sol Grill
Hacienda del Sol Guest Ranch Resort
Tel: 520-529-3500
$$$–$$$$
Voted Tucson's most romantic restaurant, this elegant fine dining restaurant is located at the exclusive Hacienda del Sol Guest Ranch in the shadow of the Catalina foothills. Dine on the patio for a spectacular view of the mountains. Contemporary American cuisine, featuring foie gras, prime rib, rack of lamb, grilled buffalo sirloin, and catch of the day, among others, is

prepared using locally sourced meats, fish, dairy, and produce grown in the resort's own organic garden, whenever possible. Award-winning wine list. This is the place to push the boat out in Tucson.

Hub Restaurant and Ice Creamery
266 E. Congress Sreet
Tel: 520-207-8201
$–$$

Located in the heart of downtown, Hub is a hip new eatery serving up elegant spins on pub foods. You'll find the usual suspects – rotisserie chicken, fish and chips, steaks, burgers, pot pies, and soups, salads, and sandwiches – but there are a few vegetarian surprises, including roasted vegetable tofu and vegetable hash. Leave room for a serving of their rich homemade ice cream. Bar and live music nightly. Open late.

Janos
3770 E. Sunrise Drive
Tel: 520-615-6100
$$$

Ensconced in elegant digs at the Westin La Paloma hotel, the celebrated Janos continues its tradition of blending French and Southwestern influences to produce one of Tucson's most rewarding gastronomic experiences. The menu changes often, but a sampler menu (a series of small courses each accompanied by a different wine) could include lobster and brie relleno, cognac-scented beef tenderloin, and lamb

sirloin marinated in lemon, basil, garlic, and olive oil. The desserts are equally entrancing, and a wine cellar with 700 selections (20 are offered each night) will keep oenophiles happy on return visits. The more casual J Bar next door is a less expensive alternative. Chef Janos is also executive chef of Kai at the Wild Horse Pass Resort in Phoenix and has also just opened another restaurant in Tucson. Closed Sun.

Lodge on the Desert Restaurant
306 North Alvernon Way
Tel: 520-320-2000
$–$$$

This pleasant restaurant is hidden in an intimate courtyard in the recently remodeled 1930s hacienda Lodge on the Desert. The young chef and his team are working hard to create a niche in Tucson for their culinary vision, and gradually building a following in Tucson. The kitchen uses organic, locally sourced foods, and dishes are imaginatively seasoned with unusual spice blends. Try the delicious organic beet salad, followed by the expertly grilled Loch Duart Organic Salmon, paired with watercress salad, lemon-mashed potatoes, and smoked paprika nuage. The ancho-chocolate torte is a winning combination of chocolate and chilli that pays homage to Tucson's proximity to Mexico. A prickly pear lemonade is a nice Sonoran Desert

touch, too, if a little sweet. It's like drinking a virgin tequila sunrise (there's a prickly pear mojito, for those who want something alcoholic). Diners can relax in front of a huge outdoor fireplace or sit inside in an attractive, airy dining room. Service is attentive and friendly. This is a hotel kitchen, so the chef is catering to a crowd, but you'd never know it. There's even a separate gluten-free menu.

Lovin' Spoonfuls Vegetarian Restaurant
2990 N. Campbell Avenue
Tel: 520-325-7766
$

Healthy eaters will be thrilled by this vegetarian and vegan restaurant, which has been winning raves for such meat- and dairy-free dishes as adzuki-bean burgers, soy bacon cheeseburger, veggie chilli dogs, and country fried "chicken." There's a gluten-free menu, too, as well as organic wine and beer. Closed for dinner Sun.

Sachiko Sushi Restaurant
3240 E. Valencia Road
Tel: 520-741-1000
$–$$

When you grow tired of tacos and enchiladas, drop by this highly regarded sushi restaurant, known for authentic preparations and reasonable prices. The menu of hot dishes, including tempura, teriyaki, and noodles, is also quite good. No lunch Sun.

Tohono Chul
7366 N. Paseo del Norte

Tel: 520-797-1222
$

It's difficult to imagine a more peaceful spot than the patio at this restaurant in Tohono Chul Park. Watch hummingbirds in the garden as you enjoy a breakfast of English scones, buttermilk pancakes or *huevos rancheros*. The lunch menu offers raspberry chipotle chicken, spinach *fettuccine alfredo*, grilled salmon, and large salads, among quite a few other choices. Come for the famous afternoon tea. You can browse the gift shop after your meal, or burn off a few calories by strolling through the desert park.

Wildflower
7037 N. Oracle Road
Tel: 520-219-4230
$$

This classy, contemporary bistro has a knack for pleasing patrons with a worldly mix of American, Asian, and European cuisines. Clear, earthy flavors are artfully assembled in such dishes as roasted rack of lamb with Dijon crust, Tuscan white-bean ravioli with wood-grilled chicken, and meatloaf with whipped potatoes. No lunch Sun.

Zinburger Wine and Burger Bar
1865 E. River Road
Tel: 520-299-7799
$–$$

Burgers get high-class treatment at this mod spot, which also has tasty, creative appetizers (try the truffle fries), thick milkshakes, pie, and, interestingly, a small but thoughtful choice of wines.

WINE COUNTRY

This may come as news to most Arizonans, but not to the White House, which has been serving fine Arizona wines since 1989

Oenophiles enjoy spending long weekends touring the state's three main wine-growing regions – southeastern Arizona, the Sonoita/Elgin area, and northern Arizona – and are discovering the many inventive ways that food, wine, and tourism are interweaving to create a new cultural experience along Arizona's backcountry highways.

Spanish monks raised vines in Arizona in the 17th century, but it wasn't until 1973 that a retired soil scientist planted the first vines in the Sonoita region, whose rich red soils, 5,000ft (1,500-meter) elevation, oak-dotted grasslands, and ideal climate soon lured others. There are now more than 50 small vineyards in what is being called Napa-Zona. A variety of grapes are grown, including Mediterranean grape varietals such as Petite Verdot, Petite Syrah, Tempranillo, Mourvedre, and Grenache. The state's first all-organic winery, Granite Creek, is now producing its first wines in northern Arizona's Chino Valley. Some wineries, such as Dos Cabezas are pairing with fine-dining restaurants to promote their wines, or, like Kokopelli Winery in Chandler, creating their own wine bars.

Critics are taking notice. Some 20 wines from eight wineries have scored an 88 or above from Wine Spectator magazine. Best of all, Arizona wineries receive more than 30,000 visitors a year, bringing dividends for those whose passion for terroir (a region's unique wine character) led them to try their luck in these rural Arizona destinations. For further information, visit www.arizonavines andwines.com.

LEFT: a tasting at Canelo Hills Vineyard and Winery.
RIGHT: ripe Cabernet grapes ready for harvest.

Visiting the Wineries

The 11 wineries in Elgin/Sonoita, Arizona's oldest wine-growing region, offer an excellent general introduction to Arizona's vineyards and winemaking.

Award-winning Callaghan Winery produces exciting wines from Mediterranean grapes. Nearby Village of Elgin Winery uses Sauvignon Blanc, Cabernet Sauvignon, and Sangiovese single varietals to create award-winning small-batch wines like Tombstone Red and has a harvest food-and-wine festival in September. Dos Cabezas, bought by winemaker Todd Bostock in 2006, saw its Viognier white and El Norte red win Governors Awards for Best in Arizona in 2007. The tasting room is next to Canela Bistro on Highway 82. Most are only open on weekends.

Nearby Willcox now has six winery tasting rooms in the historic downtown. It's best known as a grape-growing region. Musician Maynard Keenan, owner of Caduceus, the label under which he produces wines, co-owns the most famous of its wineries, Dos Cabezas, since renamed Arizona Stronghold. Film producer Sam Pillsbury, former owner of Dos Cabezas, now runs Pillsbury Wine Company, playing with new grape blends.

Page Springs Cellars (open daily), a vineyard and tasting room near Sedona, provides both grapes for Caduceus and Arizona Stronghold. Owner and winemaker Eric Glomski co-owns Arizona Stronghold and offers bistro foods and tastings of a variety of Arizona wines, including his own Rhone-style wines in the tasting room. Using Sedona as a base, you can visit 16 wineries in northern and central Arizona. Near Prescott, Granite Creek, the state's first organic winery, is a wonderful place for a picnic and to hear live music on weekend afternoons.

Top and Above: Augustfest is celebrated with wine-tasting, winery and vineyard tours, horseback rides, grape-stomping, music, and lunch at the Sonoita Vineyards Harvest Festival at Sonoita Vineyards, a winery in Elgin, Arizona.

BORDER COUNTRY

Ghost towns, Spanish missions, Old West history, and entrancing desert landscapes lure travelers to "la frontera" – Arizona's colorful borderlands

Edge places: those no-man's lands where foreign entities rub up against each other, boundaries blur, and something entirely new emerges. Arizona's border with the Mexican states of Sonora and Chihuahua is one such frontier, a geographical crossroads that has witnessed cultural confluence and collision for centuries.

The recipe begins geographically with the convergence of both the **Chihuahuan** and **Sonoran Deserts** and the **Rocky Mountains** and **Sierra Madre**. Fold in a huge expanse of volcanic basin-and-range topography rising in elevation from just over 1,000ft (300 meters) in the west to nearly 10,000ft (3,000 meters) in the east, and pierce it with one of the last free-flowing rivers in the country, the San Pedro. Then mix in half a dozen Indian cultures, 18th-century Spanish missions, 19th-century American forts and mining towns, modern retirement communities, state-of-the-art astronomical observatories, and twin border towns where cultures constantly meet and merge, and you have a unique salsa – one of the fieriest in the West.

Ecological crossroads

Begin your explorations from Interstate 10 in extreme southeastern Arizona, just over the New Mexico line. Drop south and west on Highway 80 into the **Chiricahua Mountains** via **Portal**. These high peaks are made of uplifted rhyolite, fused ash from an explosion in nearby Turkey Caldera 25 million years ago. Erosion by rainfall has created an extraordinary rockscape preserved in 17-sq-mile (44-sq-km) **Chiricahua National Monument** ❹ (tel: 520-824-3560; visitor center daily 8am–4.30pm; charge), on the western side of the Chiricahuas, south of Willcox.

To view the rocks, follow the 6-mile (10km) **Bonita Canyon Drive**, which

Main attractions

CHIRICAHUA MOUNTAINS
FORT BOWIE
BISBEE
TOMBSTONE
KARTCHNER CAVERNS
RAMSEY CANYON
TUMACACORI
SAN XAVIER DEL BAC
KITT PEAK
ORGAN PIPE CACTUS NATIONAL MONUMENT

LEFT: the interior of San Xavier del Bac.
RIGHT: Coronado National Monument.

Geronimo, posing with his wife, at Fort Sill, Oklahoma, where he remained until his death in 1909.

climbs from the visitor center through lush **Bonita Canyon** to **Massai Point**, the starting point for a short nature trail and day hikes among the rocks. Rocky Mountain and Sierra Madrean wildlife mingle in these mountains via a natural corridor running through the Chiricahuas to Mexico. Mexican plants and animals such as rare Apache fox squirrels and Chihuahua and Apache pines live side by side with species more commonly found north of the border. Of particular interest are the birds that summer in the Cave Creek area. Top of the list is the trogon, a Mexican native with a long, coppery tail and bright feathers, sulphur-bellied flycatchers, tanagers, chickadees, warblers, and a variety of hummingbirds.

Surrounding the monument is **Coronado National Forest** (tel: 520-388-8300) and **Chiricahua Wilderness**, which contain 100 miles (160km) of hiking trails and many delightful camping spots. A rough forest road traverses the mountains, but is closed by snow in winter. Check the weather forecast before starting out.

On the trail of the Apache

To the Chiricahua Apache Indians, this was the "Land of Standing Up Rocks." Led by Cochise, Victorio, and Geronimo, they successfully evaded capture by US Army troops during the 1860s and 70s, when settlers began encroaching on Apache territory, but they were eventually forced to surrender. Massai Point provides a view of **Cochise Head**, said to be the profile of the old Apache warrior. To learn more about the Apache Wars, visit nearby **Fort Bowie National Historic Site ❺** (tel: 520-847-2500; visitor center daily 8am–4.30pm). This ruined adobe outpost once consisted of barracks, officers' quarters, storehouses, a trader's store, and a hospital. It was built to protect the Butterfield Overland Mail Stage and local residents. A 1.5-mile (2.5km) self-guided trail to the ruins leaves from Apache Pass Road.

Highway 80 continues south to the 1902 copper-smelting town of **Douglas ❻** past guest ranches, heart-lifting views of the **Peloncillo Mountains**, and a roadside plaque near **Skeleton Canyon** at the spot where Geronimo

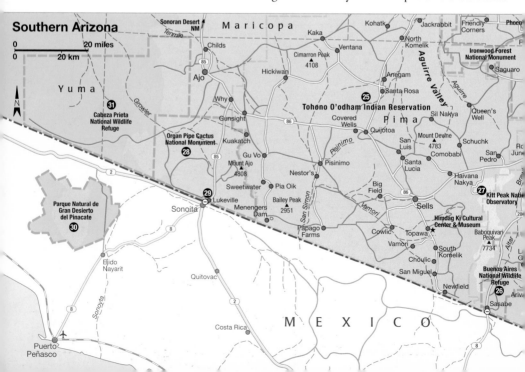

surrendered in 1886. The five-story **Gadsden Hotel** (built 1907) is a faded beauty that bills itself as "the last of the grand hotels." Once host to Theodore Roosevelt, its main attraction now is the lobby, which contains massive marble columns decorated with 14-karat gold leaf supporting a vaulted ceiling with stained-glass panels.

About 15 miles (24km) east of Douglas is the 93,000-acre (38,000-hectare) **John Slaughter Ranch Museum** ❼ (tel: 520-558-2474; Wed–Sun 10am–3pm; charge), once owned by former Texas Ranger and Cochise County sheriff John Slaughter. His 1890s house, corral, and other buildings have been restored as examples of ranch life during Arizona's territorial years. A 2,330-acre (940-hectare) section is now protected as **San Bernardino National Wildlife Refuge**.

Copper Queen

Douglas served the old copper mining town of **Bisbee** ❽, which spreads for 3 steep miles (5km) across **Mule Pass Gulch** and **Tombstone Canyon** in the 5,000ft (1,500-meter) **Mule Mountains**,

just west of Douglas. Starting out as a rowdy, cosmopolitan mining camp in 1877, early mining claims were won and lost at the faro table by hard-drinking miners and ex-soldiers. The first major mining operation began when Judge Dewitt Bisbee (who never saw the town named for him) and other San Francisco businessmen bought the **Copper Queen Mine** in 1880. But with underground copper seams running for miles into other claims, cooperation proved the only way for everyone to get rich, and the still-powerful Phelps Dodge corporation was born.

Bisbee's colorful history – lynchings, murders, miners, working girls, and hopeful immigrants – is showcased in clever, interactive exhibits at the **Bisbee Mining and Historical Museum** (tel: 520-432-7071; daily 10am–4pm; charge), housed in the 1897 **Phelps Dodge General Office Building**. Now a satellite of the Smithsonian Institution, this museum is one of the Southwest's true gems. A standout is the depiction of the Bisbee Deportation of 1917, when 1,000 striking miners were loaded at gunpoint

> *"Bisbee – the city of foul odors and sickening smells."*
> – Editor of the *Tucson Citizen*, circa 1900

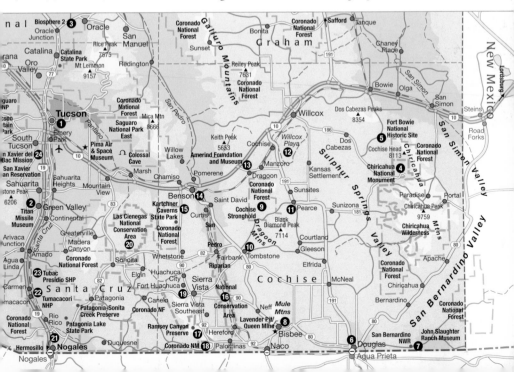

into boxcars and expelled from the state for "anti-government" activities.

Down and dirty

The other unmissable attraction in Bisbee is the **Queen Mine Tour** (tel: 520-432-2071 or 866-432-2071; daily tours 9am–3.30pm, call for reservations; charge). Visitors are equipped with yellow slickers and miner's helmets and lamps, and sit astride an old mine train for the chilly trip down the shaft with a flinty ex-miner – himself a mine of information about drilling, blasting, mining etiquette, and the cushy life of a sanitary engineer, or "shit nipper."

After yielding 8 billion pounds (3.6 billion kg) of copper, Bisbee's 33 mines (and an astonishing 2,500 miles/4,000km of tunnels) were all closed by 1975, including the yawning abyss of the **Lavender Open Pit Mine**, on the edge of downtown, which long ago swallowed a whole mountain.

Some of the Southwest's funkiest art galleries, museums, and offbeat lodgings are housed in historic buildings downtown (including the OK Jail and miners' boarding houses. Many are on

a popular self-guided historic walking tour of downtown's steep hills – you'll soon understand why postal workers in Bisbee refuse to home-deliver mail.

View the 1939 **Phelps Dodge Mercantile**, 1906 **Post Office and Library**, the 1880s **Miners Hotel** in Brewery Gulch, and the 1902 four-story, red-roofed **Copper Queen Hotel**, where you can sleep in the Theodore Roosevelt Suite, John Wayne Room (a straight shot for the Duke after a night in the adjoining saloon bar), or, if you're male, take your chances with the spectral Julia, the "soiled dove" who haunts the Ghost Room on the third floor.

Tough towns

A highway tunnel through the Mule Mountains opens onto the limestone **Chihuahuan Desert** terrain of creosote, yucca, ocotillo, and sweeping vistas of the alluring **Dragoon Mountains** to the northwest, where you can hike and camp at **Cochise Stronghold ⑨**, the warrior's hideout. Immediately ahead is the "Town too Tough to Die": **Tombstone ⑩** (tel: 888-457-3929).

Guides at the Queen Mine – former miners themselves – lead visitors on a subterranean tour.

BELOW: the weathered ruins of the guardhouse at Fort Bowie, built in 1862 to protect the Apache Pass.

The old mining town was the setting of the infamous OK Corral gunfight in 1881, which pitted US Marshal Wyatt Earp, his brothers Morgan and Virgil, and "Doc" Holliday against the Clanton and McLaury boys, ranchers whose extracurricular activities included cattle rustling and harboring stagecoach robbers. Unless you're in the mood for stage-set Wild West artifice, avoid the costumed cowboys, mock gunfights, and tourist traps, though you may get a kick out of the old **Bird Cage Theater**, where working girls plied their trade in 14 "cages" or "cribs" suspended from the ceiling.

Instead, take a walk over to the 1882 Victorian red-brick **Tombstone Courthouse State Historic Park** (tel: 520-457-3311; daily 8am–5pm; charge) to view the original courthouse setup and a reconstructed gallows. Diagrammed exhibits offer two theories about what happened during the 30-second OK Corral gunfight, in which Virgil and Morgan Earp were wounded and three members of the Clanton gang killed. The Clantons and other victims of frontier justice are buried in **Boothill Cemetery**, one of the tackiest graveyards you will ever visit – so kitsch that it's a must-see – complete with fake-looking headstones, cute epitaphs, and piped-in Willie Nelson music.

Tombstone's eateries also veer toward the hokey, but worth a look is a joint called the **Nellie Cashman Restaurant and Pie Salon**, which was once a hospital run by an Irish mining camp follower known as "the Angel of Tombstone."

Tombstone and Bisbee are resurrected mining towns. To see what happens when boom leads to bust, drive a dirt road east from Tombstone to the ghost mining towns of **Gleeson**, **Courtland**, and **Pearce** ⓫. Pearce hosted an 1894 gold rush and is now the only site with sizeable ruins (a two-story corner mercantile store, a post office, and the jail). From Pearce, paved Highway 191 heads north to Interstate 10, past **Willcox Playa** ⓬, which floods in winter to form a wetland that attracts, along with nearby **White Water Draw**, more than 10,000 sandhill cranes,

A mural decorates the walls in Tombstone, illustrating an old-fashioned photo opportunity.

A Bisbee art gallery; the former mining town has a thriving art scene.

buffs. There are excellent exhibits on the native peoples of the Americas and contemporary exhibits by some of the state's most talented native artists. This is an active research center. Important archaeological studies are co-published with the University of Arizona.

Subterranean world

From **Benson** ⓮, follow Highway 90 south for 9 miles (14km) to one of Arizona's top new visitor attractions: **Kartchner Caverns State Park** ⓯ (tel: 520-586-CAVE for reservations, 520-586-4100 for info; daily 7.30am–6pm; charge). Kartchner is a rare "wet cave," with more than 90 percent of its colorful Escabrosa limestone decorations still growing. It was discovered in 1974 by cavers Randy Tufts and Gary Tenen beneath the **Whetstone Mountains** and Kartchner Ranch. The 2.5-mile (4km) cave was kept secret for 14 years while the cavers, the Kartchner family, and state officials debated how best to develop the caverns without destroying their delicate ecosystem.

State-of-the-art technology includes misting systems in the caves,

Canada and snow geese, and an array of other waterfowl.

Located between Willcox and Benson is the fabulous **Amerind Foundation Museum** ⓭ (tel: 520-586-3666; Tue–Sun 10am–4pm; charge). This is one of the Southwest's premier private archaeological and ethnographic collections. The dream of the amateur archaeologist William Fulton, who built this lovely hacienda-style ranch in 1937 to show off his artifacts, it should not be missed by archaeology

double-lock doors to seal in moisture, and specially blasted entrance tunnels. Arizona State Parks spared no expense in doing the job right, opening the caves in 1999.

Tours leave every 20 minutes from the **Discovery Center**, xeriscaped with interpretive nature trails of varying lengths. Inside, view a 15-minute multimedia film and interactive exhibits that include a simulated cave crawl-through and virtual cave tour. You must reserve ahead; this is currently Arizona's hottest ticket. Or arrive by 7.30am to try for one of 100 tickets released daily on a first-come, first-served basis (hint: stay in the park's 60-site campground to ensure first dibs).

Rangers offer entertaining and informative talks on the porch before accompanying the tram to the cave entrance. Inside, in the **Rotunda** and **Throne Rooms** and the **Big Room**, the temperature is a steady, steamy 68°F (20°C), with paved, barrier-free walkways leading past deep mud flats and unusual formations, such as colorful shields, streaky "bacon," "fried eggs," flowing draperies, "cave popcorn,"

wavy helectites, ceiling-hanging stalactites, and floor-growing stalagmites. Record-breakers here are the 58ft (18-meter)-high Kubla Khan column and a 21ft (6-meter)-long soda straw, the longest in the United States. Both the caves and the strong conservation message being promoted are impressive. **Note:** Big Room tours are only available Oct 15–April 15.

Birding hot spots

Running parallel to Highway 90 is another impressive natural attraction. **San Pedro Riparian National Conservation Area** ⓰ (tel: 520-439-6400; visitor center daily 9.30am–4.30pm) preserves cottonwood-willow bosque along the **San Pedro River** for 100 miles (160km) between St. David and the Mexican border. Named a Globally Important Bird Area by the American Bird Conservancy, this perennial waterway supports more than 80 species of mammals, 45 reptile and amphibian species, 100 species of breeding birds, and 250 species of migrant and wintering birds. An astonishing

A Boothill grave marker.

BELOW: San Jose de Tumacacori, a mission church built by O'odham Indians, was abandoned in 1848 as a result of Apache raids.

TIP

For updates on bird sightings and rare bird alerts, call the Tucson Audubon Society on 520-798-1005.

4–10 million migratory birds lay over every year.

Bird lovers can help **Southern Arizona Bird Observatory** (tel: 520-432-1388) tag hummingbirds at **San Pedro House** near Sierra Vista in summer, or visit The Nature Conservancy's 300-acre (120-hectare) **Ramsey Canyon Preserve** ⑰ (tel: 520-378-2785; Feb–Oct daily 8am–5pm, Nov–Jan Thur–Sun 9am–4pm; tours Mar–Oct Mon, Thur, and Sat 9am; charge). A wonderful little nature center contains exhibits on the San Pedro and Ramsey Canyon ecosystem and a gift store; guided tours are offered. In August, avian migrants from Mexico, attracted by the warm Sierra Madrean environment of the **Huachuca Mountains**, include painted redstarts, eared and elegant trogons, clouds of butterflies, bats, and 14 hummingbird species, flocking in the huge sycamores and at porch feeders.

Coronado's quest

The Huachucas (highest point, **Miller Peak**, at 9,466ft/2,885 meters) are a blessing during the 100°F (38°C) heat of summer, offering breathtaking

drives with views into Mexico, camping in **Coronado National Forest**, and hiking. The 2,880-acre (1,160-hectare) **Coronado National Memorial** ⑱ (tel: 520-366-5515; visitor center daily 8am–4pm; charge) commemorates the location of what is thought to have been the first Spanish *entrada* into North America by Don Francisco Vásquez de Coronado, in 1540. Going on information from the advance party of Padre Marcos de Niza and the Moorish slave Esteban in the 1530s, the charismatic 30-year-old Spaniard financed his own expedition from Mexico City, following old Indian trails north across torrid desert and probably passing near 6,844ft (2,086-meter) **Coronado Peak**. After months of fruitless travel, Coronado's search for gold and glory was deemed a failure, but it set the stage for what would later become a massive colonization effort by Spain.

In 1877, after the Southwest had become American territory, the US Army built **Fort Huachuca** ⑲ as part of its campaign against the Apache. Of the many soldiers who fought during the Apache Wars, none was more

BELOW: San Xavier del Bac, the "White Dove of the Desert," was completed in 1797 and is still an active parish church.

respected for its bravery than the fort's black troops, known to the Apache as Buffalo Soldiers. A room in the **Fort Huachuca Historical Museum** (tel: 520-533-5736; Mon–Fri 9am–4pm, Sat–Sun 1pm–4pm; free) tells their story through memorabilia, photos, Indian artifacts, and dioramas. It is well worth a stop in the military base town of **Sierra Vista** (you'll pass right by the fort, now a training center for military intelligence). Note: due to stepped-up homeland security, only US citizens may currently visit this museum. You'll need to show driver's license and proof of car insurance, if you drive into the compound.

North of Sierra Vista, turn west on Highway 82. Look for pronghorn as you drive through 66 sq miles (170 sq km) of native grasslands at **Las Cienegas National Conservation Area ⑳** (tel: 520-722-4289) into expansive rolling ranch and wine country. If this area looks familiar, it may be because the 17,500-acre (7,100-hectare) **San Rafael Ranch**, southeast of **Patagonia**, doubled as Oklahoma during the shooting of the 1955 film of the Rodgers and Hammerstein musical. Riparian birds like vermilion flycatchers may be glimpsed in these 5,000-ft (1,500-meter) grasslands, and some 300 avian species frequent The Nature Conservancy-run **Patagonia-Sonoita Creek Preserve** (tel: 520-394-2400; Apr–Sept Wed–Sun 6.30am–4pm, Oct–Mar 7.30am–4pm, guided tours year-round Sat 9am; charge), which preserves cottonwood-willow habitat from Patagonia north through **Madera Canyon** in the Santa Rita Mountains.

Spanish Missions

Nogales ㉑, which sits astride the US–Mexico border at the junction of Highway 82 with Interstate 19, is where most Arizonans get their border-town fix. Shop 'til you drop, try Sonoran *ranchero*-style food, and, if you're in the mood for dancing, look for a bar playing lively Norteña music. **Northern Sonora** and the stretch of Interstate

19 between Nogales and **Tucson** that follows the beautiful Santa Cruz River Valley contains several 17th-century Indian missions founded by Italian Jesuit missionary Padre Eusebio Francisco Kino during the early Spanish colonial era. **Tumacacori National Historical Park ㉒** (tel: 520-398-2341; daily 8am–5pm; charge) preserves three mission churches built between 1691 and the early 1800s.

Tumacacori and its sister missions of **Guevavi** (11 miles/18km south) and **Calabazas** (15 miles/24km south) were abandoned in 1771, after Spain recalled its Jesuit missionaries and replaced them with Franciscans. The present church began construction in 1800, finishing just before Mexican independence in 1821. Apache raiding grew so bad on the unprotected Mexican northern frontier that, in 1848, the residents moved away and the mission fell into ruin. A peaceful self-guiding trail leads through the church, which remains a remarkable testimony to the skills of Indian craftsmen.

The 5-mile (8km) **Juan Bautista de Anza National Historic Trail** along the

Catholicism was brought to the region by Spanish missionaries in the late 17th-century and remains a vital cultural force.

BELOW: once a wild and wooly mining town, Tombstone is now dedicated to rehashing its Old West history for the tourist trade.

The restoration of San Xavier del Bac has returned the interior to its original brilliance.

BELOW: Organ Pipe Cactus National Monument.

Santa Cruz River connects Tumacacori to **Tubac Presidio State Historic Park** ㉓ (tel: 520-398-2252; daily 9am–5pm; charge), operated by Tubac Historical Society, which preserves part of the fort that was erected by the Spanish in 1752 to protect their missions following the 1751 Pima Indian Revolt. Apache raiding and political turmoil caused the site to be abandoned, but the settlement was revived following the 1853 Gadsden Purchase. By 1859, Tubac had become a mining boomtown and home to Arizona's first newspaper, the Weekly Arizonan, now on display in the presidio museum. With the founding of an art school in 1948, it morphed into an art colony. Popular with day-trippers, Tubac has about 100 art studios, galleries, and businesses and features a popular annual Festival of the Arts every February.

When Tumacacori was abandoned in 1848, residents moved north to **San Xavier del Bac Mission** ㉔ (tel: 520-294-2624; daily 7am–5pm; free). The "White Dove of the Desert" is considered the most beautiful of all the Kino church missions, with its classic white plaster exterior and ornate facing. It was founded as a satellite, or *visita*, of Tumacacori in 1700 and built by Tohono O'odham Indians in the late 1700s under the direction of Franciscan priests. It is still the parish church for the San Xavier Reservation today. In the 1990s, the tribe and members of a local friends' group worked with an international team to restore interior murals. Restoration of the exterior is now being undertaken.

Desert skies

The 2.8-million-acre (1.1-million-hectare) **Tohono O'odham Reservation** ㉕ sprawls west of Tucson across a surprisingly verdant desert landscape. The Tohono O'odham Nation's **Himdag Ki Cultural Center and Museum** (tel: 520-383-0211; Mon–Fri 10am–4pm; free) is a $15.2 million facility that is 7 miles (11km) southeast of Sells, in the village of Topawa, with sacred Baboquivari Peak as a backdrop. The center has a library, an archive, classrooms, and in-depth exhibits about Tohono O'Odham culture. The outer ring of the exhibit hall has special sections about government, language,

land, and food. A revolving central exhibit area currently displays artwork by 10 contemporary tribal members. The central hallway has a permanent exhibit celebrating Indian veterans of various wars. Nature paths, shady ramadas, footbridges, and an outdoor amphitheater tie the landscape to the building. A good time to visit is during the Tohono O'odham's cultural celebration on June 11, which features a prayer run, the ancient stickball game of *toka*, a film festival, *keihina* and *waila* music, and arts and crafts.

The signature cactus of this desert, the delightfully anthropomorphic saguaro, can be found throughout the desert, and seems to wave its many arms in salutes, hugs, handshakes, and finger-pointing disapproval all along the two-lane **Ajo Highway** (Highway 86). Dramatically backlit mountains, huge desert basins, and storms can be seen hundreds of miles away across an almost hallucinogenic landscape.

A distinctive landmark near the US–Mexico border is 7,734-ft (2,357-meter) **Baboquivari Peak** ("narrow about the middle" in the Tohono O'odham language), a brooding volcanic neck believed by the "People of the Desert" to be the home of their creator god, I'itoi. The **Baboquivari Mountains** lie west of the border grasslands of 116,000-acre (47,000-hectare) **Buenos Aires National Wildlife Refuge 26** (tel: 520-823-4251; visitor center daily 7.30am–4pm, closed weekends June–Aug 15), which supports pronghorn and numerous bird species, including the endangered masked quail. Desert skies here are unbelievably clear, making southern Arizona a mecca for stargazers. **Kitt Peak National Observatory 27** (tel: 520-318-8726; daily 9am–4pm, nights by reservation Sept–July only; tours 10am, 11.30am and 1.30pm; charge) has 19 optical telescopes and two radio telescopes, including the huge McGath-Pierce Solar Telescope and the 4-meter (13ft) Mayall Telescope for dark-sky viewing. A short self-guided tour takes you past the most state-of-the-art telescopes, and a visitor center offers exhibits that will keep you fascinated for hours.

The big empty

About three hours southwest of Tucson, drop south onto Highway

Undocumented immigration is a long-standing issue along the border.

BELOW: a view of Montezuma Canyon.

TIP

Singing Wind Bookshop
(tel: 520-586-2425;
daily 9am–5pm), exit
304 near Benson, is
Arizona's most unusual
bookstore. Located in
Win Bundy's ranch
house, it is known for its
wide range of books on
the Southwest. Call for
directions.

BELOW: a timelapse
photo captures
the movement of
the stars.

85 at **Why** (named for the Y in the road), and enter 516-sq-mile (1,336-sq-km) **Organ Pipe Cactus National Monument** ㉘ (tel: 520-387-6849; 24 hours; visitor center open daily 8am–5pm; charge), which preserves cactus species mainly found south of the border. Remote and lightly visited, this national monument is nestled between the torqued and twisted volcanic **Ajo** and **Puerto Blanco Mountains** and is chock full of coyotes, desert tortoises, rattlers, kit foxes, and other rarely seen desert critters. After a rainfall, brittlebush, desert marigolds, poppies, lupines, and other wildflowers burst into bloom. Allow enough time to take the 56-mile (90km) **Pueblo Blanco Scenic Drive** and 21-mile (34km) **Ajo Scenic Drive** into the backcountry to view organ pipe cactus, rare Mexican elephant trees, limberbush, and senita cactus. Many dirt roads lead to historic ranches, mines, and prehistoric Indian sites; winter is the coolest time to visit.

In 2006, the National Park Service completed a 23-mile (37km) steel fence on its southern boundary, which has successfully prevented illegal vehicle crossings through the national monument. Homeland Security will be evident during your visit to the park. Border Patrol officers patrol this area 24 hours a day, and you will encounter checkpoints where you will be asked to show identification. Overnight stays in the backcountry are no longer permitted.

Highway 85 leads south into **Sonora** and **Baja California**, via the border at **Lukeville** ㉙. Reports of drug cartel violence south of the US–Mexico border have generally been confined to the El Paso, Texas, area, and there have been no reports of increased violence in Arizona's border towns, so feel free to explore the frontera zone. If you go into Mexico only once on your travels, Lukeville may be the easiest place to do so. You must carry Mexican car insurance, which is easily available in Lukeville, and most important, have proof of citizenship. (**Note:** US residents as well as foreign nationals must now carry documentation or passports for re-entry). For more information, contact Lukeville Customs and Border Control (tel: 703-526-4200).

A few miles south of Lukeville is Mexico's **Parque Natural de Gran Desierto del Pinacate** ➌ one of the world's truly extraordinary landscapes – an ebony-hued lava land topped incongruously by Sonoran Desert vegetation. **Puerto Peñasco** (Rocky Point), 65 miles (105km) south of Lukeville, is Arizona's favorite seaside resort, and a great place to swim in the Gulf of California and enjoy endless sandy beaches.

Adjoining Organ Pipe Cactus is 86,000-acre (34,800-hectare) **Cabeza Prieta National Wildlife Refuge** ➌, a sanctuary for desert bighorn sheep. Though beautiful, travel here is by permit only, due to the presence of the **Barry Goldwater Bombing Range** on the preserve's north side. In addition to these units, three undeveloped landscape monuments have been set aside to protect the Sonoran Desert.

The 496,000-acre (200,724-hectare) **Sonoran Desert National Monument**, 60 miles (100km) southwest of Phoenix, conserves a variety of habitats, from desert to montane, including wilderness areas, and may be accessed via Interstate 8 and AZ 238, east of the Gila Indian Reservation.

The 71,000-acre (28,732-hectare) **Agua Fria National Monument**, 40 miles (65km) north of Phoenix, contains 450 prehistoric archaeological sites in scattered, remote locations around Agua Fria River Canyon. Access is via Interstate 17 at Badger Springs or Bloody Basin Road. Both units are managed by the Bureau of Land Management in Phoenix (tel: 602-580-5500).

The third unit is 129,000-acre (52,204-hectare) **Ironwood Forest National Monument**, 25 miles (40km) northwest of Tucson, which protects a rich stand of rare ironwood trees, as well as three mountain ranges and three important archaeological districts on the National Register of Historic Places. There are two main points of entry: Avra Valley Road and Red Rock exits, from Interstate 10, then southwest on Sasco Road to Silverbell Road. It is managed by the BLM in Tucson (tel: 520-258-7200).

"For the first time, I felt I was getting close to the West of my deepest imaginings, the place where the tangible and the mythical became the same."

– Edward Abbey,
about the Southwest

BELOW: lightning strikes in the desert.

The Devil's Highway

El Camino Diablo, the Devil's Highway, is a rough, unpaved route from Carborca, Mexico, to Yuma, Arizona, across one of the most overheated and desolate landscapes in the Southwest. Prehistoric people used the route to transport shells and salt from the Gulf of California. Spanish soldiers led by Melchior Diaz were the first Europeans to travel the route in 1540. More than 150 years later, missionaries Padre Eusebio Kino and Padre Garces and explorer Juan de Anza also came this way.

After gold was discovered in California in 1849, thousands traveled the Devil's Highway. Between 400 and 2,000 people died of thirst on their way to the gold fields in the 1850s, making this the deadliest immigrant trail in the United States. Many of their graves, marked by heaps of stones and makeshift crosses, are still visible.

The road is best traveled in early spring or fall using a four-wheel-drive vehicle; summer temperatures reach 120°F (49°C), and winter nights can dip below freezing. There are no services or water. Carry one to two gallons (4–8 liters) of water per person per day and pack at least two days' extra water and food, as well as spare tires. Permits are required to enter the Barry Goldwater Bombing Range and Cabeza Prieta National Wildlife Refuge.

RESTAURANTS

Prices for a three-course dinner per person, excluding tax, tip, and beverages:
$ = under $20
$$ = $20–45
$$$ = $45–60
$$$$ = over $60

Big Nose Kate's Saloon
417 E. Allen Street, Tombstone
Tel: 520-457-3107
$
The food – mostly salads, sandwiches, and pizza – is nothing to write home about, but the decor is colorful in a vaguely Victorian way, the service (by waitresses in saloon-girl costumes) is generally attentive, and the live country music is entertaining. A reasonable choice in a town that caters mostly to the tourist trade.

Bisbee Breakfast Club
75A Erie Street, Bisbee
Tel: 520-432-5885
$
Housed in a renovated former drug store in adjoining Lowell, this large, airy breakfast spot is the area's hottest ticket with the morning crowd. Retro without being pretentious, it serves up creative modern diner breakfasts and some interesting lunch selections, including a variety of unusual wraps, burgers, and salads.

Bisbee Coffee Company
2 Copper Queen Plaza, Bisbee
Tel: 520-432-7879
$
A popular daily gathering spot in downtown Bisbee that serves good coffee, pastries, and quiches and has Wi-fi.

Bisbee Grille
Copper Queen Plaza, Bisbee
Tel: 520-432-6788
$–$$
This central restaurant is a local and out-of-towner's favorite for a range of grilled foods, including ribs, burgers, and steaks. Seafood, pasta, meatloaf, and salads round out the menu.

Café Roka
35 Main Street, Bisbee
Tel: 520-432-5153
$$
Over the last 25 years, Chef Rod Kass has created an upscale, artsy environment in historic downtown Bisbee in which to present his innovative brand of northern Italian cuisine. Four-course meals may include artichoke and portobello mushroom lasagna; scallops with spinach pasta; rack of lamb; roasted duck; or grilled salmon. The menu is not extensive, but it changes frequently. Reservations are suggested, especially on weekends.

Canela Bistro
3252 Highway 82, Sonoita
Tel: 520-455-5873
$$$–$$$$
In 2005, husband-and-wife chef-owners John Hall and Joy Vargo returned to John's local ranch roots, bringing with them classical Cordon Bleu training and a passion for superbly prepared but accessible food. Many of the ingredients at this unexpectedly gourmet weekend dinner restaurant at the Sonoita–Patagonia crossroad are locally sourced. The enormous steak-frites or pork tenderloin and mac 'n' cheese have a loyal local following. Home-made soups are smooth, creamy, and vibrant, and mouth-watering Point Reyes blue cheese makes an appearance on one of the best artisanal cheese plates around.

Cantina Romantica
Rex Ranch, off Amado exit 48 on I-19, Tubac
Tel: 520-398-2914
$$$–$$$$
The dinner menu is not extensive at this rustic hacienda on the 4,000-acre (1,620-hectare) Rex Ranch north of Tubac, but in this case, small is beautiful. Grilled meats are the specialty, although you'll find a tasty selection of vegetarian dishes, including bountiful salads. Several varieties of chilli are used to great advantage, as are tequila, citrus, and prickly pear. Highlights include a pecan-crusted pork roulade with chilli sauce; grilled double-cut lamb chops with a port wine, cherry, and jalapeño jus; grilled citrus chicken and shrimp with tequila and prickly pear sauce; and wild mushroom and basil lasagna. There's no bridge across the Santa Cruz River to the ranch. You have to drive through the water. Open Wed–Sun. Seasonal closings; call for hours.

Gathering Grounds
319 McKeown Avenue, Patagonia
Tel: 520-394-2097
$–$$
This wonderful coffee house and meeting place in the center of Patagonia serves fresh-tasting, locally sourced food at incredible prices. At breakfast, there's excellent organic Fair Trade coffee to accompany substantial egg dishes and unusual muffins and pastries. At lunch, choose from interesting quiches, salads, soups, wraps, and hot and cold sandwiches. Dinner entrées are geared to healthy ranch country appetites. They run the gamut of pork and prime ribs, ribeye and New York steak, all with interesting sauces, to lighter fare like grilled Alaskan cod with avocado butter, salmon with apricot and horseradish sauce, and portobello mushrooms stuffed with risotto. Wi-fi. Dinner only on weekends.

The Grasslands Bakery and Café
3119 Highway 83, Sonoita
Tel: 520-455-4770
$–$$
This terrific little natural-foods bakery and café

makes incredibly good organic baked goods, including croissants and *streusel kuchen* and deep-dish pies with spelt flour crusts. The dining room offers homemade soups, salads, warm pasta salads, hot and cold sandwiches, quiches, and excellent desserts. Open for lunch and Sunday brunch, Thur–Sun only.

High Desert Market Café
203 Tombstone Canyon, Bisbee
Tel: 520-432-6775
$

Situated in the old Blue Sky Café, this terrific laidback local favorite is a combination market, bakery, and café with indoor and outdoor seating. They do good coffee and a large selection of baked goods, and interesting dishes such as strata savory bread pudding with sausage and spring rolls. There are also a variety of salads and sandwiches on organic whole-wheat bread. It's good for a quick, budget-friendly meal.

Longhorn Restaurant
501 E. Allen Street, Tombstone
Tel: 520-457-3405
$–$$

Everything is super-sized at this tourist-oriented Western saloon and restaurant, including the humongous hot dogs (the largest in Cochise County), ribs, steaks, and burgers. It's a perennial favorite in Tombstone, but don't expect too much.

Nellie Cashman Restaurant
117 S. 5th Street, Tombstone
Tel: 520-457-2212
$–$$$

Named for an angelic mine camp follower, this restaurant is in an 1879 building in Tombstone. The food serves mainly mainstream tourist fare – sillynamed egg dishes at breakfast, burgers and sandwiches at lunch, and standard Western dishes at dinner. Their pies are the main draw. Closed Sun.

OK Café
220 E. Allen Street, Tombstone
Tel: 520-457-3980
$

A decent choice for a breakfast of pancakes, steak and eggs, biscuits with gravy, and other traditional American fare. The lunch menu includes bison, ostrich, and emu burgers.

The Outside Inn
4907 S Highway 92,
Sierra Vista
Tel: 520-378-4645
$$

A good choice for a romantic dinner, the Outside Inn is quiet and attractive. The seafood is especially good. Patio dining is available, but the restaurant is small, so reservations are recommended. Closed Sun.

Palatiano's
601 W. 4th Street, Benson
Tel: 520-586-3523
$

If you're in the mood for fish fries, steaks, prime ribs, and other comforting American diner specials, this is your place. Popular with locals.

Ranch House Restaurant
661 N. 2nd Street, Ajo
Tel: 520-387-6226
$–$$

With a name like Ajo (Spanish for garlic), you'd think this remote town would use a lot of the stinking rose, but you'd be wrong. Never mind. This Western-themed cowboy spot will fill you up with burgers, steaks, prime rib, and other hearty fare that will keep you going.

Rosa's Little Italy
7 Bisbee Road, Bisbee
Tel: 520-432-1331
$$

Rustic Sicilian and Southern Italian food is well prepared at this small, atmospheric trattoria in Bisbee. There are numerous classic dishes, including veal piccata, *fettuccine alfredo*, and tiramisu for dessert. Popular, so make reservations. Dinner only Wed–Sun.

Salsa Fiesta
1201 W. Rex Allen Drive,
Willcox
Tel: 520-384-4233
$

A cheerful spot for authentic Mexican food in Willcox, which is not particularly known for its restaurants.

Shelby's Bistro
19 Tubac Road, Tubac
Tel: 520-398-8075
$–$$

A casual little eatery in downtown with an outdoor patio that serves soups, salads, sandwiches, and wraps at lunchtime. Weekend dinners include delicious entrées such as lavenderrubbed chicken and buffalo shrimp. Open Wed–Sat.

Tree of Life Café
Tree of Life Rejuvenation
Center, Patagonia
Tel: 866-394-2520
$–$$

Non-guests at this private residential retreat center are welcome to join residents for meals that consist of creatively prepared, beautifully presented, low-glycemic, vegetarian/vegan raw foods. The menu is globally inspired, 100 percent organic, and seasonal. Produce is grown onsite. Meals are served at set times and prix-fixe. You must make a reservation 48 hours in advance to eat here. The center offers an interesting roster of spa services, classes, workshops, treatments, and retreats, if you decide to check in. This is a fascinating and unexpected bonus in Border Country for travelers interested in alternative health and healing modalities.

Velvet Elvis Pizza Company
292 Highway 82, Patagonia
Tel: 520-394-2102
$

An eccentric, hip little place in downtown Patagonia whose thincrust, wood-fired pizza has people coming from miles away. You can get it with a variety of toppings. Wash it all down with a choice of freshly pressed juices, organic wines, or microbrews. Soups and salads are also quite good. There aren't many places to eat in Patagonia, but this place should satisfy.

Wagon Wheel Saloon
400 W. Naugle Avenue,
Patagonia
Tel: 520-394-2433 **$**

This authentic cowboy bar and restaurant has been catering to local buckaroos for more than 60 years and offers exactly what you would expect from a cowboy joint – barbecued ribs, steaks, burgers, and plenty of ice-cold beer.

INSIGHT GUIDE TRAVEL TIPS
ARIZONA & THE GRAND CANYON

TRANSPORTATION

GETTING THERE AND GETTING AROUND

GETTING THERE

By Air

Phoenix Sky Harbor (PHX; www.skyharbor.com) is Arizona's main airport. In 2010, more than 38 million passengers flew on 17 airlines to over 100 cities worldwide. Tucson International Airport (TUS; www.flytucsonairport.com) is much smaller, with 8 airlines used by more than 3.7 million passengers a year. Among the carriers serving these airports are:

From the US

American Airlines: tel: 800-433-7300; www.aa.com
Continental: tel: 800-525-0280; www.continental.com
Delta: tel: 800-221-1212; www.delta.com
Frontier Airlines:
tel: 800-432-1359;
www.frontierairlines.com
JetBlue: tel: 800-538-2583; www.jetblue.com
Southwest: tel: 800-435-9792; www.southwest.com
United Airlines: tel: 800-864-8331; www.united.com
US Airways: tel: 800-428-4322; www.usairways.com.

From Canada

Air Canada:
tel: 888-247-2262;
www.aircanada.com
WestJet: tel: 888-937-8538; www.westjet.com.

From Europe

British Airways: tel: 800-247-9297; www.britishairways.com.

Airport Taxes

Domestic flights include up to 20 percent in additional taxes to cover US Excise Tax (7.5 percent), post-9/11 security costs, and airport and facility fees. Airlines include this in the final total for the plane fare.
Important Note:
Expect delays departing US airports due to Homeland Security anti-terrorism rules. These are apt to change, so check before flying (www.dhs.gov). See also Visas and Passports, page 340.

Passengers may take one resealable 1-quart (1 liter) size clear plastic bag on board, which can contain liquids or gels in containers of 3 fluid ounces (100ml) or less. The contents of the plastic bag must fit comfortably and be completely closed/sealed and subjected to X-ray inspection separate from carry-on bag. Leave any gifts unwrapped, and take laptops out of bags for inspection by Transportation Security Administration (TSA; www.tsa.gov/travelers) personnel. Note that footwear must be removed and scanned by X-ray machines.

By Train

Amtrak offers more than 500 destinations across the US. The trains are comfortable and reliable, with lounges, dining cars, domed viewing cars, snack bars, and, in some cases, movies, live entertainment, and, on the Southwest Chief, interpretive programs organized by the National Park Service. Most routes offer sleeper cars with private cabins in addition to regular seating with pull-out foot rests that offer reclined sleeping.

Amtrak's Southwest Chief runs from Chicago to Los Angeles, across northern Arizona, with stops in Winslow, Flagstaff (bus service connects to the Grand Canyon), Williams Junction (bus service connects to Grand Canyon Railway), and Kingman, Arizona. The Sunset Limited runs from New Orleans to Los Angeles, across south-central Arizona, with stops at Tucson and Yuma.

Ask about senior citizen, military, AAA, student, and children's discounts, and Amtrak's package tours, including multi-day trips to the Grand Canyon. International travelers can buy a USA Rail Pass, good for 15, 30, or 45 days of unlimited travel on Amtrak throughout the US.

Contact Amtrak (tel: 800-872-7245; www.amtrak.com) for detailed scheduling.

By Bus

One of the least expensive ways to travel in America is by interstate bus. The largest national bus company is Greyhound (tel: 800-231-2222; www.greyhound.com). The company routinely offers Discovery Passes for 7, 15, 30, or 60 days of unlimited travel.

GETTING AROUND

To and From the Airport

Many hotels offer a free shuttle service to and from the two major airports. Several private shuttle companies offer service out of Phoenix Sky Harbor. A full listing can be found on the airport website (www.skyharbor.com). They include Arizona Shuttle (tel: 800-888-2749; www.

ABOVE: if you venture into the desert, it is recommended to have a 4-wheel drive vehicle.

arizonashuttle.com), serving Phoenix, Flagstaff, and Tucson; Shuttle "U" Prescott (tel: 800-304-6114; www.shuttleu.com), serving Prescott; and Sedona Phoenix Shuttle (tel: 800-448-7988; www.sedona-phoenix-shuttle.com), serving Sedona. From Tucson International, groups can reserve a shuttle to the city and surrounding communities through Arizona Stagecoach (tel: 520-889-100; www.azstagecoach.com). Valley Metro operates a regular connection from its METRO Light Rail to Sky Harbor, while SunTran buses include routes from downtown Tucson to the airport. Both airports have several national rental car chains available and taxi stands with reasonable rates (base charge of approximately $5, then $2–3 per mile). For more detail information on rail, bus, and rental options, read further

Orientation

While Phoenix is not the geographic center of Arizona (that honor goes to Payson, 90 miles/145km northeast) it might as well be. Tucson, Flagstaff, Yuma, Kingman, and Grand Canyon Village are all within a 2–4 hour drive and less than an hour by commuter plane. It makes sense that most explorations begin by touching down in the capital. In the north, interstate I-40 connects Kingman to Flagstaff and Albuquerque, New Mexico. Interstate I-10 in the south-central region snakes its way east from Los Angeles, California, and passes through Phoenix and Tucson. The centrally located north–south

Interstate I-17 links Flagstaff with Phoenix, then connects with I-10, or with I-8 to Yuma and San Diego, California. There are a number of paved state highways linking smaller towns throughout the state. The two Amtrak tracks run east–west and basically follow the routes of I-40 and I-10/I-8. Flying into Las Vegas, Nevada, is the quickest and easiest way to access the Arizona Strip and the North Rim of the Grand Canyon.

By Air

The following commuter airlines offer service within the region, including Phoenix, Tucson, Flagstaff, Tusayan (Grand Canyon), Las Vegas, Los Angeles, Lake Havasu City, Kingman, Show Low, and Yuma:
Great Lakes: 800-554-5111; www.flygreatlakes.com
Scenic: tel: 866-235-9422; www.scenic.com
Mesa Airlines/US Airways Express: tel: 800-428-4322; www.usairways.com
Vision Airlines: tel: 800-256-8767; www.visionholidays.com.

By Rail

The METRO light rail service, provides visitors with convenient access from Phoenix Sky Harbor International Airport to the downtown area, serving Tempe, Mesa, and Phoenix. Trains run every 10 minutes during rush hour and every 20 minutes during off-peak periods. For more information, go to www.valleymetro.org/metro_light_rail. Further expansion of the light rail service is planned over the next 15 years.

An especially memorable way to reach the Grand Canyon is aboard the Grand Canyon Railway (tel: 800-843-8724; www.thetrain.com), which runs one round-trip daily between Williams and the South Rim.

By Bus

Greyhound bus services and shuttle buses (see above) link cities in Arizona. Once there, city bus lines can be an excellent and inexpensive way of getting around. Valley Metro (tel: 602-253-5000; www.valley_metro.org) provides public transportation in the Greater Phoenix Area. Sun Tran (tel: 520-792-9222; www.suntran.com) serves the metro Tucson area and has transit centers at major destinations throughout the city. Open Road Tours (tel: 855-563-8830; www.openroadtoursusa.com) serves the South Rim of the Grand Canyon once daily, connecting in Flagstaff. The South Rim of Grand Canyon National Park provides free shuttle buses, including service from nearby Tusayan, to attractions within the park with paid entrance. The only shuttle connecting the North and South rims is provided by Transcanyon Shuttle from mid-May to mid-October (tel: 928-638-2820; www.trans-canyonshuttle.com)

By Road

Driving is by far the most convenient way to travel in Arizona, especially outside the major cities. Major roads are well maintained, although backcountry roads are frequently unpaved and some may be impassable using a regular passenger vehicle. If you plan on driving into remote areas or in heavy snow, mud, or severe weather, it's a good idea to rent a four-wheel-drive vehicle with good clearance.

Maps and Information

Your greatest asset as a driver is a good map. They can be obtained from tourism offices, service stations, supermarkets, and convenience stores. If you're traveling across the Indian reservations in northern Arizona, purchase the top-rated Indian Country road map, which is so detailed it is used by local residents.

Maps of national parks, forests, and other natural areas are usually offered as part of your entrance fee. For hikers, topographical maps are available through Trails Illustrated (www.trailsillustrated.com); these maps are often in bookstores. The most detailed topographical maps are available from the US Geological Survey (www.store.usgs.gov).

Although roads are maintained even in remote areas, it is advisable to listen to local radio stations and to check with local tourism offices for the latest information on weather and road conditions, especially in winter or if planning to leave paved roads. The Arizona Department of Transportation offers the 511 Traveler Information Service, allowing you to get information about closures, construction, delays, public transit, weather, and more by dialing 511 or logging on to www.az511.gov.

Driving in Remote Areas

If you plan on driving in uninhabited areas, carry a spare tire and extra water – at least a gallon (4 liters) per person per day. A cell phone is a good idea, too, although some areas will be out of range. Service stations can be few and far between. Not every town will have one, and many close early. It's always better to have more fuel than you think you'll need.

A word of caution: If your car breaks down on a back road, do not strike out on foot. A car is easier to spot than a person and provides shelter. If you don't have a cell phone or your phone doesn't work, sit tight and wait to be found. A compact disk may be used as a signaling device in place of a mirror. Keep cool, do not exert yourself, ration water prudently, and eat lightly.

Car Rental

Most rental agencies require you to be 21 years old or over (25 at some locations) and have a valid driver's license and a major credit card. Many take debit cards, too, and some will take cash in lieu of a credit card, but this might be as high as $500. Non-English speaking travelers must produce an international driver's license from their own country.

You will find rental car companies in most cities and airports. Rental vehicles range from economy cars to luxury convertibles, vans, and 4WD vehicles. Rates are cheap, and most companies offer unlimited mileage. But you should still shop around, preferably online, for the best rates and features. Local rental firms outside the airport are often less expensive than the national companies because they don't charge high airport fees.

It's cheaper to arrange car rental in advance. Look out for package deals that include a car: rental rates can be reduced by up to 50 percent if you buy a "fly-drive" deal.

Go over the insurance coverage provisions carefully with the agent before signing the rental agreement. Loss Damage Waiver, or Collision Damage Waiver, can be expensive, but is essential if your credit card or personal car insurance does not already include it. Without it, you'll be liable for any damage done to your vehicle in the event of an accident. You are advised to pay for supplementary Liability Insurance on top of standard third-party insurance. Insurance and tax charges can add a lot to an otherwise inexpensive rental – assume about $25–35 per day.

BELOW: watch out for wildlife.

Major rental car companies are:
Alamo: tel: 800-462-5266; www.alamo.com
Avis: tel: 800-331-1212; www.avis.com
Budget: tel: 800-527-7000; www.budget.com
Dollar: tel: 800-800-4000; www.dollar.com
Enterprise: tel: 800-736-8222; www.enterprise.com
Hertz: tel: 800-654-3131; www.hertz.com
National: tel: 800-227-7368; www.nationalcar.com
Thrifty: tel: 800-847-4389; www.thrifty.com

RV Rentals

No special license is necessary to operate a motor home (or recreational vehicle – RV for short) but they aren't cheap. When you add up the cost of rental fees, insurance, gas, and campground fees, renting a car and staying in motels or camping may be less expensive. Cruise America (tel: 800-671-8042; www.cruiseamerica.com) has RVs for rent in a variety of sizes (from 19–30ft/6–9 meters). For additional information about RV rentals, call the Recreational Vehicle Association (tel: 888-467-8464; www.rvra.org).

ACCOMMODATIONS

HOTELS, YOUTH HOSTELS, BED AND BREAKFAST

CHOOSING LODGINGS

Reservations and Prices

Grand Canyon National Park

All lodgings within the park may be booked through Xanterra Parks and Resorts, 6312 South Fiddlers Green Circle, Suite 600N, Greenwood Village, CO 80111; tel: toll-free within the United States 888-297-2757, 303-297-2757 outside the United States; www. grandcanyonlodges.com.

Chain Hotels and Motels

These are ubiquitous throughout the United States and have many fans. Some people dislike chains because they offer no variety, lack a personal touch, and are often located in the most commercial, nondescript areas of town next to busy highways. The advantage is that once you've been to a hotel run by a particular chain, even though these are usually a franchise, you can bank on certain facilities and a standard of service wherever you are in the US. For travelers wanting to focus on their vacation, this can be a boon.

Bed-and-Breakfasts

Bed-and-breakfasts vary greatly in terms of price and quality, but the one thing they have in common is that they are almost invariably in a private and/or historic home. Few have restaurants, and facilities will not be as extensive as in a regular hotel. Privacy can be an issue in older inns, but some have separate cottages with self-catering facilities, allowing you to come and go as you

please. Hosts are usually a mine of information about local sights, and this can be a great way to make life-long friends. For those travelers who enjoy the personal ambience – not to mention the afternoon teas, wine and cheese happy hours, and gourmet breakfasts found in many places – bed-and-breakfasts are a great choice.

High vs Low Season

High season prices for lodgings in Arizona (winter in the low desert in the south, and summer in the high desert in the north) can vary considerably. If you're willing to travel to Phoenix and other Sonoran Desert locales in summer, when the daytime temperatures top 100°F (37.7°C), you'll score deep discounts even in the most highly-rated lodgings. Prices in Flagstaff and other Northern Arizona locales may drop in winter, except for the Grand Canyon, where the National Park Service fixes rates with the concessionaire for the whole year.

Camping

Private Campgrounds

A nationwide network of private campgrounds, called Kampgrounds of America (KOA; tel: 406-248-7444; www.koa.com), has members in Arizona. They offer good-quality facilities, including swimming pools, restaurants, and laundries. Most accept reservations.

Camping on Public Lands

Camping inside one of Arizona's world-class national, state, or tribal parks is a major attraction for many travelers. You'll find developed campgrounds with individual tent

and RV sites that have an adjoining car parking spot, barbecue grills, picnic tables, and nearby flush toilets for about $10–25 per night – you can get more than one tent on a pitch. State park campgrounds are usually the best designed, and most have showers. Most campsites are on a first-come, first-served basis and fill by early afternoon at the most popular places (winter in the low desert and summer in the high desert mountains). Campsites in many national parks may now be reserved by calling 877-444-6777 or logging on to www.recreation.gov. A number of federal and private campgrounds may be reserved by logging on to www.reserveamerica.com. US Forest Service and Bureau of Land Management (BLM) campgrounds are usually "primitive," meaning they have designated sites and picnic tables, but usually only vault toilets. Many campgrounds have no water, so keep a 5-gallon (22 liter) water carrier in the car. The cost is low for these sites, making them an excellent budget option. Dispersed camping in nondesignated sites is allowed for free on national forest lands. Bring all you'll need and pack everything out when you leave. Aside from food and water, the most useful items are moist babywipes for general hygiene, resealable plastic bags for trash, toilet paper, and a small trowel for digging a 6in (15cm) cat hole to bury human waste in the biological layer of the soil away from precious desert water sources. Treat, filter, or boil all water to avoid giardia, a nasty bug transmitted through contaminated water at campsites downstream from cattle grazing areas.

TRANSPORTATION

ACCOMMODATIONS

ACTIVITIES

A – Z

GRAND CANYON

Best Western Grand Canyon Squire Inn
100 Highway 64, Tusayan
Tel: 928-638-2681 or toll free 800-622-6966
www.grandcanyonsquire.com
Larger and better appointed than most properties in the Best Western chain, this hotel – on a commercial strip in Tusayan, just outside the national park – offers large rooms and a plethora of distractions, including a bowling alley and tennis courts. The restaurant is your best bet for a good steak and seafood dinner if South Rim restaurants are booked. Pool, restaurant, coffee shop, bar, exercise room, sauna, air conditioning, TV. **$$**

Bright Angel Lodge & Cabins
West Rim Drive, Grand Canyon
Tel: 928-638-2631 or 888-297-2757 (reservations)
www.grandcanyonlodges.com
This rustic lodge was designed by Mary Jane Elizabeth Colter in 1935 and built on the site of Bright Angel Camp, the first tourist facility in the park. The historic turquoise-trimmed lobby features Indian motifs and a huge fireplace. There's a museum about the famous Harvey Girls in a side room as well as a fireplace made of all the rocks in the Grand Canyon. The

accommodations range from dormitory-style rooms with shared baths to private cabins with canyon views. Creature comforts are simple, but the location and price make the lodge good value. Reservations for the rim cabins should be made at least a year in advance. Restaurant, coffee shop, ice cream parlor. **$**

Canyon Plaza Quality Inn and Suites Grand Canyon
PO Box 520, Tusayan
Tel: 928-638-2673 or toll free 800-228-5151
www.grandcanyonplaza.com
Next to the IMAX theater in Tusayan, a short drive from the park entrance, this property has 232 rooms that are large, clean, and comfortably furnished, although not much above standard chain store chic. The public spaces are airy and well maintained, and the suites, though modest, are roomy enough for families. Service here is usually satisfactory. The buffet is a firm local favorite. Restaurant, bar, outdoor pool, whirlpool, air conditioning, TV. **$$**

Grand Canyon Lodge
Bright Angel Point
Tel: 928-638-2611 or 888-297-2757 (reservations)
www.grandcanyonlodges.com
A log-and-limestone lodge with 50ft (15-meter) ceilings and a glass-walled sunroom overlooking the

canyon is the centerpiece of this historic complex – the only lodging inside the park's North Rim. A few motel-style rooms are available but lack the rustic charm of the small log cabins clustered around the main building. Cabins are available in four sizes, some better appointed than others. A few have canyon views but are usually booked a year or more in advance. The dining room is wrapped in windows, but the cuisine generally falls short of the setting. No matter; the views can't be beaten. Be sure to make dinner reservations several weeks before your arrival. Restaurant, cafeteria, bar, gift shop, horseback ride concession. **$**

Grand Hotel
PO Box 3319, Tusayan
Tel: 928-638-3333 or toll free 888-634-7263
www.grandcanyongrandhotel.com
Large, comfortable, nicely appointed rooms, an airy lobby, and a dinner show featuring local Navajo dancers are among the attractions of this 127-room National Park Lodge-style motel on Highway 180/64 in Tusayan, just outside the national park. Restaurant, bar, indoor pool, fitness room, air conditioning, TV. **$$**

Havasupai Lodge
Supai
Tel: 928-448-2111
www.havasupaitribe.com
Located down inside the western Grand Canyon, in the tiny Indian village of Havasupai, this 24-room motel can only be reached via the river, by hiking in, or by riding a mule down into the canyon from the rim. All 24 rooms have two beds, private baths, and are air-conditioned and non-smoking. There are no phones or TVs. Strictly for the adventurous. **$**

Hualapai Lodge
Route 66, Peach Springs
Tel: 928-769-2636 or 888-

868-9378
www.grandcanyonwest.com
Located in the Hualapai Indian tribal village of Peach Springs about 60 miles (96km) from the popular new Skywalk attraction in Grand Canyon West, this modern lodge is the only lodging on the reservation. There are 60 oversized, comfortable rooms with amenities. Book a room on the side away from the train tracks. A concessionaire offers river rafting and other activities. Restaurant, saltwater pool, spa, fitness center, gift shop. **$**

Maswik Lodge
Grand Canyon
Tel: 888-297-2757 (reservations)
www.grandcanyonlodges.com
About 300 guest rooms and cabins are offered at this run-of-the-mill lodge, a 15-minute walk to the South Rim through the forest. The cabins tend to be a little rough around the edges, but the rooms are gradually being upgraded. Ask for a room in Maswik North if you're concerned about comfort. Restaurant, bar, gift shop, TV. **$**

Phantom Ranch
Grand Canyon
Tel: 928-638-2631 or 888-297-2757 (reservations)
www.grandcanyonlodges.com
The only lodging in the bottom of the Grand Canyon offers basic log-and-stone

BELOW: swimming at a Lake Mead resort.

PRICE CATEGORIES

Price categories are based on the cost of a double room in high season.
$ = $110 or less
$$ = $110–250
$$$ = $200–250
$$$$ = more than $250

cabins and single-sex dormitories. Make reservations as early as possible (Xanterra accepts bookings up to 13 months in advance). Meals at the dining hall are served family style and should be reserved ahead of time. Check the Bright Angel transportation desk for last-minute openings. Postcards mailed here are carried out of the canyon by mule. **$**

Thunderbird and Kachina Lodges
Grand Canyon
Tel: 888-297-2757 (reservations)
www.grandcanyonlodges.com
Sandwiched between El Tovar and Bright Angel Lodge, these low-slung vintage motels are an unfortunate 1960s anachronism in the historic district. They do, however, have some modern amenities that are lacking in the rustic lodges. You'll get the best canyon views from Kachina Lodge's second floor rooms. **$$**

El Tovar Hotel
Grand Canyon
Tel: 928-638-2631 or 888297-2757 (reservations)
www.grandcanyonlodges.com
This rustic European hunting lodge-style inn was built in 1905 of stone and Oregon pine. It offers a level of luxury not found elsewhere on the South Rim and is worth the splurge. Standard rooms

ABOVE: El Tovar Hotel.

tend to be small, although deluxe rooms and suites (which have terraces with spectacular views) are quite comfortable and several have been recently upgraded. The dining room serves the best food on the South Rim. The lobby, with Mission-style furnishings, high ceilings, a fireplace, and assorted moose and antelope heads hanging from dark log walls, is worth seeing even if you're not spending the night. Restaurant, bar, gift shop, air conditioning, TV. **$$**

PAGE AND THE ARIZONA STRIP

Best Western Arizona Inn
716 Rimview Drive, Page
Tel: 928-645-2466 or 800-826-2718
www.bestwesternarizona.com
This modern motel about a mile from downtown Page has 101 large rooms with queen-size beds and sweeping views of the desert. Outdoor pool, restaurant, bar, fitness room, air conditioning, TV. **$**

Canyon Colors Bed and Breakfast
225 South Navajo, Page
Tel: 928-645-5979 or 800-536-2530
www.canyoncolors.com
Guests enjoy cheery, modern, country-style rooms at this house in a quiet residential area of Page. The two rooms, each able to accommodate four comfortably, have queen bed, futon, bath, fireplace, TV, VCR (access to an extensive video library). A full breakfast is included in the rate. Pool, air conditioning. **$$**

Courtyard by Marriott
600 Clubhouse Drive, Page
Tel: 928-645-5000 or 800-851-3855
www.marriott.com
This pleasant, Pueblo-style hotel offers comfortable, commodious lodging adjacent to the Lake Powell National Golf Course, one of the most scenic in the state. Restaurant, bar, laundry facilities, gift shop, outdoor pool, exercise room, air conditioning, television. **$$**

Dreamkatcher's Bed and Breakfast
1055 South American Way, Big Water, UT
Tel: 435-675-5828
www.dreamkatcherslake powell.com
Detail-oriented hosts Eric and Jarod make a stay at this modern bed-and-breakfast in a small town on the Utah side of Lake Powell a memorable one. The three elegantly furnished guest rooms are plush and comfortable, with four-poster and sleigh beds, full baths, and a nice feeling of privacy; there's a TV and games in the lounge. Breakfast is a relaxing experience on the landscaped patio, with soft music playing, rich coffee on the brew, and gourmet fare, from Swedish pancakes to stuffed croissants. Rooftop hot tub is a treat after a long day's drive or hike. Worth the 15-minute drive from Page for some serious pampering, this is an oasis in the desert, in more ways than one. **$–$$**

Jacob Lake Inn
Highway 67 and 89A, Jacob Lake
Tel: 928-643-7232
www.jacoblake.com
This historic mountain inn is a welcome hub of activity in this sprawling, lonely country and the only lodging open year round. The thin-walled cabins and motel units have definitely seen better days, but the coffee shop is lively, the tasty homemade pies and other fare are filling, and the milkshakes are justly renowned. Restaurant, gift shop, gas station. **$**

Kaibab Lodge
HC 64, Box 64, Fredonia
Tel: 928-638-2389
www.kaibablodge.com
Rooms at this mountain lodge, located on Highway 67 about 18 miles (29km) from the North Rim of the Grand Canyon, are tucked away in rustic cabins at the edge of a sweeping meadow. The main lodge, built in the 1920s, has an airy lobby with log beams, a big fireplace, Adirondack-style furniture,

and TV room (there are no TVs in guest rooms). Restaurant, gift shop. Open seasonally. August is a quieter time to visit. **$–$$**

Lake Powell Resort

Lake Powell Resorts and Marinas
100 Lakeshore Drive, Page
Tel: 928-645-2433
www.lakepowell.com
This former Wahweap Hotel is a large and busy hub for tourists exploring Lake Powell. All rooms have balconies or patios, but only about half overlook the lake. The Rainbow Room serves good American and Southwestern fare and has panoramic views of the lake. Rentals of power boats, houseboats, and other watercraft are available. Two pools, fitness room, restaurant, snack bar, lounge, air conditioning, TV. **$$**

NAVAJO AND HOPI RESERVATIONS

Cameron Trading Post Motel
US 89, PO Box 339, Cameron
Tel: 928-679-2231 or 800-338-7385
www.camerontradingpost.com
The motel adjoins a busy trading post built in the early 20th century and still serving the surrounding Navajo Nation and drivers on Highway 89. Rooms are comfortable and attractive, overlooking the scenic Little Colorado River canyon and bridge. But it's the trading post itself – and the treasures it contains, including a great little restaurant – that is the real attraction. Restaurant, gift shop, TV, air conditioning, post office, gas station. **$**

Goulding's Lodge
PO Box 3600001, Monument Valley, UT
Tel: 435-727-3231
www.gouldings.com
This former trading post, just outside the tribal park, has 62 motel-style rooms with Southwestern decor and balconies. The restaurant serves typical American dishes and has spectacular views. There's a great little museum with exhibits on all the movies shot in Monument Valley and the original owners. The hotel can arrange horseback riding and backcountry tours with Navajo guides.

Restaurant, gift shop, indoor pool, tour desk, air conditioning, TV (with VCR and collection of Westerns shot in Monument Valley. Free Wi-fi. **$$**

Holiday Inn Canyon de Chelly
Navajo Route 7, Chinle
Tel: 928-674-5000 or 888-465-4329
www.holidayinnchinle.com
A good second choice if Thunderbird Lodge, inside Canyon de Chelly National Monument, is full. The 108-room modern inn is half a mile from the park. Fitness center, outdoor pool, self-serve laundry. Park tours can be arranged. Air conditioning, TV, data ports, fridge, coffee-maker, hairdryer, and iron. Children under 19 stay free and eat free in Garcia's Trading Post Mexican restaurant, located on the site of the old trading post. **$–$$**

Hopi Cultural Center
PO Box 67, Second Mesa
Tel: 928-734-2401
www.hopiculturalcenter.com
The main lodging for visitors on the Hopi Reservation, the Hopi Cultural Center motel offers 30 basic chain-style guest rooms. It's bland, but if you stay here, you are in the heart of Hopi: the museum is next door, and you can sample Hopi specialties like piki bread in the restaurant. **$**

Kayenta Monument Valley Inn
PO Box 307, Kayenta
Tel: 928-697-3221 or 800-465-4329
A busy place with large and well-kept, if predictable, lodging. The hotel is at the intersection of US 160 and 163 about 24 miles (38km) from Monument Valley Navajo Tribal Park. The restaurant serves American and Navajo fare. Restaurant, gift shop, outdoor pool, tour desk, air conditioning, TV. **$$**

Valley of the Gods Bed and Breakfast
Valley of the Gods Road
Box 310-307, Mexican Hat, UT
Tel: 970-749-1164
www.bedandbreakfast.com/utah-mexican-hat-valleyofthegodsbb.html
This famous off-the-grid B&B is located in a historic stone house overlooking spectacular Valley of the Gods, north of Monument Valley and the San Juan River, near Mexican Hat, a major put-in for river runners. The drive alone will take your breath away. The B&B is the only residence inside southeastern Utah's Cedar Mesa Cultural and Recreation Management Area, which preserves many Ancestral Pueblo ruins. The four guest rooms are comfortable in a utilitarian way, with private baths. Full breakfast is

served. Owners Claire and Gary Dorgan are very outdoor oriented and volunteer with the BLM and the Forest Service in helping conserve this beautiful location. Great hiking, bike riding, and relaxation. **$$**

View Hotel and Restaurant
Monument Valley, UT
www.monumentvalleyview.com
This handsome new hotel is the only lodging within Monument Valley Navajo Tribal Park. It is Navajo-owned (the owner is a member of the multi-generation Ortega trading family) and the low-slung structure is sensitively built in ecological harmony with its surroundings. The entire hotel is non-smoking. All the rooms in the hotel have scenic views, balconies, air conditioning, flat-screen TVs with cable, refrigerators, coffee/tea makers, and microwaves. The visitor center is next door. Wi-fi in the lobby and some guest rooms, fitness center, laundry. **$$**

FLAGSTAFF AND ENVIRONS

Abineau Bed and Breakfast
1080 Mountainaire Road, Flagstaff
Tel: 928-525-6212 or 888-715-6386
www.abineaulodge.com
Located on the edge of rustic Mountainaire, south of Flagstaff off Interstate 17, this elegant rustic lodge (formerly the Sled Dog Inn) has nine tranquil rooms on the edge of the national forest; you can hike right out the

door. All rooms have full baths, log furniture, down comforters, but no phones or TVs. There are two large living rooms with rock fireplaces, a hot tub, and sauna. Full breakfast includes home-made granola. Dinner for guests and non-guests is available in the licensed on-site restaurant on weekends. **$$–$$$**

Fall Into Nature
4555 South Lake Mary

Road, Flagstaff
Tel: 928-714-0237 or 888-920-0237
www.fallintonature.com
This modern three-suite bed-and-breakfast is down a woodsy road just southeast of town. There's hiking, horseback riding, and fishing on Upper Lake Mary. **$$**

Grand Canyon Railway Hotel and Resort
235 N. Grand Canyon Boulevard, Williams

Tel: 928-635-4010 or 800-THE-TRAIN
www.thetrain.com

A reconstruction of the 1908 Fray Marcos Hotel, this 89-room hotel at the historic train depot mixes turn-of-the-20th-century ambiance with convenience. The Western-style lobby celebrates the art of Frederic Remington; a saloon has a player piano and a beautifully carved bar from a London pub. Restaurant, bar, air conditioning, TV, indoor pool. **$$**

Hilton Garden Inn Flagstaff
350 W. Forest Meadows Street, Flagstaff
Tel: 928-226-8888
www.hiltongardeninn.com
Set on a busy commercial strip, a few minutes from downtown, this property is one of the newer hotels in town. It delivers Hilton-style efficiency. Rooms are well laid out for business people to work in, with ergonomically designed chairs and oversized desks, Wi-fi, and in-room printing to the business center, microwaves, refrigerators, and coffee makers. Hot breakfast buffet. Pool, fitness room, whirlpool, air conditioning, TV. **$$**

Hotel Monte Vista
100 N. San Francisco Street, Flagstaff
Tel: 928-779-6971 or 800-545-3068
www.hotelmontevista.com
Dark and a bit threadbare, this downtown landmark, opened in 1927, was once a favorite of celebrity guests such as John

Wayne, Clark Gable, and Spencer Tracy. You can still find some old-time charm here, but the hotel is best suited for students, backpackers, and other budget travelers. Some rooms have shared baths. Good Thai restaurant on site. Popular bar. **$**

The Inn at 410
410 N. Leroux Street, Flagstaff
Tel: 928-774-0088 or 800-774-2008
www.inn410.com
This handsome wood-frame bed-and-breakfast set on a quiet downtown lot offers nine rooms and suites beautifully decorated in styles ranging from Old West and Victorian to French Country, some with fireplace and Jacuzzi. An inviting living and dining room, big front porch and backyard garden give guests plenty of room to roam. Breakfasts are bountiful and expertly prepared. One of Arizona's most popular B&Bs. **$$–$$$**

La Posada
303 E. 2nd Street (Route 66), Winslow
Tel: 928-289-4366
www.laposada.org
Designed in the late 1920s by Mary Elizabeth Jane Colter, who considered it her masterpiece, this rambling hacienda-style hotel adjoining the train station was only open for 27 years before it was closed and

ABOVE: the Arizona Biltmore.

later gutted. Restoration began in 1997, and the hotel now offers more than 20 guest rooms furnished in the spare but elegant style of the period. The hotel's grand open spaces, with their heavy beams and vaulted ceilings, have been faithfully restored by private owners using Colter's original plans. The award-winning gourmet restaurant is a destination in itself. This is a fascinating historic site and good value. Ask for a room on the other side of the hotel from the station, or bring ear plugs.

Restaurant, bar. **$$**

Radisson Woodlands Hotel Flagstaff
1175 W. Route 66, Flagstaff
Tel: 928-773-8888 or 888-201-1718
www.radisson.com
A lobby with Italian marble floors, granite architectural details and plush furnishings set the tone of this hotel, among the most sumptuous in town. Rooms are spacious and tasteful. A Japanese restaurant and sushi bar are a pleasant surprise. Two restaurants, outdoor pool, fitness center, air conditioning, TV. **$$**

ARIZONA'S WEST COAST

Havasu Springs Resort
2581 Highway 95, Parker
Tel: 928-667-3361
www.havasusprings.com
This huge resort about 20 miles (32km) south of Lake Havasu City encompasses three motels, but the real

attraction is houseboat rentals (these are a popular item with Spring Breakers, so be advised). The vessels sleep up to 12 people and have various features, but all are equipped with bathrooms and complete galleys. **$$**

London Bridge Resort
1477 Queens Bay, Lake Havasu City
Tel: 928-855-0888
www.londonbridgeresort.com
Part Tudor mansion, part southwestern oasis and part tropical getaway, the

resort is popular with the Spring Break party crowd who come more for the pools, water sports, and open-air night club than the large condominium-style guest quarters. The bridge itself is in the backyard. Restaurant, nightclub, three pools, tennis courts, golf course, marina, boat rentals, air conditioning, TV. **$$**

Nautical Beachfront Resort
1000 McCulloch Boulevard North, Lake Havasu City

Tel: 928-855-2141 or 800-892-2141
www.nauticalinn.com
Arizona's only beachfront resort, this is a great place to bring the kids and have

fun messing about in boats on the shores of the lake. The 139 rooms and suites are light, bright, and comfortably furnished. You could easily imagine you are on vacation on an island. Rooms have TVs, refrigerators, microwaves, coffee makers, and Wi-fi access. On-site restaurant, bar, and Starbucks coffee shop. Pet friendly. **$$**

Shiloh Inn Hotel and Suites
1550 S. Castle Dome Avenue, Yuma
Tel: 928-782-9511
www.shilohinns.com
Spacious rooms, with couches, microwaves, refrigerators, and patios or balconies, are among the most comfortable in Yuma, and the well-maintained lawn is a welcome patch of green in an otherwise stark desert landscape. Suites with kitchenettes are also available. Pool, restaurant, bar, exercise room, TV, air conditioning. **$$**

Temple Bar Resort
Temple Bar
Tel: 800-255-5561
www.templebarlakemead.com
This 18-unit motel is set on the shore of Lake Mead surrounded by miles of open desert. A variety of watercraft, including ski boats, patio boats, fishing boats, and jet skis, are available for rent at a fully equipped marina. Restaurant, marina, RV facilities, TV, air conditioning. There are also inexpensive fishing cabins for rent. **$**

SEDONA AND THE VERDE VALLEY

Amara Creekside Resort
310 N. Highway 89A, Sedona
Tel: 928-282-4828 or 800-815-6152
www.amararesort.com
This top-rated boutique hotel on the banks of Oak Creek has the feel of organic architect Frank Lloyd Wright's spectacular home and studio Taliesin West in Scottsdale but with a striking modern sensibility geared toward today's travelers. The low-profile hotel is the linchpin of Sedona Center, which includes two shopping centers and restaurants, all linked by a self-guided nature trail with exhibits developed by the Sedona-based Institute of EcoTourism. The resort has 100 tranquil rooms, including 24 suites with whirlpool tubs. All have pillowtop mattresses, walk-in closets, and Aveda bath products; many overlook the creek or lawn and have patios. Creekside dining in three restaurants. Spa, heated outdoor saltwater pool, meeting rooms, Wi-fi throughout. **$$**

Briar Patch Inn
3190 N. Highway 89A, Sedona
Tel: 928-282-2342 or 888-809-3030
www.briarpatchinn.com
Set on the banks of Oak Creek a few miles north of Sedona, this historic canyon hideaway offers 18 cozy cabins with stone-and-wood-panel walls, rustic furnishings, and Indian rugs; some cabins have decks and fireplaces. Complimentary full breakfast is served in an attractive dining room or on a terrace overlooking the creek in summer, often to the strains of live classical musicians. Massage and wellness programs are available. **$$–$$$**

Enchantment Resort
525 Boynton Canyon Road, Sedona
Tel: 928-282-2900 or 800-826-4180
www.enchantmentresort.com
This famous resort has a glorious Boynton Canyon location with luxurious accommodations. Pueblo-style casitas have single rooms as well as one- and two-bedroom suites, many with living rooms, fireplaces, and patios. All are decorated in a contemporary southwestern style, and the views are universally gorgeous. The Yavapai Dining Room specializes in fine southwestern and Continental cuisine and has panoramic views of the canyon. A second restaurant, Tii Gavo, offers a more casual atmosphere. A spa with a wide range of facilities and services is also on the grounds. Four pools, two restaurants, fitness center, pitch-and-putt golf course, nature walks, mountain bike rentals, tennis courts, meeting facilities, children's program, air conditioning, TV. **$$$**

Garland's Oak Creek Lodge
PO Box 152, Oak Creek
Tel: 928-282-3343
www.garlandslodge.com
A unique historic lodge on a wooded homestead next to Oak Creek. With its roaring fires and porches with rocking chairs, the lodge offers a quintessential cabin-in-the-woods experience. Rustic but beautifully maintained, the 16 air-conditioned cabins have no phones or TVs and are surrounded by gardens. Full breakfasts, four-course dinners, and afternoon teas

are included in the price and include organic fruits and vegetables grown on site. Two-night minimum. Dinner, served family style in the cozy dining room, is open to a limited number of non-guests. Reserve well ahead; the lodge is often booked a year in advance. Dinner reservations here are like gold dust. Closed Nov–Mar and Sun. **$$$**

Sedona Motel
218 Highway 179, Sedona
Tel: 928-282-7187
www.thesedonamotel.com
A pleasant but basic, budget-priced lodging option in Sedona that offers all the scenic beauty of the redrocks at just a fraction of the cost. From here, you can walk to Uptown Sedona's restaurants and shops. **$**

MOGOLLON RIM AND THE TONTO BASIN

Grey Hackle Lodge
PO Box 145, Payson
Tel: 928-478-9980
www.greyhacklelodge.com
11 log cabins set on 4 acres (1.6 hectares) just east of Payson. Some are one-room cabins with kitchenettes; others are two-story cabins with full kitchens and fireplaces. Simply furnished, the cabins are well maintained. Private baths, TV. **$**

Kohl's Ranch Lodge
Highway 260, Payson
Tel: 928-478-4211 or 800-521-3131

www.ilxresorts.com
Set on Tonto Creek in the ponderosa pine forest east of Payson, this is an attractive, backwoods time-share resort. Cabins are quite roomy, with dining areas, kitchenettes, patios and fireplaces. Rooms in the main lodge are somewhat more modest, though several have fireplaces. All are furnished in contemporary style. Restaurant, cowboy bar, outdoor pool, horseback riding, mountain bike rentals, exercise room, putting green, playground, TV, air conditioning. **$$–$$$**

Majestic Mountain Inn
602 E. Highway 260, Payson
Tel: 800-408-2442
www.majesticmountaininn.com
Regular rooms at this attractive stone-and-timber lodge in Payson have the style and comfort of a standard motel unit. If you're looking for something more comfortable, the luxury rooms are larger and have Jacuzzi and gas fireplace. Pool, meeting facilities, TV, air conditioning. **$**

Mountain Meadows Cabins
HC 2, Box 162E, Payson
Tel: 928-478-4415
www.mountainmeadows cabins.com
Six cabins situated east of Payson under the Mogollon Rim at an elevation of 6,400ft (1,950 meters). Each has a private bath, kitchen, and fireplace. Most of the land surrounding the cabins is part of a national forest. Kitchen, TV, VCR, barbecue grill. **$–$$**

WHITE MOUNTAINS

The Commons at White Mountain Lodge
140 Main Street, PO Box 143, Greer
Tel: 928-735-9977 (cabin reservations) or 520-977-0452 (suite/lodge reservations)
www.wmlodge.com
Set in an 1892 log home overlooking Greer Meadow and the Little Colorado River – the first homestead in Greer – this country inn has loads of history and ambiance. Under new ownership, it has been converted to attractive vacation rentals. The historic lodge now has four self-contained suites, or "cottages," with kitchens, sitting rooms, and TVs. There are six freestanding log cabins, ranging from studio size to three-bedroom, three-bath, with kitchens and fireplaces or wood-burning stoves; some cabins also have whirlpool tubs. On weekends, there's a two-night minimum stay. No pets. No smoking. **$$–$$$**

Greer Lodge Resort
44 Main Street, Greer
Tel: 928-735-7216
www.greerlodgeaz.com
This large resort on the south end of the little mountain community of Greer offers an assortment of comfortable cabins overlooking the meadows and the Little Colorado River. Freestanding cabins are dog and child friendly. Many amenities are included in the room rate, including fly-fishing lessons, use of mountain bikes, binoculars, and telescopes in summer, and snowshoes in winter. Air conditioning, fireplaces, TVs. The main lodge and restaurant burned down in a fire in May 2011, but owner Doug Sandahl is already planning to rebuild; the lodge remains open, and the rest of the property is unaffected. **$$–$$$**

Molly Butler Lodge
PO Box 134, Greer
Tel: 928-735-7226
www.mollybutlerlodge.com
The first lodging in Greer (1910) was run by Mormon pioneers Molly and John Butler. After a century, it had become rather run down, but new owners are whipping the place into shape and, in 2011, there will be a grand reopening of the 11 historic cabins and suites, each remodeled and decorated with period furnishings and luxurious modern amenities. The heart and soul of the lodge is the bar and restaurant. The bar is still a lively community gathering place at the end of the day and the restaurant is popular for its fish fry, steak, and beer on Friday nights. **$**

Red Setter Cabins
44 Main Street, Greer
Tel: 928-735-7216
www.greerlodgeaz.com
Part of Historic Greer Lodge, these five attractive hand-hewn log cabins are set on the north end of the village right on the Little Colorado River, on 10 acres (4 hectares). Choose from cabins of varying sizes, from a cosy cabin that sleeps four to

an eight-bedroom cabin that sleeps up to 32 people (this building was once the award-winning Red Setter Inn Bed and Breakfast). Rooms have a French country décor, with four-poster and sleigh beds topped by cozy feather comforters. All rooms have baths or showers, TVs and phones, and access to balconies or decks overlooking the river. The largest cabin has three sitting rooms with fireplaces, and the downstairs sitting room has games, and a TV/DVD player with DVD library. Activities include private fishing and access to miles of national forest trails. **$$–$$$**

PHOENIX

Arizona Biltmore Resort and Spa
24th Street and Missouri Avenue
Tel: 602-955-6600 or 800-954-0086
www.arizonabiltmore.com
This grand hotel inspired by Frank Lloyd Wright (who acted as consultant on the project) is the last word in grace, dignity, and architectural distinction. It is situated on 39 acres (16 hectares) in what was once a remote area of Phoenix that has now been swallowed up by surrounding development. The hotel has a total of 738 guest rooms, consisting of oversize rooms in the historic hotel and a newer wing. Suites are also available in the recently opened Ocatilla, a hotel within a hotel, which provides a high-end

pampering concierge experience for guests. Two 18-hole golf courses, full-service spa, fine dining in two restaurants, bars, five swimming pools, fitness center, biking, shops, business center, air conditioning, TV, valet parking. **$$$**

Cedar Hill Bed and Breakfast
175 E. Cedar Street, Globe
Tel: 928-425-7530
www.cedarhill.
globemiamicommons.com
This inn is in the historic district of Globe and is the kind of place where guests mingle easily in a relaxed environment. Wine and snacks on arrival, and a big breakfast. A home away from home for explorations of Globe. **$**

Embassy Suites Phoenix
2333 East Thomas Road
Tel: 602-957-1910
www.embassysuites.com
This attractive, full-service, all-suites hotel is convenient both to the airport and downtown Phoenix. It is full of comforts, including a cooked-to-order breakfast in the morning. **$**

Fairmont Scottsdale Princess
7575 E. Princess Drive,

Scottsdale
Tel: 480-585-4848
www.fairmont.com
This luxurious resort sprawls 450 acres (180 hectares) at the base of the McDowell Mountains north of Scottsdale. Spanish Colonial architecture, antique furnishings, fountains, generous patios, and immaculate landscaping create a rich and exotic ambiance. The 649 spacious rooms and casitas are decorated in muted desert tones, with fine southwestern furnishings, large bathrooms and terraces. Seven restaurants serve Spanish and Mexican cuisine. Restaurants, bars, two 18-hole golf courses, tennis courts, three pools, fitness center, spa services, shops, business center, meeting facilities, TV, air conditioning. **$$$**

FireSky Resort and Spa
4925 N. Scottsdale Road, Scottsdale
Tel: 480-945-7666 or 800-528-7867
www.fireskyresort.com
Rising from the ashes of a former motel, FireSky is an energetic young boutique hotel in downtown

Scottsdale. One of the unique Kimpton resorts, this hotel takes its design cues from the elements, which are incorporated into the architecture, décor, and vibrant color scheme of the hotel. There are 204 guest rooms and suites, with soothing décor, clustered around a lushly landscaped central courtyard with areas for socializing and privacy, and enjoying the balmy Phoenix night air. The onsite restaurant Taggia features artisanal Coastal Italian cuisine crafted by one of Phoenix's leading Slow Food chefs. Two swimming pools, on-site Jurlique spa, hosted evening wine hour, free Wi-Fi throughout the resort. Room rates are very reasonable. Pet friendly. **$$**

Gainey Suites Hotel
7300 E. Gainey Suites Drive, Scottsdale
Tel: 480-922-6969 or 800-970-4666
www.gaineysuiteshotel.com
This attractive all-suites boutique hotel adjacent to Gainey Village development is a great budget option in upscale Scottsdale. The 162 recently remodeled suites range in size from studios to two-bedrooms, sleeping two to eight people. Pillow-top mattresses fully equipped kitchens, flat-screen LCD TVs with on-demand movies, CDs, and games, and free Wi-Fi throughout. Pool, outdoor hot tub, laundry facilities, and delicious complimentary hot breakfast buffet and evening hors d'oeuvres. Golf tee times at over 50 local courses can be arranged through the hotel. **$$**

Hermosa Inn
5532 North Palo Cristi Road, Paradise Valley
Tel: 602-955-8614 or 800-241-1210
www.hermosainn.com
Centrally located in a residential area between Phoenix and Scottsdale, this small historic inn includes restored portions

of the original 1930s adobe home and studio of cowboy artist Lon Megargee, which he later converted to a guest ranch and inn. Subsequent owners have added their own personal touches and retained the intimate feel of the property: lush walled gardens and winding pathways, a small swimming pool, tennis courts, 34 airy deluxe casitas, some with clerestory windows and patios around bird-filled private courtyards with their own hot tubs, villas, and the Blue Door Spa. The current owners also own the top-rated Royal Palms Hotel. This is a historic structure, so expect smaller rooms and bathrooms furnished with charming southwestern details. The onsite restaurant, Lon's, is top rated for its artisanal Western cuisine. **$$$**

Holiday Inn and Suites Phoenix Airport North
1515 N. 44th Street
Tel: 602-244-8800
www.holidayinn.com
Just minutes from Sky Harbor International Airport, this all-suites hotel offers spacious accommodations with separate bedrooms and living rooms, and contemporary furnishings. The high-rise surrounds a central courtyard with an outdoor pool. A good choice for business travelers who need extra room or for families with small children. Restaurant, bar, pool, exercise room, meeting facilities, airport shuttle, air conditioning, TV. **$$**

Hotel San Carlos
202 N Central Avenue
Tel: 602-253-4121
www.hotelsancarlos.com
Built in 1928, this multistory Italian Renaissance-style hotel was the first high-rise, fully air-conditioned, luxury hotel in downtown Phoenix and is still today, downtown's only historic boutique hotel. After undergoing a

BELOW: Royal Palms resort.

million-dollar restoration, it is slowly returning to its former glory and is a member of the Historic Hotels of America. Many of the original fixtures and fittings are intact, especially in the grand lobby, which has chandeliers, a copper-doored elevator, decorative moldings, and other details. The 128 rooms, including five Signature Suites, are cramped by today's standards and at the mercy of ancient plumbing and thin walls. Still, all have attractive period features as well as Serta Sleeper mattresses, coffee makers, cable TV, data ports, clock radios, ceiling fans, and irons. Rooftop pool, two restaurants, gift shop, barber shop. Staff are friendly and helpful, and the hotel is within walking distance of the Phoenix Art Museum and Heard Museum, and the METRO light rail stops right in front of the hotel. **$–$$**

Maricopa Manor
15 W. Pasadena Avenue
Tel: 800-292-6403
www.maricopamanor.com
When it was built in 1928, this hacienda-style bed-and-breakfast was in the countryside outside town. Now, it's in the heart of the city, a block from the busy Camelback corridor. An acre (0.4 hectare) of landscaped grounds shelter the property from the surrounding bustle. All six rooms are suites with attractive, mostly contemporary southwest furnishings. Four luxury suites have fireplaces and whirlpool tubs. Pool, air conditioning, TV, gardens, complimentary breakfast, Wi-fi throughout. **$$**

The Phoenician
6000 E. Camelback Road, Scottsdale
Tel: 480-941-8200 or 800-888-8234
www.thephoenician.com
No extravagance is overlooked at this landmark resort at the base of Camelback Mountain. Guest rooms, suites, and

casitas are lavishly furnished, with marble bathrooms, patios, Italian linens, and original art; some have travertine fireplaces. The grounds and public spaces are equally elaborate. The resort's 250 acres (100 hectares) encompass a world-class 27-hole golf course, nine pools (including a 165ft/50-meter water slide), manicured gardens, 11 tennis courts, a full-service spa, and an extensive art collection. The 11 restaurants and lounges range from Mary Elaine's, perhaps the finest French cuisine in the state, and the Praying Monk, set in a wine cellar with barrel-vaulted ceilings, brick archways and European antiques, to casual outdoor dining and an ice cream parlor. All this luxury doesn't come cheap, though you may be surprised at just how affordable a standard room can be during the sweltering summer off-season. Several bars, bike rentals, gift shops, children's program, meeting facilities, air conditioning, TV. **$$$**

Pointe Hilton Squaw Peak Resort
7677 N. 16th Street
Tel: 602-997-2626
www.hilton.com
With an elaborate water park and extensive children's program, this luxury resort is a hit with kids. Guest quarters are mostly two-room suites furnished in contemporary style with a few Spanish Colonial touches. Adults may prefer to avail themselves of the 18-hole golf course, full-service spa, tennis courts, or four pools. Jogging trails meander through immaculate grounds. Eight restaurants range from quick, casual eats to haute cuisine. Shops, air conditioning. **$$$**

Ritz-Carlton Phoenix
2401 E Camelback Road
Tel: 602-468-0700
www.ritzcarlton.com
This grand hotel across

ABOVE: Westward Look Resort.

from the Biltmore Fashion Park shopping center offers impeccable service and elegant accommodations. Antique furnishings and paintings in public spaces lend an air of Old World sophistication. Guest quarters are furnished with reproductions and have marble bathrooms. Pool, fitness center, restaurants, bar, air conditioning, TV. **$$$**

Royal Palms Resort and Spa
5200 E. Camelback Road
Tel: 602-840-3610 or 800-672-6011
www.royalpalmshotel.com
You'll feel as if you've wandered into a Mediterranean villa at this recently renovated hotel, built in the 1940s. Walled courtyards with antique fountains, gardens, antique European furnishings, and beautifully restored architectural details create an atmosphere of romance and opulence. Each deluxe casita is designed in a distinctive style, ranging from Spanish Colonial to contemporary. Other rooms aren't quite so lavishly appointed. The restaurant, T. Cook's, is considered one of the finest in the city. Bar, pool, tennis court, spa, fitness room, air conditioning, TV. **$$$**

Sheraton Wild Horse Pass Resort and Spa
Gila River Indian Community, 5594 W. Wild Horse Pass Boulevard, Chandler
Tel: 602-225-0100 or 888-218-8989

www.wildhorsepassresort.com
The Pima (Akimel O'odham) and Maricopa (Pee Posh) tribes have been renowned hosts since the 19th century, and their heritage is woven into every detail of this luxury resort, just south of Phoenix. The sight and sound of water in the desert is the central motif throughout. A replica of the Gila River meanders through the grounds. A riverside pool with waterfalls replicates the Hohokam ruins of Casa Grande. A dramatic mural retells the tribes' history in the domed lobby – itself a spectacular reference to a traditional Pima roundhouse. Pima basketry and Maricopa pottery designs adorn the two large wings containing the guest rooms. Wild horses gallop into view while coyotes can be heard yipping at night. The 500 rooms have patios or balconies and views of the golf course, Estrella Mountains or the Gila River. All have minibars, safes, phones, bath and shower, and TVs. Amenities include a 36-hole golf course, an Indian-inspired spa, horseback riding, a hiking

trail system, two tribal museums, cultural tours, boat rides on the replica river, and a nearby casino.

The resort's fabulous four-star dinner restaurant, Kai, is consistently voted top special dinner

restaurant in Phoenix. It showcases contemporary American Indian-inspired cuisine, using greens and

other foods grown on the Gila Reservation and other Indian reservations in the US. **$$$**

TUCSON

Adobe Rose Inn
940 N. Olsen Avenue
Tel: 520-318-4644 or 800-328-4122
www.aroseinn.com
Built in 1933 and enclosed by 1ft (30cm) -thick pink adobe walls, this snug bed-and-breakfast is in a quiet residential neighborhood near the University of Arizona. The six rooms and cottages are furnished in a rustic southwestern style; one room has a corner kiva fireplace. A full breakfast is included. Pool, TV, air con-ditioning, and high-speed internet connection. **$-$$**

Arizona Inn
2200 E Elm Street
Tel: 520-325-1541 or 800-933-1093
www.arizonainn.com
One of downtown Tucson's top lodgings, this elegant historic southwestern inn is just 5 minutes from the University of Arizona but feels like its own oasis. Guest rooms and suites are tastefully furnished with antiques and are mainly in casitas, with patios and fireplaces, amid 14 acres (6 hectares) of manicured grounds and gardens. Outdoor pool, ten-nis courts, massage, exer-cise room, fine dining, bar, air conditioning. Reserve well ahead. **$$**

Arizona Riverpark Inn
350 S. Freeway
Tel: 800-551-1446
www.theriverparkinn.com
Located in downtown Tucson, this attractive, small boutique hotel is a thrifty option while still offering a relaxing, resort-like setting. The 174 rooms and suites have satellite TV, microwaves, refrigera-tors, coffee/tea makers, and Wi-fi. A plentiful hot breakfast is included. On-site casual dining res-taurant, Jacuzzi, pool, pet

friendly (there's an arroyo trail for walkies). Transportation to UA cam-pus provided. Note: this hotel is often used by groups and students. **$**

Hotel Congress
311 E. Congress
Tel: 520-622-8848 or 800-722-8848
www.hotelcongress.com
John Dillinger and his gang stayed at this quirky 1919 hotel near the Amtrak sta-tion, though the clientele nowadays is mostly hip young backpackers and budget travelers willing to put up with a lot of noise. Rooms offer basic com-forts, but the place has some interesting touches such as old-fashioned radios and telephones, an internet café, a lively saloon and late-hours nightclub, and a great little coffee shop that has been featured on the Food Network. Idiosyncratic and inexpensive. Private and shared hostel rooms are available. Bar, restaurant. **$**

Lazy K Bar Guest Ranch
8401 N. Scenic Drive
Tel: 520-299-RIDE
www.lazykbarranch.com
The ranch's 24 adobe casi-tas are set in the Tucson Mountains overlooking the Santa Cruz Valley, about 16 miles (26km) northwest of Tucson. Recreational opportunities abound, with a riding program, spa, live entertainment, and cook-outs. American Plan (all meals included), pool, hot tub, volleyball and basket-ball courts, ranch store, meeting facilities, air condi-tioning. **$$$**

Lodge on the Desert
306 N. Alvernon Way
Tel: 520-325-3366 or 800-456-5634
www.lodgeonthedesert.com
Built in 1936 as a personal hacienda-style residence

on the edge of town, this boutique hotel is now just northeast of downtown Tucson. A recent multimil-lion-dollar reconstruction has doubled the size of the resort, carefully blending the old part of the hotel, consisting of historic casi-tas, well-tended gardens, cacti, and shady palms, with modern guest rooms and more amenities aimed at business travelers, such as spacious bathrooms with Jacuzzi tubs, large flat-screen TVs, fireplaces, and balconies with views of the Santa Catalina Mountains. The older casitas have plenty of charm, though: most have patios and fire-places, and some have saltillo-tiled floors and exposed beams. A new retro-style pool and pleas-ant lobby and library tie together both sides of the expanded property. The on-site restaurant, tucked away in a corner of the old part of the property, next to the original hacienda, is very attractive and is one of Tucson's hidden gems. **$$-$$$**

Loews Ventana Canyon Restaurant
7000 N. Resort Drive
Tel: 520-299-2020
www.loewshotels.com
Tucson's premier resort is an oasis of luxury and com-fort in the desert outside the city. The 398 rooms and suites are large and beautifully furnished, each with a private balcony over-looking the city or Santa Catalina Mountains. The design of public spaces, including the terraces, meeting rooms, restau-rants, and the lobby, offers an understated elegance in keeping with the desert setting. Diversions range from two world-class 18-hole golf courses, a

complete spa, and one of the best restaurants in Tucson. Two pools, eight tennis courts, fitness center, meeting facilities, restaurants and lounges, shops, bike rentals, air con-ditioning, TV, nature walks. **$$$**

Omni Tucson National Resort
2727 W. Club Drive
Tel: 520-297-2271
www.omnihotels.com
Golfers will think they have died and gone to heaven at this luxury resort in the foothills of the Santa Catalina Mountains, home of the annual PGA Tucson Open golf tournament. The 128 rooms and suites are very large and furnished in a contemporary style, some with fireplaces and/or kitchenettes, many with patios and balconies. The real attraction, however, are the two highly regarded golf courses, the most beautiful and chal-lenging in the region. Non-golfers will enjoy being pampered at the full-ser-vice spa or lounge by one of the two pools. Two res-taurants serve American and southwestern cui-sine. Tennis courts, bas-ketball courts, fitness center, nature trails, lounges, air conditioning, TV. **$$$**

El Presidio Bed and Breakfast
297 N. Main Avenue
Tel: 520-623-6151

Since 1985, innkeeper Patti Toci has run an elegant award-winning bed-and-breakfast in this 1886 house, part of downtown El Presidio Historic District. Four comfortable suites (two with private entrances) are furnished with antiques. All have telephones, TVs, complimentary beverages, fruit and snacks. Guests enjoy a full gourmet breakfast around a single table in the sunny veranda room, which looks out onto a restful flowered courtyard with fountain. Two-night minimum stay. **$–$$**

Randolph Park Hotel and Suites
102 N. Alvernon Way
Tel: 800-227-6086
www.
randolphparkhotelandsuites.com
If the elegant and historic Lodge on the Desert is beyond your budget, check out this reliable hotel next door on Alvernon Way, near downtown Tucson. It has many amenities aimed at business travelers on a budget. Room rates include a hot breakfast buffet. Rooms are not very inspiringly decorated but all are non-smoking and have microwaves, coffee makers, air conditioning, TV, and internet access.

On-site fitness center and business center with Wi-fi access, courtyard, Olympic-sized pool, pet friendly. **$**

Tanque Verde Guest Ranch
14301 E. Speedway Boulevard
Tel: 520-296-6275 or 800-234-3833
www.tanqueverderanch.com
More of a spa resort than a ranch, Tanque Verde is sandwiched between Saguaro National Park and Coronado National Forest at the base of the Rincon Mountains. The more than 70 rooms and suites are simple and comfortable with Western furnishings; many have fireplaces and/or patios. Casitas are large and sumptuous. The ranch is a destination in itself, and there's never a dull moment. Activities include trail rides, complimentary tennis lessons, nature hikes, lectures, live entertainment, and bountiful meals and cookouts, Spa, indoor and outdoor pools, horseback riding and lessons, tennis courts, fitness room, basketball and volleyball courts, children's program, airport shuttle, air conditioning. American Plan (all meals included). **$$$**

Westward Look Resort
245 E. Ina Road

Tel: 520-297-1151 or 800-481-0636
www.westwardlook.com
Not just another elegant Tucson ranch resort, Westward Look Resort has a long and interesting history. It was built around a 1912 hacienda on 80 acres (32 hectares) in the Santa Catalina Foothills. More than 200 guest rooms are all suite-sized, furnished in luxurious southwestern style, and grouped in graceful casitas that ensure complete privacy (perfect for a retreat or to get that novel finished). Abundant wildlife makes this a great place for nature lovers. Opportunities for recreation and relaxation are numerous. Facilities include three pools and whirlpools, a fitness center, a superb spa specializing in authentic, hard-to-find East Indian Ayurvedic treatments professionally carried out by well-trained therapists, a meditational labyrinth, tennis courts, a Celestron 2000 telescope, hiking on the resort's extensive nature trails, horseback riding, mountain biking, and strolls through a variety of desert gardens. A fine restaurant, the Gold Room, overlooking the city, has the best views in

Tucson. It features delicious New Western cuisine by award-winning chef Jamie West, who showcases produce he grows in the property's organic garden (chef tours available). Meeting facilities, air conditioning, TV. **$$$**

White Stallion Ranch
9251 W. Twin Peaks Road
Tel: 520-297-0252 or 888-977-2624
www.wsranch.com
Guests get an authentic taste of the Old West at this unpretentious working cattle ranch on 3,000 acres (1,200 hectares) bordering Saguaro National Park. Accommodations range from snug, stripped-down single rooms to larger and more comfortable two-bedroom suites with living rooms. The emphasis is on horseback riding, but a variety of other activities, including nature hikes, tennis, swimming, hayrides, cookouts, and a weekly rodeo, provide plenty of other diversions. Kids enjoy the petting zoo. Meals are served family style in the dining room. Stables and riding lessons, children's program, outdoor pool. American Plan (all meals included). **$$$**

BORDER COUNTRY

Beatty's Miller Guest Ranch and Orchard
2173 E. Miller Canyon Road, Hereford
Tel: 520-378-2728
www.beattysguestranch.com
This all-non-smoking, family-run backcountry retreat occupies an apple orchard adjacent to the Miller Peak Wilderness. Housekeeping units

include two apartments and four cabins, each with a bedroom, sitting room and full kitchen. Visitors have access to the hummingbird and butterfly gardens. Flame-colored tanagers and hummingbirds are the big draw for the serious birders who frequent this place. No meals served. **$**

Birders Vista Bed and Breakfast
5147 South Kino Road, Sierra Vista
Tel: 520-378-2493
www.birdersvista.com
This large, immaculately kept, modern stucco home is conveniently

located 10 minutes from Sierra Vista, Ramsey Canyon, and the San Pedro River. It offers a friendly, European-style bed-and-breakfast experience that will appeal to those who enjoy mingling with their hosts and other guests. Set on 4 acres (1.6 hectares) of open desert, and sheltered by a stand of mature pines, orchards, and landscaping that attract a variety of birds. Two bedrooms have sitting areas with private baths and entrances. A suite is available with two pretty bedrooms, sitting room, and private bath. A

full breakfast is included with room rate, including home-made organic plum jam from the on-site orchard; early birders can make arrangements for continental breakfast. Owners Johnnie and Audrey Eskue are avid and well-informed birders and extend a low-key, down-home Texan welcome and the run of their comfortable home. Amenities include TV, computer with internet access, videos, games, and library. Johnnie's carved wood sculptures and many paintings by local artists adorn the walls and are for sale. **$–$$**

Bisbee Grand Hotel
61 Main Street, Bisbee
Tel: 520-421-1909
www.bisbeegrandhotel.com
Elegantly restored Victorian bed-and-breakfast with period decor in the heart of downtown. A saloon on the ground floor evokes a spit-and-sawdust Old West atmosphere, and the theme is carried through 13 guest rooms. In some cases, private bathrooms are located down the hall. Billiard room, breakfast included. No in-room telephones or TVs. **$$**

Casa de San Pedro Bed and Breakfast
8933 S. Yell Lane, Hereford
Tel: 520-366-1300 or 888-257-2050
www.bedandbirds.com
Set on 10 acres (4 hectares) adjoining the San Pedro River, this highly rated B&B is a very

attractive base for birders hoping to add one of the 355 species of birds found here to their life lists. There are 10 guest rooms with private baths and southwestern furnishings; all have air conditioning and heat, art from local artists, Wi-fi, and most have fireplaces. Home-made pie in the afternoon and gourmet breakfasts. Gastronomic workshops include one with Bisbee's Café Roka's chef-owner Rod Kass. **$$**

Circle Z Ranch
PO Box 194, Patagonia
Tel: 520-394-2525 or 888-854-2525
www.circlez.com
Accommodations range from individual rooms to suites or private cottages in several adobe buildings at the foot of the Santa Rita Mountains about 60 miles (100km) south of Tucson. The main activities are horseback riding, pack trips, and birding at the adjoining Nature Conservancy preserve. This is a dude ranch. All rates are per week and are American Plan (all-inclusive). **$$$**

Cochise Stronghold: A Canyon Nature Retreat
PO Box 232, Pearce

Tel: 520-826-4141 or 877-426-4141
www.cochisestrongholdbb.com
Owners John and Nancy Yates have created the ultimate sky island hideaway in this delightful bed-and-breakfast on 15 acres (6 hectares) of forest land in the heart of Cochise Stronghold Canyon wilderness in southeastern Arizona. This is the place to hike, star gaze, and relax far away from everything. You can either rent the elegant Agave Suite in the stone house, which has a king bed, satellite TV, fully supplied kitchenette, hot tub, patio, and library, or to rough it in style, rent the Woodlands Yurt for a luxury campout with friends. More than a tent, this 30ft (9-meter) -diameter Mongolian yurt sleeps 10 people and is very comfy, with heating and evaporative cooling, pine floors, and queen, double, and single beds. You just bring camping gear and flashlight. A third unit, the Casita Manzanita guest house, will be available again in the near future. Gourmet breakfasts are served in-room and include mesquite-cornmeal pancakes and organic, vegetarian, and cleanly raised meat, dairy, eggs, and produce. You will need to bring food for other meals with you, or ask the Yates to provision. **$$–$$$**

Copper City Inn
99 Main Street, Bisbee
Tel: 520-432-1418 or 520-432-4254
www.coppercityinn.com
The three beautifully remodeled, southwest-themed rooms in the Copper City Inn, a three-level duplex across from the theater on Bisbee's Main Street, are just the ticket for travelers looking for slightly more refined lodgings in funky, artsy Bisbee. All have secure, keyless entry, French windows and balconies, super-comfy queen beds, large closets and bathrooms with local toiletries, a wet

bar with complimentary bottle of wine (owner Fred Miller tends bar at the excellent Café Roka restaurant nearby) and bottled water, tea and coffee facilities, and cable TV, Wi-fi, and phones. A larger room downstairs has a full kitchen. Rear sun deck. Voucher for continental breakfast at nearby High Desert Market and Café, a popular local spot, included in room rate. Note: The inn, like much of Bisbee, is reached by climbing a flight of steep stairs. There is no disabled access. **$$**

Copper Queen Hotel
11 Howell Avenue, Bisbee
Tel: 520-432-2216
www.copperqueen.com
This turn-of-the-20th-century landmark built during the heyday of the Copper Queen Mine drips with Old West atmosphere; guests have included John Wayne and Teddy Roosevelt. Rooms vary in size, are furnished with antiques, and most have been recently renovated. Restaurant, saloon, pool, TV, air conditioning. **$$**

Cross Creek Cottages
14 Cross Creek Road, Patagonia
Tel: 520-394-0054
www.patagoniaaz.com/lodging_cross_creek
This ranch in the countryside on the outskirts of Patagonia is a wonderful base for anyone on a budget wanting to make an extended exploration of the Border Country. The 20-acre (8-hectare) ranch has two cozy one- and two-bed cottages and a studio apartment on Sonoita Creek. The ranch has rescue donkeys, llamas, and an alpaca and adjoins the Native Seeds/SEARCH research center. There are beautiful views and places to walk. The owner, Regina Medley, is an artist with a gallery in Patagonia, and the former owner of the Duquesne House Bed and Breakfast. Works of art and antiques decorate each cottage, which have full kitchens, living rooms with woodstoves, separate

BELOW: Enchantment Resort.

bathrooms, and porches; the pretty studio apartment adjoining the owner's house and pool has a wet bar with continental breakfast fixings, microwave, and coffee maker. This authentic Patagonia lodging is a real find. No credit cards. Reasonable long-term rates available, if you fancy taking up residence. **$–$$**

Duquesne House Bed and Breakfast
357 Duquesne Avenue, Patagonia
Tel: 520-394-2732
www.theduquesnehouse.com
This converted former miners' boarding house is located in the artist haven of Patagonia. Each accommodation in the long, low adobe building is a separate apartment. Each of the four units has a private entrance, sitting room with day beds, bedroom, private bath and access to a large screened back porch and extensive gardens. A full home-made breakfast using some ingredients from the garden is served family style in the open dining/living room of the main house. "Bed no bread" stays on Tue and Wed are slightly reduced cost, without breakfast. Guests will find themselves wanting to linger and enjoy Patagonia's many charms. **$–$$**

The Gardens at Mile High Ranch
901 Tombstone Canyon, Bisbee
Tel: 520-432-3866
www.gardensatmilehighranch. com
Easy to miss at the top of Tombstone Canyon, this child- and pet-friendly 1920s travel motel is a great budget option. The seven non-smoking units have been attractively restored with private baths, full kitchens, pullout couches, cable TV, and Wi-fi. There are 3 acres (1.2 hectares) of mature, shady gardens, and a healthy continental breakfast is included all for less than $100/night – almost

certainly the best deal in Bisbee. Kid and pet friendly. **$**

George Walker House Bed and Breakfast
2225 W. George Walker Lane, Paradise
Tel: 520-558-2287
www.thegeorgewalkerhouse. com
This is a carefully restored 1902 pioneer homestead, 5.5 miles (9km) from Portal in the Chiricahua Mountains near the Mexican border. The large cabin has two bedrooms, one with a queen bed and the other with two double beds, and a shared bathroom. The large sitting/dining room has a woodstove, TV, extensive library, and games. The immaculate 1960s kitchen is fully stocked with food; you'll only need to bring fresh meats and produce. From May on, feeders attract Cave Creek's famous hummingbirds, and 140 of the 180 species of butterfly found in the Chiricahuas. **$$**

Larian Motel
410 E. Fremont Street, Tombstone
Tel: 520-457-2272
www.tombstonemotels.com
A classic 1950s budget motel with clean, basic, recently remodeled rooms with queen and king beds (some rooms have sleeper-sofas), private baths, cable TV, air conditioning, and free Wi-fi. **$**

Portal Peak Lodge
PO Box 364, Portal
Tel: 520-558-2223
Adjoining Cave Creek, not far from Chiricahua National Monument, the lodge's 16 rooms are attractively furnished in southwestern style. Rooms open onto a long deck, with magnificent views of the mountains. A restaurant, grocery store, and gift shop are on the premises. **$$**

Ramsey Canyon Inn Bed and Breakfast
29 Ramsey Canyon Road, Hereford
Tel: 520-378-3010
www.ramseycanyoninn.com
This stone inn is adjacent

to The Nature Conservancy's 380-acre (155-hectare) Ramsey Canyon Preserve. Six guest rooms, each with a private bath, and three apartments (across Ramsey Creek) with kitchens. A gourmet breakfast is included, served family style. There is organic shade-grown coffee and teas and choice of several amazing home-made pies made by the innkeeper using fruit from the inn's organic orchards. Note: This inn is no longer run by The Nature Conservancy, but is privately owned. **$$**

Rancho De La Osa Guest Ranch
PO Box 1, Sasabe
Tel: 520-823-4257 or 800-872-6240
www.ranchodelaosa.com
Developed by Navajo historian Louisa Wetherill in 1921, this dude ranch has been used as a quiet desert getaway by many celebrities over the years. The hacienda, built between the 1830s and 1860s, now houses two dining rooms and four sitting rooms. The Cantina is reputed to be the oldest building in the state and has been occupied continuously since the early 1700s. The Territorial-style ranch house has 21 adobe rooms furnished with Old Mexico antiques. All rooms are on the ground floor near the pool, hot tub, dining areas, and horse corrals and are non-smoking. Activities include horse-back riding, mountain biking, nature hikes, birdwatching, bocce ball, and croquet. Themed weekends include cook-outs, roundups, and other Western activities. American Plan (includes all meals and activities). **$$$**

Rex Ranch Resort and Spa
131 Amado Montosa Road, Amado
Tel: 520-398-2914 or 800-547-2696
www.rexranch.com
Where do overworked

southern Arizona innkeepers and restaurateurs go for a reasonably priced romantic getaway, a little pampering, and good food? Many say Rex Ranch, a beautiful historic ranch resort, across the Santa Cruz River just south of Tucson, where the rest of the world seems a long way away. There are 30 different types of pleasant southwest-style rooms and suites at the ranch, occupying several houses, and two casitas. All have private or shared patios, coffee makers and fridges, Wi-fi (fee extra), and all but two have private bathrooms with baths or showers. Fine dining in the ranch's well-loved Cantina Romantica Wed–Sun in high season features Continental cuisine. Pool, hot tub, meeting rooms, spa, rose gardens, fountains, yoga, horseback riding, mountain biking, birdwatching, hiking, volleyball, games room. **$$–$$$**

Shady Dell RV Park
1 Old Douglas Road, Bisbee
Tel: 520-432-3567
www.theshadydell.com
The nine restored vintage aluminum travel trailers at this funky little trailer park aren't something you see every day, even in artsy Bisbee. You get to spend the night in a classic 1950s trailer, or set up for the night in a madcap Polynesian-themed bus or dry-docked yacht. Each is comfortable and has a stove, fridge, percolator, dishes, linens, and cassette tapes of big band, early rhythm and blues, and favorite old radio programs played on reproduction vintage radios. Some also have old black-and-white TVs. Restrooms and showers are shared. **$–$$**

PRICE CATEGORIES

Price categories are based on the cost of a double room in high season.
$ = $110 or less
$$ = $110–250
$$$ = $200–250
$$$$ = more than $250

ACTIVITIES

FESTIVALS, THE ARTS, NIGHTLIFE, SHOPPING, SPORTS, AND TOURS

FESTIVALS

The following festivals and other events are listed by month, and then according to where they fall within that month. Sports events are listed separately.

2012 sees the centennial of Arizona, with state-wide celebrations and festivals. Be sure to check local listings for these once-every-hundred-years events.

January

First People's World's Fair and Powwow "Thunder in the Desert" (Tucson). Every four years, tribes from all over the country converge on Tucson for this big powwow that rings in the New Year. The next powwow is scheduled for 2016. Tel: 520-622-4900; www.usaindianinfo.org.
Quartzite Powwow Gem and Mineral Show (Quartzite): A popular gathering of gem fanatics in airstream trailers in this dusty Old West town. Tel: 928-927-6325; www.qiaaz.org.
Wings Over Willcox (Willcox). Birders flock to the flooded playas of southeastern Arizona, which attract thousands of migratory wading birds each winter, for talks and events. Tel: 800-200-2272; www.wingsoverwillcox.com.

February

Arizona Renaissance Festival (Apache Junction). Music, theater, crafts, games, and tournaments on weekends from February to early April. Tel: 520-463-2700; www.royalfaires.com/arizona.
Festival of the Arts (Tubac): The oldest event of its kind in the Southwest, this six-day arts festival at the beginning of February showcases the work of hundreds of artists, craftspeople, and musicians in the tiny arts community of Tubac, just south of Tucson. Tel: 520-398-2704; www.tubacaz.com/festival.
Gold Rush Days (Wickenburg). A melodrama, shootouts on Frontier Street, a beard-growing contest, a rodeo, a parade, arts and crafts booths, and food celebrate the Old West over three days. Tel: 928-684-5479; www.wickenburgchamber.com.
Matsuri Japanese Festival (Phoenix): Heritage Arts and Science Park in downtown Phoenix is the venue for this weekend-long festival celebrating all-things Japanese in late February. Tel: 602-262-5071; www.azmatsuri.org.
O'odham Tash Casa Grande Indian Days (Casa Grande): Coinciding with the World Championship Hoop Dance Contest, this powwow includes Indian ceremonies, a rodeo, and an arts and crafts festival. Tel: 520-836-4723.
Tucson Gem and Mineral Show (Tucson): The largest gathering of precious-stone fans in the world sells out every hotel in Tucson in February. Book ahead. Tel: 520-322-5773; www.tgms.org.
Sedona International Film Festival (Sedona): Celebrities gather in Red Rock country for this increasingly popular independent film fest. Includes classic films, premieres, and workshops. Tel: 928-282-1177; www.sedonafilmfestival.com.
Winterfest (Flagstaff): This month-long celebration of winter includes a parade, Northern Arizona University sports, arts and crafts exhibits, sled-dog races, food events, Alpine and Nordic skiing, concerts, lectures, cultural happenings, plays, and family activities. Tel: 928-774-4505; www.flagstaffchamber.com/winterfest-flagstaff.

Winterfest Jamboree (Lake Havasu City): This winter desert festival includes street fairs and powerboat races on Lake Havasu. Tel: 928-855-4115.

March

Bluegrass On the Beach (Lake Havasu City): This three-day celebration of bluegrass has moved from Parker to the shores of Lake Havasu City and features many top acts the first weekend in March. Tel: 2090785-4693; www.landspromotions.com/parkerhome.
National Festival of the West (Scottsdale): This huge four-day western festival features a western music jamboree, concerts, a huge trade show, western film festival, the Cowboy Spirit Award, a chuckwagon cookoff, mountain man rendezvous, cowboy mounted shooting, and Buffalo Soldiers re-enactment. Tel: 602-996-4387; www.festivalofthewest.com.
Heard Museum Guild Indian Fair and Market (Phoenix): Some of the best Indian arts and crafts in the West are on sale at this annual event, which also features Indian food, music, and dance. Tel: 602-252-8848; www.heard.org.
Ostrich Festival (Chandler): Includes ostrich racing, music, a parade, art exhibits, carnival rides, and an auto show. Tel: 480-963-4571; www.ostrichfestival.com.
Scottsdale Arts Festival (Scottsdale): This arts show features music and dance performances and crafts exhibitions. Tel: 480-994-2787; www.scottsdaleperformingarts.org.
Wa:k Powwow (Tucson): San Xavier del Bac Mission, south of Tucson, is the host for this Tohono O'odham celebration of Indian culture. Includes

inter-tribal dances, gourd dances, arts and crafts, food. Tel: 520-573-4000.

April

Culinary Festival (Scottsdale): Food and music are the draw at this downtown Scottsdale celebration. Tel: 480-945-7193; www. scottsdaleculinaryfestival.org.
Glendale Jazz and Blues Festival (Glendale): Glendale's longest running festival features national and local acts, artists-in-residence, arts and crafts, food, and wine tastings by local wineries. Tel: 623-930-2299; www.glendaleaz.com/events/jazzandbluesfestival.
International Mariachi Conference (Tucson): A week-long celebration of Mexican mariachi music, including workshops, concerts, an art exhibit, and a golf tournament. Tel: 520-838-3913; www.tucsonmariachi.org.
Maricopa County Fair (Phoenix): Entertainment, shopping, food booths, and a livestock fair are all part of the fun. Tel: 602-252-0717; www.maricopacountyfair.org.
Old West Founder's Days (Tombstone): A three-day festival that honors town founder Ed Schieffelin. The big deal is a re-enactment of the events leading up to the gunfight at the OK Corral at this Tombstone Old West extravaganza. Tel: 888-457-3929; www.tombstonechamber.com/founders-days.
Tucson Folk Festival (Tucson): Showcases national and regional musicians from Arizona and the Southwest and offers workshops, a gospel sing-along, a children's show, and food and craft booths. Tel: 520-319-8599; www.tkma.org.

National Park Passes

If you plan on visiting several parks on your vacation, consider buying a 12-month National Parks and Federal Recreational Lands Pass. The pass costs $80 and covers entrance fees to all federally managed parks (those managed by the National Park Service, the Bureau of Land Management, and the USDA Forest Service). It does not cover camping fees or other use fees, such as cave tours. Passes can be obtained at any park entrance station and one bonus is that fees will benefit the park where you purchase the pass. You may also purchase passes at www.store.usgs.gov/pass. For more information, call 1-888-275-8747.

Yaqui Easter (Tucson): Animistic beliefs and Christianity come together beautifully in this unique Easter celebration by Arizona's Yaqui Indian community, one of the not-to-be-missed events in the Indian year. Includes traditional Lent and Holy Week processions, re-enactments, and ceremonies merged into the nature-based Yaqui culture over the centuries. Highlights include a lenten all-night fiesta featuring the Yaqui deer dancer and Holy Week ceremonies including matachine dancers and a maypole. Tel: 520-791-4609; www.pascuayaqui-nsn.gov.

May

Cinco de Mayo (Phoenix and Tucson): Commemorating a key historic battle in Mexico's history of independence, this colorful celebration is one of the Southwest's most popular events, featuring folkloric dancing, mariachis, norteño music, and great food. Tel: 877-225-5149 (Phoenix); www.visitphoenix.com; 520-292-9326 (Tucson); www.visittucson.org.
Mountain Man Rendezvous (Williams): One of the oldest mountain men get-togethers in the West features an encampment and traditional activities such as leather work, carving, and weaponry. Tel: 928-635-1418; www.experiencewilliams.com.
Pine–Strawberry Arts and Crafts Festival (Pine): Down-home country crafts and community spirit are featured at this rural fest, with Navajo tacos served by the community center. Tel: 928-476-6537; www.pinestrawberryartscrafts.com.
Route 66 Fun Run Weekend (Seligman to Topock): Not a foot race but a classic car "run," with a festival in Kingman on Saturday that features Hualapai barbecue, booths, entertainment, and classic car judging, then a leisurely Sunday morning ride from Seligman to Topock on Route 66. Tel: 928-753-5001; www.azrt66.com.
Wyatt Earp Days (Tombstone): Gunfight re-enactments are the highlight of this Memorial Day fest, along with Old West costumes and arts and crafts. Tel: 520-457-3511; www.wyattearpdays.com.

June

Bluegrass Festival (Prescott): A summer solstice celebration of bluegrass featuring local bands. Tel: 928-445-2000; www.prescottbluegrassfestival.com.
Folk Arts Fair (Prescott): Gold panning, candle making, toy making, and other

kid-centered western arts and crafts at the Sharlott Hall Museum. Tel: 928-445-3122; www.sharlot.org.
Hon-Dah Powwow in the Pines (Pinetop): Tribes from the US and Canada get together to compete in fancy dances and grass dances on the grounds outside of a casino. Arts and crafts, food, and an Apache Sunrise dance. Tel: 800-929-8744; www.hon-dah.com.
Juneteenth Festival (Tucson): Gospel, blues, and folk music, dance, and a fun run are on the agenda at this festival at the Kennedy Park Fiesta Area. Tel: 520-883-5511.
Old Miners' Day (Chloride): The highlight of the year in the almost ghost town of Chloride is an Old West festival featuring a large parade, mock gunfights, vendors, pie-baking contests, a bake sale, raffle for door prizes, a 50-50, and food booths. Tel: 928-565-2204; www.chloridearizona.com/oldminersday.

July

Annual Hopi/Navajo Festivals of Arts and Culture (Flagstaff): The best of the best Indian artisans are featured at these popular juried shows at the Museum of Northern Arizona. Tel: 928-774-5213; www.musnaz.org.
Native American Arts and Crafts Festival (Pinetop-Lakeside): White Mountain Apache arts and crafts are featured. Tel: 928-367-4290; www.pinetoplakesidechamber.com.
Old West Days (Holbrook): Old West re-enactors, kids games, arts and crafts, food vendors, Bucket of Blood races, a quilt show, and a talent contest take place in downtown Holbrook. Tel: 928-524-6558; www.holbrookchamberofcommerce.com.
Pioneer Day Celebration (Snowflake): Snowflake's Mormon heritage is celebrated with arts and crafts and food booths. Tel: 928-536-4331; www.pioneer-days.com.

August

Fiesta de San Agustin (Tucson): A fiesta of live music, food, street dancing, and bullfighting honors Tucson's patron saint, Saint Augustine. Tel: 520-624-1817; www.tucsonsbirthday.org.
Norteño Music Festival and Street Fair (Tucson). One of the biggest music festivals in the Southwest celebrates northern Mexican music and rhythms. Tel: 520-622-2801.
Red Rocks Music Festival (Sedona): Chamber music concerts and workshops are offered by

internationally renowned musicians at this late August to Labor Day event. Tel: 877-733-7257; www. redrocksmusicfestival.com.

Southwest Wings Birding and Nature Festival (Sierra Vista): Arizona's longest-running nature festival is an educational celebration of the diversity of birds, mammals, reptiles, and insects, in the sky islands of southern Arizona. Tel: 520-226-0149; www.swwings.org.

Vigilante Days (Tombstone): A chilli cookoff, fun run, and street entertainment highlight, this Old West festival is sponsored by the Lions' Club. Tel: 520-457-3291; www. tombstonevigilantes.com.

September

Arizona Cowboy Poets' Gathering (Prescott): One of the biggest such gatherings in the West attracts the top cowboy poets in the nation. Tel: 928-445-3122; www.azcowboypoets.org.

Festival of Science (Flagstaff): A week of fascinating talks, presentations, and demonstrations by Flag's many scientists about topics from astronomy to geology and archaeology. Tel: 928-522-7090; www.scifest.org.

Fiesta del Tlaquepaque (Sedona): Mariachis, folkloric dancing, food, and continuous entertainment highlight this fiesta at Sedona's main arts and crafts marketplace. Tel: 520-282-4838; www.tlaq.com.

Gold Camp Days (Oatman): Entertainments include the international "Burro Bisket Toss" competition at this old mining community's annual celebration. Tel: 928-768-6222; www. oatmangoldroad.org.

Grand Canyon Music Festival (Grand Canyon): Internationally known classical musicians converge on the Grand Canyon for several weeks of chamber music concerts in the Shrine of the Ages Auditorium as well as blues concerts and an art show. Tel: 800-997-8285; www. grandcanyonmusicfest.org.

Navajo Nation Fair (Window Rock): The capital of the Navajo Nation is the location for the tribe's biggest fair of the year, including beauty pageant, a ProRodeo, Indian dance competitions, food, arts and crafts. Tel: 928-871-7055; www.navajonationfair.com.

White Mountain Apache Tribal Fair and Rodeo (Whiteriver): A Labor Day rodeo and powwow event in the White Mountains featuring cowboy skills, dances, arts and crafts, food, and entertainment. Tel: 928-338-4346; www.wmat.nsn.us.

October

Arizona State Fair (Phoenix): Fairground rides, concerts by big-name acts, livestock judging, food booths, and art shows are some of the attractions at this big fall month-long event. Tel: 602-252-6771; www. azstatefair.com.

Helldorado Days (Tombstone): Music, arts and crafts, a parade, a fashion show, a carnival, and gunfight re-enactments light up this Old West town. Tel: 520-457-9317; www. helldoradodays.com.

Jazz on the Rocks (Sedona): Internationally known jazz musicians are the big draw at this popular annual Jazzfest in the red rocks. Tel: 602-244-8444; www.sedonajazz.com.

London Bridge Days (Lake Havasu City): This annual celebration commemorates the 1968 dedication of the bridge in the desert with a parade, costume competitions, live entertainment, and other fun sponsored by the Rotary Club. Tel: 928-453-3444; www.golakehavasu.com.

Prescott Folk Music Festival (Prescott): Fiddle, banjo, guitar, harmonica, mandolin, dulcimer, plus singers, songwriters, and storytellers are highlighted in concerts on six stages at the Sharlot Hall Museum. Tel: 928-445-3122; www.sharlot.org.

Rex Allen Days (Willcox): Cowboy movie star Allen is honored each year with this celebration featuring a fair, rodeo, art show, and cowboy dancing. Tel: 520-384-2272; www. rexallendays.org.

Sedona Arts Festival (Sedona): A juried arts show among the red rocks. Tel: 928-204-9456; www. sedonaartsfestival.org.

Tucson Heritage Experience Festival (Tucson): More than 50 heritage and cultural associations provide food in El Presidio Park, along with music, dance, storytelling, and entertainment. Tel: 520-624-1817; www.visittucson.org.

November

Western Music Festival (Tucson): Dedicated to preserving the ways of the old cowboys, this international music festival celebrates music of the Old West. Tel: 520-743-9794; www. tucsonwesternmusicfestival.webs.com.

December

Christmas Mariachi Festival (Phoenix): Held at the US Airways Center, this extravaganza of Mexican musicians is hugely popular for the

What's On

Keeping up with the copious entertainment options throughout the state can be a daunting task. The Phoenix New Times (www. phoenixnewtimes.com), Flagstaff Live (www.flaglive.com), Sedona Monthly (www.sedonamonthly. com), and Tucson Weekly (www. tucsonweekly.com) are excellent resources with extensive music, club, and art listings. Consumer review sites such as Citysearch (www.citysearch.com), Yelp (www. yelp.com), and Chowhound (www. chowhound.com) are also useful, but take the commenter opinions with a grain of salt.

holidays. Tel: 480-558-1122; www. christmasmariachifestival.com.

Cowboy Christmas and Cowboy Poets' Gathering (Wickenburg): Cowboy poets, musicians, singers, and others involved in the ranch community get together annually to celebrate their way of life in this charming event. Includes a chuckwagon breakfast and a cowboy mass. Tel: 928-684-5479; www. wickenburgchamber.com.

Festival of the Arts (Tempe): Mill Avenue and the area around Arizona State University is the venue for this top-rated juried art show around the holidays each year. Tel: 602-997-2581; www.tempefestivalofthearts.com.

La Fiesta de Tumacacori (Tumacacori): Apache and Tohono O'odham Indian dancers, Mexican folkloric dancing, mariachi music, arts and crafts, food booths, and other entertainments draw thousands to the old Spanish mission and National Historical Park each Christmas. Tel: 520-398-2341; www.nps.gov/tuma.

Pueblo Grande Indian Market (Phoenix): Pueblo Grande Museum hosts this annual gathering of 200 Native American artisans from more than 50 tribes at South Mountain Park. Also includes singers, dancers, food booths. Tel: 602-495-0901; www.pgindianmarket.com.

THE ARTS

Theater, symphony, concerts, ballet, and art exhibitions can be found mainly in Phoenix and Tucson in central and southern Arizona, to a lesser extent in the northern Arizona communities of Flagstaff and Sedona and, seasonally, at the

Grand Canyon, which hosts a popular **Chamber Music Festival** every September (tel: 800-997-8285; www.grandcanyonmusicfest.org). In downtown Phoenix, **The Orpheum Theater** (www.orpheum-theater.com) is the place to catch dance productions and big-ticket performers and comedians, while **The Phoenix Symphony Hall** (tel: 602-495-1999; www.phoenixsymphony.org) has a steady schedule of classical music and operas. The University of Arizona in Tucson and Arizona State University in Phoenix are cultural hubs. Touring Broadway shows are held at Frank Lloyd Wright's last major venue, **Grady Gammage Memorial Auditorium** at ASU (tel: 480-965-5062; www.asugammage.com), and soul, jazz, world, classical music and more fill **Centennial Hall** on the UA campus (tel: 520-621-3341; www.uapresents.org). Flagstaff has a symphony (tel: 928-774-5107; www.flagstaffsymphony.org), as well as pop and rock performances at its own **Orpheum Theater** (tel: 928-556-1580; www.orpheumpresents.com). Winter brings chamber music to Sedona (tel: 928-204-2415; www.chambermusicsedona.org). Many of Arizona's smaller towns, pioneer communities, and Indian reservations have seasonal festivals of the arts and music, where you'll find even more cultural offerings.

NIGHTLIFE

Casinos

New casinos have been opening at a steady clip on reservations throughout the state, with 15 tribes operating 22 venues at last count. Harrah's manages the **Ak-Chin's** casino, less

Buying Tickets

The easiest way to reserve and pay for tickets is simply to call up the relevant box office or go to the venue's website and pay by credit card. Sometimes, however, you will be required to make ticket purchases through brokers and agencies such as Ticketmaster (tel: 800-745-3000; www.ticketmaster.com), Ticketweb (tel: 866-777-8932; www.ticketweb.com), and StubHub (www.stubhub.com). Unfortunately, commission and convenience fees of more than $5 per ticket almost always apply.

Shopping Malls

There are several popular outlet malls in Arizona, notably at Oak Creek in northern Arizona (tel: 928-284-2150), famed retailer Nordstrom's Last Chance outlet in Phoenix (tel: 602-248-2843; www.nordstrom.com), and Foothills Mall in Tucson (tel: 928-526-4827; www.shopfoothillsmall.com). More traditional malls include the Flagstaff Mall along Route 66 (tel: 928-526-4827; www.flagstaffmall.com), Prescott Gateway (tel: 928-442-3659; www.theprescottgatewaymall.com), Scottsdale's enormous Fashion Square (tel: 480-941-2140; www.fashionsquare.com), and Tucson's outdoor luxury mall La Encantada (tel: 520-615-2561; www.laencantadashoppingcenter.com).

than an hour's drive from Phoenix in Maricopa (tel: 800-427-7247; www.harrahsakchin.com). The **Pima-Maricopa's Casino Arizona** has two locations, on the north and south sides of Scottsdale (tel: 480-850-7777; www.casinoaz.com). On the outskirts of Tucson, the Pascua Yaqui tribe runs **Casion del Sol** and **Casino of the Sun** (tel: 800-344-9435; www.solcasinos.com) and the Tohono O'odham nation runs two casinos under the **Desert Diamond** banner and one called **Golden Ha:saň** (tel: 520-294-7777; www.ddcaz.com). For a full list, visit the Arizona Department of Gaming at www.gm.state.az.us/casinos.

Comedy Venues

Celebrity comics often sell out Phoenix's **Orpheum Theater** (see above). The journeymen and up-and-comers take the smaller stages at the Tempe branch of the **Improv** (tel: 480-921-9877; www.tempeimprov.info), as well as Scottsdale's **Comedy Spot** (tel: 480-945-4422; www.thecomedyspot.net), **Stand-up, Scottsdale!** (tel: 480-882-0730; www.standupscottsdale.com), and family-friendly **Jester'Z Improv** (tel: 480-423-1020; www.jesterzimprov.com). In Tucson, **Laff's Comedy Caffe** (tel: 520-323-8669; www.laffstucson.com) has weekly open mic nights and a new headliner every weekend.

Gay and Lesbian Venues

Most of the clubs and bars popular with the LGBT community are found in metropolitan areas. Raucous bunches descend on **Amsterdam** (tel: 602-258-6122) and a country-western crowd gathers at **Cash Inn Country** (tel: 602-244-9943; www.cashinncountry.net), both in Phoenix. In Tucson, lesbians dance and sing karaoke at **Ain't Nobody's Biz** (tel: 520-318-4838; www.thebiztuc.com), while **IBT's** (tel: 520-882-3053; www.ibtstucson.com) is popular with gay

men. For a listing of clubs and gay-friendly businesses throughout the state, visit www.gayarizona.com.

Live Music

Char's Has the Blues (tel: 602-230-0205; www.charshastheblues.com) and the **Rhythm Room** (tel: 602-265-4842; www.rhythmroom.com) are the cornerstones of the blues, rock, and R&B scenes in Phoenix. Tempe welcomes a hard-rock and alternative crowd at the **Marquee Theatre** (tel: 480-829-0607; www.luckymanonline.com) while Scottsdale country music fans fill **Handlebar-J** (tel: 480-948-0110; www.handlebarj.com) for line-dancing and live acts. In Tucson, tiki-bar **The Hut** (tel: 520-623-3200; www.huttucson.com) hosts an eclectic mix of bluegrass, surf-guitar, and world music, while **Plush** (tel: 520-798-1298; www.plushtucson.com) caters to indie rockers and the proudly divey **Boondock Lounge** showcases blues bands and singer-songwriters (tel: 520-690-0991; www.boondockslounge.com). Tucson jazz aficionados catch dinner and a show at **Cushing Street** (tel: 520-622-7984; www.cushingstreet.com) and **Kingfisher** (tel: 520-323-7739; www.kingfishertucson.com). Many of the area's casinos also book touring singers and bands.

Nightclubs

Opinions about dance clubs can be contentious, though many agree **Revolver Lounge** (tel: 480-946-2005, www.revolverlounge.com) is the swankiest place to dance in Scottsdale. **Club Congress** (tel: 520-622-8848; www.hotelcongress.com/club) in Tucson has great live acts, but also club nights that cater to folks who actually remember the 80s.

Pubs and Bars

There are countless watering holes throughout the state worth hanging your hat in. A few favorites include the two **Postino Wine Bars** in Phoenix (tel: 602-852-3939 and 602-274-5144; www.postinowinecafe.com), the **Four Peaks Brewpub** (tel: 480-303-9967; www.fourpeaks.com) in Tempe, Tucson's oldest bar **Buffet** (tel: 520-623-6811; www.thebuffetbar.com), and the **Monte Vista Cocktail Lounge** (tel: 928-774-2403; www.hotelmontevista.com/MVLounge) in a historic Flagstaff hotel.

SHOPPING

What to Buy

You'll find both the most cutting-edge and the most traditional art in this diverse state, depending on your interests. Sedona is one of the top art centers in the country. There are also numerous galleries highlighting sculpture, paintings, and other works by nationally known artists in Red Rock Country and the Old Town neighborhood in Scottsdale. Traditional homespun pioneer arts are alive and well throughout Arizona, particularly in mountain towns, where women continue to practice the old-time crafts of quilting, spinning and weaving, pie-making, and putting up preserves.

For most people, the main thrill is buying arts and crafts made by members of Arizona's Indian tribes. Each of the reservations offers places to buy locally made wares. Tribes specialize in different crafts, including woven rugs, sand paintings, *kachinas*, basketry, pottery, inlaid jewelry, beading, carving, and folk art from found materials. (See page 194 for more information.)

The Phoenix area is well known for winter production of citrus, as well as, increasingly, artisan foods such as locally raised and produced goat cheese, grass-fed beef, organically grown tomatoes, greens, and herbs. Wines from several up-and-coming vineyards in the Patagonia-Sonoita area, south of Tucson, also make excellent gifts.

Where to Shop

For sheer quantity and choice, Phoenix is still Arizona's top destination for shopping. You'll find several excellent malls and shopping centers, where you can stroll and discover unique designer clothing and gifts, stock up on basics, and even, at the internationally renowned **Biltmore Fashion Park** (tel: 602-955-8400; www.shopbiltmore.com), enjoy a weekly farmers' market. Scottsdale is well known for its Old West and contemporary art galleries as well as the state's largest concentration of shops. Tucson is the place for all things Mexican and has a popular arts cooperative in its El Presidio historic downtown area, where you can explore adobe buildings, just as in Old Mexico, and meet the artists.

In northern Arizona, **Tlaquepaque Marketplace** and the galleries spread throughout Sedona specialize in contemporary southwestern art (tel: 928-282-4838; www.tlaq.com). You'll also find the state's largest collection of New Age items, such as crystals, guidebooks to local vortexes, and numerous alternative wellness services. T-shirts dyed in Sedona's red-rock mud are on sale in many commercial stores. In Flagstaff, contemporary pioneer and Southwest-inspired creations such as split-twig figurine jewelry, innovative weavings, stained glass, and quilts can be found at **The Artists Gallery** on San Francisco Street (tel: 928-773-0958; www.flagstaffartistsgallery.com). A branch of the excellent second-hand bookstore **Bookman's** adjoins Northern Arizona University (tel: 928-774-0005; www.bookmans.com). You're also close enough to the Navajo and Hopi Indian reservations here to find excellent kachinas, rugs, baskets, pots, and silver jewelry by Indian artists at several stores along Route 66 and on San Francisco Street.

Indian Arts

Wherever you are in Arizona, simply head out to the reservations. You will find historic trading posts, such as **Cameron Trading Post** (tel: 800-338-7385; www.camerontradingpost.com) just north of Flagstaff on Highway 89 and national historic site **Hubbell Trading Post** near the New Mexico border (tel: 928-755-3254; www.nps.gov/hutr). Local Indian-made arts and crafts abound at tribally owned arts cooperatives, such as **Jerome Artists Cooperative Gallery** not far from Prescott (tel: 928-639-4276; www.jeromecoop.com), the **Colorado River Indian Tribes Library/Museum** just south of Lake Havasu (tel: 902-669-9211, ext 335; www.crit-nsn.gov) and **Navajo Arts and Crafts Enterprise** (tel: 520-871-4090; www.gonavajo.com). Each of the Hopi mesas specializes in a different craft, which can be bought directly from the artisan, local stores, or the **Hopi Cultural Center** on Second Mesa (tel: 928-734-2401; www.hopiculturalcenter.com). The White Mountain and San Carlos Apache of eastern Arizona are known for their leatherwork, beading, and basketry. The **White Mountain Apache center of Whiteriver** (tel: 928-338-4346; www.wmat.nsn.us) has arts and crafts for sale. Between Phoenix and Tucson, colorful pottery by the Maricopa may be found on the **Gila Indian Reservation** (tel: 602-963-3981; www.gilariver.org) and at gift shops at **Wild Horse Pass Resort** in Chandler (tel: 480-502-5600; www.wildhorsepass.com). In southern Arizona, fine Tohono O'odham basketry is sold at the **Tohono O'odham Cultural Center and Museum** (tel: 520-383-0211; www.tonation-nsn.gov), southwest of Tucson, and at the **Arizona-Sonora Desert Museum** in Tucson (tel: 520-883-1380; www.desertmuseum.org). Even roadside and in-home vendors, such as **Garland's Navajo Rugs** in Sedona (tel: 928-282-4070; www.garlandsrugs.com) and **D. Y. Begay's Weaving Studios** in Tselani and Scottsdale (tel: 602-538-5339), are worth a quick detour. If you're unable to visit the reservations, the **Museum of Northern Arizona** in Flagstaff (tel: 928-774-5213; www.musnaz.org) and the **Heard Museum** in Phoenix and its branches (tel: 602-346-

Parks and Historic Sites

With three national parks, six national forests, 15 national monuments and memorials, two national recreation areas, and five national historic parks, sites and trails, not to mention dozens of state and local properties, Arizona is certainly not wanting for public lands. Begin your explorations by consulting the National Park Service (www.nps.gov/state/az) and the National Forest Service (www.fs.usda.gov). A full listing of state parks and services, including camping, fishing, and festival information, is available from the Arizona State Parks Office in Phoenix (tel: 602-542-4174; www.pr.state.az.us). For an up-to-date compendium of sites that have been granted national historic landmark status, refer to the National Historic Landmarks Program (www.nps.gov/nhl/designations/listsofnhls.htm). The Bureau of Land Management (tel: 800-637-9152; www.blm.gov/az) is yet another source of excellent information on public property.

8190; www.heard.org) are excellent places to buy authenticated Indian art pieces. Each museum has annual Indian marketplaces where you can buy juried pieces.

Souvenirs

Among Arizona's unique gifts are the copper bells designed by architect Paolo Soleri and manufactured and offered for sale at the experimental futuristic Soleri villages of **Arcosanti** and **Cosanti** (tel: 928-632-7135; www.arcosanti.org). Gifts inspired by Prairie Architecture founder Frank Lloyd Wright can be purchased at his former home and school at **Taliesin West** in Scottsdale (tel: 480-860-2700; www.franklloydwright.org) and **Biltmore Fashion Park** at the Arizona Biltmore Hotel on Camelback Road (tel: 602-955-6600; www.arizonabiltmore.com), which he helped design. Pottery made by Mark Arnegard can be purchased from **Arne Ceramics** on Route 66 (tel: 928-779-0429; www.arneceramics.com), just west of downtown Flagstaff. The art centers at Sedona (tel: 928-282-3809; www.sedonaartscenter.com) and Tubac (tel: 520-398-2371; www.tubacarts.org) each have excellent gift shops. You'll also find pottery aplenty in the former mining towns of Bisbee (try Poco Loco; tel: 520-432-7020) and Jerome, which have now been taken over by artists. Pick up cowboy duds at **Spur Western Wear** in Tombstone (tel: 520-457-9000; www.spurwesternwear.com) and classics of southwestern literature at the wonderfully jumbled **Singing Wind Bookstore** in Benson (tel: 520-586-2425). **Visions Fine Art** in Sedona (tel: 928-203-0022; www.visionsfineart.com) has an exhaustive catalog of modern works, and a rotating collection of legendary Arizona artist Ted DeGrazia's paintings, drawings, sculptures, ceramics, and jewelery can be viewed and purchased at **DeGrazia's Gallery** in the Sun (tel: 520-299-9191; www.degrazia.org).

Food

Food lovers will want to bring home a taste of the Southwest. In southern Arizona, **El Charro** (tel: 520-622-1922; www.elcharrocafe.com), the country's oldest Mexican restaurant, sells its salsas in jars, along with other chilli-infused items. Prickly pear cactus jellies and syrups made by the Tohono O'odham Indians are on sale at the **Arizona Sonora Desert Museum** (tel: 520-883-1380; www.desertmuseum.org), which holds an annual Tohono O'odham fall harvest festival. At farmers' markets throughout

Spring Training: Where to See Your Favorite Team

As many as 1.2 million fans have attended spring training games in southern Arizona in one season. Below is a list of where US baseball teams do their spring training. Locations do change periodically, so check www.cactusleague.com before heading to the ball park.
Anaheim Angels, Tempe Diablo Stadium, Tempe; tel: 480-350-5205; www.tempe.gov/diablo
Arizona Diamondbacks, Salt River Fields, Talking Stick; tel: 480-270-5000; www.saltriverfields.com
Chicago Cubs, Hohokam Park, Mesa; tel: 480-644-4451; www.hohokamstadium.com
Chicago White Sox, Camelback Ranch, Glendale; tel: 623-302-5000; www.camelbackranchbaseball.com
Cincinnati Reds, Goodyear Ballpark, Goodyear. tel: 623-882-3130; www.goodyearaz.gov
Cleveland Indians, Goodyear Ballpark, Goodyear. tel: 623-882-3130; www.goodyearaz.gov
Colorado Rockies, Salt River Fields,

Talking Stick; tel: 480-270-5000; www.saltriverfields.com
Kansas City Royals, Surprise Recreation Campus, Surprise; tel: 623-222-2222; www.surpriseaz.gov
Los Angeles Dodgers, Camelback Ranch, Glendale; tel: 623-302-5000; www.camelbackranchbaseball.com
Milwaukee Brewers, Maryvale Baseball Park, Phoenix; tel: 623-245-5500; www.phoenix.gov/sports/marystad.html
Oakland Athletics, Phoenix Municipal Stadium; tel: 602-392-0074; www.phoenix.gov/sports/phxmuni.html
San Diego Padres, Peoria Sports Complex, Phoenix; tel: 623-773-8720; www.peoriasportscomplex.com
San Francisco Giants, Scottsdale Stadium; tel: 480-312-2856; www.scottsdaleaz.gov/stadium
Seattle Mariners, Peoria Sports Complex, Phoenix; tel: 623-773-8720; www.peoriasportscomplex.com
Texas Rangers, Surprise Recreation Campus, Surprise; tel: 623-222-2222; www.surpriseaz.gov

the state and some delicatessens, you'll find local goat cheese from **Black Mesa Ranch in the White Mountains** (tel: 928-536-7759; www.blackmesaranchonline.com); olive oil from olives grown at **Queen Creek Olive Farm and Mill** (tel: 480-888-9290; www.queencreekolivemill.com), southeast of Phoenix; organic tomatoes raised near Bisbee; grass-fed beef from Date Creek Ranch, Wickenburg (tel: 928-231-0704; www.datecreekranch.com); and fresh-pressed apple cider from **Stout Mills** in Willcox (tel: 520-384-3696; www.cidermill.com), among other "locavore" items. These make superb picnic fare while traveling or for a special Taste of Arizona carry-on meal on the plane ride home. Remember to eat them up before landing, though. Customs will require you to dispose of any fresh items.

SPORTS

Outdoor Activities
Hiking

It would be a shame to visit Arizona's stunning low and high desert country and not get out on a trail and hike, no matter what your fitness level. Trails for all levels of walker can be found

throughout the state, from strolls on urban trails, botanical gardens, and resort grounds in Tucson and Phoenix to challenging backcountry hiking in the Grand Canyon and other national, state, city, and tribal parks and national forests.

Ranger-led hikes on public lands are a great way to learn about the desert and stay safe in an unfamiliar landscape. The Sierra Club also offers guided hikes on weekends in many venues; contact their local chapter to find out what is happening in your local area (tel: 602-253-8633; www.arizona.sierraclub.org). Winter is the best time to hike in the low desert; summer in the high country.

Seasoned desert hikers set out in the cool post-dawn hours during the hot summer season and return by late morning; heat builds up in Arizona's rocks throughout the afternoon and continues to radiate into the surrounding landscape even after sunset, so evening hikes remain quite warm even though you are out of the direct sun.

Take precautions. Bring a quart (1 liter) of water for a short hike, a gallon (4 liters) for a full day out, and eat salty, high-energy snacks. Wear sturdy, supportive hiking shoes, a broad-brimmed hat, high SPF factor sunscreen, sunglasses, and breathable fabrics that can be rolled down to cover exposed skin.

Cycling

Several organizations provide information on trails, races, group tours, and other events. The Greater Arizona Bicycling Association (www. bikegaba.org) and the Arizona Bicycle Club (www.azbikeclub.com) have chapters throughout the state.

Mountain Biking

Mountain bikers are a more rugged breed than cyclists, and the steep and dusty trails of Arizona attract some of the world's best. For trail information, race and ride listings, classes, and volunteer opportunities contact The Mountain Bike Association of Arizona (www.mbaa.net). Visit Mountain Bike Arizona (www.mountainbikeaz.com) for user-submitted trail descriptions and the Southern Mountain Bike Association (tel: 520-358-4438, www.sambabike.org) to participate in organized rides.

Fishing

Fishing licenses are required and can be obtained from the Arizona Game and Fish Department (2222 W. Greenway Road, Phoenix, AZ 85023; tel: 602-942-3000; www.azgfd. gov). Fishing on the White Mountain Apache Indian Reservation (Wildlife and Outdoor Recreation Division, PO Box 220, Whiteriver, AZ 85941; tel: 928-338-4385; www.wmatoutdoors. org) and San Carlos Apache Indian Reservation (PO Box 1240, San Carlos, AZ 85550; tel: 928-475-2343; www.sancarlosapache.com) require a tribal fishing license.

Kayaking, Canoeing, Rafting

Arizona offers an abundance of both whitewater and flatwater paddling. For information on routes and conditions, consult the agency that manages the river or lake. Other sources of information are paddling clubs and outdoor gear retailers. For Grand Canyon outfitters and information, visit the Grand Canyon River Outfitters Association at www.gcroa.org.

Skiing

Arizona has four downhill skiing areas. Arizona Snowbowl is only 14 miles (22.5km) from Flagstaff and will be the first resort in the state to have snowmaking (tel: 928-779-1951; www.arizonasnowbowl.com). For a smaller option in the Flagstaff area, skiers sometimes choose Elk Ridge in Williams (tel: 928-814-5038; www. elkridgeski.com). On the east-central

border of the state is the largest ski resort, Sunrise Park, which has 65 trails (tel: 928-735-7669; www. sunriseskipark.com). Residents of Tucson take to the slopes at Ski Valley in Mount Lemmon (tel: 520-576-1321; www.skithelemmon.com). For cross-country skiing, Flagstaff Nordic Center (tel: 928-220-0550; www.flagstaffnordiccenter.com) has 25 miles (40km) of groomed trails, instruction, and equipment rentals.

Birding

Arizona – the southern region in particular – is a legendary birding destination, with hundreds of species spotted and popular yearly ornithological celebrations (see Festivals, above). Phoenix is home to the local chapter of the Audubon Society (tel: 602-468-6470; az.audubon.org). Visit the Arizona Field Ornithologists' website (www.azfo.org) for articles, report sightings, checklists and more. You can also join in the many birding events organized by the Southeastern Arizona Bird Observatory (tel: 520-432-1388; www.sabo.org).

Participant Sports

Golf

There are scores of public and private golf courses as well as full-fledged golf resorts throughout the state. For a complete list, contact the Arizona Golf Association (7226 N. 16th Street, Suite 200, Phoenix, AZ 85020; tel: 602-944-3035; www.azgolf.org) or pick up a copy of Golf Arizona magazine (www. golfarizonamagazine.com).

Tennis

There are public tennis courts in just about every city and large town in Arizona, though avid players may find it more convenient to stay in a hotel with courts. Contact the city or county Parks and Recreation Department for locations and hours. For information on tournaments, lessons, and leagues, contact the Arizona Tennis Association (7335 E. Indian Plaza, Suite 124, Scottsdale, AZ 85251; tel: 480-970-0599; www.arizonatennis.org).

Spectator Sports

Professional and amateur football, baseball, golf, hockey, auto racing, and horse and dog racing take place exclusively in Phoenix and Tucson. The rest of the state is rural: spectator sports here are most likely to be exciting PRCA-rate pro rodeos. Details are noted below in the sporting event calendar and in a special box on

Baseball Spring Training. For general information on Arizona sports news and schedules, visit www.azcentral.com.

Sporting Events

January

Rillito Park (Tucson): Horse racing in Tucson takes place at this track on First Avenue throughout the winter season. Tel: 520-293-5011; www. rillitodowns.com.

Tostito's Fiesta Bowl (Tempe): One of the major college football bowl games and part of the Bowl Championship Series. Tel: 480-350-0911; www. fiestabowl.org.

Waste Management Phoenix Open (Scottsdale): Played on picturesque TPC Golf Course in Scottsdale, this PGA golf tournament (formerly the **FBR Open Golf Tournament**) is one of the oldest and most revered. Tel: 602-870-0163; www. wastemanagementphoenixopen.com.

February

All-Arabian Horse Show (Scottsdale): Arabian horses strut their stuff at this event, the largest of its kind in the world. Tel: 480-515-1500; www. scottsdaleshow.com.

Cactus League Baseball Spring Training (various venues): Games are held in February and March. For information about teams and venues, see box. For information on current schedule, check with www. cactusleague.com.

Parada del Sol and Rodeo (Scottsdale): A Jaycee fundraiser at WestWorld that includes a three-day PRCA-sanctioned rodeo with five performances. Tel: 480-990-3179; www.paradadelsol.us.

Scottish Highland Games (Phoenix): The caber toss, pipes and drums, dance, and other Celtic events highlight this popular event for kilt fans. Tel: 602-431-0095; www. arizonascots.com.

Silver Spur Rodeo (Yuma): A PRCA pro-rodeo sponsored by the Jaycees, followed by cowboy dancing. Tel: 928-344-5451; www.yumajaycees.org/rodeo.

Tucson Rodeo – La Fiesta de los Vaqueros (Tucson): Bareback riding, steer wrestling, saddle bronco riding, tie-down roping, team roping, bull riding, and women's barrel racing are the highlights at this big winter rodeo. Tel: 520-741-2233; www. tucsonrodeo.com.

March

Accenture Match Play Tournament (Marana): Annual PGA event held in the Tucson area. Tel: 520-572-8000;

www.pgatour.com.
Arizona Rattlers (Phoenix): The Arena league football team plays home games at downtown Phoenix's US Airways Center from March to July. Tel: 480-985-3292; www.azrattlers.com.
RR Donnelly Founder's Cup (Phoenix): Women golfers compete at this new LPGA tournament in the Phoenix area each spring. Tel: 386-274-6200; www.lpga.com/lpgafounderscup.aspx.

April

Arizona Diamondbacks (Phoenix): Arizona's major league baseball team, and 2001 World Series Champion, plays regular season home games at Chase Field from April to September. Tel: 602-514-8400; www.dbacks.com.

May

Whiskey Row Marathon (Prescott): One of the toughest marathons in the US attracts runners from all over the country. Also includes a half-marathon, a 10K, and a 2-mile (3km) fun run. Tel: 928-445-7221; www.whiskeyrowmarathon.com.

June

Grand Canyon State Summer Games (Phoenix): The multi-sport, multi-age games attract amateur athletes from throughout Arizona. Native American games take place at Fort McDowell. Tel: 480-517-9700; www.gcsg.org.
Phoenix Mercury (Phoenix): The women's professional basketball team, and two-time WNBA champion, plays home games at downtown Phoenix's US Airways Center from June to September. Tel: 602-252-9622; www.wnba.com/mercury.
Pine Country Pro Rodeo (Flagstaff): A long-running event in northern Arizona's capital featuring rodeo events. Tel: 928-526-3556.

July

Cowpunchers Reunion Rodeo (Williams): Real cowboys test their skills at this Old West rodeo event in the pines. Tel: 928-635-1418; www.azcowpunchers.com.
Prescott Frontier Days Rodeo (Prescott): Considered the oldest rodeo in the West, this famous gathering draws cowboys from all over the country and also has fireworks, a parade, and a cowboy golf tournament. Tel: 928-445-3103; www.worldsoldestrodeo.com.

August

Arizona Amateur Championship (various): A popular tournament

among enthusiastic amateur golfers. Tel: 602-944-3035; www.azgolf.org.
World's Oldest Continuous Rodeo (Payson): Another contender for world's oldest rodeo, Payson pulls out the stops for its biggest event of the year. Tel: 928-474-5242; www.paysonrimcountry.com.

September

Arizona Cardinals (Phoenix): The NFL team plays home games at University of Phoenix Stadium from September to January. Tel: 800-999-1402; www.azcardinals.com.
Arizona State University Sun Devils (Tempe): The ASU varsity football team plays at Sun Devil Stadium from September to December. Tel: 480-727-0000; www.thesundevils.com.
University of Arizona Wildcats (Tucson): The UA varsity football team plays at Arizona Stadium on the UA campus. Tel: 520-621-2287; www.arizonawildcats.com.
Phoenix Greyhound Park (Phoenix): Located just north of Sky Harbor International Airport, this popular track offers nightly greyhound racing year round and betting from locations all over Phoenix. Fine dining and meeting rooms. Tel: 602-273-7181; www.phoenixgreyhoundpark.com.
Tucson Greyhound Park (Tucson): Year round greyhound racing and betting can be found in Tucson at this greyhound park. Tel: 520-884-7576; www.tucsongreyhound.com.

October

Phoenix Coyotes (Glendale): The NHL hockey team plays at the Jobing.com Arena from October through April. Tel: 480-563-7825; www.phoenixcoyotes.com.
Phoenix Suns (Phoenix): The NBA team plays physical, fast-paced basketball games at US Airways Center from October to April. Tel: 602-379-7867; www.nba.com/suns.
Turf Paradise Race Course (Phoenix): Located just north of Sky Harbor International Airport, this horse racing venue has horse racing from 1pm to 6pm daily from October through May. Restaurant, sports bar, family picnic park. Tel: 602-942-1101; www.turfparadise.com.

November

El Tour de Tucson Bicycle Race (Tucson): One of the largest perimeter bicycling event in the US, this charity fundraiser bike race is a very popular spectator event. Tel: 520-745-2033; www.pbaa.com.
Phoenix International Raceway (Phoenix): The Kobalt 500 NASCAR

race is held at this auto raceway outside Phoenix every November. Tel: (866) 408-7223; www.phoenixraceway.com.

December

Arizona and Livestock Show and Rodeo (Phoenix): The last rodeo of the year is one of the biggest. Followed directly by the Arizona National Horse Show in January. Tel: 602-258-8568; www.anls.org.

SIGHTSEEING TOURS AND EXCURSIONS

Specialist Holidays

Clubs, organizations, and tour operators offer countless themed itineraries throughout the state. **Old Pueblo Archaeology Center** in Tucson (tel: 520-798-1201; www.oldpueblo.org) and the **Archaeological Conservancy** in Albuquerque, New Mexico (tel: 505-266-1540; www.americanarchaeology.com) run trips to important ancient Pueblo sites. The **Grand Canyon Field Institute** (tel: 866-471-4435; www.grandcanyon.org/fieldinstitute) specializes in hikes that educate on the nature, people and geology of the park. To visit little-seen parts of the state by bike or kayak, book a single or multi-day trip with Scottdale's **Arizona Outback Adventures** (tel: 480-945-2881; www.aoa-adventures.com). **High Lonesome Eco Tours** out of Sierra Vista run birding tours (tel: 443-838-6589; www.hilonesometours.com). Serious duffers can find package deals in Tucson and Phoenix through **Golfpac** (tel: 888-848-8941; www.golfpactravel.com).

Guided Tours

Active families will find multiple options for hiking, biking, and kayaking through the state from **Backroads** (tel: 800-462-2848; www.backroads.com) and **Off the Beaten Path** (tel: 800-445-2995; www.offthebeatenpath.com). **Elderhostel** (tel: 800-454-5768; www.roadscholar.org) and **Smithsonian Journeys** (tel: 877-338-8687; www.smithsonianjourneys.org) offer a variety of trips with an educational bent. **OARS** (tel: 800-346-6277; www.oars.com) is the best known rafting company on the Colorado, but all licensed rafting outfitters can be found through the **Grand Canyon River Outfitters Association** (www.gcroa.org).

A – Z

A HANDY SUMMARY OF PRACTICAL
INFORMATION, ARRANGED ALPHABETICALLY

A

Admission Charges

Entrance fees at most attractions and museums typically range from $5–20/person, with discounts often available for children aged 12 or younger, senior citizens aged 65 and older, and families of 4 or more. Visit www.arizonaguide.com to find regularly updated deals on food, attractions, activities, lodging and more.

B

Budgeting for Your Trip

The financial crisis has left currencies in constant flux. The euro and pound won't go as far as they used to in the United States but Arizona is still a much more affordable destination than New York City and other tourist magnets. Allow $100–150 per day for good-quality hotels for two people, although really memorable hotels and bed-and-breakfasts tend to run you closer to $200 per night. At the other end of the spectrum, Arizona has attractive national forest, desert, and lakeside campgrounds with full facilities for $5–20 per night, and hostels and very bare bones motel lodging can be found for less than $50. You can probably get away with $40 per day per person for basic meals if you stick to diners, cafes, markets, and inexpensive restaurants and don't drink alcohol. Meals in better restaurants cost a lot more (see Restaurant sections at the end

of relevant chapters for a guide) but if you're determined to visit that famous high-end establishment and don't have the cash, one insider trick is to eat lunch there: you'll find many of the items on the dinner menu at much lower prices and still get to say you've eaten at a hip eatery. Budget at least $4 per gallon for gas costs for your rental car; most economy vehicles get approximately 30 miles (48km) per gallon. Light rail, buses, and other public transportation in cities like Phoenix and Tucson are just a few dollars per ride, allowing you to get around for much less.

C

Children

The Grand Canyon can turn us all into wide-eyed youngsters, but it is just one of many sites that appeals to kids. Cowboy towns with staged shootouts, water parks, chuck wagons, powwows, horseback riding and rafting trips are all sure to please. Reduced admission rates at many museums and attractions (usually for those under 12) make budgeting a little easier. Still, parents might need some time to themselves. Many higher-end hotels and resorts can contact babysitting services. Some even provide the occasional "Parents' Night Out" where children are entertained with group activities while Mom and Dad hit the town.

Climate

Temperature: Arizona spans half a dozen climate and life zones, but by

and large, you will find sunny skies, low humidity, and limited precipitation. Climate varies widely with elevation. Climbing 1,000ft (300 metres) is equivalent to traveling 300 miles (500km) northward. In temperature, traveling from the lowest to the highest points in Arizona is like traveling from Mexico to the north of Hudson Bay in Canada. In Tucson, for example, it's possible to sun yourself at the poolside in the morning and ski atop nearby Mount Lemmon in the afternoon.

When to Visit

The northern region averages around 73 percent sunshine; the southern part of the state averages around 90 percent. Yearly rainfall averages 12ins (30cm); much of it falls in brief, intense thunderstorms during the summer "monsoon" season, when dry washes (arroyos) and narrow canyons are prone to flash floods and dangerous to travelers. Wind velocity

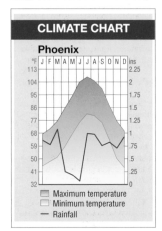

CLIMATE CHART

Phoenix

- Maximum temperature
- Minimum temperature
- Rainfall

in cities is under 8mph (13kmh), although exposed and high-elevation areas tend to be gusty.

Average temperatures in low-elevation Phoenix and Tucson reach 100°F (38°C) in summer and fall, but often soar to 110°F (43°C) or higher for long periods. Nights are warm and pleasant, usually ranging from 65°F (18°C) to 75°F (24°C). Winter and early spring are the ideal seasons to visit Phoenix and Tucson, with average daytime temperatures from 65°F (18°C) to 75°F (24°C); night time temperatures dip into the 30s°F (below zero °C). It's not unknown for southern Arizona to experience a frigid snap with snowfall in January. Come prepared. Phoenix gets about 7ins (18cm) of rain per year. Tucson, at a slightly higher elevation, gets 11ins (28cm).

It's a very different story in Flagstaff, capital of northern Arizona, 145 miles (230km) to the north at the base of the San Francisco Peaks, the highest mountains in the state. Temperatures here range from 75°F to 80°F (24°C to 27°C) in summer and fall to around 15°F (-10°C) in winter. Due to a long-running drought, annual precipitation in Flagstaff now averages 12.5ins (30cm), most of it falling in July, August, and January. Winter is very cold but generally sunny, with deep snows falling at times. Average snowfall at the Arizona Snowbowl in the San Francisco Peaks is 260ins (660cm). Spring is a mixed blessing in northern Arizona, bringing with it strong winds, as the jetstream changes direction from the northwest to the south, via the Gulf of California, the sources of those tropical storms in summer.

At its hottest, the South Rim of the Grand Canyon reaches 90°F (32°C). Temperatures run about 20°F (11°C) hotter at Phantom Ranch at the bottom along the Colorado River. Flash flooding is common during the monsoon season.

The weather is more comfortable and the crowds generally lighter in spring and fall, with average daytime highs from 65°F (18°C) to 75°F (24°C). Nights are chilly.

Winter is quiet at the South Rim, although rooms may be hard to come by over the Christmas holiday, when El Tovar and other hotels put on special activities. Temperatures slip below freezing nightly, and snowstorms are common, although this can be a great time to do a river trip in the Grand Canyon, which stays relatively warm and mild. Expect icy conditions on roads and trails and occasional road closings due to snow.

ABOVE: when in the desert, be sure to wear appropriate clothing (including a hat) and plenty of sunscreen to protect your skin.

The North Rim is about 1,000ft (300 meters) higher than the South Rim and is significantly cooler and breezier, with summer highs around 75°F (24°C). Evening and morning can be nippy, even in summer. The North Rim is blanketed with as much as 200ins (510cm) of snow in winter and is closed from mid-October to mid-May.

What to Wear

Think cool and comfortable. With few exceptions, western dress is informal. A pair of jeans or slacks, a polo or button-down shirt, and boots or shoes are appropriate at all but the fanciest places and events. Shorts or capris and light shirts are suitable for most situations in the warmer months, although it's a good idea to have a sweater or jacket for evenings, high elevations, or overly air conditioned shops and restaurants.

Hot, jagged, uneven desert paths will quickly make mincemeat out of light sandals and tennis shoes. Be sure to bring a well-fitting, comfortable, and sturdy pair of hiking shoes or boots, or outdoor sandals for outdoor activities (see Outdoor Adventures chapter, pages 88). Try to break them in before a big hike. Lightweight, wicking fabrics will make walks and hikes much more enjoyable. During the "monsoon" season in summer, temperatures can plummet with the rains, and waterproof parkas and pants should be on hand if you plan to be away from shelter.

In the high desert summer and in fall and spring elsewhere, layering is the name of the game. Mornings and nights are chilly enough to necessitate long pants and jackets, sweaters or fleeces. As the sun comes out, the layers come off. Backpackers may want to consider purchasing convertible pants with zippered legs. Rain gear, thin gloves and a wool or fleece hat can be handy for quick shift in weather.

Prepare for winters in the mountains to be cold and snowy, though sunny with dry air. Again, layering is highly recommended. Polyester or micro-fiber base layers, fleece, merino wool, and soft shell jackets are all good choices for active outdoors activities. A single thick coat may not be enough for the range of temperatures. Those layers will also come in handy (though fewer will be necessary) during the cold winter nights and mornings at low altitude.

A high-factor sunblock, wide-brimmed hat, and sunglasses are essential year round, even if the day starts out cloudy. The sun is merciless, especially in the desert, where shade is scarce.

Crime and Safety

In general, Arizona is very safe. Be cautious in backcountry areas, which occasionally, but rarely, have unbalanced individuals and antisocial survivalists. Avoid hiking and camping alone in remote areas, if you are a woman, and keep to yourself. There is some gang activity in Phoenix and Tucson, but most travelers should have little to worry about. While in the street, use your common sense. Don't carry around large sums of money or expensive video/camera equipment. Walk purposefully and don't make eye contact with unwelcome strangers or respond to come-ons. Don't travel alone at night. Ask the staff in your hotel for advice about areas that should be avoided.

Customs Regulations

You can bring into the US the following duty-free items: one liter of alcohol, if over 21 years of age; 200 cigarettes, 50 cigars (not Cuban), or 2kg of tobacco, if you're over 18; and gifts worth up to $100 ($800 for US citizens). Travelers with more than $10,000 in US or foreign currency, traveler's checks, or money orders must declare these upon entry. Meats, fruits, vegetables, seeds, or plants (and, note, even sealed prepared foods from them) are not permitted and must be disposed in the receptacles provided before entering. For more information, contact US Customs and Border Protection (tel: 877-227-5511; "Know Before You Go" document on www.cbp.gov).

D

Disabled Travelers

Under the Americans with Disabilities Act (ADA), accommodations built after January 26, 1995, and containing more than five rooms must be useable by persons with disabilities. Older and smaller inns and lodges are often wheelchair-accessible. For the sight-impaired, many hotels provide special alarm clocks, captioned television services, and security measures. To comply with ADA hearing-impaired requirements, hotels have begun to follow special procedures; local agencies may provide TTY and interpretation services. Check with the front desk when you make reservations to ascertain to what degree the hotel complies with ADA guidelines. Ask specific questions regarding bathroom facilities, bed height, wheelchair space, and availability of services. Restaurants and attractions are required to build ramps for those with limited mobility. Many major attractions have wheelchairs for loan or rent. Some provide menus, visitors' guides, and interpreters for hearing- and seeing-impaired guests.

Paved trails suitable for use by travelers with disabilities can be found in many parks, including the Grand Canyon. Wheelchairs are available for temporary day use at Canyon View Information Plaza and Yavapai Observation Station at the South Rim. Wheelchair accessible tours can be arranged through any lodge transportation desk (tel: 928-638-0591), and several whitewater rafting companies operating in the Grand Canyon offer rafting trips for people with disabilities with advance notice. Grand Canyon National Park publishes an Accessibility Guide, which has information on park facilities that are accessible to visitors with disabilities. It's available from NPS Information Centers, by writing to PO Box 129, Grand Canyon, AZ 86023, or through the park's website: www.nps.gov/grca/planyourvisit/accessibility.htm.

The Society for the Accessible Travel and Hospitality (tel: 212-447-7284; www.sath.org) publishes a quarterly magazine on travel for the disabled.

E

Embassies and Consulates

Foreign embassies are all located in Washington, DC. Phone numbers include UK (tel: 202-588-6500); Germany (tel: 202-298-4000); France (tel: 202-944-6000); Australia (tel: 202-797-3000); New Zealand (tel: 202-328-4800); Canada (tel: 202-682-1740); Ireland (tel: 202-462-3939); and South Africa (tel: 202-232-4400). Contact the US State Department for street addresses and other countries' embassy and consulate information (tel: 202-647-4000; www.state.gov/s/cpr/rls).

G

Gay and Lesbian Travelers

Phoenix is home to a large gay and lesbian community, and there are a growing number of gay-friendly stores and bars, nightclubs, and restaurants. You'll find news and entertainment listings for Phoenix in Echo Magazine, a free bi-weekly that is distributed in cafés, bookstores, and bars (tel: 888-324-6624; www.echomag.com). For information on virtually anything, from lodging to HIV/Aids resources in Phoenix, contact 1N10 – a gay and lesbian community youth center – open between 10am and 10pm seven days a week (www.1N10.org). You can reach the Arizona Aids hotline at 602-234-2752. The Tucson Weekly Observer (www.tucsono_bserver.com) has information on the gay scene in Tucson.

Traveling as a gay person in rural Arizona is likely to be more challenging. Lesbians, and to a lesser degree, gay men have a small presence in college and liberal arts towns like Flagstaff and Sedona, but are largely underground elsewhere, due to conservative attitudes. A helpful overview of gay resources throughout the state can be viewed at www.gayarizona.com.

Electricity

The United States uses 110 to 120 volts AC (60 cycles). If visiting from outside North America, you may require an electrical adapter for any electronics or appliances you want to bring. Electrical outlets accept the standard North American plug with two flat parallel pins.

H

Health and Medical Care

Health Coverage and Pharmacies

It's vital to have medical insurance when traveling in the US. Although hospitals are obligated to provide emergency treatment to anyone who needs it whether or not they have insurance, you may have to prove you can pay for treatment of anything less than a life-threatening condition. Know what your policy covers and have proof of the policy with you at all times or be prepared to pay at the time service is rendered. Popular chain CVS Pharmacy has several 24-hour locations in Phoenix and one in Tucson (www.cvs.com).

BELOW: a Saguaro cactus.

Health Hazards

Altitude Sickness

This is not a serious consideration in most parts of the state, although people traveling from sea level may feel uncharacteristically winded at elevations as low as 6,000–7,000ft (1,800–2,100 meters). The sensation usually passes after a few days. Symptoms, including nausea, headache, vomiting, extreme fatigue, light-headedness, and shortness of breath, intensify over 10,000ft (3,000 meters). Although the symptoms may be mild at first, they can develop into a serious illness. It's best to acclimatize gradually when you are coming from sea level. Spend a few days at a lower elevation, then move higher.

Cactus

To avoid being pricked, stay on trails and wear long pants and sturdy boots. Some people may have allergies to the prickly varieties of these beautiful desert plants.

Dehydration

Drink plenty of fluids and, if outdoors, carry bottles of water and a high-energy snack to eat. The rule of thumb is one gallon (four liters) of water per person per day, and at least one quart (one liter) for shorter walks. Don't wait to get thirsty; start drinking as soon as you set out. Dehydration and salt deficiency can lead to heat exhaustion. It's best to moderate or avoid alcohol and caffeine, drink plenty of water and take time to acclimatize to the heat if you are not accustomed to it. Also avoid the sun at its hottest: 2–4pm.

Drinking Water

All water from natural sources must be purified before drinking. Giardia is found throughout the West, even in crystal-clear water, and it can cause severe cramps and diarrhea. The most popular purification methods are tablets or filters or by boiling water for at least five minutes.

Flash Floods

Sudden downpours – even those falling miles away from your location – can fill canyons and dry riverbeds with a deadly roaring torrent of water and mud that will sweep away everything in its path. Travelers should be especially careful during the summer "monsoon" season (July to September). Avoid hiking or driving in arroyos or narrow canyons, and never try to wade or drive across a flooded stream. If rain begins to fall, or you see rain clouds in the distance, move to higher ground. It's impossible to outrun or even outdrive a flash flood. Take action before water levels begin to rise.

Frostbite

Symptoms of frostbite, which occurs when living tissue freezes, include numbness, pain, blistering, and whitening of the skin. The most immediate remedy is to put frostbitten skin against warm skin. Simply holding your hands for several minutes over another person's frostbitten cheeks or nose may suffice. Otherwise, immerse frostbitten skin in warm (not hot) water. Refreezing will cause even more damage, so get the victim into a warm environment as quickly as possible. If one person is frostbitten, others may be too.

Heat Stroke

Long, uninterrupted periods of exposure to high temperatures can lead to heat stroke, which means that the body's core temperature rises to a dangerous level and its normal cooling system – reddening and sweating – is overwhelmed. To head off problems, keep major arteries in your neck cool by wearing a wet bandanna or cotton shirt with a collar. If you start to feel dizzy and fuzzy-brained, feel muscle weakness and start to stumble, and your skin has become pale and dry rather than red and sweaty, immediately begin spraying yourself with water or, better yet, pour it on you. This creates evaporative cooling and is the fastest way to recover. You can also lie down in a dark room with a wet sheet over you and the air conditioning on. Whatever you do, don't jump into cold water in a pool: it can send your body into shock. Heat stroke is a common problem for light-eyed, light-haired Europeans from northern climates and is a potentially serious condition, so don't ignore the telltale signs.

Hypothermia

This occurs when the core body temperature falls below 95°F (35°C). At altitude, combinations of alcohol, cold, and thin air can produce hypothermia. Watch for drowsiness, disorientation, and sometimes increased urination. If possible, get to a hospital, otherwise blankets and extra clothing should be piled on for warmth. If necessary, skin-to-skin contact is effective. Don't use hot water or electric heaters and don't rub the skin. The elderly should be careful in extremely cold weather.

Sunburn

Even a couple of hours outdoors can result in sunburn, so protect yourself with a high-SPF sunscreen (be sure to put it on 15 minutes or so before going out in the sun), polarized sunglasses, and a broad-brimmed hat. The elderly and the ill, small children, and people with fair skin should be especially careful. Excessive pain, redness, blistering, or numbness mean you need professional attention. Minor sunburn can be soothed by taking a cool bath or using aloe vera gel.

Insects and Animals

Gila Monsters

North America's only venomous lizard, found in the Sonoran Desert, looks menacing but is easily recognized and rarely encountered.

Insects

Bees are abundant, which should concern only those allergic to bee stings. Carry an Epi pen to be safe when traveling. The kissing bug is an unusual-looking black insect with an unpleasant bite. There are fire ants and some varieties of wasp. Their sting can be painful but isn't dangerous unless you're allergic to their venom. Cedar gnats, or no-see-ums, are one of the most annoying of bugs, starting in May when they, like many bugs, begin to hatch. They get into eyes, ears, noses, mouths, and hair and deliver a nasty bite that can swell and give flu-like symptoms. If camping or hiking among junipers (cedars, in pioneer slang), use fine-mesh netting and a tent with no-see-um-proof windows. Deer flies, a particularly large biting fly, may also be found in Four Corners locations and will present an annoyance to hikers.

The bite of a black widow spider and tarantula and the sting of a pale-colored desert scorpion's tail can pack a punch, but are rarely a serious health threat to adults. Scorpions are nocturnal, so use flashlights and never walk barefoot in the desert. They often hide in recesses, dark corners, and old wood piles and like to crawl into protected places, so shake out clothes or sleeping bags that have been on the ground and check your shoes before slipping into them in the morning.

Snakes

Arizona has two venomous snakes: rattlesnakes and coral snakes. Only about three percent of people bitten by a rattlesnake die, and these are mainly very small children. Walk in the open, proceed with caution among rocks, avoid dark and overgrown places where snakes lurk, shake out bedding or clothing that has been lying on the ground, and wear sturdy hiking boots. Snakes often lie on roads at night because of the residual heat radiating from the pavement, so use a flashlight if walking on a paved road after dark. Most important: Keep your hands and feet where you can see them, and don't let children poke under rocks or logs.

Snakebite kits are good psychological protection but there is controversy over how effective they are. If bitten, first, stay calm, to avoid circulating the venom through your body more rapidly. Then apply a tourniquet lightly above the bite toward the heart. Try to identify the species and go immediately to the doctor.

Internet

Internet connectivity on some older foreign laptops and handheld computers may not work in the US. You may need to purchase a global modem before leaving home or a local PC-card once you arrive in the US. For more details, check www.teleadapt. com. There are fewer cyber cafés and business centers than in years past, but many public buildings, parks, coffee houses, and restaurants offer WiFi access as a visitor incentive. You'll have fewer options in rural areas, but most lodgings offer WiFi hot spots, though charges often apply. Public libraries almost always have free Wi-fi. Check www.openwifispots. com for updated maps of free Wi-fi locations throughout the US.

Media

Television

All major cities have channels affiliated with major networks and local stations, as well as a vast number of cable hookups and satellite dish offerings. Hotel rooms usually have cable TV, but you often have to pay to watch movies (Pay Per View). Newspapers give daily and weekly information on TV and radio programs, and satellite TV programming has a program guide through the remote.

Money

Credit cards are very much part of life in Arizona, as in other parts of the US. They can be used to pay for pretty much anything, and it is also common for car rental firms and hotels to place a temporary deposit on your card. Rental companies may oblige you to pay a large deposit in cash if you do not have a card.

You can also use your credit card to withdraw cash from ATMs. Before you leave home, check which ATM system will accept your card and what conversion charges you will incur. It is advisable to contact your issuing bank and inform them of your travel plans so they do not freeze your account because of fears of fraud. The most widely accepted cards in the US are Visa, American Express, MasterCard, and Discover Card. Diners Club, and Japanese Credit Bureau.

Foreign visitors may wish to take US dollar traveler's checks to Arizona since exchanging foreign currency – whether as cash or checks – can prove problematic. An increasing number of banks offer foreign exchange facilities, but this practice is not universal. Some department store chains offer foreign currency exchange. Many, but not all, shops, restaurants, and other establishments accept traveler's check in US dollars and will give change in cash. Alternatively, checks can be converted into cash at the bank.

American dollars come in bills of $1, $5, $10, $20, $50, and $100, all the same size. The dollar is divided into 100 cents. Coins come in 1 cent (penny), 5 cents (nickel), 10 cents

(dime), 25 cents (quarter), 50 cents (half-dollar), and $1 denominations. There is no Value Added Tax (VAT) in the US but cities charge a sales tax, usually 7–8 percent of the sale. Car rental companies charge both sales tax and service fees.

Newspapers and Magazines

Every city and most large towns have a local newspaper. For national and international news, along with local and regional events, check the following papers.

The state's largest newspaper is the Arizona Republic (tel: 602-444-8000; www.azcentral.com). Tucson's paper is the Arizona Daily Star (tel: 800-695-4492; www.azstarnet.com). The Tucson Citizen (tel: 520-573-4614; www. tucsoncitizen.com) is a free weekly newspaper based in the same building as the Daily Star with information on what's happening and current events.

Northern Arizona's leading newspaper is the Arizona Daily Sun (tel: 928-774-4545; www. azdailysun.com), one of the oldest newspapers in the West. Indian news can be found in the Navajo-Hopi Observer (tel: 928-226-9696; www. navajohopiobserver.com) and the Navajo Times (tel: 928-871-1130; www.navajotimes.com). The Yuma Daily Sun follows events in Yuma (tel: 928-539-6857; www.yumasun. com). And the Lake Powell Chronicle has information on Lake Powell and

BELOW: a signpost welcoming you to historic Bisbee.

Page (tel: 928-645-8888; www. lakepowellchronicle.com).

Also available are the New York Times, Los Angeles Times, Washington Post, USA Today, and the Wall Street Journal. You're better off looking at the websites of overseas newspapers; except for in a few hotels and specialty bookstores, as they are nearly impossible to find.

The following magazines feature profiles of interesting destinations and local people, as well as restaurant listings and a calendar of events: Arizona Highways (tel: 800-543-5432; www.arizona_highways.com) and Tucson Lifestyle (tel: 520-721-2929; www.tucsonlifestyle.com).

O

Opening Hours

US stores are often open seven days a week and, except for Sundays, tend to stay open into the evening, especially in tourist areas. Government businesses are usually only open on weekdays from 8 or 9am to 4 or 5pm. US post offices are usually open at 8am and close around 5 or 5.30pm, open for limited hours on Saturdays, and are always closed on Sundays and holidays.

P

Postal Services

The opening hours of federal post offices vary between central, big-city branches, and those in smaller towns or suburbs; but all open Monday to Friday and some open also on Saturday mornings. Ask hotel or motel personnel for the opening hours of the post office nearest you or check www.usps.com. Drugstores and hotels sometimes have a small selection of stamps. There are stamp-vending machines in the lobbies of most post offices as well as Automated Postal Centers that allow you to use a credit card to ship mail. ATM machines also often sell stamps for domestic postage.

Large envelopes over 13oz (369 grams) must now be sent by two- to

Emergencies

In case of emergency, dial 911 to contact the police, fire, or ambulance service.

three-day Priority Mail in the US or Media Mail, if the envelope contains printed materials. The fastest service offered by the post office is Express Mail, which guarantees next-day delivery to most destinations within the US, and delivery within two to three days to foreign destinations by Global Express Mail. Private courier services offering overnight and two-day delivery are usually the most reliable, although more expensive than the US Post Office. Ground delivery, taking an average of five days, is very popular. The two main courier services are FedEx: (tel: 800-463-3339; www.fedex.com) and UPS: (tel: 800-742-5877; www.ups.com).

R

Religious Services

There is no official state religion in the United States or Arizona, but Christmas Day is recognized as a federal and state holiday. The majority of Arizonans who identify themselves as religious identify as Protestants or Catholics. Arizona is home to more Mormons than most states outside of Utah, but Mormons still make up a very small percentage of the population. Judaism, Buddhism, Hinduism and other major world religions have only a tiny presence, which is concentrated almost exclusively in the urban areas.

T

Telephones

Pay phones can be found in transportation hubs, gas stations, shopping malls, and convenience stores. The cost of making a local call from a pay phone for three minutes is 25–50 cents. To make a long-distance call from a pay phone, use either a prepaid calling card or your credit card: dial 1-800-CALLATT, key in your credit card number, and wait to be connected. In most areas, local calls have now changed to a 10-digit calling system, using the area code.

Cell phones: American cell phones use GSM 1900, a different frequency from other countries. Only foreign phones operating on GSM 1900 will work in the US. You may be able to take the SIM card from your

Public Holidays

Public holidays in the US include: New Year's Day (January 1), Martin Luther King Day (third Monday in January), President's Day (third Monday in February), Memorial Day (last Monday in May), Independence Day (July 4), Labor Day (first Monday in September), Columbus Day (second Monday in October), Veterans' Day (November 11), Thanksgiving (fourth Thursday in November), and Christmas Day (December 25).

home phone, install it in a rented cell phone in the US, and use it as if it's your own cell phone. Ask your wireless provider about this before leaving. Cell phones can be rented for about $50 a week in the US. Also available are GSM 1900-compatible phones with prepaid calling time, such as those offered by T-Mobile (www.t-mobile.com). Be aware that you probably won't be able to pick up a signal in remote rural areas. Check the coverage before starting out.

Dialing Abroad

To dial abroad (Canada follows the US system), first dial the international access code 011, then the country code. If using a US phone credit card, dial the company's access number below, then 01, then the country code.

Sprint, tel: 10333
AT&T, tel: 10288.
Country codes:

Australia	61
New Zealand	64
South Africa	27
United Kingdom	44

Tipping

Service personnel expect tips in Arizona. The accepted rate for baggage handlers is $1 per bag. For others, including taxi drivers and waiters, 15–20 percent is the going rate, depending on the level and quality of service. Sometimes tips are included in restaurant bills for those dining in groups. Moderate hotel tipping is around $1 per bag or suitcase handled by porters and bellboys. Room service often adds service charges, but feel free to slip them an additional $1–2. You should tip a doorman or concierge if he or she holds your car or performs other services. It is not necessary to tip housekeeping staff unless you stay several days, then budget about $2–3 per day.

Time Zones

Arizona operates under Mountain Standard Time (GMT -7) from mid-November to mid-March and Mountain Daylight Time (GMT -6) from mid-March to mid-November. Except for the Navajo Nation lands, the state does not observe daylight saving time.

Tourist Information

Below is a list of tourist information offices in Arizona. Most can provide maps, accommodations and dining recommendations, and other suggestions for local attractions and services. Where addresses are provided, the offices are open to the public during regular business hours:

Arizona Office of Tourism
Tel: 866-275-5816
www.arizonaguide.com

Bisbee Chamber of Commerce
Tel: 520-432-5421
www.bisbeearizona.com

Flagstaff Visitors Bureau
One East Route 66, Flagstaff
Tel: 928-774-9541 or 800-842-7293
www.flagstaffarizona.org

Grand Canyon Chamber of Commerce
Tel: 928-638-2901
www.grandcanyonchamber.com

Lake Havasu City Convention and Visitors Bureau
420 English Village, Lake Havasu City
Tel: 800-242-8278
www.golakehavasu.com

Navajoland Tourism Office
Tel: 928-871-6436
www.discovernavajo.com

Nogales–Santa Cruz County Chamber of Commerce
123 W. Kino Park Way, Nogales
Tel: 520-287-3685
www.nogaleschamber.com

Page–Lake Powell Chamber of Commerce
34 S. Lake Powell Boulevard, Page
Tel: 928-645-2741
www.pagechamber.com

Phoenix Visitors Information Center
125 N. Second Street, Suite 120, Phoenix
Tel: 877-225-5149
www.visitphoenix.com

Pinetop–Lakeside Chamber of Commerce
Tel: 928-367-4290 or 800-573-4031
www.pinetoplakesidechamber.com

Prescott Chamber of Commerce
Tel: 928-445-2000
www.visit-prescott.com

Rim Country Chamber of Commerce
100 W. Main Street, Payson
Tel: 928-474-4515 or 800-672-9766
www.rimcountrychamber.com

Scottsdale Convention and Visitors Bureau
Tel: 480-421-1004
www.scottsdalecvb.com

Sedona–Oak Creek Canyon Chamber of Commerce
331 Forest Road, Sedona
Tel: 928-282-7722 or 800-288-7336
www.visitsedona.com

Sierra Vista Convention and Visitors Bureau
21 E. Wilcox Drive, Sierra Vista
Tel: 800-288-3861
www.visitsierravista.com

Sonoita–Elgin Chamber of Commerce
Tel: 520-455-5498
www.sonoitaelginchamber.org

Tempe Convention and Visitors Bureau
Tel: 866-914-1052
www.tempecvb.com

Tombstone Chamber of Commerce
Tel: 888-457-3929
www.tombstone.org

Tonto Basin Chamber of Commerce
Tel: 800-404-8923
www.tontobasinchamber.org

Tucson Convention and Visitors Bureau
100 S Church Avenue, Tucson
Tel: 520-624-1817 or 800-638-8350
www.visittucson.org

Williams–Grand Canyon Chamber of Commerce
200 W. Railroad Avenue, Williams
Tel: 928-635-1418
www.experiencewilliams.com

Yuma Convention and Visitors Bureau
202 N. Fourth Avenue, Yuma
Tel: 928-783-1897 or 800-293-0071
www.visityuma.com

V

Visas and Passports

Foreign travelers to the United States (including those from Canada and Mexico) must carry a valid passport; a return plane ticket is also normally required. A visa is required for visits of more than 90 days. Visitors needing a visa should apply to the American embassy or consulate in the city or country where they live permanently. As part of the application process, travelers may need to schedule an interview and fingerprint scan. Processing fees start at $140.

Tourists or business travelers from countries participating in the Visa Waiver Program, such as the UK, can stay up to 90 days in the US without a visa. Travellers eligible for the program must register online via the website of the Electronic System for Travel Authorization (tel: 703-526-4200; https://esta.cbp.dhs.gov/esta) at least three days before they travel. An approved application remains valid for up to two years, or until the traveler's passport expires. It also entitles the holder to multiple entries into the US during this period.

For the most current information, contact the U.S. Department of Homeland Security at www.dhs.gov.

W

Weights and Measures

The United States uses the Imperial System throughout the country. You will see the occasional use of liters and meters, but in general measurements are done in inches, miles, ounces, pounds, gallons, etc.

BELOW: a road sign in Arizona provides clear directions.

FURTHER READING

Guides

Ancient Ruins of the Southwest: An Archaeological Guide, by David Grant Noble. A detailed guide to major archaeological finds throughout the deserts of the Southwest, with ample coverage of Arizona.
Arizona's Ghost Towns and Mining Camps: A Travel Guide to History, by Philip Varney. The second edition of a popular illustrated guide to what remains from the old West.

History and Culture

And Die in the West: The Story of the O.K. Corral Gunfight, by Paula Mitchell Marks. An extensive and unbiased account of the events surrounding the most famous shoot-out of the "Wild West."
Arizona: A Cavalcade of History, by Marshall Trimble. An anecdotal history.
Book of the Hopi, by Frank Waters. A pioneering work on the culture, spiritualism, stories and traditions of the Hopi by a novelist.
Book of the Navajo, by Raymond Locke. The sixth edition of a scholarly cultural history of the Navajo, first published in the 1970s.
The Exploration of the Colorado River and its Canyons, by John Wesley Powell. Powell's original account of his harrowing 1874 trip through the Grand Canyon.
Geronimo: The Man, His Time, His Place, by Angie Debo. A detailed account of the great Indian chief, with a focus on the Apache Wars.
Revenge of the Saguaro, by Tom Miller. An eccentric account of traveling in the towns around Tucson.

Nature

Desert Solitaire, by Edward Abbey. Abbey's ode to the desert and national parks has especially powerful passages on the Grand Canyon, as well as Glen Canyon before the flood.
Downcanyon, by Ann Zwinger. An account of a naturalist's journey down the Colorado.
The Man Who Walked Through Time, by Colin Fletcher. An evocative and engrossing account of a 1963 hike from one end of the Grand Canyon to the other.
Roadside Geology of Arizona, by Halka Chronic. An entry in an excellent series of guides that introduces the geological wonders of the Southwest as seen through the car window.
Sonoran Desert Spring / Sonoran Desert Summer, by John Alcock. Two books of observations from the desert by a dedicated naturalist.

Fiction

The Bean Trees, by Barbara Kingsolver. Kingsolver's 1988 debut novel of a young woman who flees her Kentucky home and finds herself working in a garage in Tucson.
Bisbee '17, by Robert Houston. Inspired by a true story, this short novel tells the tale of a copper miner strike in dusty Bisbee a century ago.
The Dance Hall of the Dead, by Tony Hillerman. The second of Hillerman's popular Lieutenant Joe Leaphorn mysteries set on the Navajo reservation.
The Dark Wind, by Tony Hillerman. Hillerman's second mystery to feature Jim Chee, the younger, more earnest counterpart to Joe Leaphorn.
Days of Plenty, Days of Want, by Patricia Preciado Martin. A collection of short stories set within Arizona's Mexican-American community.
The Laughing Boy, by Oliver La Farge. Subtitled "A Navajo Love Story," this short novel won the Pulitzer in 1915.
Riders of the Purple Sage, by Zane Grey. One of the great Westerns, still poignant and exciting 100 years after it was written.
Skinwalkers, by Tony Hillerman. Perhaps the most famous of the Leaphorn/Chee mysteries, this page-turner involves a triple murder on the Navajo reservation.

Other Insight Guides

Insight Guide: Arizona is a top-selling title in our flagship series, with superb photography and in-depth background reading on the state's history and culture.
Insight CityGuides provide detailed and local insight into the vibrant cities of the USA. Titles include *New York City, San Francisco,* and *Las Vegas.*
Insight Step by Step Guides provide precise itineraries and recommendations from a local, expert writer for dining, lodging, and sightseeing; titles include *Boston* and *New England.*
Insight Smart Guides are packed with information, arranged in a unique A–Z format that helps you find what you want quickly and simply. Titles include *Orlando* and *San Francisco.*

Send Us Your Thoughts

We do our best to ensure the information in our books is as accurate and up-to-date as possible. The books are updated on a regular basis using local contacts, who painstakingly add, amend and correct as required. However, some details (such as telephone numbers and opening times) are liable to change, and we are ultimately reliant on our readers to put us in the picture.

We welcome your feedback, especially your experience of using the book "on the road". Maybe we recommended a hotel that you liked (or another that you didn't), or you came across a great bar or new attraction we missed. We will acknowledge all contributions, and we'll offer an Insight Guide to the best letters received.

Please write to us at:
 Insight Guides
 PO Box 7910
 London SE1 1WE
Or email us at:
 insight@apaguide.co.uk

TRANSPORTATION ACCOMMODATIONS ACTIVITIES A–Z

ART AND PHOTO CREDITS

Alamy 30, 71, 105, 189, 210, 243, 296/297, 303
Arizona Office of Tourism 4T, 7BL/ML/MTL, 36 B/M/T, 37T, 68/69, 114/115, 125T, 145, 162B, 163B, 212, 242T, 245, 261, 262T, 302
AWL Images 142, 144/T, 146, 162T, 180, 256
Bisbee Mining and Historical Museum 62, 64
Corbis 37B, 96, 148, 257, 262, 265/T, 304
Richard Cummins 227T
Fort Verde State Historic Park 252
Grand Canyon Lodge 137
Grand Canyon National Park 135T, 140, 194T, 222
Getty Images 219
Heard Museum Collection 9B
George H. Huey 195B
Istockphoto 1, 21, 26, 41, 42, 45, 50, 77, 79, 81R, 83, 85, 89, 91, 95, 97, 100, 101, 104L, 128, 132, 133, 134/T, 138, 139, 158, 167, 172, 173, 185T, 191T, 214/215, 226, 248, 252T, 254/T, 258, 259/T, 264T, 266, 267
Kerrick James 12/13, 14/15, 149, 206B, 267T
Catherine Karnow 192R
NASA 163T
National Forest Service/Kari Geer 84, 99, 260, 266T
National Park Service Micahel Quinn 70, 130/131, 131T, 136T
Nature PL 263
APA Richard Nowitz 2/3, 4B, 5B,

6B/MR/TL, 6/7, 7BR/MR/TR, 8B/T, 9M/T, 10B/T, 11L/R, 14/15, 18, 19B/T, 20B/T, 22, 23, 27, 32, 33, 34R, 38, 43, 44, 46, 47, 51, 61, 66, 67, 72/73, 74, 75, 76, 78. 80L/R. 81L, 84, 88, 90, 92/T, 93, 94, 98, 102, 103, 104R, 106, 107, 108, 109, 111, 112, 113, 116/117, 118/119, 120, 121B/T, 124, 125B, 126, 127, 132T, 135, 136, 139T, 140T, 150, 151, 152/T, 154/T, 155, 156, 157, 159/T, 164/165, 166, 169/T, 170, 172T, 174, 175/T, 176, 178/T, 179/T, 181, 182, 183/T, 184, 185, 187/T, 188, 189T, 190, 195T, 196/197, 198, 199B/T, 200, 201, 202/T, 203/T, 204, 206T, 207/T, 208, 209/T, 211, 212T, 216, 217, 220, 223, 224/T, 225/T, 226T, 227, 228, 234, 235, 236/T, 237, 238/T, 239/T, 240/T, 241/T, 242, 243T, 273L/R, 274, 275, 277/T, 278/T, 279/T, 280/T, 281/T, 282, 283/T, 284L/R/T, 285/T, 266, 267/T, 292, 293, 296T, 297/T, 298/T, 399/T, 300, 301T, 302T, 303T, 305, 308, 310, 311, 312, 313, 314, 315, 317, 320, 321, 324, 326
Painted Desert Inn 260T
Phoenix Art Museum 222T
Smithsonian Institution/National Museum of American Art 35T
Stephen Trimble 28, 29, 186, 192/T
Superstock 143, 272
Tom Till 194B, 270/271
US Library of Congress 24L/R, 25, 31, 34B/T, 35B, 39, 48, 49, 56, 57,

54, 55, 56L/R, 57, 58/59, 60, 63, 65, 110, 158T, 190T, 191, 210T, 218, 261T, 294
Werner Forman 264

PHOTO FEATURES

86/87
Arizona Office of Tourism 86/87, 86BL, 87M/TR, Istockphoto 86BR, 87BR

232/233
All photos Heard Museum Collection, except 232/322 Richard Nowitz

246/247
Istockphoto 246/247, 246BL, 247BL/BR/TR, APA Richard Nowitz 247ML, Alamy 246MR

290/291
Alamy 290/291, 291M, Camera Press 290BL, 291BR, Istockphoto 290BR, 291TR,

Map production: original cartography Colourmap Scanning, updated by Apa Cartography Department

© 2012 APA Publications UK Ltd

Production:
Tynan Dean
Linton Donaldson
Rebeka Ellam

INDEX

Main references are in bold type